Logic and Contemporary Rhetoric

The Use of Reason in Everyday Life

TENTH EDITION

Howard Kahane

Late of
University of Maryland
Baltimore County

Nancy Cavender

College of Marin

THOMSON

TM

WADSWORTH

Australia • Canada • Mexico • Singapore • Spain
United Kingdom • United States

THOMSON

★ ™

WADSWORTH

Publisher: Holly J. Allen
Philosophy Editor: Steve Wainwright
Assistant Editors: Lee McCracken, Barbara Hillaker
Editorial Assistant: John Gahbauer
Technology Project Manager: Julie Aguilar
Marketing Manager: Worth Hawes
Marketing Assistant: Andrew Keay
Marketing Communications Manager:
   Laurel Anderson
Executive Art Director: Maria Epes

Composition Buyer: Ben Schroeter
Print Buyer: Doreen Suruki
Permissions Editor: Stephanie Lee
Production Service: Penmarin Books
Text Designer: Paula Shuhert and Image House
Copy Editor: Kevin Gleason
Cover Designer: Bill Stanton
Cover Image: Paul Zwolak / Marlena Agency
Compositor: Stratford Publishing Services
Cover and Text Printer: Malloy, Inc.

Printed in the United States of America
2   3   4   5   6   7   09   08   07   06

Thomson Higher Education
10 Davis Drive
Belmont, CA 94002-3098
USA

Thomson Learning Academic Resource Center
Asia (including India)
Thomson Learning
5 Shenton Way
#01-01 UIC Building
Singapore 068808

Australia/New Zealand
Thomson Learning Australia
102 Dodds Street
Southbank, Victoria 3006
Australia

Canada
Thomson Nelson
1120 Birchmount Road
Toronto, Ontario M1K 5G4
Canada

UK/Europe/Middle East/Africa
Thomson Learning
High Holborn House
50–51 Bedford Row
London WC1R 4LR
United Kingdom

ISBN 0-534-62604-1

In memory of Howard Kahane, 1928–2001

Contents

*I do not pretend to know what many
ignorant men are sure of.*

—Clarence Darrow

*To know that we know what we know,
and that we do not know what we do not
know, that is true knowledge.*

—Henry David Thoreau

We have met the enemy and he is us.

—Walt Kelly's "Pogo"

*Education is not simply the world of
abstract verbalized knowledge.*

—Aldous Huxley

*Many people would sooner die than
think. In fact, they do.*

—Bertrand Russell

*You can fool too many of the people too
much of the time.*

—James Thurber

PREFACE

The tenth edition of *Logic and Contemporary Rhetoric* is dedicated to Howard Kahane, who died in 2001 after a long battle with heart disease. Although Howard wrote a number of books, this one was his favorite because he believed passionately in helping people think critically about the world they live in and the decisions they make. His method was to apply logical principles in a practical way to analyze contemporary political and social issues, rather than to focus on the mathematical structure of logic. (This is why there is so little formal logic in the book, although he did write a formal logic text that is still in use.) The approach, now known as "critical thinking," was used by a few philosophy teachers when the first edition appeared in 1971, but Howard's book helped to popularize the movement and was widely imitated.

One of his regrets was letting his editor talk him into the title—which he thought was too high flown and out of keeping with his nuts and bolts approach. He wanted to call it Crap Detection—a title that suited his method as well as his style, and in his case, the old adage "the style is the man" was never more apt—right down to the wry quips and parenthetical asides. What you read in the book was what you got in the man, which is why his voice is so strong. (He couldn't stand the mind-numbing rhetoric so common in many textbooks.)

Howard had immense common sense, a droll wit, and the zeal of a missionary for unmasking hypocrisy, exposing political shenanigans (on the left and right), and debunking wrong-headed beliefs. But more than anything else, he thought that an informed and responsible citizenry was the cornerstone of democracy and that it was his job to make people aware of the snares in the system. This is why he took such pains to show how we could be manipulated by the media, the advertisers, the political system, and, unfortunately, our textbooks. And this is why he urged students to analyze and question those in authority—even their teachers. It is a tribute to the man and his ideas that *Logic and Contemporary Rhetoric* is still going strong in its fourth decade.

The purpose of this tenth edition of *Logic and Contemporary Rhetoric,* as of the previous nine, is to help students improve their ability to reason well about problems they encounter in everyday life and about issues that are debated in the social/political arena. (The intent certainly is not to move students to the right or left on the political spectrum but rather to help them move *up* on the scale measuring rational sophistication.)

The text contains examples and exercise items drawn from a broad range of sources — television programs, advertisements, literary works, political speeches, newspaper columns, the Internet, and so on. Students get to sharpen their ability to think critically by reasoning about important topics and issues — abortion, astrology, capitalism, corruption, drugs, diets, doublespeak — instead of examples concerning sophomores dating seniors or all Greeks being mortal. It quotes from writings, comments, and testimony of Aristotle, Molefi Kete Asante, Woody Allen, Ambrose Bierce, Winston Churchill, Linda Chavez, Dostoevsky, Rush Limbaugh, Bill Moyers, Geraldo Rivera, Sara, Duchess of York, William Shakespeare, Adlai Stevenson, Alice Walker, Barbara Walters, Oprah Winfrey, and hundreds of others.

Examples are drawn from astrological predictions, Budweiser commercials, Bush and Kerry political doings, syndicated columnists, works of literature, and hundreds of other sources. Instead of the made-to-order cartoons that appear in some other texts, *Logic and Contemporary Rhetoric* contains drawings by the likes of David Levine, Edward Sorel, Tom Toles, George Booth, Jack Ziegler, and many others, and comic strips featuring *Calvin and Hobbes, Andy Capp, Doonesbury, Boondocks, Peanuts,* and *Dennis the Menace,* and others to illustrate points in a lively and interesting manner. The trademark of *Logic and Contemporary Rhetoric* always has been, and still is, ease of comprehension and the presentation of up-to-date and interesting material. Textbooks need not be dull!

NEW TO THE TENTH EDITION

The principal changes in this edition are these:

1. Hundreds of old examples have been replaced by more up-to-date items culled from the (sadly) thousands of new candidates. For example, political items concerning the Bush administration, the 2004 presidential campaign, and the election of George W. Bush to a second term in office have replaced outdated ones.
2. Dozens of old exercise items have been replaced by new ones.
3. Although some of the text again has been rewritten to improve organization, style, and flow, the general subject matter covered by this new edition has not changed. But several changes have been made, including a substantive revision of Chapter 8. The quick appraisal method of analyzing arguments has been dropped, and a more comprehensive analysis of an argument has been added using the critical thinking tools explained throughout the text, including a discussion of the premises and conclusion, overall validity, fallacious reasoning, use of language, and worldviews. The point of this revision is to give students some idea of how they might analyze arguments using what they have learned in previous chapters.

   In addition, a new section has been added to Chapter 11, "News as Entertainment," that discusses the increasing tendency in the media of crafting news items into Hollywood action stories to shape their message and capture the public's interest. Many new examples have been drawn from the cataclysmic events of the past few years: the September 11 terrorist attack on the World Trade Center, the war on terrorism, the war in Afghanistan, and the Iraq War. And finally, the selected list of periodicals has been restored to the book, by popular demand.

ORGANIZATION OF THE TEXT

The thought that sparked the original organization of material in *Logic and Contemporary Rhetoric* way back in 1969–1970 was that student reasoning about everyday topics could be improved by acquainting them with a few basic principles of good reasoning and, in particular, by enlightening them concerning common ways in which people are taken in by fallacious arguments and reasoning in everyday life. But a close examination of the ways in which reasoning, in fact, goes wrong in everyday life shows that it does so in a majority of cases first because of a lack of sufficient (or sufficiently accurate) background information; second, because of the psychological impediments (wishful thinking, rationalization, prejudice, superstition, provincialism, and so on) that stand in the way of cogent reasoning; and third, because of a poor understanding of the nature and quality of the various information sources.

Taking account of this insight has resulted in a book that divides into eight parts, as follows:

1. *Good and Bad Reasoning:* Chapter 1 introduces students to some basic ideas about good and bad reasoning, the importance of having good background beliefs, in particular of having well-pruned worldviews, as well as some very rudimentary remarks about deduction and induction and the three overarching fallacy categories employed in chapters 3, 4, and 5.
2. *Deduction and Induction:* Chapter 2 contains more detailed material on deductive and inductive validity and invalidity.
3. *Fallacious Reasoning:* Chapters 3, 4, and 5 discuss fallacious reasoning, concentrating on how to avoid fallacies by becoming familiar with the types most frequently encountered in everyday life. The point is to help students increase their ability to spot fallacious reasoning by discussing the most common types of fallacious argument and by providing students with everyday life examples on which to practice.
4. *Impediments to Cogent Reasoning:* Chapter 6 discusses wishful thinking, rationalization, provincialism, denial, and so on, and how to overcome them. It explains the attractiveness and mistaken nature of belief in the paranormal and other pseudosciences. In some ways, this is the most important chapter in the book, because these skewers of rational thought so severely infect the thinking of all of us. (Some instructors pass over this chapter on the grounds that the topic is more appropriately taught in psychology classes, not in classes primarily concerned with critical reasoning. But the reality here is that many students do not take the relevant psychology classes and that those who do often are provided with a purely theoretical account divorced from the students' own reasoning in everyday life, not with a "how-to" discussion designed to help them overcome these obstacles to rational thought.)

5. *Language:* Chapter 7 discusses the ways in which language itself can be used to manipulate meaning, for instance, via doubletalk and long-winded locutions. (This chapter also contains a section, not common in critical-thinking texts, on the linguistic revolution that has tremendously reduced the use of sexist, racist, and other pejorative locutions in everyday discourse; and it also has a few things to say about the use of politically correct (PC) locutions.)

6. *Evaluating and Writing Cogent Essays:* Chapter 8 deals with the evaluation of extended argumentative passages—essays, editorials, political speeches, and so on. Chapter 9 addresses the writing of these kinds of argumentative passages. (Instructors are urged not to pass over Chapter 9 and urged to have students write *at least* two argumentative papers during the semester. Writing is very likely the best way in which we all can learn to sharpen our ability to reason well. Writing is indeed nature's way of letting us know how sloppy our thinking often is. But it also is the best way to learn how to sharpen our ability to think straight.)

7. *Important Sources of Information:* Chapter 10 discusses advertising as an information source (singling out political ads for special scrutiny); Chapter 11, the media (television, newspapers, radio, books, and magazines), in particular, the mass media; and Chapter 12, public school textbooks. (For many people, these are the most important sources of information about how the world works. Instructors are urged not to pass over the chapter on the media too quickly: In this day and age, so much that happens in our lives depends on our being able to assess accurately what the media—in particular, the mass media—tell us.)

8. *More on Cogent Reasoning:* The Appendix provides additional material on deduction and induction (including a few words about syllogisms); cause and effect; scientific method; and so on.

Note also that a section at the back of the book provides answers to selected exercise items. It should be remembered, however, that most of the exercise items in this text are drawn from everyday life, where shades of gray outnumber blacks and whites. The answers provided thus constitute author responses rather than definitive pronouncements. Similar remarks apply to the answers to the remaining exercise items provided in the *Instructor's Manual* designed to accompany *Logic and Contemporary Rhetoric.*

THE UNIQUE NATURE OF LOGIC AND CONTEMPORARY RHETORIC

This book is unique among critical reasoning texts in bringing together all of these apparently diverse elements, in particular, in stressing the importance of overcoming natural impediments to cogent reasoning; in bringing to bear good background information when dealing with everyday problems; and in so extensively discussing the most important information sources. In this complicated modern world, all of us are laypersons most of the time with respect to most topics; the ability to deal effectively with the "expert" information available to us via the media, textbooks and periodicals—to separate wheat from chaff—thus is crucial to our ability to reason well about everyday problems, whether of a personal or of a social/political nature.

Although the text contains much discussion of theory, this is *not* a treatise on the theory of cogent and fallacious reasoning. Rather, it is designed to help students learn *how* to reason well and *how* to avoid fallacious reasoning. That is why so many examples and exercise items have been included—arranged so as to increase student sophistication as they progress through the book—and why exercises and examples have been drawn primarily from everyday life. Learning how to reason well and how to evaluate the rhetoric of others is a skill that, like most others, requires practice, in this case practice on the genuine article—actual examples drawn from everyday life.

This text provides students with a good deal more than the usual supply of exercise items, but perhaps the most important are those requiring them to do things on their own: find examples from the mass media, write letters to elected officials, do research on specified topics. (The *Instructor's Manual,* available to adopters of the text, suggests several other kinds of student activities—for example, classroom debates on issues of the day—that dovetail nicely with the spirit of the text.)

A true critical reasoning course, or textbook, is unthinkable in a closed or authoritarian society and antithetical to the indoctrination practiced in that kind of culture. The authors of this text take very seriously the admonition that eternal vigilance is the price of liberty. Citizens who think for themselves, rather than uncritically ingesting what their leaders and others with power tell them, are the absolutely necessary ingredient of a society that is to remain free.

ACKNOWLEDGMENTS

Many thanks to the publisher's reviewers for this tenth edition: Steve Adkison, Idaho State University; Robert B. Covert, Coastline Community College; Paul Mattick, Adelphi University; and Kerri K. Morris, University of Alaska, Anchorage.

Thanks also to the others who have aided in the preparation of this and previous editions, including Professors Thomas Allen, California Polytechnic University, San Luis Obispo; Don Anderson, Pierce College; Anatole Anton, San Francisco State University; Gary L. Baran, Los Angeles City College; Lawrence Beloof, West Hills Community College; William Bonis, California State University, Long Beach; Gene Booth, University of New Mexico; Donald Burrell, California State University, Los Angeles; Henry C. Byerly, University of Arizona; Joseph Campbell, Washington State University; Alice Cleveland, College of Marin; Monte Cook, University of Oklahoma; Rosemary Cook, Saybrook Institute; Wally Cox, Regent University; Leland Creer, Central Connecticut State University; Robert Cogan, Edinboro University; David Detmer, Purdue University, Calumet Campus; R. V. Dusek, University of New Hampshire; Frank Fair, Sam Houston State University; Dana R. Flint, Lincoln University; Marilyn M. Fry, Coastline Community College; Sidney Gendin, Eastern Michigan University; Norman L. Geisler, Liberty University; James A. Gould, University of South Florida; J. Anthony Greybasch, Central State University; Paul J. Haanstad, University of Utah; Max O. Hallman, Merced College; Alan Hausman, Hunter College; James Heffernan, University of the Pacific; John Hernandez, Palo Alto College; Mark Herron, National University; J. Thomas Howald, Franklin College; John L. King, University of North Carolina; Charles Landesman, Hunter College and CUNY Graduate Center; Donald Lazere, California Polytechnic State University; Herschel Mack, Humbolt State University; Patrick Maher, University of Pittsburgh; Reed Markham, California Polytechnic University, Pomona; Judith McBride, somewhere in Arizona; Thomas McKay, Syracuse University; Donna Monahan, College of Marin; David Morgan, University of Northern Iowa; Clayton

Morgareidge, Lewis and Clark College; Gonzalo T. Palacios, University of the District of Columbia; Ray Perkins, Jr., Plymouth State University; Linda Plackowski, Delta College; Nelson Pole, Cleveland State University; Merrill Proudfoot, Park College; Malcolm Reid, Gordon College; Vincent Riccardi, Orange Coast College; Paul O. Ricci, Cypress College; Paul A. Roth, University of Missouri; Arent H. Schuyler, Jr., University of California, Santa Barbara; Robert Schwartz, University of Wisconsin—Milwaukee; Roger Seanom, University of British Columbia; S. Samuel Shermis, Purdue University; Pamela Spoto, California State University, Chico; Douglas Stalker, University of Delaware; Ben Starr, Modesto Junior College; Joan Straumanis, Kenyon College; John Stroupe, Western Michigan University; Gregory P. Swartzentruber, Villanova University; Roye Templeton, University of Maryland, Baltimore County; John Titchener, University of Maryland, Baltimore County; and Perry Weddle, California State University, Sacramento.

Finally, our very special thanks to the students of Whitman College, the University of Kansas, Bernard Baruch College of CUNY, the University of Maryland Baltimore County, and the College of Marin.

NANCY CAVENDER
Mill Valley, California

What is the use of philosophy, if all it does is enable you to talk . . . about some abstruse questions of logic, etc., and if it does not improve your thinking about the important questions of everyday life?

—Ludwig Wittgenstein

"Congratulations, Dave! I don't think I've read a more beautifully evasive and subtly misleading public statement in all my years in government."

*C*artoon *commentary on the state of contemporary rhetoric.*

It's much easier to do and die than it is to reason why.

—H. A. Studdert Kennedy

Read not to contradict and confute, nor to believe and take for granted . . . but to weigh and consider.

—Francis Bacon

You can lead a man up to the university, but you can't make him think.

—Finley Peter Dunne

You can lead me to college . . . but you can't make me think.

—Sweatshirt update seen at Duke University

Ignorance of reality provides no protection from it.

—Harold Gordon

Reason is logic, or reason is motive, or reason is a way of life.

—John Le Carré

Chapter

1

GOOD AND BAD REASONING

There is much truth to the old saying that life is just one problem after another. That's why problem solving is one of life's major preoccupations. **Reasoning** is the essential ingredient in problem solving. When confronted with a problem, those of us who are rational reason from what we already know, or have good reason to believe, or can find out, to new beliefs useful in solving that problem. The trick, of course, is to reason well. This book is about good reasoning—about how to reason well in everyday life—whether dealing with personal problems or those of a social or political nature.

Fortunately, no one is an island. We all have available to us a great deal of knowledge others have gained through experience and good reasoning—accurate information and well-intended advice available to anyone who reaches out for it. Unfortunately, not all information is created equal. Charlatans and fools can speak as loudly as saints or Nobel Prize winners. Self-interest often clouds the thinking of even the brightest individuals. The trick when evaluating the mountain of verbiage we all are exposed to is to separate the nourishing wheat from the expendable chaff. One way to become good at doing this is to think a bit about what makes reasoning good (cogent), as opposed to bad (fallacious).

1. REASONING AND ARGUMENTS

Here is a simple example of reasoning about the nature/nurture issue:

> Identical twins sometimes have different IQ test scores. Yet these twins inherit exactly the same genes. So environment must play some part in determining a person's IQ.

Logicians call this kind of reasoning an **argument.** In this case, the argument consists of three statements:

1. Identical twins often have different IQ test scores.
2. Identical twins inherit the same genes.
3. So environment must play some part in determining IQ.

The first two statements in this argument give reasons for accepting the third. In logic talk, they are said to be **premises** of the argument; and the third statement, which asserts the **claim** made by the argument, is called the argument's **conclusion.**

In everyday life, few of us bother to label premises or conclusions. We usually don't even bother to distinguish one argument from another. But we do sometimes give clues. Words such as *because, since,* and *for* usually indicate that what follows is a premise of an argument. *Therefore, thus, consequently,* and *so* generally signal conclusions. Similarly, expressions such as "It has been observed that . . . ," "In support of this . . . ," and "The relevant data are . . . " are used to introduce premises, while expressions such as "The point of all of this is . . . ," "The implication is . . . ," and "It follows that . . . " are used to signal conclusions. Here is a simple example:

> *Since* it's always wrong to kill a human being [premise], it *follows* that capital punishment is wrong [conclusion], *because* capital punishment takes the life of [kills] a human being [premise].

Put into textbook form, the argument looks like this:

1. It's always wrong to kill a human being.
2. Capital punishment takes the life of (kills) a human being.
∴3. Capital punishment is wrong.[1]

Of course, an argument may have any number of premises and may be surrounded by or embedded in other arguments or extraneous material.

In addition to using transitional words such as *since, because,* and *therefore,* we sometimes employ sentence order—the last sentence in a series stating an argument's conclusion—and occasionally even express a conclusion in the form of a question. During the 2004 presidential primaries, for example, an enthusiastic Democrat gave her reasons for backing John Kerry. She was sure he had the best chance of defeating George Bush and was doubtful that any other candidate could defeat him. She stated her conclusion in the form of a rhetorical question: "Doesn't it make sense to vote for Kerry?" (But she was wrong.)

---

[1] The symbol ∴ often is used as shorthand for the word *therefore* and thus indicates that a conclusion follows.

We should also note that, in daily life, premises and even the conclusions of arguments sometimes are omitted as understood. Life is short, and we don't always bother to spell out matters that are obvious or not at issue or can be taken for granted. In the IQ example given earlier, for instance, the premise that IQ differences must be due either to genetic or to environmental factors was omitted as generally understood. When assessing arguments, we should by all means add omitted premises of this kind when they are relevant.

EXERCISE 1-1

Identify the premises and conclusions in the following arguments. (A few are from student exams—modestly edited.)[2]

Example
Argument
   The barometer is falling sharply, so the weather is going to change.
Argument Structure
   Premise: The barometer is falling sharply.
   Implied premise: Whenever the barometer falls sharply, the weather changes.
   Conclusion: The weather is going to change.

1. Since everyone deserves health care, and more than 40 million Americans don't have medical insurance, the United States should institute national insurance.

2. The Bush administration's argument for the war in Iraq (before shifting justifications): Saddam Hussein has weapons of mass destruction that are a threat to us, and he has links to al Qaeda. The United States should go to war and depose him.

3. *The Economist:* "It is difficult to gauge the pain felt by animals because pain is subjective and animals cannot talk."

*4. William Shakespeare: "Forbear to judge, for we are sinners all."

5. Aristotle: "The Earth has a spherical shape. For the night sky looks different in the northern and the southern parts of the Earth, and that would be the case if the Earth were spherical in shape."

*6. The government thinks 18-year-olds are responsible enough to vote and mature enough to fight a war, so why can't they drink alcohol?

7. We're never going to find cures for diabetes, cancer, Alzheimer's, and a lot of other diseases unless we use the most promising research available. Stem cell research is the way to go.

8. America is a society that values its freedoms. Censorship clearly has no place in a society that values its freedoms. It curtails independent thought, and it discourages people from examining societal problems.

---

[2] Starred (*) items are answered in a section at the back of the book.

9. College costs big bucks. When you put out that kind of money, you should be able to decide where your money goes. Students shouldn't have to take introductory courses if they don't want to. Besides, you don't need those basic courses for lots of careers.

2. Exposition and Argument

Of course, only those groups of statements that provide reasons for believing something form arguments. Thus, anecdotes are not usually arguments, nor are most other forms of **exposition.** But even in these cases, arguments often are implied. Here is a sales clerk talking about the difference between two digital cameras, an Olympus and a Kodak. "Well, the Olympus has 4.1 megapixels and the Kodak has only 2.2. They both have terrific image quality, but the Olympus is better for cropping and enlarging your prints. The Kodak is $300 less, but it's not as high-powered." Although the clerk's remarks contain no specific argument because no conclusion is drawn, a conclusion is definitely implied. You should choose the Olympus if you want a more high-powered camera; otherwise you should choose the Kodak.

The point is that talk generally is not aimless. A good deal of everyday talk, even gossip, is intended to influence the beliefs and actions of others and thus constitutes a kind of argument. In the camera example, the clerk provided information intended to convince the customer to draw either the conclusion, "I'll buy the Olympus because the range of options is worth the extra $300 to me," or the conclusion, "I'll buy the Kodak because high-powered options aren't worth $300 more to me." In other words, the point of the clerk's chatter was to sell a camera. Similarly, advertisements often just provide product information rather than advance explicit arguments, yet clearly every such ad has an implied conclusion—that you should buy the advertised product.

Nevertheless, it is important to understand the difference between rhetoric that is primarily expository and discourse that is basically argumentative. An argument makes the claim, explicit or implicit, that one of its statements follows from some of its other statements. It at least implies that acceptance of its conclusion is justified if one accepts its premises. A passage that is purely expository gives us no reason to accept any "facts" it may contain (other than the implied authority of the writer or speaker, as, for example, when a friend tells us that she had a good time at the beach).

Exercise 1-2

Here are several passages. (Some are from student papers—again, modestly edited.) Indicate which contain arguments and which do not, label the premises and conclusions of those passages that do (as you did in the previous exercise), and explain why you think the other passages do not contain arguments.

Example

Passage from an Agatha Christie novel: "M. Hercule Poirot, having nothing better to do, amused himself by studying her without appearing to do so. She was, he judged, the kind of young woman who could take care of herself with perfect ease wherever she went. . . . He rather liked the severe regularity of her features and the delicate pallor of her skin. He liked the burnished black head with its neat waves of hair, and her eyes—cool, impersonal and gray."

Evaluation: This is not an argument. The author says Poirot judged (reasoned) that the woman could take care of herself but does not describe his reasoning. And the rest of the passage simply says that Poirot liked certain features of the young woman.

*1. If we keep burning so much coal and oil, the "greenhouse" effect will continue to get worse. But it will be a disaster if that happens. So we've got to reduce dependency on these fossil fuels.

2. SUVs are a menace. They suck up gas, and they roll over easily. I'm for raising taxes on them until they're taxed off the planet.

3. Tuition for state colleges should be lowered. Lots of students drop out of school because they can't afford it and there's not enough financial aid to go around. If they go to school and work, it takes them forever to get their degrees.

*4. My summer vacation was spent working in Las Vegas. I worked as a waitress at the Desert Inn and made tons of money. But I guess I got addicted to the slots and didn't save too much. Next summer my friend Hal and I are going to work in Reno, if we can find jobs there.

5. Legalizing prostitution is bound to increase sexually transmitted diseases. And look what it would do to women. It can't help but lead to their degradation. Besides, most people don't like the idea, anyway.

6. I've often wondered how they make lead pencils. Of course, they don't use lead; they use graphite. But I mean, how do they get the graphite into the wood? That's my problem. The only thing I can think of is maybe they cut the graphite into long round strips and then cut holes in the wood and slip in the graphite.

7. Some people in the field of medicine are keen on embedding computer chips inside the body, but I've got a problem with that. True, the chips could provide helpful medical information if I'm unconscious or something, which I guess is the main reason for doing it, but I don't want to make that kind of information available to the government or anyone else, for that matter, who might want to invade my privacy.

8. Why is there so much opposition to using animals for medical research? We know medical research saves the lives of humans. True, some animals suffer in the process, but it's worth it in the long run. After all, most people value the lives of humans more than animals.

*9. Descartes: "Good sense is of all things in the world the most equally distributed, for everybody thinks himself so abundantly provided with it, that even those most difficult to please in all other matters do not commonly desire more of it than they already possess."

10. Lauren Hillenbrand, *Seabiscuit:* "To the gleeful shriek of the crowd, Seabiscuit and Ligaroti ripped out of the gate side by side. There was no clear strategy in either camp; each rider wanted the lead immediately. It was Seabiscuit who got it, tearing toward the first turn with his head in front."

11. Why shouldn't public schools take donations from private business? The government doesn't expend enough money to repair the buildings, let alone pay teachers a decent salary. Besides, big business would demand more for its money—like higher standards and better discipline.

12. Alexis de Tocqueville, *Democracy in America:* "Men will never establish any equality with which they will be contented. . . . When equality of condition is the common law of society, the most marked inequalities do not strike the eye: when everything is nearly on the same level, the slightest are marked enough to hurt it.

    Hence the desire for equality always becomes more insatiable in proportion as equality is more complete."

3. Cogent Reasoning

Reasoning can be either **cogent** (good) or **fallacious** (bad). We reason cogently when we satisfy the following conditions:

1. The premises of our reasoning are **believable (warranted, justified),** given what we already know or believe.
2. We consider all likely **relevant information.**[3]
3. Our reasoning is **valid,** or **correct,** which means that the premises we employ provide good grounds for accepting the conclusion we draw.[4]

When all three of these conditions of cogent reasoning are not satisfied, reasoning is said to be **fallacious.** Note, by the way, that in daily life, we often speak of *arguments* as being fallacious or cogent, even though, strictly speaking, it is reasoners—individuals— who reason either fallaciously or cogently. Life is short, and we often speak imprecisely when context makes clear what is intended.

Believable Premises

The first condition of cogent reasoning requires that we bring to bear whatever we already know or believe—our relevant **background beliefs** and information—to determine whether we should or shouldn't accept the premises of an argument being evaluated. Take, for instance, the first premise of the capital punishment argument discussed earlier—the premise making the claim that taking the life of a human being always is wrong. Most of us are not pacifists—we don't believe that it always is wrong to take a human life. Bringing that background belief to bear thus should make us see the first

---

[3] Satisfying this extremely stringent requirement is usually beyond the ability of most of us most of the time. The point is that good reasoners try to come as close as possible to satisfying it, taking into account the importance of drawing the right conclusion and the cost (in time, effort, or money) of obtaining or recalling relevant information. (One of the marks of genius is the ability to recognize that information is relevant when the rest of us fail to notice.)

[4] Provided we know nothing else relevant to the conclusion. Note that reasoning from an unjustified premise may still be cogent if it also employs justified premises that sufficiently support its conclusion. Note also that the term *valid* sometimes is used more broadly than we have used it here. For a more comprehensive account of valid reasoning, see Howard Kahane and Paul Tidman, *Logic and Philosophy,* 9th edition (Belmont, Calif.: Wadsworth, 2003).

premise of the capital punishment argument as questionable. So we should not accept the conclusion of that argument unless further reasons are presented in its support. (On the other hand, those of us who *are* pacifists obviously should reason differently.)

By way of contrast, consider the stated premise of the following argument:

> Serena Williams must be a terrific tennis player. She won the Wimbledon championship in 2003. (The implied premise is that anyone who took a first at Wimbledon must be an outstanding athlete.)

Tennis fans know that the Wimbledon grand slam championship is one of the most demanding tennis competitions in the world, and acceptance of the stated premise (that Williams won the tournament) was warranted by plenty of background information.

It's interesting to notice that, in effect, evaluating a premise of an argument by bringing background beliefs to bear entails constructing another argument whose conclusion is either that the premise in question is believable or that it isn't. For example, when evaluating the capital punishment argument discussed before, someone who is not a pacifist might construct the following argument: "I believe that it isn't wrong to kill in self-defense, or in wartime, or to kill those guilty of murder. So I should reject the premise that taking a human life always is wrong."

This brings to mind the fact that in daily life we often are exposed to **assertions,** or **claims,** that are not supported by reasons or arguments. Clearly, it is not rational to accept these assertions without evaluating them for believability, and, obviously, their correct evaluation requires us to do exactly what we do when evaluating the believability of the premises of an argument—namely, bring to bear what we already know or believe. Evaluating unsupported assertions thus involves just part of what is done when we evaluate arguments.

No Relevant Information Passed Over

The second criterion of cogent reasoning requires that we not pass over relevant information. In particular, it tells us to resist the temptation to neglect evidence contrary to what we want to believe.

Here, for instance, is the substance of remarks made in spring 2000 by a student at a top-notch university concerning his virtually daily concentration on stock trading (making him what is called a "day trader"):

> When I started college in 1998, I noticed that lots of students were spending a good deal of time playing the stock market and making a bundle. They quoted statistics on how stocks had been going up dramatically for several years in this new, high-tech economy. So I borrowed $1000 from my parents [nice to have parents like that] and took a flyer on an Internet startup, quickly turning my investment into $2500, which I then reinvested in other high-tech stocks. Hey, why not get in on this booming economy and rising stock prices?

Underneath this student's rhetoric, there was an implied argument, namely this:

It's smart for me to spend lots of time investing in stocks.

Stock prices, especially of high tech stocks, have been going up rapidly for several years now.

The economy is booming.

So stock prices will continue to go up and I'll make my bundle.

Alas, this student, as many others, was wiped out when the Nasdaq (principally high-tech stocks) crashed in 2000 and 2001. His reasoning neglected several important points.

First, as a potential investor ought to find out before investing, stock prices don't always go up. They often go down, sometimes way down. In the past, every stock market boom eventually ended, and stock prices declined.

Second, when you speculate in the stock market, you compete against experienced managers of huge holdings, professionals with a great deal more relevant information than any ordinary investor can have. (That's one reason why smart investors choose highly rated, professionally managed mutual funds rather than trying to pick their own winners.)

Third, day traders, like stock investors in general, must pay a fee every time they trade a stock, an expense that must be overcome by rising stock values. (The problem broker fees pose to stock investors is similar to the one confronting people who bet on the horses—in that case, the track takes a commission on winnings in every race, making it difficult for all but the most knowledgeable experts even to break even.)

And finally, time spent day trading inevitably takes away from other activities, including (yes, it's true) studying for classes, which is more likely to pay off better, financially and otherwise, in the long run.

Notice, by the way, that every one of these points can be figured out by an intelligent person who thinks carefully about the matter, so that it would make perfect sense for students who are tempted to day trade to at least obtain relevant information about past stock market booms. If getting rich by gambling on stocks were that easy and safe, wouldn't just about everyone be rich by now? When someone performs a service for you, in this case as a broker, don't they always charge for their services? Don't I have more important things to do (like studying) than gambling on a more-or-less daily basis?

The moral here is that when we neglect relevant evidence, we do not reason cogently. Contrary to the old saying, what you don't know *can* hurt you.

Valid Reasoning

The third criterion of cogent reasoning requires that the premises of an argument genuinely support its conclusion; or, as logicians like to say, it requires that an argument be **valid,** or **correct.** It is vitally important to understand that the validity of an argument has nothing whatever to do with the truth of its premises or conclusion. Validity concerns the nature of the *connection* between the premises and conclusion of an argument, not the truth or believability of its premises. Determining that an argument is valid tells us that *if* we are justified in believing in its premises, *then* we also are justified in believing in the truth of its conclusion. It doesn't tell us *whether* its premises are true. An argument thus can be perfectly valid and have completely false premises, and even have a false conclusion. Here is an example:

1. The Cleveland Indians have won more World Series games than any other major league team. (False premise, alas!)
∴2. They have won more World Series games than the New York Yankees. (False conclusion.)

The argument is valid because if the beloved Indians *had* won more World Series games than any other major league team, then, obviously (well, it's obvious to baseball fans), they would have won more World Series games than the Yankees. The argument is valid, even though its premise and conclusion both are false. It's valid because anyone who is justified in believing its premise is justified in believing its conclusion.

4. TWO BASIC KINDS OF VALID ARGUMENTS

Premises may correctly support conclusions in two fundamentally different ways. The first way yields *deductively valid* arguments; the second, *inductively valid* (or inductively strong) arguments.[5]

Deductive Validity

The fundamental property of a **deductively valid** argument is this: If all of its premises are true, then its conclusion must be true also, because the claim asserted by its conclusion already has been stated in its premises, although usually only implicitly.

Here is an example of a very simple deductively valid argument:

1. If this wire is made of copper, then it will conduct electricity. (Premise)
2. This wire is made of copper. (Premise)
∴ 3. This wire will conduct electricity. (Conclusion)

Taken alone, neither premise makes the claim that the wire will conduct electricity; but taken together, they do. We cannot imagine what it would be like for both premises of this argument to be true, yet its conclusion turn out to be false. Indeed, it would be contradictory to assert both of its premises and then to deny its conclusion.

It is important to see that it is the **form** of this argument—namely:

1. If some sentence, then a second sentence.
2. The first sentence.
∴ 3. The second sentence.

that makes it deductively valid, not the truth values of its statements. Letting the capital letter *A* stand for the first sentence and *B* for the second sentence, the *form* of the argument can be stated this way:

1. If *A* then *B*.
2. *A*.
∴ 3. *B*.

---

[5] Some authorities believe that there is at least one other kind of legitimate argument—namely, the kind in which various alternatives are evaluated. The authors of this text incline to the view that evaluative arguments fall into one or the other of the two basic kinds about to be mentioned. Note also that some authorities restrict the use of the term *valid* so that it refers only to deductively good arguments, even though in everyday life inductively strong arguments generally are said to be valid. In addition, note that the reasoning process called "mathematical induction" happens to be a kind of deductive reasoning. (Terminology sometimes is misleading.)

Clearly, every argument having this form is deductively valid, another example being this argument:

1. If <u>Sonia reads Vogue magazine</u>, <u>then she's up on the latest fashions</u>.
2. <u>Sonia reads Vogue magazine</u>.
3. <u>She's up on the latest fashions</u>.

Logicians, by the way, call the form of this argument, and every argument having this form, **modus ponens.**

It's very important to clearly understand that the deductive validity of an argument guarantees that its conclusion is true *only if* its premises are true. Determining that an argument is deductively valid thus tells us just that *if* its premises are true, *then* its conclusion must be true also; it doesn't tell us *whether* its premises are true and thus doesn't tell us *whether* its conclusion is true.

Here, for instance, is a deductively valid argument having the form *modus ponens* that contains one true and one very likely false premise and thus does not guarantee the truth of its conclusion:

1. If more people read Agatha Christie's mystery novels than read Shakespeare's plays, then her novels must be better than his plays. (False premise?)
2. Her novels have been read by more people than have Shakespeare's plays. (True premise)
∴ 3. Her novels must be better than his plays. (False conclusion?)

Of course, a deductively valid argument that contains a false premise may, luckily, have a true conclusion. But that would be a matter of luck, not of good reasoning.

The fact that a deductively valid argument cannot move from true premises to a false conclusion constitutes its chief characteristic and great virtue. But deductive arguments are limited. They cannot yield conclusions that are not at least implicit in the premises from which they are derived. *Inductive* reasoning is needed to perform this task.

Inductive Validity

Inductively valid (inductively strong) arguments, unlike deductively valid ones, have conclusions that go beyond what is contained in their premises. The idea behind valid induction is that of *learning from experience.* We often observe patterns, resemblances, and other kinds of regularities in our experiences, some quite simple (sugar sweetening coffee), some very complicated (objects moving according to Newton's laws—well, Newton noticed this, anyway). Valid inductions simply project regularities of this kind observed in our experiences so far onto other possible experiences.[6]

Here is a simple example of an inductively valid argument, of the kind sometimes called *induction by enumeration,* expressed by a rather smart child in Jacksonville, Florida, explaining why he is doubtful about the existence of Santa Claus:

> The tooth fairy turned out not to be real. The Easter Bunny turned out not to be real. So I'm beginning to wonder about Santa.

---

[6]As well as those experiences we can't have but might have if we had lived millions of years ago or if, say, we could go into the interior of the sun without being incinerated.

Admittedly this is a small sample, but perhaps not for a four-year-old with a limited range of experience.

We use inductive reasoning so frequently in everyday life that its nature generally goes unnoticed. Being informed about induction is a bit like being told that we've been speaking prose all our lives. We start drawing perfectly good inferences of this kind (and some klinkers) at a very early age. By age five or six, the use of induction has taught us a great many of the basic truths that guide everyday behavior—for instance, that some foods taste good and some don't, the sun rises every morning and sets every evening, very hot things burn the skin, some people are trustworthy and some aren't (something most of us seem to need to relearn over and over), and so on.

The great virtue of inductive reasoning is that it provides us with a way of reasoning to genuinely new beliefs, not just to psychologically new ones that are implicit in what we already know, as in the case of valid deductions. However, this benefit is purchased at the cost of an increase in the possibility of error. As remarked before, the truth of the premises of a deductively valid argument guarantees the truth of its conclusion; but the premises of a perfectly good induction may all be true and yet its conclusion be false. Even the best "inductive leap" may lead us astray, because the patterns noticed in our experiences up to a given point may not turn out to be the exact patterns of the whole universe. This happens all too often in daily life—for example, when a restaurant that has served excellent food many times in the past fails us on a special occasion. But it sometimes happens even in the lofty realm of theoretical science. Physicists, for instance, believed for a long time that asbestos does not conduct electricity—a belief supported by very good, very strong inductive reasoning—but then discovered that all substances, including asbestos, conduct electricity when cooled down close to absolute zero.

Nevertheless, rational people use induction in formulating their ideas about how things are going to turn out, whether in ordinary, everyday circumstances or in the rather special ones scientists bring about in the laboratory. Induction, thinking of Winston Churchill's famous remark about democracy, is the worst way to expand one's knowledge except for all of the other ways (guessing, wishful thinking, astrology, and so on).

EXERCISE 1-3

Which of the following passages (modestly edited to make them more straightforward than arguments often are in daily life) do you think are deductively valid? Inductively valid? Defend your answers, showing the structure of those you believe to be valid.

1. My doctor told me to take Tylenol (actually, acetaminophen, the active ingredient in Tylenol) when I get a headache, and I've done that. Well, the stuff has cured my headaches, but it also has made me feel drugged. I've apparently just been trading a headache for a drugged feeling. So I figure that if I take it again to cure this headache, the result will be the same. I'm switching back to aspirin.

2. If I buy these potato chips, I know I'm going to eat the whole bagful at one sitting. But if I do that, I'll upset my stomach. Well, then, if I buy this tempting item, my guts are going to get upset again. Satan, get thee behind me!

3. My father has always voted for Republican candidates, and my mother has also. Hah! Now that I'm old enough to vote, I'm going to vote Democratic. That'll show them.

Calvin is no match for Miss Wormwood, who easily reads between the lines of Calvin's attempts at ingratiation.

4. On the other hand, even though both of my parents are stuck on *Law and Order,* I'm going to watch that program anyway. What the heck. I've always found it fascinating and expect because of that that I usually will. Rebellion can go too far.

5. SOME WRONG IDEAS ABOUT COGENT REASONING

Having just presented three standards of cogent reasoning and having explained the nature of valid deduction and induction, perhaps we need to mention several recently voiced ideas about logic and good reasoning. According to these modestly trendy ways of looking at the topic, what counts as good reasoning is "culturally relative," or "gender-relative," or even (popular among students) "individually relative." We hear talk of "feminine logic," supposedly different from the "male logic" taught in logic classes (often by female logicians, but let that pass), and of "black intelligence," different from the "Eurocentric" variety foisted on us by white males, as though what makes reasoning good differs from group to group, race to race, or one sex to the other. We all too often hear students say things such as "That may well be true for you, but it isn't true for me" and listen to academics talk disparagingly of "Aristotelian linear reasoning," as opposed to a more "intuitive" type of reasoning, and so on.

But there is no truth to these ideas about what constitutes good reasoning. It is the height of folly to conclude, say, that an argument having the form *modus ponens* is not valid. Think, for example, what it means to assert seriously that all human beings have a right to life and then in the next breath to claim, equally seriously, that a particular human being, Smith, has no right to life. What sense is there in first saying that if Jones has been to China, then he's been to Asia, and then asserting that he has indeed been to China but not to Asia? Yet accepting reasonings that violate the standards of deductive logic

A wise person hears one word and understands two.

—Jewish proverb

Reading between the Lines

The expression "reading between the lines" has several meanings. One captures the idea of grasping an intended thought that is not expressed, another of getting more information from a statement or argument than it explicitly—or even implicitly—contains, still another of noticing what rhetoric either deliberately or accidentally hides. Reading between the lines often is the essential ingredient in assessing a good deal of the everyday talk we all encounter, in particular political rhetoric and (interestingly) advertisements.

Take the Bufferin ad that states, "No regular aspirin product reduces fever better." Reading between the lines of this ad, we should conclude that Bufferin does *not* reduce fever better than some competing products, because if it did, the ad would make that stronger claim ("Bufferin reduces fever better than any other aspirin product") rather than the weaker one that none reduces fever better. The point is that our own background beliefs should lead us to expect an advertisement to make the strongest claim possible and thus lead us to at least tentatively conclude that a less strong claim is made because stronger claims would be false.

Reading between the lines is the linguistic equivalent of "sizing up" other people—for example, of gleaning information about their beliefs or likely actions from their overt behavior or way of saying something. A good poker player, for instance, looks for signs of bluffing—some players often unwittingly signal a bluff by increasing chatter or by nervous behavior; others do so by feigning lack of concern. Similarly, intelligent voters try to size up political candidates by looking for nonverbal clues and by reading between the lines of campaign rhetoric. (More will be said about campaign rhetoric in Chapters 7 and 10.)

---

means precisely accepting some sorts of contradictory assertions or other, because the point of the principles of valid deduction (including the valid principles of mathematics) is to assure that we do not contradict ourselves when we reason from one thing to another. (That's why, to take just one of a thousand examples, double-entry bookkeeping works.)

Similarly, what reason could there be for violating the standards of good inductive reasoning—for denying what experience teaches us? That a large majority of the scientists who laid the groundwork in physics, chemistry, and biology were white males is totally irrelevant to the truth of their basic ideas and theories. *The way the world works does not differ depending on the race or sex of those trying to discover the way the world works!* That is why, to take an everyday example, it is foolish to toss away money on homeopathic medicines: Medical science has shown, over and over again, by means of inductive reasoning, to say nothing of very highly confirmed general biological principles, that homeopathy does not work. The point cannot be stressed too heavily. There simply is no truth whatsoever to the idea that standards of good reasoning differ from group to group, male to female, or person to person.

There is, however, a good deal of truth to three much different ideas. One is that self-interest, prejudice, and/or narrowmindedness do in fact often lead people to reason

invalidly. Bigotry has a bad name for good reason. Another is that self-interest often motivates us to neglect the values or interests of others, even when we share those values, so that some groups or individuals find their interests frequently neglected. For instance, rich people who believe fairness requires that everyone ought to have an equal chance when starting out in life often forget about equality of opportunity when they argue for the elimination of all inheritance taxes; in families in which both parents work, husbands notoriously tend to paper over their failure to share household and child-rearing duties; in the business world, high executives, while asserting their belief in equal rights for all, frequently overlook the ways in which women, Latinos, and blacks are often passed over for corporate advancement. In all of these cases, the problem is not with the principles of good reasoning. It is with the fallacious nature of the ways in which these principles sometimes are employed.

Those who champion other sorts of "logics" than the standard variety thus may well be mistaken in their target. They attack the principles of good reasoning rather than the failure of their opponents to employ these perfectly good (indeed the *only* good) standards of reasoning correctly or to reason from acceptable moral or other kinds of values.

A good deal more will be said in later chapters on these matters, in particular about moral and other value claims. For now, the point is just that we must distinguish the principles of good reasoning, which are the same for all, from the ways in which these principles are employed (sometimes fallaciously), and from the differing values that enter into the premises of different reasonings.

6. BACKGROUND BELIEFS

Earlier, we characterized cogent reasoning in terms of three conditions: the validity of connections between premises and conclusions, the believability of premises, and the discovery and use of relevant information. Clearly, satisfaction of the last two of these three conditions requires the employment of background beliefs. That is why bringing one's background beliefs to bear often is the most important task in evaluating an argument for cogency.

Consider, for example, the argument frequently heard in the early 1980s that AIDS is essentially a gay plague inflicted on homosexuals as punishment for their perverse sexual conduct (a claim still occasionally heard). The key premise of this argument was that AIDS can be transmitted sexually only via homosexual conduct, a premise that was supported by the evidence that in the United States a large majority of those reported early on to have the disease were indeed homosexuals. But people with good background information did not accept this argument. For one thing, they knew that in other places around the world—for instance, in Haiti and parts of Africa—large numbers of heterosexuals also had contracted AIDS via sexual behavior. And for another, those familiar with some of the basic scientific ideas concerning disease had theoretical (which means higher-level inductive) reasons for believing that AIDS could be transmitted via heterosexual behavior, as are syphilis, hepatitis B, herpes, and so on.

The point is that contrary to the old saying, ignorance is *not* bliss. It just renders us incapable of intelligently evaluating claims, premises, arguments, and other sorts of rhetoric we all are subject to every day. When evaluating arguments and issues, we can't bring relevant beliefs to bear if we don't have them, and we cannot make good judgments if what we believe is off the mark.

7. KINDS OF BACKGROUND BELIEFS

Background beliefs can be divided up in many different ways, an important one being a separation into beliefs about **matters of fact** and beliefs about **values.** It is a factual question, for example, whether capital punishment is practiced in every society (it isn't); it is a question of values whether capital punishment is morally justified (is it?). In dealing with most social or political issues, we need to separate claims that are about matters of fact from those concerning values, because these two different sorts of claims are defended, or justified, in different ways. The statement, for example, that a given state has a death penalty is proved true, or false, by an examination of relevant government records; the judgment that capital punishment is, or isn't, morally justified as the punishment for heinous crimes is determined by bringing to bear an accepted moral code, or subjective intuitions.[7]

Background beliefs also can be divided into those that are *true* and (unfortunately) those that are *false.* Someone who believes, for example, that capital punishment exists as a practice in every society has a false belief; those who believe that every society punishes murderers in one way or another has a belief that is true. An important reason for regularly testing our background beliefs in terms of our experiences and of what we

---

Knowledge not renewed quickly becomes ignorance.

—Peter Drucker

---

[7] Philosophers and others disagree seriously concerning the question whether there are such things as objective moral principles that all clear-minded, rational individuals are bound to see as correct, or whether moral right and wrong is a matter of subjective opinion—of feelings that can, and perhaps do, differ from person to person. More will be said on the topic of values in Chapter 8.

> Those who do not remember the past are condemned to relive it.
>
> —George Santayana

learn from others is precisely to weed out background beliefs that are false. Education consists in a lot more than simply learning a mountain of facts; it also has to do with weeding out beliefs that turn out to be false (or unjustified).

Beliefs also differ as to how firmly they are or should be held. We feel completely sure, completely confident, of some beliefs (for example, that the sun will rise tomorrow); less sure, but still quite confident, of others (for example, that the United States will still be in existence in the year 2050); and a good deal less sure, but still mildly confident, of others (for example, that we won't get killed some day in an auto accident). The trick is to believe firmly what should be believed, given the evidence, and believe less firmly, or not at all, what is less well supported by evidence.

All of this relates directly to decisions we have to make in everyday life. Wise individuals take into account the probability of one thing or another happening and thus of the confidence they should place in their beliefs about what to do. That's a large part of the truth behind familiar sayings such as "A bird in the hand is worth two in the bush."

8. WORLDVIEWS OR PHILOSOPHIES

As we grow up from childhood into adults, we tend to absorb the beliefs and standards of those in the world around us—our families, friends, and culture. It is no accident that so many of us have the same religious affiliation, or lack of same, as do our parents, that we accept the principles and standards of our own society, and so on.

These beliefs constitute an important part of our **worldviews** or **philosophies**.[8] They tend to be the most deeply ingrained and most resistant to amendment of all of our background beliefs. They become so much a part of us that we often appeal to them without consciously realizing we have done so. They are so intricately woven into the fabric of our belief systems that we often find it hard to isolate and examine individual strands. And when we do examine them, our natural tendency is to reaffirm them without thought and to disparage conflicting claims and evidence, quickly dismissing evidence that might count against them.

Most of these beliefs are general—for example, that killing always is morally wrong, that there is some good in virtually all human beings, or that we all die sooner or later. But not all are. Belief in a monotheistic deity, for instance, or rejection of such a belief, is a particular belief.

But in spite of the example just cited, more general beliefs usually (that is, generally!) are more important than beliefs that are particular, or less general, because they tell us about a wider range of cases and thus tend to be more useful in everyday life. Believing that it rarely rains in July in Los Angeles, for instance, clearly is more useful than believing merely that it won't rain there, say, on July 16, 2010. That is why most of the important beliefs in one's worldview are general and also why most important scientific

---

[8] Including religious beliefs in the case of those who have religious convictions.

pronouncements are general—indeed, often extremely general. (Newton's laws, for example, don't just tell us about apples falling from trees or even just about items of all kinds falling toward the Earth. They also tell us about the motion of the Earth around the sun, about the motion of all planets around the sun, about how tides rise and fall, and, in fact, about the motions of all objects whatsoever.) It also is why it is so important, and useful, to expand our worldviews to contain at least a few modestly well-founded beliefs about important scientific theories—for example, about the theory of the evolution of all life on Earth.

9. INSUFFICIENTLY GROUNDED BELIEFS

Most of us have strongly held beliefs about a great many controversial issues, and so we tend to respond automatically to arguments about these matters. We feel confident that we know whether marijuana or cocaine should be legalized, whether we should privatize social security, whether this candidate or that is more likely to serve all of the people equally if elected to office, and so on. We hold these beliefs, often very strongly, even though a good deal of the time we have insufficient justifying background knowledge and have engaged in too little thought to be able to support our beliefs intelligently or defend them against informed objections. What, for example, do we usually know about candidates running for seats in the United States House of Representatives? (In 2004, a significant number of voters did not even know the names of both major party candidates

---

The worldviews of political parties are implied in the words and phrases they use repeatedly in their discourse. University of California linguist George Lakoff came up with a list of words used over and over in the speeches and writings of conservatives and liberals. It's worth examining them to figure out the dominant worldviews reflected in the language.*

Conservatives: "character, virtue, discipline, tough it out, get tough, tough love, strong, self-reliance, individual responsibility, backbone, standards, authority, heritage, competition, earn, hard work, enterprise, property rights, reward, freedom, intrusion, interference, meddling, punishment, human nature, traditional, common sense, dependency, self-indulgent, elite, quotas, breakdown, corrupt, decay, rot, degenerate, deviant, lifestyle."

Liberals: "social forces, social responsibility, free expression, human rights, equal rights, concern, care, help, health, safety, nutrition, basic human dignity, oppression, diversity, deprivation, alienation, big corporations, corporate welfare, ecology, ecosystem, biodiversity, pollution, and so on."

What worldviews did you come up with?

*Taken from Lakoff's book *Moral Politics: How Liberals and Conservatives Think,* University of Chicago Press, 2002.

Compare the worldview reflected in this gem, excerpted from a 1950s women's magazine, to your worldview.

The Good Wife's Guide

- Prepare yourself. Take 15 minutes to rest so you'll be refreshed when he arrives. Touch up your make-up, put a ribbon in your hair and be fresh-looking. He has just been with a lot of work-weary people. . . .
- Listen to him. You may have a dozen important things to tell him, but the moment of his arrival is not the time. Let him talk first—remember, his topics of conversation are more important than yours. . . .
- Make the evening his. Never complain if he comes home late or goes out to dinner, or other places of entertainment without you. Instead, try to understand his world of strains and pressure and his very real need to be at home and relax. . . .
- Don't complain if he's late home for dinner or even if he stays out all night. Count this as minor compared to what he might have gone through that day. . . .
- Don't ask him questions about his actions or question his judgment or integrity. Remember, he is the master of the house and as such will always exercise his will with fairness and truthfulness. You have no right to question him. . . .
- A good wife always knows her place.

—*Housekeeping Monthly,* May 13, 1955

for congressional seats in their districts; fewer still could name both candidates for state legislatures in their districts. Could you?) Too often we base our vote on our party affiliation (that is, our political beliefs), not on the merit of individual candidates. Clearly, then, weeding out insufficiently grounded background information is vital if we are to improve our reasoning about important, to say nothing of relatively trivial, matters. (It also might be a good idea to find out something about candidates for various offices before stepping into a booth and casting our ballots.)

Having well-supported background beliefs is particularly important with respect to those basic background beliefs that make up our worldviews. Worldviews are like lenses that cause us to see the world in a particular way or filters through which we process all new ideas and information. Reasoning based on a grossly inaccurate or shallow worldview tends to yield grossly inaccurate, inappropriate, or self-defeating conclusions (except when we're just plain lucky), no matter how smart we otherwise may be. Sometimes the harm is relatively minor (gamblers who waste a few bucks playing "lucky" lottery numbers; astrology column readers who arrange vacation times to fit their sign), but at other times the harm can be more serious (people with an overly rosy view of human nature who get taken by sharp operators; misanthropes who miss out on the benefits and joys of trusting relationships).

It is worth noting here that widespread failure to revise worldviews often results in serious political and social unrest and injustice. E. M. Forster captures this poignantly in his novel *A Passage to India,* in which he depicts intense conflicts in colonial India between English masters and their conquered Indian subjects. Believing themselves socially and racially superior, the English relegate the Indians to subordinate positions, never allowing them equality under the British raj. The insensitivity of the British to the plight of their subjects is met with resentment, distrust, anger, and threats of violent retaliation by the Indians. (To make matters worse, the Indians are divided from each other by differing religious and cultural beliefs.) Very few of the British or Indians Forster depicts ever revise their biases and prejudices in the light of new information—for instance, in the light of obvious evidence about the competence of individual Indians or the glaring prejudice of English officials. The novel makes a compelling case for a widespread reexamination of worldviews and other background beliefs if human beings are to arrive at a peaceful, nonexploitative coexistence on planet Earth.

Obviously, then, we need to examine our background beliefs, in particular, those that make up our worldviews, for consistency and believability, and we need to amend them so as to square with newly acquired information. The point is that having a good supply of background beliefs is not just a matter of filling up one's "tank" with gallons of facts. It is at least equally important to improve one's existing stock of beliefs by weeding out those that experience proves to be false, to sharpen vague beliefs, and to replace crude beliefs with those that are more sophisticated—beliefs that penetrate more deeply into the complexities of life and the world.

Socrates is said to have claimed that the unexamined life is not worth living. While clearly an exaggeration, there surely is a great deal of truth in this idea. By the same token, there is a large dose of truth in the idea that an unexamined worldview is not likely to be worth holding, in particular because it will contain little more than an accumulation of the ideas and prejudices of others. Examining worldviews allows us to take control of our lives by actively sorting out our fundamental beliefs, testing them against ideas and information that point to conclusions contrary to what we already believe, and making whatever revisions are indicated in the light of what we have learned. *Doing this helps us to become our own person rather than just a passive follower of others!* Unfortunately, there is a natural human tendency, stronger in some than in others, to hang on to old, comfortable beliefs, come what may. To reason cogently, we need to fight this natural human tendency (discussed further in Chapter 6).

EXERCISE 1-4

1. Using the Internet, go to google.com and search for "I have a dream" under the exact phrase option. Figure out which parts of the speech state or imply Martin Luther King's philosophy, and explain his worldview.

2. Here is a Japanese bar association official, Koji Yanase (quoted in *Newsweek*, February 26, 1996), explaining why there are only half as many lawyers in his country as there are in the Greater Washington, D.C., area alone: "If an American is hit on the head by a ball at the ballpark, he sues. If a Japanese person is hit on the head he says, 'It's my honor. It's my fault. I shouldn't have been standing there.'" Explain the two different worldviews implied in Yanase's observation.

3. Find at least one item on the Internet or in the mass media (a newspaper or magazine article or a television program) that seems to be based on a worldview contrary to the one you yourself hold. Explain your choice.

4. Find at least one item on the Internet or in the mass media that reflects a typically American point of view you happen to share, and explain what makes it typically American. (This is not as easy to do as it sounds. Recalling the content of the box on E. M. Forster's novel may help prod your memory.)

5. Describe a situation in which you changed your mind on some more or less fundamental belief, and explain what convinced you to do so. (This is a very difficult question for many people to answer, another bit of evidence for the fact that much of what goes on in the accumulation and emendation of important background beliefs happens only on the edge of consciousness.)

EXERCISE 1-5

1. Bring your background beliefs to bear and evaluate the following passage:

   During the 1999 House Judiciary impeachment hearings, a CNN reporter asked Republican Representative Mitch McCollum if it wasn't a mistake to impeach President Clinton along strictly party lines (every Republican on the relevant House committee voted "aye," every Democrat "nay"). He replied that the Republicans on the committee weren't voting for political reasons. After all, from a strictly political point of view, they would want Clinton to remain in office, so that Vice President Al Gore didn't become president.

2. The tax bill passed by Congress in the spring of 2003 was the second large tax break in three years. The Bush administration claimed that the average tax cut would be $1,000, but that was because tax breaks to the rich were so large. As Laura Tyson, Dean of the London Business School, pointed out (in *Business Week*, August 11, 2003), "Payroll taxes that pose the heaviest burden for most American families have been left untouched while the top marginal income tax rate, the capital-gains tax, and the dividend tax [all of which benefit the wealthy] have been reduced." Nevertheless, the bill was popular with lots of lower-income taxpayers who liked it because they thought it would probably cut their own tax bills. Bring your background beliefs to bear and reason about whether these people were right in thinking the bill benefited them. (Carry out the reasoning by thinking about what would be likely to happen when the bill became law.)

*3. A *Time* magazine story headlined "China's Arms Race: The World's Most Populous Country Wants the World's Best Military," claimed that "Beijing [China's capital, for those whose grasp of geography is not up to snuff] is buying and spying its way to superpower status." It listed China's annual military budget as $10.9 billion. What figures do you need to know, even if just approximately, to evaluate *Time*'s spin on the story? If you have this knowledge, what is your judgment? If you don't, a tiny bit of research will be in order here.

EXERCISE 1-6

How do the ideas expressed in the following excerpt from an essay by British philosopher Bertrand Russell compare with those in your own worldview and other background beliefs?

> The aesthetic indictment of industrialism is perhaps the least serious. A much more serious feature is the way in which it forces men, women, and children to live a life against instinct, unnatural, unspontaneous, artificial. Where industry is thoroughly developed, men are deprived of the sight of green fields and the smell of earth after rain; they are cooped together in irksome proximity, surrounded by noise and dirt, compelled to spend many hours a day performing some utterly uninteresting and monotonous mechanical task. Women are, for the most part, obliged to work in factories, and to leave to others the care of their children. The children themselves, if they are preserved from work in the factories, are kept at work in school, with an intensity that is especially damaging to the best brains. The result of this life against instinct is that industrial populations tend to be listless and trivial, in constant search of excitement, delighted by a murder, and still more delighted by a war.

Russell's essay, by the way, appeared in the June 1921 issue of the *Atlantic Monthly*. (The more things change, the more they remain the same?)

EXERCISE 1-7

Here is an excerpt from a speech delivered to the Utah chapter of NOW in May 1997 by Elizabeth Joseph in which she argues that polygamy is beneficial to women in the modern world:

> I've often said that if polygamy didn't exist the modern American career woman would have invented it. Because, despite its reputation, polygamy is the one lifestyle that offers an independent woman a real chance to "have it all." . . .
>
> As a journalist, I work many unpredictable hours in a fast-paced environment. The news determines my schedule. . . . Because of my plural marriage arrangement, I don't have to worry [about coming home late]. I know that when I have to work late my daughter will be surrounded by loving adults with whom she is comfortable and who know her schedule without my telling

them. My eight-year-old has never seen the inside of a day-care center, and my husband has never eaten a TV dinner. And I know that when I get home from work, if I'm dog-tired and stressed-out, I can be alone and guilt free. It's a rare day when all eight of my husband's wives are tired and stressed at the same time.

It's helpful to think of polygamy in terms of a free-market approach to marriage. Why shouldn't you or your daughters have the opportunity to marry the best man available, regardless of his marital status? . . .

Polygamy is an empowering lifestyle for women. It provides me the environment and opportunity to maximize my female potential without all the trade-offs and compromises that attend monogamy. The women in my family are friends. You don't share two decades of experience, and a man, without those friendships becoming very special. . . . [P]olygamy [is] the ultimate feminist lifestyle.

Compare Joseph's view to your own on marital arrangements. Do you find her ideas persuasive? Does your worldview jibe with hers? Why or why not? Most of us think of monogamy as "natural," yet polygamy has been common throughout the world at different times in history. (Although Utah outlawed the practice in the nineteenth century as a condition of statehood, the antibigamist law is rarely enforced in that state. Estimates put the number of polygamists in Utah in the tens of thousands, even though it's impossible to verify the statistics, given the illegal nature of the activity.) Portions of Joseph's speech were reprinted in the February 1998 issue of *Harper's Magazine*.

10. Two Vital Kinds of Background Beliefs

Background beliefs obviously differ greatly in their importance. Two kinds that are extremely important concern the *nature of human nature* and the *reliability of information sources*.

The Nature of Human Nature

Good beliefs about what we ourselves and other people are like constitute a vital part of everyone's worldview. They are crucial in applying what we know to the problems encountered in everyday life, whether of a personal or a social nature. When can we trust our friends? Is an instructor to be believed who says that students are graded solely on the quality of their exams and not on agreement with the instructor's personal opinions? Will people be sufficiently motivated to work diligently under a socialistic system? Are large numbers of elected officials motivated by selfish interests that frequently override their sense of duty to those who have elected them?

Fortunately, we don't have to start constructing theories about human nature from scratch, since other people, including some of the great writers (Shakespeare, Aristotle, Darwin, Freud), have been at the task for some time now. (Of course, tapping these sources has its risks. Freud, for instance, had some way-off-target ideas on the subject to go along with some extremely penetrating ones.) But even common everyday sayings contain a mother lode of wisdom. Blood *is* thicker than water, and power *does* tend to corrupt, even if it is doubtful that the female of the species is any more vain than the male.

The Reliability of Information Sources

Thoughts about the accuracy, sufficiency, and truthfulness of information sources constitute another vital kind of background belief. As with computers, so also with the human mind: "Garbage in, garbage out." We therefore need constantly to reassess the reliability of important information sources—television, newspapers, magazines, friends, the Internet, teachers, textbooks, and so on. Under what conditions are these sources likely to provide truthful or, at least, sensible information or opinions? When are alleged experts likely even to possess the truth, much less be motivated to tell it to us straight? When are they likely to be prejudiced in ways that may cloud their judgment? We can't assume automatically that a source is reliable without some *reason* for believing this. As lamented a while back, many people seem to think that if they read it in print or hear it on the TV evening news, then it must be true. Sophisticated reasoners, however, realize that these information sources do not always furnish "the truth, the whole truth, and nothing but the truth"; they don't necessarily provide us with "All the news that's fit to print" (the *New York Times* motto), instead sometimes shaving matters either out of ignorance or from self-serving motives. Intelligent viewers of the scene thus try to determine when these sources are likely to be reliable and when not. That is why a whole chapter in this text, Chapter 10, deals with advertising as an information source; Chapter 11 with the reliability of the media; and another chapter, Chapter 12, with public school textbooks as information sources.

11. Science to the Rescue

The mention of Darwin and Freud a while back brings to mind the central place that science plays in modern life and in the construction of accurate stocks of background beliefs—in particular, in the formulation of sensible worldviews. Although no information source is absolutely reliable and no theory exempt from at least a small measure of doubt, the most reliable, the most accurate information comes from the well-established sciences of physics, chemistry, biology, and, to a lesser extent, psychology, the social sciences, and the applied sciences such as engineering. The scientific enterprise is an organized, ongoing, worldwide activity that builds and corrects from generation to generation. The method of science is just the rigorous, systematic, dogged application of cogent inductive reasoning, mixed with all sorts of deductive—including mathematical—reasoning from what has so far been observed over many centuries to theories about how the universe and the many things in it have functioned and are likely to function. Theories falsified by experience are tossed out, no matter whose pet ideas happen to get stepped on. Absolutely no one, starting from scratch, could hope to obtain in one lifetime anything remotely resembling the sophisticated and accurate

[9]Note, however, that psychology has just recently come out of its infancy. Note also that there is more chicanery in medical research (because of the profit motive?) than in most other areas of science.

conclusions of any of the sciences, even if that person were a Galileo, Newton, Darwin, and Einstein all rolled into one. *It is foolish indeed to dismiss what science has to say on any topic without very careful thought and without having extremely important reasons for doing so!*[9]

Indeed, one justification for requiring all high school students to take at least one course in a physical or biological science is to allow them to gain an understanding of the great rigor with which scientific principles are tested and proved. But another, easier way to come to understand the power of science as compared to other ways of finding about the world is to think carefully about the thousands of everyday items available to us today that did not exist 300 years ago, products that owe their existence to the tremendous advances in scientific theory that have been made since the days of Galileo and Newton. Without science, there would be no automobiles, no airplanes (not to mention spacecraft), no telephones, electric lightbulbs, air conditioning, or other electric devices of any kind (certainly no computers!), no batteries, no aspirin or other common painkillers, no anesthetics (alcohol used to be the painkiller used during amputations), no antibiotics (or even knowledge of the existence of microbes and thus the extreme importance of cleanliness), no ways to purify drinking water, no indoor plumbing, no eyeglasses, no insulin for diabetics, . . . the list goes on and on. Instead there were plenty of mosquitoes and flies (and fly paper) everywhere on summer days, and people made do with commodes, outhouses, and well-drawn drinking and washing water. In those days, doctors could cure only a handful of ailments, horse dung and its foul smell were everywhere in every city and town, lighting after dark was furnished by candles or oil lamps, and so on. Before the existence of the scientific, modern, industrial world, the average life span almost everywhere was less than 50 years, much less in most societies.

Of course, to avoid having beliefs contradicted by scientific theory or to successfully apply scientific principles in dealing with everyday problems, one does have to have at least a casual acquaintance with what science has to say on various topics. The problem is that large numbers of people have no idea what science is up to and have only the tiniest stock of scientific facts about the nature of the world.

According to a 2002 National Science Foundation (NSF) study on the state of science understanding, although many Americans realize that almost everything used in everyday life owes its existence to scientific research and theories, few understand the general way in which scientists go about their business. Researchers found that 70 percent of Americans surveyed have no understanding of the scientific process (up 6 percent from the 1996 study). Similarly, a great many people are ignorant about basic scientific information. In the NSF study, for instance, only 54 percent correctly answered the question as to how long it takes the earth to orbit the sun (one year). Not surprisingly, the study also revealed that "belief in pseudoscience is relatively widespread and growing."

Unfortunately, it isn't just the average person (or average college graduate?) who is more or less illiterate when it comes to science. Even those who need to know about specific scientific results in order to do their jobs adequately are frequently remiss in this way. During a quite severe drought in California, one government official defended his inaction by stating that "One problem [in deciding whether to enact water rationing measures] is that we have only 110 years of [precipitation] records. Our statistics [on California droughts] aren't very good." Yet, just prior to that time, a U.S. Geological Survey study of giant Sequoia tree rings had yielded a record going back more than 2,000 years.

Here is Isaac Asimov, one of the best-known popularizers of science (also famous for his science fiction), explaining why cheating in science is so rare, why getting caught is almost inevitable sooner or later, and thus why scientists on the whole are so much more trustworthy (when they're doing science!) than, say, politicians and other "public servants."

Self-Correction

Every once in a while—not often—scientists discover that one of their number has published false data or has plagiarized someone else's work.

This is always deeply embarrassing, especially since these days such news usually receives wide publicity in the nonscientific world.

In some ways, however, these scandals actually reflect credit upon the world of science. Consider:

1. Scientists are, after all, human. There is enormous pressure and competition in the world of science. Promotion and status depend on how much you publish and how soon you publish, for the lion's share of credit comes if you are first with an important theory or observation. Under these circumstances, there is great temptation to rush things; to make up some data you are sure you will eventually find anyway that will support your theory; or to help yourself to someone else's work. The surprise, really, is not that it sometimes happens, but that it doesn't happen much more often. Scientists resist the pressure marvelously well.

2. When it does happen, the mere fact that it is so publicized is a tribute to scientists. If it were a common event, or if people expected scientists to be corrupt, it would make smaller headlines and drop out of sight sooner. Single cases of scientific corruption, however, will be talked about for years and inspire articles and books by the score. It's really a compliment.

3. Cases of scientific misbehavior point out how difficult it actually is to carry them out successfully, or even for very long. . . . [A] vital principle in scientific research is that nothing counts until observations can be repeated independently and there, almost inevitably, anything peculiar is uncovered. Science is self-correcting in a way that no other field of intellectual endeavor can match.

4. It is scientists themselves who catch the frauds; no one else is equipped to do so. The point is that scientists do catch them. There is never any cover-up on the grounds that science itself must not be disgraced. However embarrassing the facts may be, the culprit is exposed pitilessly and publicly. Science is self-policing in a way that no other field is.

5. Finally, the punishment is absolute. Anyone who proves to have violated the ethics of scientific endeavor is ruined for life. There is no second chance, no vestige of status. He or she must drop out, forever disgraced.

Add to all this the fact that scientific ethics requires all scientists to labor to find flaws in their own observations and theories—and to publicize these flaws when they find them—and you will understand how stern the requirements are and how astonishing it is that scandal is so infrequent.

—From *SciQuest* (February 1982).
Reprinted by permission of the author.

Students sometimes defend their ignorance of science by arguing that they only need to know the science, if any, that is relevant to the job they will perform after graduation from college. But this is a serious mistake. For one thing, it isn't possible to know now what basic scientific ideas will be relevant to a job held several years down the pike. (It isn't really possible, except in unusual cases, to know what sort of job it will *be,* much less what kinds of knowledge are going to be relevant to it.) In this increasingly technological age, more and more jobs require at least a general idea of what science has to say about various topics.

More to the point, a rudimentary understanding of science also is of immeasurable value when dealing with all sorts of everyday problems that aren't related to earning a living. Consumers spend millions of dollars every year on over-the-counter nostrums that don't work, or may even be harmful, because they don't know simple scientific facts—for instance, that no remedies they can buy will cure the flu-like infections common in winter. (A friend of ours who had a hearing problem wasted six months having his back manipulated by a chiropractor before going to a physician who removed wax from his ear and restored normal hearing.[10]) Every day, people throw their money away on get-rich-quick schemes that defy the most basic principles of economics. Large sums are wasted on fortune tellers, mediums, and other charlatans who science has proved over and over again cannot deliver the promised goods. (This point is discussed a bit more in Chapter 6.)

Students often are put off science by the sheer complexity of the subject matter. Biology, for example, has to be an extremely complicated science, given that the human body contains trillions of cells, each one of which contains millions of atoms and subatomic particles (did you know this?). So the bad news is that every science quickly gets over the heads of almost all lay people. But the good news is that with only modest perseverance, people who are reasonably intelligent can learn enough about science to greatly improve their everyday reasoning and thus their chances of success in everyday life. (Clearly, similar remarks apply to mathematics, particularly to arithmetic and simple algebra—note the confusion that occasionally results in supermarkets when the power goes out and clerks need to actually add and subtract to figure out what is owed.)

EXERCISE 1-8

The 2002 National Science Foundation study mentioned a while back was based in part on a quiz given to determine how much American adults know about the nature of the world. Answer the following true/false questions that were part of this quiz.

1. Lasers work by focusing sound waves.
2. Antibiotics kill viruses as well as bacteria.
3. The earliest human beings lived at the same time as the dinosaurs.
4. Human beings developed from earlier species of animals.

---

[10]The point is not to knock all chiropractors but to stress the need for care when consulting experts of any kind.

If some of these are a bit difficult for you to answer, you might take comfort in the fact that only the following percentages of the adult Americans answered the questions correctly:

1. 45   3. 48
2. 51   4. 53

SUMMARY OF CHAPTER 1

Reasoning is the essential ingredient in solving life's problems. This chapter discusses some of the fundamentals of good reasoning and presents an overview of the material to be covered later on the topic of reasoning well in everyday life.

1. Reasoning can be cast into arguments, which consist of one or more *premises* (reasons) offered in support of a *conclusion*. In real life (as opposed to in textbooks), arguments usually are not labeled and divided from surrounding rhetoric, nor are their premises and conclusions neatly specified. But clues generally are given. Words such as *because, since,* and *for* usually signal premises; *hence, therefore,* and *so,* conclusions.

2. Not all groups of sentences form arguments. They may be anecdotes or other types of *exposition* or *explanation.*

3. Reasoning is either *cogent* (good) or *fallacious* (bad). Cogent reasoning must satisfy three criteria: It must (1) start with justified (warranted, believable) premises, (2) include all likely relevant information, and (3) be *valid* (correct).

4. There are two basic kinds of valid reasoning: *deductive* and *inductive.* The fundamental property of a *deductively valid* argument is this: If its premises are true, then its conclusion must be true also. This is so because the conclusion of a deductively valid argument already is contained in its premises, although usually implicitly, not explicitly. (Note that a deductively valid argument may have false premises. What makes it valid is that *if* its premises are true, then its conclusion must be also.) Unlike deductively valid arguments, those that are *inductively valid* (correct, strong) have conclusions that go beyond the claims made by their premises, projecting patterns stated in the premises onto additional cases.

5. There is no truth to claims about there being such things as "feminine logic," different from "male logic. Logic is not "gender-relative." Similarly, there is no truth to the idea that something exists called "black logic," different from the "Eurocentric" variety espoused by white male teachers. Good reasoning does not differ from sex to sex or race to race; it is not in any way tied to ethnicity. Furthermore, with respect to facts, at any rate, the idea embodied in the idea that "It may well be true for you, but it isn't true for me," is without merit, as is the academic talk of there being something called "Aristotelian linear reasoning," different from a more "intuitive" type of reasoning. (But more needs to be said, and will be, about beliefs concerning values. The point made in this chapter is that, however we may arrive at value beliefs, reasoning from those beliefs

must employ the same principles of logic as does reasoning about purely factual matters.)

6. Background beliefs can be divided in many ways, one being into beliefs about *matters of fact* (snow is white) and beliefs about *values* (Jane Austen's novels are better than those of Stephen King). (Note that when speaking of beliefs here, we have in mind a broad sense covering everything accepted as true, or very likely true, and all value judgments and convictions.)

7. Beliefs also, of course, can be divided into those that happen to be true and those that are false. They also can be differentiated in terms of how firmly they are or should be held, and with respect to whether they concern particular events (Jones went to the show last Wednesday) or those that are general (Copper conducts electricity).

8. Our most important beliefs, taken together, make up our *worldviews* or *philosophies.* They are particularly important because they enter into decisions of all kinds—about what to do or what to believe—that we need to make in everyday life. *Examples:* We all die sooner or later; it's always wrong to betray a friend; the best way to find out about how things work is to use induction and deduction. Note that, although most beliefs in our worldviews are general—even extremely general—a few are not. *Example:* We don't know whether there is or isn't a God (part of the worldviews of agnostics).

9. Unfortunately, we all tend at least sometimes to hold a belief without sufficient reason for doing so—for example, when complicated social or political issues are discussed. This is true even with respect to some of the beliefs that make up our worldviews. But worldviews, just as any beliefs, need to be carefully examined: Does evidence support them? Do we really value this more than that? Having an accurate supply of background beliefs is not just a matter of regularly acquiring more beliefs but also of pruning those we already have.

   We tend to absorb the beliefs of those around us as we mature from children into adults. Our worldviews, in particular, tend to grow out of family values, religious training, peer group attitudes, cultural heritages, and so on. We often hold these vital beliefs uncritically—indeed, often without realizing that we hold them. Good critical reasoners, on the contrary, try to become aware of and to critically evaluate their background beliefs, especially those making up their worldviews.

10. Beliefs about human nature are of vital importance when reasoning in daily life, because the success or failure of everyday interactions depends on them. Whether we can trust this sort of person or that is an example. That is one reason why reading the writings of great literary and scientific figures is so useful (in addition to being entertaining).

    Beliefs about the accuracy and truthfulness of information sources also are of great importance, because, as the saying goes, "Garbage in, garbage out." We can't reason well from poor or false information. That is why later chapters in this book deal with several important information sources.

11. Because science plays such an important part in everyone's life these days, it behooves us to become as well acquainted as we can, and as time permits, with the scientific view of the world and with the ways in which scientists come to their conclusions. No one on their own could possibly discover even a tiny fraction of what scientists have learned over hundreds of years about the way the world works. (Those who don't see the importance of science in their own lives should reflect on how much we depend, every day, on the fruits of scientific investigations. *Examples:* electrical devices, painkillers and other modern medicines, toilet paper.) Unfortunately, most people do not have even a reasonably good grasp of what science is up to.

Peanuts by Charles Schulz. ©1999 United Feature Syndicate, Inc.
Reprinted by permission of United Feature Syndicate, Inc.

A canine induction by enumeration.

Truth is more of a stranger than fiction.

              —Mark Twain

Man has such a predilection for systems and abstract deductions that he is ready to distort the truth intentionally; he is ready to deny the evidence of his senses in order to justify his logic.

            —Fyodor Dostoevsky

The pure and the simple truth is rarely pure and never simple.

            — Oscar Wilde

Every man is encompassed by a cloud of comforting convictions, which move with him like flies on a summer day.

            —Bertrand Russell

Chapter

2

More on Deduction and Induction

1. Deductive Validity

In Chapter 1, we distinguished between deductively valid and inductively valid arguments. Here now is a discussion of some of the basic principles of deductive reasoning, which, by the way, the vast majority of people find quite intuitive.

As pointed out in Chapter 1, different arguments may have the same **form,** or **structure.** Here are two arguments that have the same form—namely, *modus ponens:*

   (1)   1. If it's spring, then the birds are chirping.
         2. It is spring.
    ∴3. The birds are chirping.
   (2)   1. If a world government doesn't evolve soon, then wars will continue to occur.
         2. A world government isn't going to evolve soon.
    ∴3. Wars will continue to occur.

In Chapter 1, we noted that the form of *modus ponens* can be indicated this way:

   1. If *A* then *B*.
   2. *A*.
  ∴3. *B*.

Now, here is another commonly occurring deductively valid form, called ***modus tollens:***

Form: 1. If *A* then *B*.
            2. Not *B*.
        ∴3. Not *A*.
Example: 1. If it's spring, then the birds are chirping.
            2. The birds aren't chirping.
        ∴3. It isn't spring.

Here is still another commonly occurring deductively valid argument form, usually called **hypothetical syllogism:**

Form: 1. If *A* then *B*.
            2. If *B* then *C*.
        ∴3. If *A* then *C*.
Example: 1. If we successfully develop nuclear fusion power, then power will become cheap and plentiful.
            2. If power becomes cheap and plentiful, then the economy will flourish.
        ∴3. If we successfully develop nuclear fusion power, then the economy will flourish.

And here is the deductively valid form called **disjunctive syllogism:** [1]

Form: 1. *A* or *B*.
            2. Not *A*.
        ∴3. *B*.
Example: 1. Either Bush won in 2004 or Kerry did.
            2. Bush didn't win.
        ∴3. Kerry did.

Note that, while the first premise is true, the second, unfortunately for Kerry, is false, as is the conclusion. Nevertheless, the validity of this argument guarantees that *if* both its premises had been true, *then* so would its conclusion have been true.

Finally, here are several argument forms of a different kind (all but the first two are called *syllogisms*): [2]

Form: 1. No *F*s are *G*s.
        ∴2. It's false that some *F*s are *G*s.
Example: 1. No police officers accept bribes.
        ∴2. It's false that some police officers accept bribes. (Uh, huh.)

Form: 1. All *F*s are *G*s.
        ∴2. If this is an *F*, then this is a *G*.
Example: 1. All salamis are tasty.
        ∴2. If this is a salami, then it is tasty. (No dispute on this one.)

---

[1] Strictly speaking, in spite of their names, *disjunctive syllogism* and *hypothetical syllogism* are not syllogisms.

[2] See the appendix and also Howard Kahane and Paul Tidman, *Logic and Philosophy,* 9th edition (Belmont, Calif.: Wadsworth, 2003), for additional material on deduction and induction.

Form: 1. All *F*s are *G*s.
             2. All *G*s are *H*s.
          ∴3. All *F*s are *H*s.
Example: 1. All TV evangelists have high moral standards.
             2. All who have high moral standards live up to those standards.
          ∴3. All TV evangelists live up to high moral standards. (Proven by history.)

Form: 1. All *F*s are *G*s.
             2. This is an *F*.
          ∴3. This is a *G*. (Note that this is *not* the form called *modus ponens!*)
Example: 1. All elected officials always tell the truth.
             2. George Bush (the younger) is an elected official.
          ∴3. George Bush (the younger) always tells the truth. (Ho, ho, ho!)

Form: 1. All *F*s are *G*s.
             2. No *G*s are *H*s.
          ∴3. No *F*s are *H*s.
Example: 1. All males are chauvinist pigs.
             2. No chauvinist pigs are likeable.
          ∴3. No males are likeable.

Form: 1. No *F*s are *G*s.
             2. Some *H*s are *F*s.
          ∴3. Some *H*s are not *G*s.
Example: 1. No foreigners can be trusted.
             2. Some newborn babies are foreigners.
          ∴3. Some newborn babies cannot be trusted. (Obviously.)

In daily life, arguments tend to get strung together into larger arguments leading up to a point, a grand conclusion or **thesis.** Here is an example (with logical structure exhibited to the left) in which the conclusion of the first argument is used as a premise in the second, and the conclusion of the second is used as a premise in the third, and final, argument:

1. If *A* then *B*.	1. If a world government doesn't evolve soon, then wars will continue to occur.
2. If *B* then *C*.	2. But if they continue to occur, then nuclear weapons will proliferate.
∴3. If *A* then *C*.	3. So if a world government doesn't evolve soon, then nuclear weapons will proliferate.
4. If *C* then *D*.	4. But if they proliferate, then a nuclear war will be inevitable, sooner or later.
∴5. If *A* then *D*.	5. Which proves that if a world government doesn't evolve soon, we'll end up fighting a nuclear war sooner or later.
6. Not *D*.	6. But it's ridiculous to think we'll actually have a nuclear war (that is, it's false that we'll have such a war).
∴7. Not *A*.	7. So a world government is going to evolve soon (that is, it's false that a world government won't evolve soon).

Reprinted with special permission of King Features Syndicate.

Humorous use of disjunctive syllogism. General Halftrack's reasoning is this: Either the box is too small, or we're not running this camp right. But it's false that we're not running this camp right. So the box is too small. Build a bigger one. Just as we often do in daily life, Halftrack omits a premise as understood—namely, the premise that it's false that the camp is not being run right.

EXERCISE 2-1

1. Invent deductively valid arguments having the forms *modus ponens, modus tollens, disjunctive syllogism,* and *hypothetical syllogism.*

2. Use the conclusion of one of the arguments you have just constructed as a premise in another argument that is deductively valid.

2. DEDUCTIVE INVALIDITY

Any argument that doesn't have a deductively valid form is said to be **deductively invalid.**[3] The number of deductively invalid argument forms is legion, but a few occur so frequently that they've been given names. Here are two examples (to give the flavor):

Fallacy of **denying the antecedent:**
Form: 1. If *A* then *B.*
           2. Not *A.*
      ∴3. Not *B.*
Example: 1. If abortion is murder, then it's wrong.
           2. But abortion isn't murder.
      ∴3. Abortion isn't wrong.

The conclusion doesn't follow: Even supposing abortion isn't murder, it may be wrong for other reasons.

Fallacy of **affirming the consequent:**
Form: 1. If *A* then *B.*
           2. *B.*
      ∴3. *A.*

---

[3] A deductively invalid argument may still be a good argument if it is inductively correct. Arguments that have the forms about to be discussed are bad because they are neither deductively valid nor inductively correct.

Example: 1. If Bush is still president, then a conservative is now president.
2. A conservative is now president.
∴3. Bush is still president.

The conclusion doesn't follow: Some other conservative may now be president.

EXERCISE 2-2

1. Invent an argument having the form of the fallacy *denying the antecedent,* and then show that it is deductively invalid by explaining how its premises might be true when its conclusion is false.

2. Do the same with an argument having the form *affirming the consequent.*

3. SYLLOGISMS

A lot more needs to be said about invalid reasoning and will be in later chapters, in particular, Chapters 3, 4, and 5, where various other kinds of fallacious reasoning are discussed. But let's now discuss a few more matters concerning the deductively valid reasonings called **syllogisms.**

We said before that arguments having the form called *hypothetical syllogism,*

1. If *A* then *B*.
2. If *B* then *C*.
∴3. If *A* then *C*.

are not true syllogisms (at least not in the sense intended by Aristotle, the inventor of syllogistic logic[4]) while those having the form

1. All *A*s are *B*s.
2. All *B*s are *C*s.
3. All *A*s are *C*s.

are the genuine article. What makes one the real thing and the other not? The difference between these two kinds of arguments that makes the difference should become clear in the following little exposition as to the nature of syllogisms in traditional syllogistic logic.[5]

In traditional syllogistic logic, a **categorical proposition** is a subject-predicate proposition that asserts or denies a relationship between a **subject class** and a **predicate class.** There are exactly four kinds of categorical propositions (with one variation): **universal affirmative** (A propositions), having the form "All *S* are *P*" (*example:* "All sinners are betrayers."); **universal negative** (E propositions), having the form "No *S* are *P*"

---

[4]Obviously, something has changed since days of old, and that is why, for example, argument forms such as *hypothetical syllogism* now sometimes are thought of as the genuine article. The point is that Aristotle and Aristotelians, until recently, would not have considered these other forms to be syllogisms.

[5]For now, let's just note that we replace the *A*s, *B*s, and *C*s in the form of *hypothetical syllogism* by whole sentences, as in "If Art goes to the show, then Betsy will stay home, but the *A*s and *B*s in "All *A* are *B*" are replaced by subjects of sentences, or predicates, as in "All women are fickle."

(*example:* "No chess players are imbeciles."); **particular affirmative** (I propositions), having the form "Some *S* are *P*" (*example:* "Some men are chauvinists."); and **particular negative** (O propositions), having the form "Some *S* are not *P*" (*example:* "Some logicians are not nitpickers."). The one common variation is that statements such as "Socrates is a man," having as their subject a particular item rather than a class of items, are often honorifically considered to be A propositions.

A **syllogism** is an argument containing three categorical propositions, two of them premises, one a conclusion. Here is one of the original examples (dechauvinized):

Syllogism	*Traditional Symbolization*
All humans are mortal.	MAP
All Greeks are human.	SAM
∴ All Greeks are mortal.	∴ SAP

The term *P,* the predicate of the conclusion, is said to be the syllogism's **major term;** the term *S,* the subject of the conclusion, its **minor term;** and the term *M,* which occurs once in each premise but not in the conclusion, its **middle term.** Every syllogism has exactly three terms (none used equivocally), each one repeated twice but not in the same proposition. There are hundreds of different syllogistic forms (figure out how many), but, of course, only some are valid. The one given above is valid, whereas the syllogism "All Greeks are human; all humans are mortal; therefore, all mortals are Greek" is not.

The valid syllogism about Greeks being mortal is said to be in the **mood** AAA (for obvious reasons). (In this case, the syllogism is said to be in the *first figure,* and its *form* is said to be AAA-I, but let's pass over this complication.) There are, of course, other moods (and figures). Here, for instance, is a syllogism in the mood AII (it happens to be in the third figure): [6]

Syllogism	*Traditional Symbolization*
All things made out of grass are green.	MAG
Some things made out of grass are cigarettes.	MIC
∴ Some cigarettes are green.	∴ CIG

EXERCISE 2-3

1. Invent a deductively valid syllogism that has the same form as the valid syllogism about Greeks being mortal just mentioned.

2. Invent another deductively valid syllogism in some other mood (but not the mood AII).

3. Now invent a deductively invalid syllogism, and explain why you think that it is not valid.

---

[6] In the Middle Ages, students determined the validity of syllogistic forms by reciting a chant containing a name for each of the valid cases in each figure. For example, the name "bArbArA" occurs in the chant for the first figure, indicating that the form AAA-1 is valid. For more about syllogisms, including an explanation as to how a syllogism's figure is determined, see Howard Kahane and Paul Tidman, *Logic and Philosophy,* 9th edition (Belmont, Calif: Wadsworth, 2003).

*4. Explain why *disjunctive syllogisms* are not true syllogisms in the sense intended by Aristotle. (Try to do this before looking at the answer in the back of the book.)

4. Indirect Proofs

Another common everyday kind of reasoning is called an **indirect** or a **reductio ad absurdum** (reduce to an absurdity) proof. We reason in this way when we assume the opposite of what we wish to prove and then deductively derive a conclusion claimed to be false, indeed, often contradictory or otherwise absurd. The point is that if we validly reason to an obviously false conclusion, then our original assumption must be false and hence its negation—the thing we wish to prove—must be true. Here is an example:

> Assume for the moment that President Clinton offered a night's stay in the Lincoln Room in the White House in return for campaign contributions. Then, since doing so would definitely be at least shady, if not illegal, Clinton would have done something shady if not illegal. But Clinton is an honorable man, so we can be sure that he did not do anything shady or illegal. Therefore, the assumption that Clinton offered a stay in the Lincoln room in return for money must be false. (Notice that the fact that Clinton did, according to most viewers of the scene, rent out the Lincoln bedroom does not detract from the fact that the reasoning in this indirect argument is deductively valid. It just means that one of the premises of this argument must be false.

An indirect proof can be defeated in either of two ways. One is by showing that there is a mistake in reasoning. (In our example, there is no mistake in reasoning. The argument is deductively valid, which just means that if its premises are true, then its conclusion must be true). The other way is to show that at least one of its premises (other than the assumed premise) is false. (In our example, the likely premise would be . . . ?)

5. Tautologies, Contradictions, and Contingent Statements

A **tautology** is a statement that is *logically,* or *necessarily,* true or is so devoid of content as to be practically empty (and thus true because completely empty statements, making no claim, cannot be false).[7] *Example:* "Scott Peterson did it, or he didn't." A **contradiction** is a statement that is necessarily false (because it contradicts itself). *Example:* "Scott Peterson did it, and he didn't do it." All other statements are said to be **contingent.** *Example:* "Scott Peterson didn't do it."

We can determine the truth value of a contradiction or of a tautology by logical—deductive—means alone, without the need for any empirical investigation or inductive reasoning. But determining the truth or falsity of a contingent statement requires observation by ourselves or others and, usually, the employment of inductive reasoning. *Example:* Tasting and disliking cooked vegetables several times has led many people to

---

[7] Note that logicians often use the term *tautology* in a more restricted manner, so as to cover only the logical truths provable by means of what is called *sentential logic.*

conclude inductively that in general they will dislike cooked vegetables. (Note that there is no contradiction between always disliking cooked vegetables in the past and liking them sometime in the future. Nor does this past dislike guarantee that they always will be disliked in the future.)

EXERCISE 2-4

Which of the following are tautologies, which contradictions, and which contingent statements? Defend your answers. (Be careful; at least one of these is sneaky.)

1. Either Ralph Nader ran for president of the United States in 2004, or a lot of newspapers were mistaken.

2. Either Ralph Nader was on the ballot in Georgia in 2004, or he wasn't.

*3. Nader didn't campaign both for the presidency and for the vice presidency.

4. Snow is always white, except, of course, when it isn't.

5. The media always report the news accurately.

6. No politicians ever keep any of their campaign promises.

7. Those who laugh last, laugh best.

8. I learned in school that 2 + 2 always equals 4, but I don't believe it.

9. Either you're in favor of an equal rights amendment to the Constitution, or you're against it.

10. Trespassers will be shot and then they'll never trespass again.

11. If you don't play the state lottery, you can't win it.

12. If I didn't get all of the first ten questions here right, then I did get them all right.

6. INDUCTIVE VALIDITY (CORRECTNESS) AND INVALIDITY (INCORRECTNESS)

As indicated before, we can think of induction as a kind of *patterning*. Perhaps the simplest form of induction is the one called **induction by enumeration,** mentioned in Chapter 1. In this kind of inductive reasoning, we reason from the fact that all *A*s observed so far are *B*s to the conclusion that all *A*s whatsoever are *B*s. For example, a study of 100 members of Congress no doubt would show that they all accept campaign contributions from lobbyists intent on influencing legislation, and finding this out would count as good evidence for the inductive conclusion that all 535 members of Congress accept funds of this kind.

Obviously, some inductions of this kind are better than others and make their conclusions more probable. While there are several modestly different theories about how to determine the probability of the conclusions of enumerative inductions, almost all agree on a few points.

Greater sample size yields greater probability. The more instances in a sample (the instances observed so far), the greater the probability of a conclusion based on that sample. A sample of 100 members of Congress who accept campaign contributions from lobbyists provides a higher degree of probability that all do than a smaller sample, say, of 50 members. The point is that more of the same sort of evidence doesn't change the conclusion of an induction; rather, it changes the degree of probability of that conclusion and thus changes the strength of belief a rational person should have in it.

More representative samples yield higher probabilities than those that are less representative. The quality of a sample is even more important than its size. (Indeed, the higher its quality, the smaller a sample needs to be to yield a given degree of probability.) When sampling apples in a barrel, for instance, it won't do just to sample a few from the top (the classic case); after all, rotten apples are more likely to be at the bottom than at the top of a barrel. Samples that neglect possible rotten apples at the bottom of metaphorical barrels are said to be *biased* or *unrepresentative*. Obviously, the less biased, more representative a sample, the higher the degree of probability of an inference based on that sample.

One definite counterexample shoots down an enumerative induction. The most important reason that inductive reasoning is superior to many other kinds (for example, of the superstitious or the pseudoscientific variety to be discussed later) is that it does not allow us to pass over evidence that indicates a pet theory is false. For example, if one woman who takes a birth control pill as directed gets pregnant, then no valid enumerative induction about the pill's effectiveness can be drawn. (Note that it still may be possible to draw other kinds of valid inductive inferences, including the statistical kind to be discussed shortly.)

However, it often is hard to be sure that what looks like a counterexample really is one. A woman on birth control pills who becomes pregnant, for instance, may have accidentally neglected to take the pills properly, and we may not be aware of that fact. The moral is that it is risky to reject an enumerative induction on the basis of one counterexample, or even two, unless we are very sure that at least one is a genuine counterexample. But when we are sure, then an enumerative induction in question must be rejected.

Reasoning by Analogy

Several other kinds of inductive reasoning are very similar to enumerative induction, including reasoning by **analogy.** In one version of this kind of inductive reasoning, we reason from the similarity of two things in several relevant respects to their similarity in another. Thus, if we know that two people have similar tastes in books, art, food, music, and TV programs and find out that one likes to watch *Mystery!* on public television (PBS), then we're justified in concluding by analogy that the other probably does also.

The trouble is that every two things resemble each other in an indefinitely large number of ways. Only *relevant* resemblances count in drawing correct analogies. But what makes a resemblance relevant? The answer is background beliefs about how, in general, things hang together. For example, if the stock market rises and falls in concert with ups and downs in the Olympic elk population over several years, only fools are likely to conclude that the two will fluctuate together in the future, because so much background information contradicts this idea. On the other hand, if stocks were to rise and fall over several years in concert with ups and downs in retail sales, we could reason by analogy that the next change in one will produce a similar change in the other. (Of course, given all of the other factors relevant to stock market prices, an induction of the kind just described would have to be assigned a very modest degree of probability.)

In another version of analogical induction, we reason from the fact that all examined items of a certain kind have a particular property to the conclusion that a particular as yet unexamined item of that kind will be found to have that property. Finding out that, say, 100 members of Congress accept money from lobbyists, we can conclude by this kind of analogy that a certain other member probably also does so.

As this last example shows, analogical inductions are much safer, and thus have a higher degree of probability, than their enumerative counterparts, because they have much weaker conclusions. Concluding, for example, that a particular member of Congress accepts money from lobbyists is a much weaker, hence safer, prediction than that all members of Congress do so.

Statistical Induction

When drawing a sample from a population, we often find that not all of the examined *A*s are *B*s, so that we cannot draw a valid enumerative induction. But having found that a certain percentage of the *A*s have the property in question, we can conclude by a **statistical induction** that the same percentage of the total population of *A*s have that property. Having found, say, that 480 of the first 1,000 observed tosses of a given coin land face up, we can conclude that 48 percent of all of the tosses with that coin will land face up (thus learning, incidentally, that the coin probably is slightly biased in favor of tails, as many coins are).

Of course, what was said about the quality and, hence, the degree of probability of enumerative inductions also applies to the statistical variety. The larger the sample employed and the more representative it is, the higher the degree of probability of a statistical induction based on that sample.

Higher-Level Inductions

More general, **higher-level** inductions can be used to evaluate those that are less general. For example, we use higher-level induction when we conclude that an automobile engine eventually will wear out or need to be repaired, even though it has run perfectly for 100,000 miles. We overrule a low-level conclusion telling us that because the car has run perfectly so far, it will do so forever, by appeal to a higher-level, more general induction such as this one: All mechanical devices with moving parts checked up on so far have eventually worn out or needed to be repaired, so very probably this particular mechanical device (the engine in question) also eventually will wear out or need to be repaired.

More general inferences, based on larger samples about more kinds of items, usually have higher degrees of probability than do those that are less general. That is why an enumerative induction about a particular automobile is overruled by a more general one about many mechanical devices. (There are, in fact, even higher-level reasons for tossing out this low-level induction by enumeration—for example, scientific inductions concerning basic principles of physics and chemistry having to do with the effects of friction.)

Reasoning to Causal Connections

When we reason inductively, we often are looking for explanations, or **causes.** For instance, early investigators of the connection between cigarette smoking and lung cancer, emphysema, and heart disease wanted to determine by means of statistical inductions whether smoking *causes* these death-dealing diseases. They found that smokers contract these diseases much more frequently than nonsmokers, and heavy smokers more than light. That is, they discovered a statistical link between smoking cigarettes and contracting these diseases. Finding no higher-level evidence to the contrary, they concluded that cigarette smoking does indeed cause these life-threatening illnesses. (That some people smoke like chimneys and never come down with these illnesses doesn't prove the contrary, but it does suggest that part of the cause of these diseases must be some other, very likely genetic, factor.[8])

The inductive patterns discussed in this chapter are relatively neat and simple. Enumerative induction is an example. But in daily life, and in particular in scientific theorizing, inductive reasoning often is much more complicated and may involve mathematical reasoning (a kind of deductive reasoning) as well. We believe cigarette smoking causes lung cancer, for example, not just because a certain percentage of those who smoke get that deadly disease but also because the percentage of those who do not smoke and get lung cancer is much lower than for those who do smoke. It is the comparison of the two groups that proves the point. (In fact, the reasoning linking smoking and lung cancer is even more complicated than we have indicated here. For instance, we haven't mentioned how theorists ruled out certain other causal possibilities by carefully selecting the individuals in their samples to rule out the effects of other likely carcinogens.)

Concatenated Inductions

The cigarette/cancer example just discussed brings to mind the fact that in the vast majority of scientific cases, the reasoning employed is of the kind that can be called **concatenated**—a joining together of inductions and deductions in the discovery of a *pattern* that fits what has been observed or previously reasoned to. In scientific reasoning, inductively confirmed theories of several disciplines typically are brought to bear to reach a conclusion. This is done, for example, in determining the types and significance of the food our ancestors ate before the time of recorded history. Carbon 14 dating is used to determine the approximate date at which, say, animal feces, now fossilized, were deposited at an archeological dig; chemical analysis to reveal what kind of food it was (grain, meat, and so on) and that it was eaten by human beings and not other animals—

---

[8] See the section in the appendix concerning necessary and sufficient conditions.

all of this coupled with anthropological theories about how this sort of food fit into the everyday diet of people in those days. Knowledge of this kind may then be used as part of the evidence in theories about the migrations of ancient peoples and the dispersal of and changes in various kinds of grains, fruits, and domesticated animals.

EXERCISE 2-5

1. What is the difference between an induction by enumeration and analogical reasoning? Provide an example (not mentioned in the text) of each.

2. Explain in your own words what the difference is between an induction by enumeration and a statistical induction. Provide an example (not mentioned in the text) of a valid statistical induction.

3. What is meant by saying that an inference is a higher-level induction? Provide an example (not mentioned in the text).

7. A MISCONCEPTION ABOUT DEDUCTION AND INDUCTION

There is a widespread but erroneous idea about the difference between deductive and inductive validity. This is the idea that in deductively valid reasoning, we go from the general to the particular, while in inductively valid reasoning, we move from the particular to the general. But little can be said in support of this idea. For instance, the deductively valid argument

1. All Republican politicians are to the right of John Kerry.
∴2. All who are not to the right of John Kerry are not Republican politicians.

moves from the general to the equally general, while the inductively valid argument

1. Bill Clinton made promises during the 1992 campaign that he didn't keep.
2. Bill Clinton made promises during the 1996 campaign that he didn't keep.
3. George Bush (the younger) made promises during the 2000 campaign that he didn't keep.
∴4. George Bush very likely won't keep all the promises he made during the year 2004 campaign.

moves from the particular to the equally particular. And the inductively valid argument

1. So far, all presidential candidates of the Republican party have been male.
∴2. The next Republican party presidential candidate will be male.

moves from the general to the particular, not the other way around.

So there isn't much truth to the old idea that deductive reasoning moves from the general to the particular, while inductive reasoning moves from the particular to the general. More accurately, when we reason deductively, we reason to conclusions already contained (implicitly or explicitly) in our premises; when we reason inductively, we move to conclusions by extending patterns or resemblances from one set of events to another set.

Some of those who argue otherwise claim that the idea of deduction moving from the general to the particular is intended to be true only for syllogistic reasoning. Thus, the valid syllogism "All humans are mortal; Socrates is human; therefore, Socrates is mortal," does indeed move from the general to the particular. The trouble, of course, is that this is not true for the vast majority of other valid syllogisms, including the one mentioned a while back, whose conclusion is that all Greeks are mortal.

8. REASONING COGENTLY VERSUS BEING RIGHT IN FACT

Reasoning correctly and getting a true conclusion are unfortunately not the same thing. We can reason correctly and get a false conclusion, and we can reason fallaciously and get a true conclusion.[9] *Examples:* Scientists in times past reasoned correctly from what was known then to the conclusion that superconductivity occurs only at temperatures very close to absolute zero, but we now know that this conclusion is false. Astrology buffs reason incorrectly that they will have a good day from the fact that a newspaper column says they will or that the stars are in a certain position in the sky, and then luckily they do have a good day (for completely different reasons having nothing whatever to do with astrology or where the stars happen to be).

On the whole, it's a lot better to reason incorrectly to true—right—conclusions than it is to reason well to false ones.[10] *But the most likely way to be right, in the long run, is to reason correctly!* When people who follow astrology columns thereby do better than they otherwise would have, they're just extremely lucky, not smart. (They're also an extremely rare species of speculator.) In daily life, however, people often equate being smart with being successful, as though success proves reasoning has been cogent. It doesn't, nor does failure prove reasoning fallacious. That's life. Smart people, as they say, "play the odds"—they try to reason well and take their chances in this not quite best of all possible worlds, and *in the long run in most cases, they do a lot better than those whose reasoning is excessively fallacious.*

SUMMARY OF CHAPTER 2

1. Different arguments may have the same form, or structure. *Modus ponens, modus tollens, hypothetical syllogism,* and so on, are deductively valid argument forms. Note that in everyday life, arguments frequently get strung together, leading to a grand conclusion, a *thesis.*

2. But lots of other forms are deductively invalid. *Affirming the consequent* and *denying the antecedent* are examples of deductively invalid argument forms.

3. A *categorical proposition* asserts or denies a relationship between a *subject class* and a *predicate class.* There are four kinds of categorical propositions: *universal affirmative* (A propositions), having the form "All *S* are *P*"; *universal negative* (E propositions), having the form "No *S* are *P*"; *particular affirmative* (I propositions), having the form "Some *S* are *P*"; and *particular negative* (O

---

[9] In philosophical jargon, we can be *epistemologically right* although *ontologically wrong,* and we can be *epistemologically wrong* but *ontologically right.*

[10] Philosophical slogan: "I'd rather be epistemologically wrong and ontologically right than vice versa, but the best way to be ontologically right is to be epistemologically right." (Philosophical jargon can be just as opaque as that of every other discipline.)

propositions), having the form "Some *S* are not *P.*" Statements such as "Socrates is a man," having as their subject a particular item rather than a class of items, are often honorifically considered to be A propositions.

A *syllogism* is an argument containing three categorical propositions, two of them premises, one a conclusion. *Example:* "No foreigners are trustable. Some newborn babies are foreigners. Therefore, some newborn babies cannot be trusted." The predicate of the conclusion of a syllogism is said to be its *major term;* the subject of the conclusion, its *minor term;* and the term that occurs once in each premise but not in the conclusion, its *middle term.* Every syllogism has exactly three terms (none used equivocally), each one repeated twice but not in the same proposition. There are hundreds of different syllogistic forms (figure out how many), but, of course, only some are valid. *Example:* The syllogism "All Greeks are humans; all humans are mortals; therefore, all mortals are Greek" is not valid.

The *mood* of a syllogism is determined by the kinds of propositions it contains. Thus the syllogism just mentioned is in the mood AAA.

4. In an *indirect* or *reductio ad absurdum* proof, we assume the opposite of what we wish to prove and then deductively derive a conclusion claimed to be false, contradictory, or otherwise absurd. The point is that if we reason validly to a false, or absurd, conclusion, then our original assumption must be false and hence its negation—the thing we wish to prove—must be true.

5. A *tautology* is a statement that is *logically,* or *necessarily,* true or is so devoid of content as to be practically empty. *Example:* "Madonna is world-famous, or she isn't." A *contradiction* is a statement that is necessarily false (because it contradicts itself). *Example:* "Madonna is world-famous and she isn't." All other statements are said to be contingent. *Example:* "Madonna is talented and world-famous."

The truth values of contradictions and tautologies can be determined by logical—deductive—means alone, but the truth or falsity of contingent statements cannot. They are justified by observation or by reasoning, part of which must be inductive, from what we and/or other people have observed.

6. There are several kinds of valid, or correct, inductions. One is *induction by enumeration,* in which we infer from the fact that all As observed so far are Bs to the conclusion that all As whatsoever are Bs.

In general, the larger or the more representative a sample, the greater the probability of an induction based on it. Note that one definite counterexample invalidates an induction. (But we have to be sure that it really is a counterexample.)

Analogical reasoning is very much like induction by enumeration, the chief difference being that analogies yield conclusions about just one case (which is why they have higher degrees of probability than corresponding enumerative inductions), whereas enumerative inductions typically concern a great many.

Statistical inductions also are similar to the enumerative variety, but they move from the fact that a certain percentage of a sample has a given property to the conclusion that the same percentage in the population at large has that property.

We can use more general, *higher-level* inductions to correct, or overrule, lower-level ones. If experience shows that all mechanical devices eventually wear out or need to be repaired, then it isn't reasonable to conclude that a particular auto engine will not, even though it has run perfectly for 100,000 miles.

Inductive reasoning often is used to discover *causes,* as in the case of the statistical induction linking cigarette smoking and various life-threatening diseases.

Reasoning called *concatenated* often brings new evidence together with several already inductively established conclusions, combined with deductive reasoning, to obtain a further conclusion. This is especially true in the sciences. *Example:* Anthropologists or evolutionary theorists reason from principles of physics and chemistry in reaching conclusions from newly discovered evidence.

7. It often is said that deductively valid reasonings move from general premises to particular conclusions, while inductively valid reasoning moves from particular premises to general conclusions. But this is not correct. *Examples:* The deductively valid argument "If you jump off the Brooklyn Bridge, then you'll be killed. So if you aren't killed, you haven't jumped off the Brooklyn Bridge," moves from the particular to the particular. (By the way, the form of this inference—"If *A* then *B;* therefore, if not-*B* then not-*A*—is sometimes called *contraposition.*) The inductively valid reasoning "If Dan Rather has obtained power, then he has been corrupted by it. He has obtained power. Hence, he has been corrupted by it," moves from the particular to the equally particular (employing *modus ponens,* by the way).

8. Life being what it is, reasoning correctly sometimes results in drawing false conclusions, even from a true premise. *Example:* The person who, having loaned a friend money many times before and having always been repaid, loans the friend money again and gets stiffed. Furthermore, again life being what it is, reasoning fallaciously sometimes results in drawing true conclusions, even sometimes from false premises. *Example:* risking one's life savings at a dice table in Las Vegas employing the "double the bet" method (discussed in the appendix) and winning a small fortune.

But, still again, life being what it is, *in a large majority of cases,* those who reason cogently do better, often a great deal better, than those who reason fallaciously.

"Having concluded, Your Highness, an exhaustive study of this nation's political, social and economic history, and after examining, Sire, the unfortunate events leading to the present deplorable state of the realm, the consensus of the council is that Your Majesty's only course, for the public good, must be to take the next step."

Question-begging advice, following oracular rule number 1: Make pronouncements as empty as possible to minimize the chance of being wrong.

Chapter

3

FALLACIOUS REASONING—1

We said in Chapter 1 that we reason fallaciously when we fail to satisfy all three of the requirements of cogent reasoning. Accepting premises that we should doubt makes us guilty of the fallacy *questionable premise;* neglecting relevant evidence guilty of the fallacy *suppressed evidence;* and drawing conclusions not sufficiently supported by evidence guilty of the fallacy *invalid inference.*

Of course, we must remember that the arguments encountered in daily life tend to be vague, or ambiguous, and premises, and even conclusions, sometimes are omitted as understood. As a result, everyday arguments often can be construed in different ways. Consider the following key line in a TV beer commercial:

More people in America drink Budweiser than any other beer.

Taken literally, this isn't an argument, but it clearly implies that the listener also should drink Bud. So its import might be put this way:

1. More people in America drink Budweiser than any other beer. (Premise)
∴2. You, too, should drink Budweiser. (Implied conclusion)

Construed in this way, the ad does contain an argument, but the argument is defective because it contains an invalid inference. That a beer is the most popular does not imply you should drink it. The most popular beer may not be the best beer, and, anyway, perhaps you should drink a cheaper beer and save money or not drink any beer at all. We could, however, just as well restate the argument this way:

1. More people in America drink Budweiser than any other beer. (Premise)
2. The most popular beer is the best beer. (Implied premise)
3. You should drink the best beer. (Implied premise)
∴4. You should drink Budweiser. (Implied conclusion)

Now the argument is valid but contains at least two questionable premises—that the most popular beer is the best beer and that you should drink the best beer.

Like the Budweiser example, most fallacious arguments can be stated in more ways than one. So there often isn't a single "right" label to apply to fallacious reasoning. This doesn't mean that there aren't plenty of wrong labels to apply, and it surely doesn't mean that merely applying a plausible label is sufficient. The point is to understand *why* an argument is fallacious and why a particular label can be shown to be right. In the case of the Budweiser ad, for instance, it's important to see that being the most popular beer is not by itself sufficient reason for most people to conclude that they should go out and buy it. Labeling just helps us to see that an argument is fallacious (*if it is!*) and helps us to understand why it is fallacious.

Notice, by the way, that in calling the argument itself fallacious, rather than reasoners who may have been taken in by it, we have employed the shortcut way of talking mentioned in Chapter 1. To be precise, we should have said, for example, that anyone who was persuaded by it would be guilty of fallacious reasoning.

Although all fallacious reasoning falls into one or more of the three broad categories just mentioned, over the years a number of other, narrower fallacy species have been identified that crosscut the three basic types.[1] These labels have come into common use because experience has shown them to be helpful in spotting fallacious reasoning.

Let's now discuss some of the more important of these common fallacy categories and also add some comments concerning the broad fallacy category *questionable premise.*

1. APPEAL TO AUTHORITY

One of the most serious errors in reasoning is to accept the word of someone, in particular an alleged authority, when we should be suspicious. We all have to appeal to experts for information or advice—only fools don't do so with some regularity. In this technological age we all are nonexperts in most fields. Accepting the word of an authority,

---

[1] That is, some instances of a narrower fallacy species may fall into one of the three broad genuses and some into another. Several hundred fallacy categories have been discussed in the literature, but no single source discusses all of them. Only those that occur frequently are discussed in this text, which means that our list is not exhaustive by any means. But the division into the three broad master categories *questionable premise, suppressed evidence,* and *invalid inference* is exhaustive. For more on this master fallacy classification scheme, see Howard Kahane, "The Nature and Classification of Fallacies," *Informal Logic: The First International Symposium,* edited by J. Anthony Blair and Ralph H. Johnson (Inverness, Calif.: Edgepress, 1980). Perhaps the best book on the history of fallacy theory is C. L. Hamblin's *Fallacies* (Newport News, Va.: Vale, 1986—reprinted from an earlier edition).

alleged or genuine, when we shouldn't makes us guilty of the fallacy called **appeal to authority.**

But which appeals are proper and which fallacious? Clearly, it isn't a good idea to believe that an authority is reliable without having good reason for doing so. Some alleged authorities don't have the expertise they claim; others can't be relied on to tell it to us straight rather than feed us something more self-serving. Anyway, in some cases we need to do some of our own thinking and research.

So when seeking expert advice, three basic questions need to be addressed if we want to avoid committing the fallacy of *appeal to authority:*

1. Is the source likely to have the information or good judgment we need?
2. If so, can we trust the authority to tell it to us straight?
3. Do we have the time, desire, and ability to reason the matter out for ourselves (or to understand the expert's reasoning, so that we don't have to rely merely on the authority's word)?

We usually know right away whether we have the needed time and inclination, but the other questions often are rather difficult to answer. However, a few rules of thumb should prove helpful.

Some Authorities Are More Trustworthy than Others

Individuals who are regarded as authorities or experts are not created equal. Some are smart, others stupid; some are well trained in their field, some not; some are more or less honest (a completely honest person being a rarity in any case), others pretty much untrustworthy.

Characters who are less than completely ethical are found in every profession, but some fields attract this type more than others. The fields of law, financial advising, and politics, for instance, notoriously attract sharp operators, but even the ministry is not without its Elmer Gantrys and Jim Bakkers, and doctors who prescribe unneeded surgery are not unknown in the history of medicine.

Anyway, the personal interests of experts are bound now and then to conflict with their duties to clients. Professionals are human, after all, just like the rest of us. Politicians elected to the United States Congress are bound to savor the perks, fame, power, and excitement that goes along with their jobs (who wouldn't?), making it rather difficult for them to refuse the fat cat "campaign contributions" (bribes?) needed to gain reelection, and thus more difficult still for them to tell voters the straight truth on important issues. (Remember, though, that politics is the art of compromise and, in particular, that candidates do need to get elected to do good work, so they often need at least to shade the truth for that purpose. See the section in Chapter 10 on political rhetoric for more on this point.)

So when considering expert reasoning or pronouncements, we always need to make a judgment about believability. Does the authority have an axe to grind, a personal interest that might be furthered? Lawyers who speak out against no-fault auto insurance, as they usually do, have to be looked at with a jaundiced eye precisely because the point of no-fault insurance is to reduce legal costs. When members of Congress vote against gun laws, in spite of strong public sentiment favoring gun control in the wake of the tragedies at Columbine and elsewhere, we aren't being overly skeptical if we wonder whether their judgment has been warped by campaign contributions from interested parties or by narrow constituent interests.

On the other hand, we should be inclined, other things being equal, to accept the word of dentists who urge their patients to brush and floss regularly and of doctors who exhort us to quit smoking cigarettes, precisely because dentists make money when patients get cavities, and doctors profit when people get cancer, have heart attacks, or come down with emphysema. (Sad but true.) Advice to brush regularly or to quit smoking thus is more likely to be motivated by a professional intent to serve the interests of clients rather than by a desire to further selfish interests.

Authorities in One Field Aren't Necessarily Experts in Another

Famous athletes and movie stars who endorse all sorts of products in television commercials are good examples of professionals speaking outside their fields of expertise. There's no reason to suppose that someone who knows how to act, or to hit home runs, knows any more about washing machines, or shaving cream, than anyone else. The fact that Britney Spears is paid to endorse Pepsi Cola, or Tiger Woods to tout Nike products, proves nothing about the quality of these products, nor is there any reason to suppose that Catherine Zeta-Jones (for T-Mobile) has any special knowledge about telephone companies. Yet most of us, irrationally, are suckers when it comes to celebrity TV commercials.

Learn How Best to Appeal to Authorities

It generally is easy to know which sorts of experts to appeal to. Sick people need to consult doctors; someone sued for divorce, a lawyer. It's a lot more difficult to find experts in a particular profession who know their stuff and can be relied on. But even after finding them, we need to become adept at picking their brains. Experts often throw up roadblocks to understanding, especially by overwhelming us with professional lingo. They frequently find it tedious to explain complicated matters to laypeople, and, anyway, they may not want to spend the time and effort necessary to do so.

It also is true that laypeople often are unable to follow the complicated reasonings of trained professionals, medical specialists being a case in point. But it usually is possible to get at least a rough idea of what authorities are up to if we are persistent and if we insist that they translate their professional lingo into ordinary discourse. It's hard not to be intimidated by professional jargon or by an authoritarian aura, but it is well worth the effort to resist that sort of intimidation.

Check the Past Records of Alleged Experts

Professional sports has a saying that when in doubt you should go with a winner. Similarly, when expert advice is needed, it makes sense to go with a winner—someone whose track record is good. Those who have been right in the past are more likely than others to be right in the future, other things being equal. Remember, however, that other things are not always equal. Auto mechanics get out of touch with the latest technology, lawyers who have made their pile become lazy, and textbook writers (with at least two obvious exceptions!) may eventually go over the hill.

Of course, judging alleged experts by their track records requires that we know their records, not just their reputations. During the Gulf crisis and war, television viewers were inundated with the prognostications of well-known figures with high-flown titles, such as Henry Kissinger, secretary of state under President Nixon; Zbignew Brzezinski, head of the National Security Council under President Carter; and Dean Rusk, secretary of state under President Kennedy. Taken in by what some people have called the "halo effect," many viewers automatically accepted the words of these "elder statesmen" without checking up on their records while in office, a grave mistake given the dismal performance of so many highly placed government officials. As for that "elder statesman" Henry Kissinger, his image was tarnished during the controversy over his alleged war crimes, including his policy-making role in Vietnam and the bombing of Cambodia. This didn't discourage him from weighing in on the Iraq War, though, which he strongly defended. It's a good idea to check out the credentials of elder statesmen before accepting their opinions on any war.

Understand What Authorities Can Be Expected to Know

All experts definitely are not created equal. It isn't just that some alleged authorities, as we mentioned before, don't know what they claim to know, or that some aren't completely on the up-and-up. It's also that a good deal more is known about some topics than about others and that some information is much more expensive to obtain than others. True experts in some fields thus are more reliable than those in others.

We all are forced by the nature of modern life to seek advice and expert performance from doctors, lawyers, auto mechanics, and other kinds of trained (and often licensed) professionals. But we can't expect the same sorts of definitive answers to our questions or solutions to our problems when consulting these authorities as we can, say, when consulting physicists or chemists. Medicine, for example, while based on biological theory, still is an art: Doctors cannot always be sure of their diagnoses or of how to treat an ailment; the best of them are bound to be mistaken in their judgments now and then. Lawyers cannot be sure how jurors or judges will respond to evidence. Ministers do not have direct lines to a higher authority.

Become Your Own Expert on Important Controversial Topics

When authorities disagree on a topic of importance, the rest of us need to become our own experts, turning to authorities for evidence, reasons, and arguments, but not conclusions. This is especially true with respect to social and political matters, because experts themselves disagree so much on these issues and because we have to watch out for the intrusion of self-interest into their stated judgments and opinions. Politicians, for example, may be beholden to special interests (as we noted before) or simply be going along with a misguided tide of public opinion. Conservative commentators generally see things differently than do those who are liberal.[2]

But politics is not by any means the only topic where the reasons and reasonings of experts should count for much more than their conclusions. Judges and juries, for example, too often uncritically accept the opinions of psychologists concerning the sanity of those charged with crimes, rather than delving into the reasons behind those opinions. After all, different opinions often can be obtained just by consulting other psychologists.[3] This holds true even in fields like medicine, where we tend to trust the opinions of experts. For instance, a woman who is advised to have a hysterectomy might be wise to seek a second opinion from another physician. (Women with relevant background information know that many unnecessary hysterectomies are performed for conditions that can be treated by less invasive means.)

Note, by the way, that most fallacious appeals to authority fall under the broader category *questionable premise,* because underlying the acceptance of the word of an authority is the implicit premise that it is wise to do so. In other words, the fallacy *appeal to authority* is committed by acceptance of expert advice or information when it isn't wise to do so, perhaps because the authority isn't likely to have the information we desire or may have a serious conflict of interest.

Before going on to a discussion of other fallacies, perhaps notice should be taken of the flip side of the fallacy of *appeal to authority*—namely, failure to take the word of authorities when we should. After all, salespeople frequently do give us the relevant facts straight; TV news programs do provide us with a good deal of useful information, even if they don't provide us with "the whole truth, nothing but the truth"; politicians sometimes do put aside self-interest and speak out against powerful interests. Being careful when evaluating information sources does not mean becoming completely cynical.

2. INCONSISTENCY

We commit the fallacy of **inconsistency** when we are persuaded to accept the conclusion of an argument that contains self-contradictory statements or statements that contradict each other.[4] Obviously, if two statements are contradictory, then one of them must be false.

Consider, for example, the ways in which inconsistencies intrude into campaign rhetoric. (Campaign rhetoric: The pronouncements of most politicians most of the time.) Candidates for public office do not explicitly say *A* and then immediately assert not-*A*.

---

[2]Although labels such as "conservative," "libertarian," "liberal," "right-wing," and "left-wing" tend to be vague and ambiguous, they still have some content: Those labeled by these terms do tend to differ in their viewpoints, and critical reasoners need to take these differences into account.
[3]This observation conforms to B. Duggan's Law of Expert Testimony: "For every Ph.D. there is an equal and opposite Ph.D." See Paul Dixon, *The Official Rules* (New York: Delacorte, 1978), for more on irreverent, pithy sayings like Duggan's law.
[4]Recall the discussion in Chapter 2 about tautologies, contradictions, and contingent statements.

Instead, the contradictory nature of their pronouncements is concealed in one way or another. For instance, in the same speech, a candidate may assure voters that various government services or payments will significantly be increased (to curry the favor of voters who will profit from them), promise large tax reductions (to gain the support of those burdened by high taxes), and favor a huge reduction in the national debt (to appeal to voter beliefs about the virtues of governmental thrift).[5] That is how the vast majority of candidates for high office, including President Clinton in 1992 and in 1996, President Bush in 2000, and both major presidential candidates in 2004, have played the game. But government services and benefits cost money, and a majority of government expenses are fixed (most notably interest payments on previously contracted debts), so that a package of increased services and benefits coupled with significant tax and public debt reductions can be regarded as inconsistent in the absence of a plausible explanation as to how this trick is going to be performed. (In recent times, extremely high military expenditures, lobbied for by the "military-industrial complex," have made this trick even more difficult than it otherwise would be.) Adding up the figures is one way of determining whether candidates are being consistent, and hence believable, when they promise us the moon. One of the consequences of inconsistent fiscal policies became apparent when the second President Bush initiated major tax cuts in 2001 and 2003, then escalated military expenditures for the Iraq War by tens of billions of dollars and added

Government rules and regulations often require manufacturers to list the ingredients in their products, thus providing consumers with important information. And this, of course, is all to the good. But consumers still need to be wary, in spite of the good information food labeling regulations provide. For one thing, government labeling regulations sometimes are not as adequate as they might be. For another, advertisers often distort the information provided.

Take, for example, the requirement that producers of many kinds of foods list the amounts of fat, saturated fat, and cholesterol in their products. While excellent as far as it goes, this labeling requirement does not go far enough, because it doesn't require the listing of transfatty acids, perhaps the least healthy kind of fat in many processed food products, much worse even than cholesterol. Advertisers, as should be expected, take advantage of this glitch in food labeling requirements and in consumer lack of knowledge. For example, they often tout foods as heart-healthy because they are very low in cholesterol while neglecting the fact that they contain large amounts of transfatty acids or saturated fats (also very unhealthy). But government regulations do require that fine-print lists of product ingredients mention partially hydrogenated fats. So *knowledgeable* consumers, who know that "partially hydrogenated" means transfatty acids, can avoid getting taken in by sharp advertising. You can't expect manufacturers to advertise negative information about their products, a point discussed further in Chapter 10.

[5] Their argument thus can be put this way: If elected, I won't destroy the government services and payments you want, I will significantly reduce taxes, and I will reduce the national debt. Therefore, you should vote for me.

Cartoon by Tom Meyer.

prescription drug benefits for seniors to the budget. The result was a national deficit for 2003/2004 of $413 billion, the largest in history for a single year.

One reason that politicians get away with inconsistent claims or arguments so often is that voters, being human, tend to see political issues from the point of view of their own self-interest, just as they see personal problems and conflicts with friends and family. Self-interest tends to make us more blind than usual both to fair play and to cogent reasoning. Lots of cigarette smokers, for example, argue against a ban on the sale of cigarettes, on the grounds that we all have a right to ingest harmful substances if we are so inclined, but most of them also, inconsistently, argue against the legalization of heroin because it is harmful to health. Extremist African Americans who get on their high horses about prejudice against blacks have been known at the same time to inconsistently preach hatred of whites.

But when evaluating the various kinds of rhetoric encountered in everyday life, it is important that we don't misjudge deliberately equivocal, ironic, or humorous rhetoric. It won't do, for example, to brand the literally contradictory bumper sticker that says "Good enough isn't good enough" as contradictory, since it isn't intended to be taken literally. It says, in a humorous way, that we should do better than merely minimally well.

Note that there are ways to be guilty of the fallacy of *inconsistency* in addition to the obvious one of being inconsistent within a single argument or statement. The example

Mike Peters, 1986. Reprinted by permission of United Feature Syndicate, Inc.

above about politicians who, in the same speech, promise lots of government services, lower taxes, and a reduction in the national debt is a case in point. So are the cigarette smokers, also just mentioned, who are against making cigarettes illegal while at the same time are against legalizing the use of heroin.

Another way to be inconsistent is to *argue one way at a given time and another way at some other time, or when talking to one person and then to another.* Of course, there is nothing wrong with changing one's mind—of believing *A* at one time and not-*A* at another. That, after all, is the point of learning from experience. It is when we continue to hang on both to *A* and to not-*A,* trotting out one for use when reasoning about one thing and the other when reasoning about something else, that we are guilty of being inconsistent.

In politics, being inconsistent over time or from audience to audience is called "blowing with the wind." What is popular with constituents in one place or at one time may not be in another. Circumstances thus push politicians into being inconsistent in order to

---

We have just gone to some lengths to describe inconsistency as a serious mistake. Yet others have railed against being consistent; witness Ralph Waldo Emerson's famous remark, "A foolish consistency is the hobgoblin of little minds, adored by little statesmen, philosophers and divines."

But there need be no inconsistency in accepting both sides of this coin, provided we notice that consistency is an ambiguous concept. One sense requires us to be consistent in what we believe at any given time. This is roughly the sense meant in this chapter. The other requires us to be consistent now and forever, to stick to our guns no matter what contrary evidence we encounter. This, one must suppose, is the kind of consistency Emerson intended to disparage.

keep up with the latest trends in public opinion or to placate particular audiences. Candidates for office try as much as they can to tell people what they want to hear, and different people want to hear different things. When George W. Bush ran for office against Al Gore in 2000, he often mentioned the dangers of the United States overstepping its bounds as the world's only superpower—an issue of concern to some Americans. In the second debate with Gore, he said, "If we're an arrogant nation, they'll resent us. If we're a humble nation but strong, they'll welcome us." But three years later, he decided to invade Iraq without United Nations approval or widespread international support. In his comments to law enforcement agents just before the war in Iraq, he said, "Saddam Hussein is a danger and that's why he will be disarmed one way or another." Either he was inconsistent for politically expedient reasons or his worldview underwent a profound change in the intervening years between the debate and the war.

To some extent, we all engage in this sort of inconsistency—politicians are just better at it than most of the rest of us. Occasionally, we do so deliberately, with conscious intent. But often we are trying to fool not just or even the other guy but rather ourselves. Virtually all of us, for instance, are against cheating others, yet at one time or another we can't resist the temptation to do so to our advantage while providing reasons (excuses) to justify what we have done; for example, the excuse that most other people do it, so it's not wrong for us to do so. (This point is discussed at greater length in Chapter 6, where impediments to cogent reasoning are the subject.)

It also needs to be noticed that large organizations have an interesting way to be inconsistent that tends to be rather hard to notice: they have one representative speak out of one side of the mouth while another speaks from the other side. Let's call this sort of chicanery *organizational inconsistency,* thinking of a large organization as a kind of artificial person. (In regarding this as a fallacy, we are, of course, stretching that concept a bit, but for a good purpose, namely, to call attention to this threat to consistent reasoning.)

Another kind of organizational inconsistency occurs when it seems expedient to ignore company policy. For instance, a few days before the Olympiad's opening ceremonies in the 1998 Nagano games, Nike swooshes were seen everywhere on CBS—not just on athletes in Nike ads, but on the hats, jackets, gloves and snow boots of CBS network correspondents in their pregame coverage. Yet the CBS ethical handbook clearly prohibits advertiser identification during a broadcast outside of the time devoted to billboards or commercial messages. As an example, ". . . a request for permission to include an advertising logo on the desk of a broadcaster must continue to be, rejected" (*CBS News Standards,* p. 2). When substantial sums of money are at stake, it is clearly more expedient for CBS's practice to be inconsistent with its stated policy. (For more on this and related matters, see *The Nation,* November 30, 1998.)

The CBS chicanery just mentioned also illustrates another way to be inconsistent, namely, by *saying one thing while doing another.* (Calling this a fallacy again stretches that concept to serve everyday purposes. Strictly speaking, saying one thing and doing another does not make one guilty of a fallacy, because it does not involve an inconsistency between one claim, idea, or argument and another. We include this discussion here because it is important to be on guard against those who engage in this sort of shady behavior.)

Of course, mention of the inconsistencies of all these politicians should not blind us to the fact that they are not the only ones who are guilty of being inconsistent. The rest

Moon Mullins. Reprinted by permission of Tribune Media Services.

of us aren't exactly paragons of virtue where consistency is concerned. Feminists who argue against different "roles" for males and females, yet who don't reciprocate when given expensive engagement rings, or who always leave the driving to their husbands, along with the spanking of errant children, surely are inconsistent.[6]

Inconsistency often is connected in people's minds with hypocrisy—with pretending to believe what one in fact does not, or to be what one is not. The vast majority of candidates for office in the United States during the past 40 years or so have run on platforms opposing legalization of drugs even though lots of them smoked dope or sniffed cocaine (including Al Gore and George W. Bush?). (Forget about the fact that virtually all of them also drank alcohol or smoked cigarettes.) Bill Clinton did own up to smoking marijuana but notoriously claimed that he did not inhale (ho, ho, ho). Should we say that those who were inconsistent in this way were guilty of the sin of *hypocrisy*? Of course, the presidents just mentioned were pikers at the game compared to Anthony Comstock, who in the 1930s led the fight against pornography, with some success, all the while amassing what one aficionado described as a "magnificent collection" of the stuff.

Readers may note, when they have completed reading the three fallacy chapters in this text, that a good deal more time is spent on the first two fallacies in this chapter than on any of the others. The reason is that these two are very likely the most important. The importance of the fallacy of *appeal to authority* is obvious: We all are nonexperts about most of the things that matter in everyday life and therefore regularly have to appeal to authorities for information and advice. The importance of the fallacy of *inconsistency* also should be obvious: It lies in the crucial importance of consistency to cogent reasoning. *At least one of a set of inconsistent statements must be false!*

That is why trying to be consistent is very likely the best way to improve the quality of one's stock of background beliefs (a point to be discussed again later). Having reasoned to a particular conclusion, consistency requires that we ask ourselves whether we would be willing to carry through that line of reasoning when it applies to other cases. If not, then we must give up that line of reasoning or admit to the intellectual crime of being *inconsistent.*

---

[6] See the article by Cynthia Tucker, *Atlanta Constitution* editorial page editor, that ran in many newspapers on March 30, 1996.

3. STRAW MAN

While the broad fallacy category *suppressed evidence* seldom is mentioned in traditional logic texts, several species of this genus are given great play. One of these is the fallacy **straw man,** which is committed when we misrepresent an opponent's position, or a competitor's product, or go after a weaker opponent or competitor while ignoring a stronger one.[7]

Straw man has always been a stock-in-trade of advertisers. A Holiday Inn TV spot run several years ago was typical of the genre. It pictured someone telephoning a competitor to find out whether they had a motel in Fargo, North Dakota, and being told no, then asking if there happened to be one in the area and being told yes, in Cleveland, Ohio. (This spot wasn't as effective as it might have been because lots of viewers had no idea how far Cleveland is from Fargo.) In the same vein, a U.S. Postal Service commercial once pictured competitors trying to deliver packages with rickety old planes that fell apart on camera; IBM once touted its laser printers by comparing them with those of a pseudo-competing product unable to collate printed material and therefore not really in competition with the printers IBM was touting.

The expression *invidious comparison* often is used to characterize this kind of sleaze. Of course, politicians wouldn't engage in this sort of chicanery, would they?

4. FALSE DILEMMA AND THE EITHER-OR FALLACY

In traditional logic, a *dilemma* is an argument that presents two alternatives, both claimed to be bad for someone, or some position. (Dilemmas are discussed further in the appendix.)

The general form of a dilemma can be put this way:

Either P or Q.
If P then R.
If Q then S.
Therefore, either R or S.

Sometimes the undesired outcomes R and S are identical, sometimes quite different. Here is an example in which they are not quite the same: "Either our fellow citizens are good or they're bad. If they're good, laws to deter crime aren't needed. But if they're bad, laws to deter crime won't succeed. So laws to deter crime either are not needed or won't succeed."

A **false dilemma** is a dilemma that can be shown to be false. One way to do this is to demonstrate that the premise having the form "Either P or Q" is false by showing that there is at least one other viable possibility. This is called "going between the horns" of the dilemma. In the case of the dilemma just mentioned, a viable alternative is that our fellow citizens may be both good (in some ways) and bad (in others).

---

[7]Note, however, that some cases of this fallacy do not fall into the category of *suppressed evidence*. Should we, by the way, replace the name "straw man" by, say, "straw person" or perhaps "false characterization"?

Another way to defeat a dilemma is to challenge one or both of its other two premises. This is called "grasping the horns" of the dilemma. We might challenge the crime law dilemma, for example, by arguing that even if some citizens are bad, they still can be deterred by laws specifying harsh penalties.

False dilemmas usually are a species of the genus *questionable premise* because any set of statements that sets up a false dilemma needs to be questioned. (Note, by the way, that we can have false trilemmas, false quadrilemmas, and so on.)

The **either-or fallacy** (sometimes called the *black-or-white fallacy*) is very similar to that of *false dilemma*. We're guilty of this fallacy when we mistakenly reason from two alternatives, one claimed to be bad (that is, to be avoided) so that we ought to choose the other alternative. The general form of the fallacy is this:

Either *P* or *Q*.
Not *P*.
Therefore, *Q*.

where there is at least a third viable alternative, or it is questionable that *P* is bad. For example, "You have to vote either for the Republican or for the Democratic candidate. But you shouldn't vote for the Republican. So you should vote for the Democrat." A third alternative in this case would be to vote, say, for the Green party candidate (this is like going between the horns of a dilemma), and some people would challenge the claim that you shouldn't vote for the Republican candidate (this would be like grasping a dilemma by its horns).

5. BEGGING THE QUESTION   *avoid the ?*

When arguing, either with ourselves or with others, we can't provide reasons for every assertion and then reasons for the reasons, and so on. Some of what we assert must go unjustified, at least for the moment. But when we assume as a premise some form of the very point that is at issue—the very conclusion we intend to prove—we are guilty of the fallacy of **begging the question.**[8] In this sense *to beg* means "to avoid." When the premise simply states another version of the conclusion, the question of proof is avoided, or *begged*. (The fallacy of *begging the question* usually falls into the broad category *questionable premise* because a statement that is questionable as a conclusion is equally questionable as a premise.)

---

[8] In a sense, all deductively valid arguments beg the question, because what is said by their conclusions already is said in their premises. In the typical case, part of an argument's conclusion is said in one premise, part in another. That is the point of valid deduction; anyone who accepts the premises of a deductively valid argument and yet rejects its conclusion is guilty of being inconsistent. The difference in the case of the fallacy of *begging the question* is that the premises state the claim of the conclusion in a way that those who reject the conclusion also will reject the premises for being just as questionable as the conclusion.

[9] Cited by Richard Whately in his excellent book *Elements of Logic* (London, 1826). Whately's fallacy classification is more like the one used in this text than are those of any other text in use today.

In real life, of course, this fallacy rarely, if ever, has the form

A.
Therefore, *A.*

Few would be taken in by anything so obvious. Instead, a premise may state a conclusion in different but equivalent words, so that the conclusion is not so obviously begged. This is the way in which the question is begged in one of the classic textbook cases (from the 19th century—human gullibility tends to remain constant): "To allow every man unbounded freedom of speech must always be . . . advantageous to the state; for it is highly conducive to the interests of the community that each individual should enjoy a liberty, perfectly unlimited, of expressing his sentiments."[9]

Although the traditional fallacy of *begging the question* deals primarily with questions that are at issue, say, as in a debate, over time it has come to have a broader range so as to cover other sorts of questions. Thus, to take a textbook example, we can be said to be guilty of this fallacy when, having asked why chloroform renders people unconscious, we accept the answer that it does so because it is a soporific (a soporific being defined as something that induces sleep).

Doctors and other sorts of professionals are frequent perpetrators of this version of *begging the question,* but they aren't by any means the only ones who set us up for it. Indeed, many times questions are begged quite innocently. Here is an example taken from an article on exclusive men's clubs in San Francisco. In explaining why these clubs have such long waiting lists, Paul B. "Red" Fay, Jr. (on the roster of three of the clubs) said, "The reason there's such a big demand is because everyone wants to get in them."[10] In other words, there is a big demand because there is a big demand. Fay inadvertently (we hope) gave another version of the conclusion in the premise, and thus avoided the question of proof.

Note that the fallacy begging the question also has been broadened over time so as to cover cases in which a premise is different from the conclusion of an argument but is controversial or questionable for the same reasons that typically might lead someone to question the conclusion.

Evading the Issue

One effective way to beg the question at issue is simply to avoid it entirely. Doing this makes one guilty of the fallacy **evading the issue.** This approach succeeds when those taken in fail to notice that the issue has been evaded. Perhaps the best way to hoodwink an opponent or dodge a barbed question is to make it appear that the issue or question is indeed being addressed. Politicians frequently evade an issue concerning a complicated problem (the homeless, the national debt, whatever) by speaking instead about the pressing need to solve it. Savvy citizens are not taken in by this sort of chicanery.

---

[9]Cited by Richard Whately in his excellent book *Elements of Logic* (London, 1826). Whately's fallacy classification is more like the one used in this text than are those of any other text in use today.
[10]Quoted in "The Chosen Few," by Adair Lara, *San Francisco Chronicle,* July 18, 2004.

For example, at a White House news conference on July 17, 2003, a reporter asked the second President Bush if he took personal responsibility for including in his State of the Union address earlier that year the disputed claim that Saddam Hussein had tried to buy uranium oxide in Niger, Africa. Bush replied, "I take responsibility for putting our troops in action. And I made that decision because Saddam Hussein was a threat to our security and a threat to the security of other nations. . . . I take responsibility for making the decision, the tough decision to put together a coalition to remove Saddam Hussein." By claiming to take responsibility for actions that had nothing to do with the question, Bush managed to evade the issue entirely.

Politicians are past masters at evading the issue. When they are asked hard questions in interviews, they skirt the subject with responses like "That's a complex issue . . ." and then shift into the message they want to give. Or they claim the question isn't relevant, which clears the way for topics they do think are relevant. Or they say things like "That's a good question, but before going into that I want to discuss . . ." and then go on to spin their own point of view. Evading the issue is so important to politicians that many of them hire media trainers to help them perfect the art.[11]

6. QUESTIONABLE PREMISE—QUESTIONABLE STATEMENT

As we noted earlier, most examples of the fallacies discussed so far fall into the broader category of *questionable premise.* But not all species of questionable premise have received specific names in the literature. So when a premise that is not believable is spotted in an argument and none of these more specific labels apply, we have to fall back on the general term **questionable premise.** That is what we did earlier when we pointed out that a statement in a Budweiser commercial constituted a questionable premise.

Knowing for a fact that a statement is false obviously is a very good reason for questioning it—indeed, for dismissing it. Thus, when a colleague was alleged to be incompetent on grounds that she was an alcoholic, one of the authors of this text rejected the charge on the basis of personal knowledge that the allegation was false. But often we ought to question a statement just because we have no good reason to think it true, even though we also don't have any reason to doubt it. When evidence is lacking, reason requires holding judgment in abeyance.

Remember, though, that hearing something from a trustworthy expert often counts as a reason for believing it to be true. For example, the fact that the overwhelming majority of scientists believe the burning of fossil fuels, such as oil and coal, is polluting the air and causing a rise in worldwide temperatures ought to constitute good reason for believing that there very likely is a "greenhouse effect" resulting from the use of these fuels.

Finally, it is worth remembering here that in everyday life statements generally do not come labeled as premises or conclusions and also that not all persuasive discourse is put into argumentative form. So there is a good deal of merit in expanding the fallacy of *questionable premise* so that it becomes, say, *questionable statement.*

---

[11] For more on this see a fascinating article on media training, "Answer the &%$#* Question" in *Columbia Review of Journalism,* January/February, 2004.

7. Suppressed (Overlooked) Evidence

The general fallacy category **suppressed evidence,** introduced earlier along with *questionable premise* and *invalid inference,* has not received much attention in the fallacy literature, perhaps because theorists tend to see the suppression of evidence as an error in reasoning but not as a fallacy (as they define that concept). Whether thought of as a fallacy or not, however, it is important that we learn how to bring relevant evidence to bear on an argument and learn how to avoid being taken in by others when they suppress evidence.

Of course, people who suppress evidence often do so inadvertently, one reason that a more all-encompassing label for the fallacy might be **overlooked evidence,** or perhaps *slighted evidence.* It's easy, when strongly committed to a particular side of an issue, to pass over arguments and reasons on the other side. In recent years, advocates on both sides of issues such as capital punishment, abortion, the legalization of marijuana, the depiction of violence on TV, and the legalization of prostitution, frequently have been guilty of slighting evidence damning to their side of the issue. Those opposed to "three strikes and you're out" legislation, for instance, tend to neglect the ways in which this kind of law might protect society from repeat offenders; those in favor don't like to talk about the high costs associated with keeping people in jail long past the age at which the vast majority of criminals have ceased to commit violent crimes, or about the fact that a great many of those sentenced under these laws have not committed violent or even serious crimes.

We all, of course, sometimes are motivated by more crass considerations than mere overzealousness. Self-interest is a powerful motivator of deliberately shady reasoning, as is self-deception. (More will be said in Chapter 6 concerning the unfortunate fact that human beings are notorious self-deceivers.)

Anyway, the point of becoming familiar with the fallacy *suppressed evidence* is to sharpen one's ability to spot cases in which relevant evidence is being passed over, whether by others or by ourselves. We need, in particular, to learn how to carry through reasoning so as to see whether all likely relevant information has been considered.

Take, for instance, the accounts widely circulated in early 2000 about how the tax burden has shrunk to its lowest level in 40 years, with those earning under $30,000 (half

---

Shall I tell you what it is to know? It is to say you know when you know, and to say that you do not know when you do not know; that is knowledge.

> —Attributed to Confucius (which means that
> we do not know for sure that he said it)

We don't want to be too hasty, or too picky, in leveling a charge of begging the question. Although what Confucius is quoted as saying is literally question begging, it is very likely that what he meant to say (if he actually said it) is that a large part of wisdom is to know what you do and what you don't have good reason to believe and, by implication, not to believe what you do not have good reason to believe. Excellent advice, indeed.

Tokenism: Note that Clint equates his notion of half way with fairness.

of all taxpayers in the year 2000) paying a mere 2 percent of all income taxes. The strong implication of these stories was that the bottom half of taxpayers cannot complain, since they pay such a small amount of all taxes. Overlooked (on purpose? accidentally? out of ignorance?) was the fact that other kinds of taxes are a much greater burden to the bottom 50 percent of income earners than are income taxes. For example, as pointed out in *The Washington Monthly* (June 2000), social security taxes are a greater burden than income taxes for 74 percent of the population, according to the Joint Economics Committee of the Congress. (Look up their figures!) In addition, most of these stories failed to note that when all taxes whatsoever are added up, the bottom half of the population pays a higher percentage of their incomes in taxes than do those in the very high-income groups. It's surprising how often politically or economically driven arguments can be shot down by carrying through a line of reasoning in this way.

This is true with respect not just to arguments themselves but also to proposals for action (which, in any case, do imply arguments). Consider, for example, the proposal (in a letter to the *San Francisco Chronicle*) that suggested instituting a higher bridge toll for the low-mileage, high-polluting cars generally driven by rich people than for high-mileage, low-polluting cars driven by others. The point was to raise money in a way that would be fair by hitting those who could afford it most and who pollute the most. But the writer neglected to consider the monstrous traffic jams that would result from requiring toll booth attendants to determine the rate of gas mileage of every car passing

Many people have trouble distinguishing between having no evidence or proof for a claim and having evidence or proof that the claim is false. But having no evidence, say, that vitamin C helps us fight the common cold is quite different from having evidence that it does not do so. Similarly, a lack of clinical proof that marijuana has certain medicinal benefits is much different from having clinical proof that it does not. Lack of *clinical proof,* by the way, also is quite different from having no good evidence whatsoever concerning marijuana's medicinal benefits. In fact, there is a good deal of such "anecdotal" evidence.

through their gates. So the writer's suggestion was completely impractical, as good critical reasoners would quickly figure out by bringing to bear the overlooked evidence just mentioned. When proposals for action are made, good critical reasoners try to figure out how what is proposed might work out in actual practice—in the real world. (Recently, when students in a critical reasoning class were given this example, one savvy student pointed out that there are indeed ways to charge higher tolls for low-mileage, high-polluting cars than for those that get high mileage and pollute less—namely, by having tolls paid electronically, as some bridges in fact now do, and (as none do) have tolls differ from one kind and year of car to another. Is this practical?)

For lots of us, becoming adept at bringing to bear suppressed or overlooked relevant information is perhaps the most difficult knack required by good reasoning. Sometimes the difficulty is compounded by our limited understanding of the issue at hand. Take, for example, the Environmental Protection Agency's decision in 2002 to omit, for the first time in six years, the chapter on global warming from its annual federal budget. The *New York Times* (September 15, 2002) reported that industrial lobbyists were "praising the decision, contending that carbon dioxide, which is believed to cause global warming, is not a pollutant." In one sense the lobbyists were right—carbon dioxide is not a pollutant; it's a natural gas—but scientists would argue that it has the side effect of trapping heat and thus causing temperatures to rise. Understanding the fallacious reasoning in the lobbyists' argument requires most of us to do a bit of research.

8. TOKENISM

Tokenism—mistaking a token gesture for the real thing, or accepting a token gesture in lieu of something more concrete—is another common fallacy.

Sometimes, of course, the token gesture is accepted because nothing else is likely to be forthcoming. A longtime corporation employee who is "retiring" early might just as well accept the token gift of a wristwatch. But we often fall for token gestures because we fail to see their true nature. For example, in 1998, Nike announced it was cutting ties with four Indonesian factories that assembled its products because the companies refused to comply with Nike standards for wage levels and working conditions. Considering the fact that Nike employs up to 500,000 workers worldwide and has been repeatedly accused of using factories with sweatshop conditions, its decision to drop four factories seems little more than a token gesture. (Note in passing that no on-the-line workers overseas making Nike shoes receive anything close to what is the minimum wage in the United States and that, as of 2001, almost all Nike products still are made under sweatshop conditions.)

> In the Italian film *Il Postino* (*The Postman*), the big politician promises, again, that pipes will be built so that the people can have indoor running water, and he actually has construction begin before the election. People again vote him into office, and—surprise—construction immediately stops. Voters have again been suckered by a token gesture and only wake up to that fact when it is too late to make a difference.

As might be expected, tokenism is one of the politician's best friends. When, in June 2000, George W. Bush, then Texas governor, stayed the execution of a convicted felon so as to leave time for DNA tests, his action was taken by some observers to rebut the claim that Bush denied the convicted all of their political rights by failing to use his power of granting 30-day stays of execution. But his action in this case was obviously a token gesture, since, with the one exception of his pardon of a dramatically innocent person, he had failed to act in 131 cases of people on death row, including several in which those convicted were generally held to be clearly innocent or had not been fairly tried.

Actually, his token gesture was a variation on a related ploy—namely, behaving or speaking one way when the heat is on, and another when it isn't sufficiently hot to force change. For as long as possible, Bush satisfied those of his Texas constituents and his financial supporters who favored being "tough on criminals," changing when a wider constituency was being wooed during his presidential campaign, much as Texan Lyndon Johnson did on race way back in the 1960s.

SUMMARY OF CHAPTER 3

All fallacious reasoning falls into one or more of the three broad categories of *questionable premise, suppressed evidence,* and *invalid inference.* But other fallacy categories, crosscutting these broad ones, have come into common use.

1. *Appeal to authority:* Accepting the word of alleged authorities when there is not sufficient reason to believe that they have the information we seek or that they can be trusted to provide it to us (for example, when they have a vested interest), or doing so when we ought to figure the matter out for ourselves. *Example:* Taking the word of power industry executives that nuclear plants are safe.

    When appeals must be made to authorities, we should remember that some are more trustworthy than others, and in particular, we should be wary of experts who have an axe to grind. We also should pay attention to the track records of alleged authorities.

2. *Inconsistency:* Accepting the conclusion of an argument that has self-contradictory statements or statements that contradict each other. These contradictory assertions may be made (1) by one person at one time and place, (2) by one person at different times or places (without explaining the contradiction as a change of mind based on reasons), or (3) by different representatives of one institution. While not, strictly speaking, a fallacy, we need to note when there is a contradiction between what someone says and what that person does. *Example:* President Clinton's campaign promise that he would lift the ban on gays in the military compared with his actual performance on the matter.

3. *Straw man:* Misrepresenting an opponent's position or a competitor's product to make it easier to attack them or to tout one's own product as superior, or attacking a weaker opponent while ignoring a stronger one. *Example:* A U.S. Postal Service commercial that pictured a competitor's plane that fell apart on camera.

4. *False dilemma:* A dilemma that can be shown to be false either by "going between the horns" of the dilemma or by "grasping its horns." *Example:* Refuting the dilemma about the futility of laws to deter crime by pointing out that there is a third alternative—namely, that many citizens are both good and bad.

The *either-or (black-or-white)* variation occurs when an argument based on the assumption that there are just two viable alternatives, one of which is bad (so the other has to be chosen), although there is at least one other viable alternative. *Example:* Refuting the argument that you should vote for John Kerry because the only alternative is George W. Bush by pointing to a third possibility, say, voting for Ralph Nader (or if you live in Florida or Ohio, by not voting for a presidential candidate?).

5. *Begging the question:* Assuming without proof the question, or a significant part of the question, that is at issue, or answering a question by rephrasing it as a statement. *Example:* In explaining why exclusive men's clubs have such long wait lists, "Red" Fay said, "The reason there is such a demand is because everyone wants to get in them." One way to beg the question is to avoid it entirely and thus evade the issue. *Example:* An elected official who answers queries about what will be done for the homeless by speaking instead about the need to provide adequate housing for everyone.

6. *Questionable premise—questionable statement:* Accepting a less than believable premise or other statement. *Example:* Accepting the claim that Budweiser is the best beer as a reason for deciding to switch to Bud. (Note that the five fallacies just described are variations of this broader fallacy but that not all species of *questionable premise* have special names.)

7. *Suppressed (overlooked) evidence:* Failing to bring relevant evidence to bear on an argument. *Example:* Advocates on both sides of the debates about the merits of "three strikes and you're out" laws who slight sensible arguments and objections of their opponents.

8. *Tokenism:* Accepting a token gesture in lieu of the real thing. *Example:* Being satisfied with campaign rhetoric when there is little likelihood of serious intent to carry through.

EXERCISE 3-1

Determine which fallacies (if any) occur in the following passages and state reasons for your answers. Note: Some items may contain more than one fallacy.

Example

Passage: Heard in a debate concerning capital punishment: "Capital punishment is morally wrong. After all, murder is just as wrong when committed by a government as it is when done by an individual person."

Evaluation: The speaker *begged the question at issue.* To say that capital punishment is murder is to say that it is a morally wrong killing (note that only wrongful killings are considered to be murder). But the issue was whether capital punishment—governmental killing—*is* murder, so to assume without argument that it is begs the question.

*1. Overheard in a laundry: "What makes me think abortion is murder? When my pediatrician refused to perform an abortion for me, she said she wouldn't be a party to murder. Babies and childbirth are her business, you know."

*2. President Lyndon Johnson: "I believe in the right to dissent, but I do not believe it should be exercised."

3. An item from the *New York Times* Service, March 2000: In 1988 Maureen Dowd, *New York Times* reporter, asked President Bush (the father of George W.) how he could justify claiming that he was a good candidate for blacks when he did nothing to influence the Reagan administration against watering down civil rights laws during his eight years as vice president. Bush replied, "But I helped found the Yale chapter of the United Negro College Fund."

4. Joe Morgan, announcing a Giants-Marlins baseball game and commenting on the Marlin pitcher: "He's been a little erratic, which explains why he hasn't been consistent."
   1) Appeal to authority -- how expert on that person
   3) Straw man - misrep. opp. position

5. Comment by gossip columnist Liz Smith a week after the attack on the World Trade Center, when the stock market was falling fast. ". . . the most important thing for citizens of any age—for themselves and for their Uncle Sam and as a tribute to the thousands who likely died—should be to call a broker and buy stock in American companies this week, and next week and the next."

6. Excerpt from the second President Bush's 2004 State of the Union address: "A strong America must also value the institution of marriage. . . . Congress has already taken a stand on this issue by passing the Defense of Marriage Act signed in 1996 by President Clinton. That statute protects marriage under federal law as the union of a man and a woman, and declares that one state may not redefine marriage for other states. Activist judges, however, have begun redefining marriage by court order, without regard for the will of the people and their elected representatives. On an issue of such great consequence, the people's voice must be heard. If judges insist on forcing their arbitrary will upon the people, the only alternative left to the people would be the constitutional process. Our nation must defend the sanctity of marriage."

7. Eric Jubler, in an article in which he argued that America should "open up" its wilderness areas: "The purist [conservationist] is, generally speaking, against everything . . . the purist believes that those who do not agree with him desire to 'rape the land.'"
   7 overlooked evidence
   2 inconsitancy

8. Calvin Coolidge is alleged to have been the first to say this: "We must keep people working—with jobs—because when many people are out of work, unemployment results."

9. In an interview with Sarah, Duchess of York, Larry King asked whether she was friends with Prince Charles. She replied, "Well, Larry, the important thing is that I have great respect for the royal family."

10. Argument in a student essay: "Prostitution should not be legalized because it encourages the breakdown of the family. Nevada, where prostitution is legal in ten counties, has the highest divorce rate in the nation, almost twice as high as the national average."
    6 Questionable statement

11. Notice from the Hyatt Regency Hotel in New Orleans: "We are pleased to confirm your reservation. It will be held on a space-available basis."

12. It is reported that when Socrates was condemned to death his wife cried out, "Those wretched judges have condemned him to death unjustly!" To which Socrates is said to have replied, "Would you really prefer that I were justly condemned?"

inconsistent

13. An article on Nike's Asian factories (*Time,* March 30, 1998) addressed a question asked by an anti–sweat shop activist: "Can't they find more money to pay the workers?" (Labor activist Jeff Ballinger estimated that Vietnamese workers were paid 57 cents per pair of shoes, typically selling for $90—see *Extra! Update,* June 1998). *Time*'s response to the question was "The short answer is no. Corporations pay the going rate for labor wherever they are."

14. Question to artist's model: "Why did he paint you so often?" Answer: "Because I'm his model."

*15. From a Dr. Joyce Brothers newspaper column: "Question: You should be more fearful of rape at home because rapes occur more frequently in private homes than in back alleys. Answer: TRUE. Studies indicate that more rapes are committed in the victim's home than in any other place. Almost half took place in either the victim's home or the assailant's; one fourth occurred in open spaces; one fifth in automobiles; one twelfth in other indoor locations."

16. From *Slander,* by Ann Coulter, on the attitudes of liberals: "The liberal catechism includes hatred of Christians, guns, the profit motive, and political speech, and an infatuation with abortion, the environment, and race discrimination (or in the favored parlance of liberals, 'affirmative action')."

17. From a *New Republic* review of the James Michener book *Iberia:* "Michener leads off his chapter on bullfights with an argument between your quintessential American and Spaniard about brutal sports—which the Spaniard wins by pointing out that more young men get killed and maimed every year playing American football than in the bullring."

18. In June 1997, President Clinton was praised in some circles for using his line-item veto to slash 38 military construction projects, costing $289 million, that Congress had added to the Pentagon's military construction proposal. He allowed 207 projects to stand, totaling more than $500 million—increasing the overall construction budget to nearly $9 billion.

19. A *Washington Monthly* article on celebrity chefs (July/August, 2001) quoted Evan Kleinman, chef of Angeli Café in Los Angeles as saying, "Basically when it comes to food and food supply, I find it frightening that something so fundamental to life has been left to people whose only concern is profit. . . . I mean as far as I can see, because of that, there are only two kinds of people putting food in their mouths—the ones who have lost the notion that food is something made by human hands and then there are the others . . . for whom there's still some link with food as a culture of nurturance."

20. Paraphrase of part of a letter to the editor (*Washington Post National Weekly Edition,* March 13–19, 1989): "It's true that the Ayatollah Khomeini has gone too far with his death sentence for author Salman Rushdie [because of

his "outrageous" book *The Satanic Verses*], but Rushdie also has gone too far by offending all Moslems. I am a strong believer in the freedom of speech. However, books like Rushdie's only create hatred and division and weaken the ties of people to each other. Therefore, his book and others like it should be abolished."

21. When Calvin Klein was asked what the secret of his success was, he answered, "I make clothes women want to wear."

22. A politician touting the United States as a "do-gooder" nation for its humanitarian efforts around the world pointed out that in 2001 alone the United States gave a total of $15 billion in foreign aid to many countries in need of basic goods.

*23. Sociologist James Q. Wilson: "I am not about to argue [as some sociobiologists do] that there is a 'sympathy gene.' But there must be some heritable disposition that helps us explain why sympathy is so common."

24. The second President Bush in a televised interview with Diane Sawyer (December 16, 2003), explaining why he doesn't read the newspapers: "I get my news from people [in his administration] who don't editorialize. . . . They give me the actual news, and it makes it easier to digest, on a daily basis, the facts."

25. In attacking a proposed equal rights amendment to the state constitution of Iowa, Pat Robertson argued that the proposal was part of a "feminist agenda . . . a socialist, anti-family political movement that encourages women to leave their husbands, kill their children, practice witchcraft, destroy capitalism and become lesbians."

26. A commercial aired in the 1998 election campaign that uses President Clinton's sex scandal as the theme. The announcer asks, "Should we reward Democratic plans for more big government? More big spending? Should we reward their opposition to more welfare reform? And should we reward not telling the truth?"

    "That is the question of this election. Reward Bill Clinton. Or, vote Republican."

27. From "Intelligence Report" by Lloyd Shearer in *Parade* magazine (November 5, 1978): "This past September, [Bob Hope] refused to cross a picket line at the Chicago Marriott Hotel, where 1500 guests were waiting for him at a dinner of the National Committee for the Prevention of Child Abuse. W. Clement Stone, the insurance tycoon who contributed $2 million to the Nixon campaign fund in 1972, tried to negotiate a temporary halt of picketing so that Hope could enter the hotel. When Stone failed, Hope returned to the Drake Hotel, where he videotaped a 15-minute spot to be shown at the dinner. Hope, who belongs to four show business unions, later explained that he had crossed a picket line many years ago and subsequently had to apologize to labor leader George Meany. He promised then never to cross another." (This is a rather old example, but still very instructive.)

28. Jorg Haider, Nazi sympathizer and Austrian Parliament member, in response to an interview with a *Time* magazine reporter (*Time,* February 14, 2000):

    Time: Why did you praise Hitler's employment policies?
    Haider: I think it was only one sentence out of a big debate. My opponents took out one sentence and made a campaign against me, and it was not possible for me to explain myself.

29. Ad for an International Correspondence School journalism course: "Every successful writer started that first story or article with no previous experience. William Shakespeare, Alexander Dumas, Harold Robbins, Danielle Steel, Barbara Cartland—any famous writer you can name started just like you."

30. *Extra! Update* (April 2003) included two quotes on religion by Bill O'Reilly on *The O'Reilly Factor.*

    March 11, 2003: Both sides of the debate [on whether to invade Iraq] are saying God is on their side. . . . I think both sides are wrong. Nobody knows for sure what the absolute right thing to do is. We can only have opinions. Thus, it's intellectually dishonest to be claiming God is on your side when only God knows for sure what the right thing to do is."

    December 4, 2002: "I'm telling you, I'm telling you that President Bush is doing what Jesus would have done."

31. Walter Burns, in an article in which he argues for capital punishment: "When abolitionists speak of the barbarity of capital punishment . . . they ought to be reminded that men whose moral sensitivity they would not question have supported [it]. Lincoln, for example, albeit with a befitting reluctance, authorized the execution of 267 persons during his presidency . . . and it was Shakespeare's sensitivity to the moral issues that required him to have Macbeth killed."

32. Phyllis Schlafley, an outspoken opponent of the women's liberation movement, in her book *The Power of Positive Women:* "The second dogma of the women's liberationists is that, of all the injustices perpetrated upon women through the centuries, the most oppressive is the cruel fact that women have babies and men do not. Within the confines of women's liberationist ideology, the abolition of this overriding inequality becomes the primary goal."

"If the coach and horses and the footmen and the beautiful clothes all turned back into the pumpkin and the mice and the rags, then how come the glass slipper didn't turn back, too?"

---

*T*wo important factors in critical or creative thinking are the ability to bring relevant background information to bear on a problem and to carry through the relevant implications of an argument or position to determine whether they hang together. The cartoon above illustrates the second of these factors: The child carries through the reasoning in the Cinderella story and finds it wanting. The first factor might be illustrated by a child who realizes there are millions of chimneys for Santa Claus to get down in one night and wonders how he could possibly manage to do so in time.

How happy are the astrologers, who are believed if they tell one truth to a hundred lies, while other people lose all credit if they tell one lie to a hundred truths.

—Francesco Guicciardini

It ain't so much the things we don't know that get us into trouble. It's the things we know that ain't so.

—Artemus Ward

Chapter

4

FALLACIOUS REASONING—2

Most instances of the fallacies discussed in the previous chapter fall into the broad fallacy categories *questionable premise* or *suppressed evidence*. Most of the fallacies to be discussed in this and the next chapter belong to the genus *invalid inference*.

1. *AD HOMINEM* ARGUMENT

There is a famous and perhaps apocryphal story lawyers like to tell that nicely captures the flavor of this fallacy. In Great Britain, the practice of law is divided between solicitors, who prepare cases for trial, and barristers, who argue the cases in court. The story concerns a particular barrister who, depending on the solicitor to prepare his case, arrived in court with no prior knowledge of the case he was to plead, where he found an exceedingly thin brief, which when opened contained just one note: "No case; abuse the plaintiff's attorney." If the barrister did as instructed, he was guilty of arguing **ad hominem**—of attacking his opponent rather than his opponent's evidence and arguments. (An *ad hominem* argument, literally, is an argument "to the person.")

Politicians on both sides of the aisle commit this fallacy. On the right: When Newt Gingrich called John Kerry a "Jane Fonda anti-war Democrat," he was guilty of *ad hominem*. Anyone who knows Jane Fonda's anti-Vietnam stance will get the suggestion that Kerry is a bad guy. This allegation ignores the fact that Kerry served in the Vietnam War with distinction before he protested the war and that he took a stand against that particular war, not against all wars. On the left: When Ralph Nader announced on *Meet the Press* that he was running for president in the 2004 election, he said, "George Bush is a giant corporation masking as a human being." Whereas Bush certainly had strong corporate ties, the *ad hominem* description is a caricature intended to ridicule him.

It is important not to confuse *ad hominem* arguments with those in which the fallacy is *straw man*. The difference is that *straw man* attacks misrepresent an opponent's position, whereas those that are *ad hominem* abuse an opponent directly.

Attacks on Character or Credentials Sometimes Are Relevant

Although attacks on a person usually are irrelevant to that individual's arguments or claims, sometimes they are very relevant indeed. Lawyers who attack the testimony of courtroom witnesses by questioning their expertise or character are not necessarily guilty of arguing *ad hominem*. In the O. J. Simpson case, for example, defense lawyers certainly were not guilty of arguing *ad hominem* when they showed detective Mark Fuhrman to have perjured himself on the witness stand. Fuhrman's lie about not having used racial epithets was not directly relevant to the case at hand (it had nothing to do with whether Simpson was guilty of murder), but it certainly was relevant to judgment about Fuhrman's credibility as an expert witness.

Similarly, courtroom witnesses often express opinions or arguments against which the typical layperson is unable to argue directly. When doctors, lawyers, or other experts testify, often the best we can do is try to evaluate their honesty or judgment. Evidence that a psychologist testifying in court has been convicted of perjury, or spends a great deal of time testifying in court, would be good reason to prefer the conflicting testimony of experts on the other side of the case.

Of course, negative evidence concerning an expert rarely proves that the authority's pronouncements are false. At best, character attacks just provide grounds for disregarding their testimony, not for deciding that it is false. If a doctor who advises operating on a patient turns out to be held in low esteem in the profession, it is rash to conclude that *therefore* no operation is necessary.

What has just been said about attacking the credentials of experts applies to organizations and their pronouncements as well. For example, that a research organization receives most of its funds from the pharmaceutical industry and also regularly issues reports favorable to drug company interests constitutes a very good reason to be suspicious of its output.

Guilt by Association

One of the important variations on *ad hominem* argument is that of **guilt by association.** According to an old saying, people can be judged by the company they keep. But is this true? Is it rational to judge people in this way?

The answer is that it is—up to a point and under certain circumstances. In the absence of contrary evidence, a man frequently seen in the company of several different women known to be prostitutes is rightly *suspected* of being connected with their occupation. Similarly, a person who frequently associates with several known agents of a foreign government is rightly suspected of being an agent of that government.

But suspicion is very different from certitude. Judgments based on a person's associations rarely have a high degree of probability. Suspecting that someone uses the services of prostitutes is much different from knowing that he does. (It is, however, good reason to look further, assuming we care enough about the matter.) Someone frequently in the company of prostitutes may turn out to be a sociologist conducting an investigation. A person often seen in the company of foreign spies may turn out to be a friendly counterspy or even just an associate.

2. Two Wrongs Make a Right

Those who try to justify a wrong by pointing to a similar wrong perpetrated by others often are guilty of the fallacy sometimes called **two wrongs make a right** (traditional name: *tu quoque*—"you're another"). For example, in the year 2000 presidential election, over 1900 Palm Beach County, Florida, citizens voted for two candidates for the

---

The Handbook of Political Fallacies, *by British political philosopher and reformer Jeremy Bentham (1748–1832), is one of the classic works on political rhetoric and fallacies. Here are excerpts from his account of the first of four "causes of the utterance of [political] fallacies" (another excerpt appears in Chapter 6).*

First Cause . . . : Self-conscious Sinister Interest

[I]t is apparent that the mind of every public man is subject at all times to the operation of two distinct interests: a public and a private one. . . .

In the greater number of instances, these two interests . . . are not only distinct, but opposite, and that to such a degree that if either is exclusively pursued, the other must be sacrificed to it. Take for example pecuniary interest: it is to the personal interest of every public man who has at his disposal public money extracted from the whole community by taxes, that as large a share as possible . . . should remain available for his own use. At the same time it is to the interest of the public . . . that as small a share as possible . . . should remain in his hands for his personal or any other private use. . . . Hence it is that any class of men who have an interest in the rise or continuance of any system of abuse no matter how flagrant will, with few or no exceptions, support such a system of abuse with any means they deem necessary, even at the cost of probity and sincerity. . . .

But it is one of the characteristics of abuse, that it can only be defended by fallacy. It is, therefore, to the interest of all the confederates of abuse to give the most extensive currency to fallacies. . . . It is of the utmost importance to such persons to keep the human mind in such a state of imbecility that shall render it incapable of distinguishing truth from error. . . .

Students inclined to complain that too many of the fallacy examples in this text come from politicians should seriously reflect on Bentham's remarks, especially because government today deals with so many matters that determine the quality of all of our lives.

same office, thus invalidating their ballots. Democratic party representatives claimed that the vast majority of these double votes resulted from confusion brought on by an illegally designed ballot, thwarting voter intent. A Republican party spokesperson dismissed their complaint by pointing out that in the 1996 presidential election over 15,000 ballots in Palm Beach County were invalidated for that reason, without creating a huge uproar. But surely, the fact that the 1996 election had a problem does not justify having the same problem in the year 2000.

Similarly, Cynthia Tucker, editorial page editor of the *Atlanta Constitution,* was guilty of this fallacy when, after pointing out how the rich and powerful often are given special privileges, she wrote in a March 1996 article, "These revelations make the case for affirmative action. People of color, who rarely have power or connections, are just seeking the same favors available to those who [already] have them." Clearly, the fact that the governor of California and several regents of the University of California had used their influence to get children admitted into state universities (one of Tucker's examples) does not justify special treatment for nonwhites who lack special access. The one kind of wrong doesn't make the other kind right.[1] (Wouldn't the proper remedy in the sort of cases just mentioned be to stop special favors for the offspring of the rich, powerful, or famous?)

Fighting Fire with Fire

Like most other fallacies, *two wrongs* seems plausible because of its resemblance to a more legitimate way of reasoning—in this case to the plausible idea that we sometimes are justified in "fighting fire with fire." Killing in self-defense illustrates this nicely. We feel justified in fighting one evil (the unjustified attack on our own life) by doing what otherwise would constitute another evil (taking the life of the attacker). So the fallacy *two wrongs make a right* is not automatically committed every time one wrong is counteracted by another. The crucial question is whether the second wrong is genuinely needed to fight, or counteract, the first.[2]

Two Wrongs and Hypocrisy

The fallacy *two wrongs make a right* also sometimes seems plausible—not fallacious—for another reason: Those who argue this way may intend to imply that their opponents are being hypocritical, and often this charge is accurate and may even have some merit. The town drunk isn't the one to tell us we've had one too many and are making fools of ourselves, even if we are. (That's the import of the reply, "You're a fine one to talk.") Similarly, the philanderer who finds out about his wife's infidelity is hardly the one to

---

[1] There may, of course, be other reasons for having affirmative action programs—for example, to make up for earlier harms perpetrated on the underprivileged, to "level the playing field." The point here is that it won't do to argue that because the other guy has special access, so should you, given the better solution that no one receives special treatment.

[2] This passes over questions concerning retributive justice. If retributivists are right, we sometimes are justified in punishing those guilty of unfairly harming others even though in doing so we fail to fight the original harm (or fail to rehabilitate the criminal or deter others from similar offenses).

complain that she has deceived him. But when we become outraged at the "chutzpah" of our accusers, we shouldn't lose sight of the fact that their hypocrisy doesn't justify our own failures.

Common Practice and Traditional Wisdom

As the traditional Latin name *tu quoque* suggests, the fallacy *two wrongs make a right* originally was intended to cover only those cases in which an individual or group responds to a charge by charging the accuser or accusers with a similar crime. But over time, it has come to take in related, indeed overlapping, sorts of fallacious arguments. One of these is **common practice,** committed when a wrong is justified on the grounds not that one other person or group, but rather lots of, or most, or even all others do the same sort of thing. Here is a typical example (from the *San Francisco Chronicle,* February 17, 1993):

> Bank of America Corp. Chief Executive Officer Richard Rosenberg yesterday said he was surprised by the public outcry about the bank's plan to cut branch employee hours and some benefits. [This was the bank's euphemistic way of disguising the reduction of full-time employees to the status of part-timers, with lower pay and reduced fringe benefits.] . . . The bank's CEO firmly defended the way the company was reducing staff following its merger with Security Pacific Corp. "I couldn't understand how we could be torn apart on this issue when we've been moving toward part-timers since 1985 and Wells Fargo and virtually every other retailer has been doing the same thing," he said. "To pick on us alone doesn't make sense."

Forgetting the fact that others also were "picked on," Bank of America's CEO clearly was guilty of the fallacy of common practice.

A related fallacy, sometimes called **traditional wisdom,** is committed when a wrong or an unsuitable practice is justified on grounds that it follows a traditional or accepted way of doing things. We do, of course, want to learn from past experiences, so we shouldn't assume that *just because* things have been done certain ways in the past, that way must be the right, or best, way now. All innovations go against past practices—from the introduction of plows that dig deeper furrows (resisted by North African farmers on the grounds that their fathers and grandfathers had farmed the traditional way) to the elimination of practices based on racial, religious, or gender bias in the United States or to do away with practices based on the caste system in India, which force "untouchables" to do dirty work, such as collecting "night soil." (Interestingly, new methods of planting seeds without plowing at all may make deep furrow plowing obsolete in its turn.)

In some cases, practices that once made perfect sense no longer do because of changing circumstances or increased knowledge. In others, the fallacy in arguing for the retention of common practices is due to the wrongheadedness or unfairness of those old ways of doing things. Those who benefit from these practices find it hard to entertain the idea that there could possibly be anything wrong with them (a matter to be mentioned again in Chapter 6, where impediments to cogent reasoning are discussed). In England, for instance, women for centuries had no legal rights under the common law. It wasn't just that women were disenfranchised. Fathers could marry a daughter to whomever they pleased,[3] and after marriage a woman's husband became the owner of her property. It took a very long time for these and similar legal injustices to be rectified; they were defended, for one thing, on the grounds that women had no legal rights because they never had had any. (In 19th-century England and America, the idea that women should have the vote was met with great hilarity in all-male circles of power, and political cartoons in newspapers and magazines poked fun at "lady suffragettes.")

It's often easier to see the questionable nature of customs in distant times or other cultures than in one's own. Consider the centuries-old tradition in some Middle Eastern countries of "honor" killing, the practice of killing girls or women who have sexual relations out of wedlock. In the Arab world, an unchaste woman brings shame on the family and sometimes the relatives themselves kill her to "cleanse the honor" that has been soiled. Hundreds of women are killed for reasons of honor each year. Yet activists trying to tighten the laws against honor killings are faced with massive opposition that portrays their campaign as an assault on Arab ways. The traditional wisdom is that an unchaste woman deserves to die.

Similar remarks apply to other societies, a very important example being India, where there also is the inhuman practice of murdering a wife whose family fails to come up with a sufficiently large dowry. Note also that in many Middle Eastern and African countries, traditional wisdom requires that young girls, just before puberty, be given a clitorectomy so as to reduce the temptation to engage in sex out of wedlock.

Of course, those who conform to these customs see them as good; it is other people, both inside and outside these cultures, who find fault with them. The point is that traditional beliefs need to be reevaluated and changed when found wanting.

But, again, we don't want to go overboard. Every change brings with it risks that may not have been calculated correctly. The "three strikes and you're out" bills, for example, were generally enacted without careful consideration of the likely consequences of such a serious departure from past practice. The point of such a bill is to assure that those who repeatedly commit serious violent crimes are not released from jail to again commit heinous offenses. But most of these measures enacted so far fail to distinguish correctly between seriously violent repeat felons and others or to consider the cost of incarcerating criminals long past the time when they are likely to commit violent crimes (most of which are committed by young men). They also fail to take account of the motivation these bills provide for two-time losers to shoot to kill rather than allow themselves to be captured and tried a third time.

W. Somerset Maugham summed things up nicely when he said, "Tradition is a guide, not a jailer."

3. IRRELEVANT REASON (NON SEQUITUR)

Traditional logic textbooks often discuss a fallacy called *non sequitur* (literally, "it does not follow"), usually described as being committed when a conclusion does not follow logically from given premises. In this sense, any fallacy in the broad category *invalid in-*

---

[3] Successful resistance to this paternal power forms an important subplot in 18th-century novelist Henry Fielding's psychologically insightful novel *Tom Jones,* made into a charming movie in the 1960s, a must-see for all movie buffs.

ference can be thought of as a *non sequitur.* But other writers describe this fallacy more narrowly.

Let's replace the ambiguous term *non sequitur* with the expression **irrelevant reason,** used to refer to reasons or premises that are irrelevant to a conclusion when the error doesn't fit a narrower fallacy category such as *ad hominem* argument or *two wrongs make a right.*

Both before and after the outbreak of the 1991 war in the Persian Gulf and the Iraq War in 2003, many Americans railed against antiwar demonstrators on grounds that they were giving the Iraqi leaders the idea that Americans were too soft to go to war, too decadent to take the number of casualties winning might require. (The same charge was leveled against Vietnam War protesters 20 years or so earlier.) This charge may well have been true (Iraq certainly misjudged American resolve), but it was irrelevant to the protesters' arguments against waging war with Iraq (or to those who protested against our fighting in Vietnam).

Sometimes irrelevant arguments defy all logic. Shortly after the attack on the World Trade Center, Michael Kelly had this to say in "Pacifist Claptrap."

> Organized terrorist groups have attacked America. These groups wish the Americans to not fight. The American pacifists wish the Americans to not fight. If the Americans do not, the terrorists will attack America again. And now we know such attacks can kill many thousands of Americans. The American pacifists, therefore, are on the side of future mass murders of Americans. They are objectively pro-terrorist.[4]

Ah, those crafty pacifists. Little did we realize the murderous intent lurking beneath the surface.

How about this excerpt from a United Airlines commercial?

> We humans are a social animal. That's why United flies to more places than any other airline.

This commercial says that the reason United flies to more places is that "we humans are a social animal," a fact that is totally irrelevant to [United's] flying to more places than competing airlines. Their use of the phrase "that's why," implying that a reason follows which supports a conclusion, is completely off base. The appeal of United's spiel is to emotion, not to brain power, not to reason. Note, by the way, that a reason is not automatically irrelevant just because it is false. For example, the old superstition about walking under a ladder bringing bad luck is false, but it isn't irrelevant to the question whether a person should or shouldn't engage in this practice; were it true, it would be a very good reason indeed for not walking under ladders.

Note also that a reason may be irrelevant when looking at a matter from one point of view but not from another. Take, for example, the remark by a psychological clinician, quoted in *Science News* magazine, that abandoning the old and standard ways of classifying mental disorder in favor of new ones "will result in denial of insurance coverage for treatment of serious psychological disturbances." Looked at from the point of view of psychiatric *theory,* this remark is irrelevant, but from the point of view of psychiatric *practice,* it is very relevant indeed.

---

[4] *Washington Post,* September 26, 2001, quoted in *Extra!,* November/December, 2001.

© Dan Wasserman, *The Boston Globe,* Tribune Media Services

A humorous (we hope) equivocation.

4. EQUIVOCATION

A term or expression is used *equivocally* in an argument when used to mean one thing in one place and another thing in another.[5] Accepting an argument that is invalid because we are fooled by an equivocal use of language makes us guilty of the fallacy that you will not be surprised to learn is generally called **equivocation.**

When a TV evangelist said that we all should stop sinning and "be like Jesus," someone in the audience expressed doubt that he was up to that, pointing out that, after all, "Jesus is the son of God." In reply, the evangelist told the doubter that he could indeed stop sinning because, "You're the son of God, too." But the evangelist was guilty of *equivocation,* because the doubter meant that Jesus is the son of God in the special way that (according to Christian doctrine) only Jesus is held to be, while the evangelist had to mean that the doubter was the son of God in the metaphorical sense in which (again according to Christian theology) we all are children of God.

Equivocation is a common fallacy because it often is quite hard to notice that a shift in meaning has taken place. As might be expected, given human nature, less than com-

[5]As used in everyday life, the term *equivocation* often connotes the use of equivocation to deceive. As used here, it does not necessarily carry this connotation. We do, of course, have to remember that equivocation is frequently employed in daily life to make invalid arguments appear to be valid.

pletely ethical manipulators frequently take advantage of the ease with which people can be fooled in this way. The sugar industry, for instance, once advertised its product with the claim that "Sugar is an essential component of the body . . . a key material in all sorts of metabolic processes," neglecting the fact that it is *glucose* (blood sugar), not ordinary table sugar (sucrose), that is the vital nourishment. It's true, of course, that table sugar does turn into blood sugar in the body, but it provides that necessary ingredient without also providing the other sorts of vital nutrients found in fruits, grains, and other more complete food sources that contain plenty of sucrose.

Advertisements of this kind for food and other health products are successful because a large majority of consumers know very little about how the body functions—what sorts of food are required for good health and what sorts are unhealthy. They tend to get their information about these vital matters from television commercials, other advertisements, and TV talk shows. So they are ready-made suckers for every fad that comes down the pike. For example, many food products have been advertised as especially healthy because they are low in cholesterol, or even cholesterol-free, while containing the usual (high) levels of fats, which the body then uses to make cholesterol. The ambiguity taken advantage of here is, again, the difference between what is in a food and what is in the bloodstream. Low blood cholesterol levels are good; low food cholesterol levels combined with high fat content definitely are not good. (Note that some foods advertised to be cholesterol free, or even fat free, contain partially hydrogenated oils, much less heart healthy than the fats listed on packages by law.)

Sometimes legal action is taken against companies for misleading advertising. When Phillip Morris was sued for deceiving smokers into thinking "light" cigarettes were less harmful than regular ones, a company spokesman said that the word *light* referred to taste, not content, but surely he was equivocating. Most smokers would tend to think that "light" meant that the cigarettes had less tar and nicotine—if only to rationalize their bad habit. (More on this case is in Chapter 10.)

Interestingly, terms that can be used either relatively or absolutely, like *rich* and *poor,* sometimes cause trouble. Poverty, for instance, is exceedingly unpleasant anywhere, at any time. But the poor in the United States today are richer in absolute terms with respect to material wealth than the vast majority of people who lived in days of old or who live today in the so-called "third world" countries of Africa, Central and South America, and Asia. This important truth is masked by the fact that the term *poor,* in its relative sense, does apply to those Americans who are poor compared to other Americans, although rich compared to most people who lived in the past or who live in third world countries today. (Do we make ourselves perfectly clear?)

But Ambiguity Often Serves Useful Purposes

Students sometimes get the idea that *ambiguity,* certainly equivocation, always is bad. But it isn't. Ambiguous uses of language, especially metaphorical ones, and even equivocations, can be employed for all kinds of good purposes. The well-known psychologist, Carl Rogers, for example, used equivocation very effectively in the following passage to emphasize a point:

> As a boy I was rather sickly, and my parents have told me that it was predicted
> I would die young. This prediction has been proven completely wrong in one

> It is he that sitteth upon the circle of the earth.
>
> —Isaiah 40:22
>
> ## Ambiguity
>
> *Almost any statement can be interpreted in various ways if we have a mind to do so. The Bible is a happy hunting ground for those intent on taking advantage of the ambiguity of natural languages, because so many people take what it says to be the word of the Ultimate Authority. This passage from Isaiah was once used to prove that the Earth is flat, but when the discoveries of Copernicus, Kepler, and Newton made the idea of a flat Earth untenable, the Isaiah quote was reinterpreted to prove that those who wrote the Bible knew the Earth is a sphere.*

sense, but has come profoundly true in another sense. I think it is correct that I will never live to be old. So I now agree with the prediction that I will die young.[6]

Ambiguous uses of language also serve to grease the wheels of social intercourse. Benjamin Disraeli, the 19th-century British prime minister, often used ambiguity to soften his replies to letters, while still coming close to being truthful, as in his reply to an unsolicited amateur manuscript: "Many thanks; I shall lose no time in reading it." (In most other contexts, of course, equivocation of this kind is rightly considered to be rather sneaky.)

Ambiguity also serves very useful purposes in literature, particularly in metaphoric passages. It enables writers to introduce multiple meanings quickly into a text in a way that adds significance to what is being said by drawing attention to often rather subtle connections without hitting us over the head with them. For example, the title of Joseph Conrad's great novel *Heart of Darkness* doesn't refer just to the central part of the African jungle but also captures some of the moral horror of the principal character, Kurtz, succumbing to the dark temptations of colonial African life, and by extension it draws attention to the corruption and depravity "civilized" people are capable of when they give in to their base instincts. It also suggests the appalling abuses of power resulting from the exploitation of Africans and their lands by European colonials at the turn of the century. The ambiguity lurking in the title of Conrad's novel thus prepares us for the complex moral issues addressed in his classic work.

5. APPEAL TO IGNORANCE

When good reasons are lacking, the rational conclusion to draw is that we just don't know. But when we greatly desire to believe something, it's tempting to take the absence

---

[6]Carl Rogers, *Journal of Humanistic Psychology* (Fall 1980).

In 1950, when Senator Joseph R. McCarthy (Republican, Wisconsin), was asked about the fortieth name on a list of 81 names of people he claimed were communists working for the United States Department of State, he responded that "I do not have much information on this except the general statement of the agency that there is nothing in the files to disprove his communist connections."

Many of McCarthy's followers took this absence of evidence as proof that the person in question was indeed a communist, a good example of the fallacy of *appeal to ignorance*. This example also illustrates the importance of not being taken in by this fallacy. McCarthy never backed up his charges with a single bit of relevant evidence, yet for several years he enjoyed great popularity and power, and his "witch hunt" ruined many innocent lives before, finally, McCarthy and "McCarthyism" were brought down in congressional hearings that revealed the true character of this miserable person.

of evidence, and thus absence of refutation, as justification for believing that it is true. Doing this makes us guilty of the fallacy **appeal to ignorance** (traditionally known as *argumentum ad ignorantiam*). Some people have argued, for example, that we should believe there is no intelligent life on other planets anywhere in our galaxy, since no one has been able to prove that there is; indeed, until recently, when the existence of other planets was confirmed, it was sometimes argued that there were no planets anywhere other than our own tight little island.

The fallacy in this sort of reasoning can be seen by turning it on its head. If appeals to ignorance could prove that no life exists on other planets, then it equally well could prove just the opposite. After all, no one has proved that life does *not* exist on any of these planets. In the absence of good evidence for a claim, the right thing to do is to be *agnostic* on the issue, to neither believe nor disbelieve. Ignorance proves nothing, except, of course, that we are ignorant. During the Iraq War, the Bush administration could have said that the opposition was guilty of appeal to ignorance when it claimed that because no weapons of mass destruction were found, there must not be any hidden weapons. As of this writing, they still haven't been found, but you never know—they may turn up.

There are, however, cases in which the failure of a search does count against a claim. That happens when whatever is searched for would very likely have been found if it existed. Given all the sky watching that has gone on in the past 10,000 years, the claim that there exists a planet-sized object between Earth and Mars is disproved by the failure of anyone to observe it. Similarly, the failure to find evidence of a virus in a blood test justifies a doctor's conclusion that we aren't infected with that virus. These are cases not of reasoning from ignorance but rather of reasoning from the *knowledge* that we would have found the item looked for if it had been there to find.

Note, however, the importance of *appropriately* searching. That telescopes have searched the sky for several hundred years, and naked eyes for thousands, without spotting a god up there proves absolutely nothing about the existence of a god in the sky, since deities are not conceived of as the kind of entities that can be seen in this way.

6. COMPOSITION AND DIVISION

The fallacy of **composition,** also sometimes called the *salesman's fallacy,* but more accurately the *consumer's fallacy,* is committed when someone assumes that a particular item must have a certain property because all of its parts have that property. Auto dealers, for example, frequently try to get prospective customers to fall for this fallacy by touting low monthly payments while neglecting total costs, hoping their marks will assume that if the monthly payments are low, then the total cost must be low also. Washers and dryers used to be sold by telling customers that it takes "only 50 cents a day" to buy one. Of course, 50 cents a day adds up to $365 in two years (a lot of money until rather recently), something buyers seldom thought to figure out even though the arithmetic involved is on the grade school level.

The fallacy of **division** is committed when we assume that all (or some) of the parts of an item have a particular property because the item as a whole has it. The fallacy of *division* thus is the mirror image of the fallacy of *composition.* While infrequently fallen for in everyday life, cases do happen. An example is concluding that all the rooms in a large, fancy, hotel must be large, as guests often do when making reservations at places such as the posh Plaza Hotel in New York (where in fact lots of rooms are rather tiny).

7. SLIPPERY SLOPE

In a typical *slippery slope* argument, an action is objected to on the grounds that once it is taken, another, and then perhaps still another, are bound to be taken, down a "slippery slope," until some undesirable consequence results. According to a slightly different version, whatever would justify taking the first step would also justify all the others, but since the last step isn't justified, the first isn't, either.

Arguing that a slope is slippery without providing good reason for thinking that it is, or when the slope clearly is not, makes us guilty of the fallacy of the **slippery slope.** For example, a Canadian-style "single-payer" health care system has often been objected to on grounds that it is a kind of socialized medicine and that its adoption would lead to socialized insurance of all kinds, socialized railroads, airlines, and so on, without sufficient reason being presented for believing this would be the case. (Are there any?) It also sometimes is argued that whatever would justify a single-payer system of health care

---

Earlier editions of this text at this point had a section on a variation of the fallacy *slippery slope* called the *domino theory.* Back in the nasty old Cold War days, dominoes were alleged to be in danger of falling all over the globe. Perhaps the chief reason advanced by the Johnson and Nixon administrations for our involvement in the war in Vietnam was that if Vietnam fell to the communists, the rest of Southeast Asia would also, and then countries in Central America (Nicaragua, El Salvador, and so on) and even parts of South America (in particular, Chile). Although we were defeated in Vietnam, it is primarily communist dominoes that have fallen—perhaps the reason that the domino theory has gone out of fashion.

also would justify all sorts of other socialistic measures, again without justifying this conclusion.

Note, however, that some slopes may well be slippery. The *slippery slope* fallacy is committed only when we accept without further justification or argument that once the first step is taken, the others are going to follow, or that whatever would justify the first step would in fact justify the rest. Note, also, that what some see as the undesirable consequence lurking at the bottom of the slope others may regard as very desirable indeed (as socialists do in the case just mentioned).

SUMMARY OF CHAPTER 4

1. *Ad hominem argument:* An irrelevant attack on an opponent rather than on the opponent's evidence or arguments. *Example:* Lee Alcorn's racist attack on Senator Joseph Lieberman. Note, however, that not all character attacks are fallacious, as they may not be when challenging the integrity of an allegedly expert witness.

   We're guilty of the variation on this fallacy called *guilt by association* when we judge someone guilty solely on the basis of the company that person keeps.

2. *Two wrongs make a right:* Justifying a wrong by pointing to a similar wrong perpetrated by others. *Example:* Defending affirmative action for "people of color" on the grounds that privileged whites often get special treatment. Note, however, that when fighting fire with fire, what would otherwise be a wrong often isn't, as when someone kills in self-defense.

   Although there is an air of hypocrisy to a charge coming from an equally guilty party, this doesn't make an accurate charge any less on target.

   Variations: Common practice, in which a wrong is justified because commonly engaged in. *Traditional wisdom,* in which a wrong is justified because that's the way things always have been done.

3. *Irrelevant reason:* Trying to prove something with evidence that is or comes close to being irrelevant. (Some other term, such as *ad hominem argument,* may also apply.) *Example:* Countering the claims of antiwar protesters by arguing that antiwar talk tells the enemy we don't have the resolve to fight.

4. *Equivocation:* Using a term or expression in an argument in one sense in one place and another sense in another. *Example:* The TV evangelist's use of the expression "son of God" to refer to Jesus Christ and to a parishioner. Note, however, that intentional ambiguity, even equivocation, is not always fallacious. It isn't, for example, when used for metaphoric effect.

5. *Appeal to ignorance:* Arguing that the failure to find evidence refuting a claim justifies believing that it is true. *Example:* Senator Joseph McCarthy's claim that 81 State Department employees were communists because there was no proof that they were not. Note, however, that the failure of *appropriate* searches sometimes does support rejection of a claim.

6. *Composition:* Assuming that an item has a certain property because all or most of its parts have that property. *Example:* Assuming a commodity is inexpensive because of low installment payments.

Division: Assuming that all or most parts of an item have a property because the whole item has it. *Example:* Assuming the rooms in a large hotel are large.

7. *Slippery slope:* Accepting a claim that a slope is slippery when no or insufficient reason has been presented to justify that claim. *Example:* Arguing that adoption of a single-payer health plan will lead to adoption of all sorts of other socialistic measures.

Exercise 4-1

Determine which fallacies (if any) occur in the following short passages and justify your answers (as you did when working on Exercise 3-1). (Some of these passages may contain fallacies discussed in the previous chapter.)

1. Letter to the editor, *San Francisco Chronicle:* "What, again? Another jab at the CIA by [columnist and reporter] Jack Anderson? . . . All countries have spy organizations. Most of them sometimes overstep the bounds of propriety. Why single out our own outfit?"

2. From a conversation overheard in early 1994 during a large social event:

   She: I don't see what's so bad about how the Clintons have done in the White House. They're doing pretty good as far as I'm concerned.
   He: Boy, you are gullible. They've been playing dirty power politics since the day they, ah, he, took office.
   She: Really? How do you know?
   He: They're Arkansas politicians, aren't they? Arkies are next to Okies.

3. Charlton Heston (then president of the NRA), in an interview after the 1999 shootings at Columbine High School, told ABC's *This Week* that he opposed President Clinton's attempt to limit handgun purchases to one a month. "Before you know it, it becomes no guns."

*4. Football player Roger Craig, on George Seifert's promotion to head coach of the San Francisco 49ers: "I think George will do an excellent job, because he's been searching for a head coaching job for some time, and what better place to start his head coaching job." (In fact, Seifert did have an excellent record with the 49ers before being canned.)

5. From a 1972 article in the *Hartford Courant* on the possibility of women priests in the Catholic Church: "Citing the historic exclusion of women from the priesthood, . . . the study [of a committee of Roman Catholic bishops] said '. . . the constant tradition and practice, interpreted as divine law, is of such a nature as to constitute a clear teaching of the Ordinary Magisterium [teaching authority of the church].'"

*6. Bumper sticker seen in California when a handgun bill was before voters of that state:

   Gun Registration Equals Mass Extermination
   First Register Guns, Then Register the Jews

7. (In this case, the question is what fallacy, if any, Momma failed to put over on her son.)

Momma by Mell Lazarus. Courtesy of Mell Lazarus and Field Newspaper Syndicate.

8. Jan Berger in the *Baltimore Evening Sun:* "Weeks of patient investigation have revealed that the gas leaked at Bhopal [India—with thousands of casualties] because something went wrong."

9. Rush Limbaugh on opponents to the war in Iraq (quoted in the *Baltimore Sun,* March 9, 2003): "I want to say something about these anti-war demonstrators. No let's not mince words, let's call them what they are: anti-American demonstrators."

10. Claim made by opponents of an initiative to legalize marijuana for medicinal purposes: "It would be foolish to permit the sale of marijuana to seriously ill people on the recommendation of their physicians. That just opens the floodgates to the complete legalization of that dangerous drug."

11. A letter to the editor of *Connoisseur* magazine defended a previous article favoring bullfighting from "the protesting letters you are sure to receive," by reminding readers that bulls selected for the arena live twice as long as those destined for McDonald's and die in a far more noble fashion.

12. Jacob Neusner in "The Speech the Graduates Didn't Hear": "Few professors actually care whether or not they are liked by peer-paralyzed adolescents, fools so shallow as to imagine professors care not about education but about popularity."

*13. Indian mystic Vivekananda: "There is no past or future even in thought, because to think it you have to make it present."

14. From a conversation with a friend (not verbatim): "Sure, I've told you before that I believe everyone's opinion counts on moral matters like abortion. But not *everyone's* opinion counts—I wouldn't want Hitler's to count. Well, [name deleted] isn't a Hitler, but she sleeps around like sex was going out of style next week or something. She's just a slut, and she's broken up at least one marriage I know about. Why should her opinion count on anything? Why should we listen to her opinion on the abortion business?"

15. Jules Crittenden, an embedded journalist for the *Boston Herald* in the Iraq War, defended himself from criticism for bringing home some illegal "souvenirs" from Iraq (*Boston Herald,* April 23, 2003): "I understand and share the world's

concern about the disappearance of legitimate Iraqi national treasures that are in fact treasures of human civilization," Crittenden wrote in an open letter to journalists in this country. "However, those are matters separate from the time-honored tradition among soldiers of bringing home reminders of some of the most intense experiences of their lives. There was no exception to that historical practice in this war . . . [until reporters and soldiers were subject to search by federal agents on returning to the United States]."

16. Argument heard all too frequently in introductory philosophy classes: "We're perfectly entitled to believe there is a God. After all, every effort by atheists to prove otherwise has failed."

17. Lewis Carroll, in *Through the Looking Glass:* " 'You couldn't have it if you did want it,' the Queen said. 'The rule is jam tomorrow and jam yesterday—but never jam *today.*' 'It must sometimes come to jam today,' Alice objected. 'No it can't,' said the Queen. 'It's jam every *other* day: today isn't any *other* day, you know.' "

18. Senator Jennings Randolph, during the debate on the equal rights amendment, dismissed arguments by feminists who testified before Congress by referring to these women as a "small band of bra-less bubbleheads."

19. Robert Ringer in *The Tortoise Report* touting gold as an investment: "Two thousand years after the human flesh had disappeared, the gold that adorned it [an ancient Egyptian corpse] remained virtually unchanged. That's a real hard act for paper money to follow."

20. Margaret Morissey, an anti-garbage activist, was interviewed on *As It Happens,* a Canadian news program (February 2002) about her arrest for blocking trucks from dumping garbage on a hill overlooking St. Brides, Newfoundland. The arrest occurred despite the fact that it was illegal to use the hill as a dumpsite. When she asked the mayor why the dumping was still allowed, he said, "We've been doing it for 30 years."

21. Overheard on the bus to Atlantic City: "I just play the quarter slots when I go to Atlantic City. That way, I don't lose too much money."

22. Peter O'Rourke, California Office of Traffic Safety, *San Francisco Chronicle:* "It isn't that our freeway system can't handle the cars; it's that congestion bottlenecks the system and prevents the smooth flow of traffic."

*23. Sigmund Freud: "Our own death is . . . unimaginable, and whenever we make the attempt to imagine it we can perceive that we really survive as spectators."

24. Excerpt from an article in *Extra!* (June 2003) critical of embedding journalists with military units during the Iraq War: "Embedding was the brainchild of Assistant Defense Secretary Victoria Clarke, formerly with Hill and Knowlton, the PR firm infamous for promoting the false baby-incubator story during the first Gulf War."

25. St. Augustine, in *De Libero Arbitrio:* "See how absurd and foolish it is to say: I should prefer nonexistence to miserable existence. He who says, I prefer this

to that, chooses something. Nonexistence is not something; it is nothing. There can be no real choice when what you choose is nothing."

26. Michael Kinsley, well-known writer and former cohost of the TV program *Crossfire,* after admitting to doing paid speeches before various groups (the suggestion was that his fees were payola), declined to state how much he was paid, saying, "I do staged debates—mini *Crossfires*—before business groups. If everyone [others in the media] disclosed, I would." (Quoted in the *New Yorker,* September 12, 1994.)

27. Item from the *Philadelphia Inquirer* (August 28, 2003) about an atheist, Sherrie Wilkins, suing a school board in Camden, New Jersey, over school uniforms: "Citing the equal protection clause of the U.S. Constitution, Wilkins' lawsuit argues that atheists should have the same rights as religious parents [since the school district allows parents to opt out of the requirement on religious grounds]. . . . [Furthermore] as an atheist, Wilkins said in court documents, she objects to the uniforms because they 'hinder her children's creativity . . . and freedom of expression.' Uniforms also symbolize militarism, which she opposes, she said."

28. A lobbyist, whose job is to get people to call or write to members of Congress, responding to the charge that this sort of activity makes the "political playing field" uneven (because big money can afford these endeavors much better than small): "Everyone knows that the playing field isn't level in this country in the business arena, or in others for that matter. Nobody complains about that. Why fuss about the funding for what I do?"

29. Excerpt from a letter to the editor of the *Pacific Sun* (September 2000): "Nowhere on the official Ralph Nader website is there any mention of concern about how women are treated in the media. I can't help but infer that this kind of human dignity is not high on his agenda."

30. On a *Larry King Live* TV show (November 29, 2000), Republican Senator John McCain defended the acceptance of the Florida presidential election results by saying that the votes in the disputed counties had been counted and recounted and that, although there were ways in which the 2000 election in Florida could have been better conducted, we should remember that many elections in the past have been less than perfect; for instance, in Illinois in 1960 (the year John F. Kennedy was elected president amidst claims of chicanery in Illinois and Texas).

It's dangerous to conclude that A is the cause of B just because B follows A.

Chapter

5

FALLACIOUS REASONING—3

Let's now continue our discussion of fallacious reasoning with several fallacies that generally fall into the broad category *invalid inference.*

1. HASTY CONCLUSION

The fallacy of **hasty conclusion** is committed when we draw a conclusion from relevant but insufficient evidence. This fallacy is committed in many different ways and circumstances, ranging from judging political candidates primarily on the basis of 30-second TV commercials to concluding that a neighbor is having an affair on the basis of one or two suspicious clues.

Of course, if we mere human beings were as lucky as Hercule Poirot or Miss Marple, or the other famous fictional detectives, our overly hasty conclusions would frequently turn out to be correct. Here, for example, is the archetype of the great fictional detective, Sherlock Holmes, making one of his amazing "deductions" when first introduced to Dr. Watson in Sir Arthur Conan Doyle's *A Study in Scarlet:*

> Here is a gentleman of the medical type, but with the air of a military man. Clearly an army doctor, then. He has just come from the tropics, for his face is dark, and that is not the natural tint of his skin, for his wrists are fair. He has undergone hardship and sickness, as his haggard face says clearly. His left arm has been injured. He holds it in a still and unnatural manner. Where in the tropics could an English army doctor have seen much hardship and gotten his arm wounded? Clearly in Afghanistan.

What Holmes observed about Watson was consistent with all sorts of other possibilities that in real life might have been actualities. Doctors don't look that much different from other professionals. Some men with a military air (whatever that might be) never have been in the military. Among Englishmen in those days, when Britain ruled the waves, naval military men were just as common as army types. Tanned faces can result from exposure to nontropical sunlight. A still and unnatural arm carriage may be the legacy of a childhood accident, a haggard expression due to anguish at the loss of a close relative. And even supposing the person in question were a military man who had been wounded in battle in Afghanistan, he still might just have come from a funeral in Italy, South Africa, Brighton, or Timbuktu. The conclusion drawn by Holmes may have been a good guess, but stated with the typical Holmes air of infallibility, it surely was hasty.

2. SMALL SAMPLE

Statistics frequently are used to project from a sample to the "population" from which it was drawn. This is the basic technique that underlies several kinds of inductive reasoning and is the method employed by most polls—including those conducted by Gallup, Harris, and the Nielsen television ratings. But when we accept a conclusion based on a sample that is too small to be a reliable measure of the population from which it was drawn, we are guilty of the fallacy of the **small sample,** a variety of the fallacy *hasty conclusion.* No sample of 100 to 500 voters, for instance, can possibly be depended on to accurately reflect the entire voting population of the United States.

Scientists, of all people, aren't supposed to commit statistical fallacies (or any fallacies, for that matter), but they're human, just like the rest of us. In an interesting, one might say comical, example (*Human Nature,* March 1979), researchers drew a conclusion about the mating vocal responses of primate species based on a sample of three human couples (each observed engaged in sex exactly once), a pair of gibbons, and one troop of chacma baboons.

The general question as to when a sample is sufficiently large is extremely difficult to answer and is a matter of great interest to statisticians and other scientists. Obviously, though, all other things being equal, the larger the percentage of a population from which a sample is drawn, the more confident we can be that it reflects that population as a whole.

3. UNREPRESENTATIVE SAMPLE

In addition to being large enough, a good sample should be *representative* of the population from which it is drawn. Indeed, the more representative a sample is, the smaller it needs to be to be significant. When we reason from a sample that isn't sufficiently representative, we commit the fallacy of the **unrepresentative sample** (sometimes called the fallacy of **biased statistics,** although that name also applies to cases where known statistics that are unfavorable to a theory are deliberately suppressed).

> Sample size does not overcome sample bias.
>
> —Saying popular among statisticians

The example just mentioned, about primate mating responses, illustrates the fallacy of the *unrepresentative sample* as well as that of the *small sample*. For one thing, only three of the dozens of primate species were checked—chimps, gorillas, lemurs, tarsiers, and so forth, may be quite different. (In fact, orangutans turn out to be much different from all other primates in their sex practices.) For another, there is plenty of reason to believe that no sample of three human couples could possibly be representative of all *Homo sapiens,* given the tremendous variety of sex practices engaged in by members of our species.

As usual, relevant background information is crucial when we try to determine whether a sample is likely to be representative of the population from which it was drawn (or is likely to be sufficiently large, for that matter). Good reasoning *always* requires good background information.

4. QUESTIONABLE CAUSE

We commit the fallacy of **questionable cause** when we label something as the cause of something else on the basis of insufficient or unrepresentative evidence, or when doing so contradicts well-established, high-level theories.[1] (*Questionable cause* is a broader version of the traditional fallacy *post hoc, ergo propter hoc,* literally "after this, therefore because of this." Note that the fallacy *questionable cause* often overlaps that of *hasty conclusion* or of *small sample.*)

As just mentioned, it isn't easy to determine whether a sample is sufficiently large or representative. This is true in particular because judgments on these matters often depend on seeing the relevance of background information and *bringing it to bear.* All too often, people make judgments about causal connections on the basis of observed correlations, often quite small, that contradict very general, very well-confirmed, and quite easily understood higher-level theories about what sorts of causes can result in what kinds of effects. People often do so because they lack the relevant and *accurate* background information; sometimes they are motivated by wishful thinking to ignore contrary evidence or theories (a topic to be discussed at some length in the next chapter).

Many people have little or no understanding of the general way in which things work in this world. As they experience life, they don't try to figure out how things work in general or attempt to gain some of the knowledge that has been gleaned over time by others. Instead, they attend almost exclusively to immediate events and problems. They may see science as some kind of magical box from which gadgets like television sets, computers, and jet planes are extracted by bearded drudges with German accents or by youthful nerds. Having relatively little background information to bring to bear on experience, they are unable to assess either the adequacy of evidence or the possibility that a general idea might be true. Think, for instance, of those who fall for regimens that supposedly reduce body fat in certain parts of the body (such as the hips) by exercising

---

[1] This doesn't mean that these higher-level theories are exempt from refutation. Evidence that persistently runs contrary even to the highest-level, most general scientific theories eventually, and sometimes rather swiftly, overturns them, as, for example, old ideas about the motions of continents, and related matters, were overturned by evidence favoring the currently held theory concerning plate tectonics.

The Small Society. Reprinted by permission of the Washington Star Syndicate, Inc.

It isn't always easy to determine what is the cause of what.

muscles in those locations, ignorant of the well-known fact that the body doesn't burn body fat in that way. Or consider those who believe in ESP in spite of the failure of every scientific test to confirm its existence.

For many people economics is just as baffling as are the hard sciences. Critics were inclined to blame the second President Bush for the downturn in the economy during his years in office. But the fact that there was a recession during his first couple of years in office does not prove that his policies caused the economy to slow down. (In fact, the bloated stock market, during the highly prosperous Clinton years, was one of several indicators that the economy would eventually go south.) The economic well-being of the United States depends on many complex factors, here and around the world, that a president does not and cannot control. This doesn't mean that by promoting unsound economic policies a president cannot be a part of the cause of an economic downturn. The point is that it is simplistic to give him the lion's share of the blame without further argument.

The fallacy *questionable cause* also sometimes is committed because items are incorrectly classified—poorly sorted into different kinds. Any items, no matter how different from each other, have some things in common, so that there always is some reason for grouping them together in our thoughts. When we classify items to discover cause/effect relationships, we need to make sure we have bunched together just the right sorts of cases. In some areas of the United States, for instance, a larger percentage of nonwhite children do poorly in school compared to students who are white, a fact that has led some people to conclude that being nonwhite is the *cause* of their doing less well in school (that there is a genetic difference involved here), an interesting and very serious example of the fallacy *questionable cause*.[2]

---

[2]Notice that in the United States, nonwhite is an ethnic, not a racial, category. Most Americans who think of themselves as African American are racially both of white (European) and African American (African) descent; a few are of African and Asian stock; and a very few are descended from European, African, and Asian forebears (Tiger Woods being a well-known example). Similar remarks apply to members of many other groups. Mexican Americans, for example, tend to be

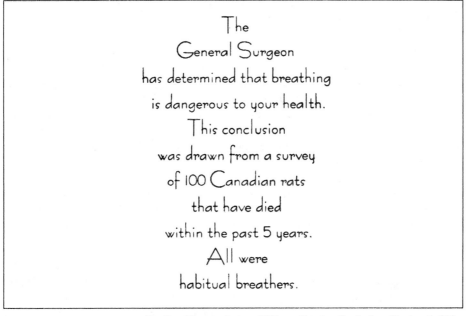

Greeting card humor illustrating some fallacy or other, no doubt.

Unfortunately, conclusions drawn from studies in the field of education are prone to oversimplification. A front-page article in the *San Francisco Chronicle* on the problems caused by using noncredentialed teachers for California schools cited a study that found "high schools with the fewest credentialed teachers had the highest failure rates on the math portion of the exit exam."[3] After a lengthy discussion of statistical evidence and recommendations that all teachers be credentialed, brief mention was made of the fact that the group also found that ". . . inexperienced teachers were also overwhelmingly concentrated in schools with the neediest students." This calls into question the cause of student failure. Did they fail because they had inexperienced (noncredentialed) teachers or because the students were so needy that even experienced teachers couldn't bring them up to grade level? Clearly a questionable cause.

As might be expected, the statistical variety of *questionable cause,* in which a mere statistical correlation is taken to provide proof of a causal connection, is quite common. It's true that every statistical correlation has some significance and, in the absence of reasons to the contrary, increases the likelihood (probability), however slightly, that there also is a causal connection between the things correlated. But when there are reasons to

---

descended from European (chiefly Spanish) and Asian forebears. Interestingly, the exact or even approximate place of origin of the Asian peoples who originally populated Mexico is hotly disputed by anthropologists and other scientists.

[3] See the *San Francisco Chronicle* article, December 12, 2002, citing a study by the Center for the Future of Teaching and Learning, in Santa Cruz.

the contrary, or when the statistical sample in question is too small or unrepresentative, we make a mistake in jumping to the conclusion that we've found a causal connection.

Sometimes alleged causal connections based on statistical surveys are too silly to take seriously, because they are so obviously contrary to well-supported background beliefs. An example is the theory that smoking marijuana causes college students to get better grades, based on one dubious statistical study in which marijuana smokers averaged slightly higher grades than nonsmokers. This theory actually gained modest acceptance in some, ah, . . . "high"-minded circles during the 1970s. (And what are the background beliefs that should make you doubt smoking dope causes an increase in grades?)

It's often very hard, if not impossible, for the layperson to evaluate statistical claims on complicated or technical subjects. Sometimes, the best that nonexperts can do is try to find the best professional advice they can. But sometimes they can evaluate these claims by employing the method described in the following excerpt from a *Psychology Today* article on statistical reasoning:

> *"What do the other three cells look like?"* This slogan should always be invoked to assess covariation [the statistical connection] of events. . . . To determine the effectiveness of chiropractic treatment, for example, one needs numbers from four "cells." How many people were cured after being treated by a chiropractor? How many were not cured after such treatment? How many people got better without treatment? How many didn't get better and went untreated?

Most of us are impressed when we see first cell statistics and fail to realize that we usually need to know about one or more of the others to determine whether we've found a causal connection or just a statistical one. Reading, say, that about two-thirds of those treated by chiropractors get better proves nothing about the effectiveness of chiropractors; it may be that two-thirds of those with similar complaints who were not so treated also got well, or even that three-quarters did (in which case we would have some evidence that chiropractors harm patients more than they help them.)

5. QUESTIONABLE ANALOGY

We reason by *analogy* when we conclude from the observed similarity of two or more items in some respects to their similarity in another.[4] Sports fans, for example, reasoned by analogy when they concluded that the 2004 Olympic Games would be fun to watch, given that they were in previous years. Caffeine lovers do so when they reason from the fact that coffee has kept them awake several nights in a row to the conclusion that drinking it again tonight will keep them awake.[5] The general form of such reasoning is that the items mentioned are alike in certain respects, so they will be alike in some other way.

---

[4]Analogical reasoning thus is very similar to *induction by enumeration.* Indeed, the latter can be thought of as a kind of analogical reasoning.

[5]Recall, though, the earlier discussion of the fallacy *questionable cause.* It isn't easy to be positive that it's the coffee keeping us awake.

But we aren't always justified in reasoning by analogy. When we do so anyway, we are guilty of the fallacy of **questionable analogy,** sometimes referred to as **faulty comparison.**

Analogical reasoning can be fallacious for several different reasons. The sample on which it is based may be too small or not sufficiently representative, it may conflict with conclusions drawn by higher-level reasoning, or there may be a lack of relevant similarity between the items implied to be alike. Here is an example based on a much too small sample:

> I've won at blackjack twice in a row by drawing a card when holding cards total-ing 18, so I conclude by analogy that I'll win next time I draw on 18.

This analogy also is defective because it ignores the higher-level theory of probability, which says that your chances of success when drawing on 18 are quite low.

In some cases, the analogy is so wide of the mark that its questionable nature should be obvious. For example, after the prisoner-abuse scandal at the Abu Ghraib prison, Saudi Arabian Daud al-Shiryan was quoted in the media saying "This will increase the hatred of America, not just in Iraq but abroad. . . . Abu Ghraib was used for torture in Saddam's time. People will ask now what's the difference between Saddam and Bush. Nothing!" The analogy is so wide of the mark that it hardly needs explaining. President Bush didn't authorize the prison abuse, to begin with, and the abuse that did occur, though bad enough in its own right, was in no way comparable to the torture and killing that went on under Hussein.

Not uncommonly, questionable analogies surface in a court of law. In 2003 many American tourists were annoyed to discover that credit card companies were charging a currency conversion fee for items purchased abroad. One irate customer filed suit against Visa and MasterCard for intentionally hiding the fee from cardholders. (It only appears—occasionally—in cardholder agreements, buried in legal jargon.) The attor-ney for MasterCard argued, "That's not hiding, that's not concealing—that's how busi-ness is done in this country." The defense went on to explain that "while consumers nat-urally understand that commercial suppliers of goods and services impose a mark-up over their costs, the proposed decision would condemn as 'embedding' the standard practice that a seller tells its customer its price to them, not which part of the price re-flects its cost and which part its mark-up." However, to compare hidden credit card fees to the undisclosed markup of commercial goods is certainly questionable. The consumer knows the cost of an item in a retail store because it is clearly marked on the price tag, but when using a credit card abroad, the consumer has no idea of the total amount be-cause of the hidden conversion fee.

Some analogies are easily seen to be fallacious, others as clearly apt. But the evalua-tions of still others often require a good deal of thought. Consider this analogy in a let-ter to the editor arguing against stricter handgun control laws: When a drunk driver runs over a child, we go after the driver, not the car. When someone kills a child with a gun, we go after the gun. But shouldn't we go after the person who murders with a gun, not the gun itself? In this case, there clearly is a relevant resemblance between the two cases—killing with a car or with a gun—so there is something to the analogy. But there also are important differences, as there often are, and the question is whether they are both relevant and sufficient to make the analogy questionable. For example, private au-tos are an extremely important kind of transportation in our society; banning their use would dramatically change all sorts of things in everyday life. Handguns serve few legitimate purposes in private hands; AK-47s and the like, none at all; restricting their use would make relatively little difference in most of our lives. Furthermore, most auto deaths result from accidents or negligence, rarely from deliberate intent to murder. Guns frequently are used deliberately to murder other people. Note that the letter writer omits the fact that, when people use guns for nefarious purposes, we go after the gun user as well as the gun itself, and also the fact that we outlaw autos believed to be unsafe to drive. The point of all of this is that we don't want to label analogies questionable, or apt, too quickly; in some cases we need to consider all sorts of factors. Good critical reasoners need to become adept at bringing background information to bear when evaluating analogies, just as most other sorts of reasoning.

This example also illustrates the difficulty in bringing one's relevant background beliefs to bear when evaluating an argument. All of the relevant differences just mentioned are common knowledge, yet we all often fail to bring information of this kind to bear when evaluating an argument. (Did you in this case?)

Before turning to a discussion of other fallacies, perhaps it should be noted that we need to distinguish between *explanatory* analogies used to explain and *argumentative* analogies used to prove a point. When we argue or reason analogically, we present evidence for a conclusion; when we use an analogy to explain, we merely liken the thing explained to something already familiar. In Plato's famous analogy of the cave, for example, the people in the cave who merely see the shadows of things are likened to those who restrict themselves to the ever-changing world of everyday experience, while the people who come out into the sunlight and see the objects themselves are likened to the philosophers who reason to the unchanging reality that lies behind everyday experiences. The analogy explains Plato's ideas about a world beyond that of mere everyday experiences, but it doesn't prove that there is such a world or in any way argue that there is. (Plato himself very likely intended his cave myth to be explanatory, not argumentative, but it often is construed otherwise.)

The point here is that we shouldn't accuse those whose analogies are intended to explain of being guilty of the fallacy *questionable analogy*. (They may, of course, serve very poorly to explain, but that is another matter.) Anyway, as just remarked, explanatory analogies sometimes are mistakenly taken to prove what they merely explain, and in this case we are indeed justified in accusing those who do this of the fallacy *questionable analogy*.

Finally, we need to notice that in everyday life it often is difficult to determine whether an analogy is intended to explain or to prove; no doubt some are intended to serve both purposes. In any case, as with explanations in general, it is hard to separate the mere explanatory nature of an analogy from its power to persuade. (Recall, for example, the salesperson's explanation about cameras in Chapter 1, where the intent was to persuade a customer to buy a camera, not merely to explain the differences between one set and another.)

6. QUESTIONABLE STATISTICS

Statistics always seem so precise and *authoritative*. It sounds so much more believable, for instance, to claim that the typical child watches an average of 4,286 acts of violence on TV by age 18 rather than just that kids typically watch an awful lot of TV violence. But how could anyone know such an exact fact? There would have to be a lot of guess-work and extrapolation from very small samples to arrive even at an informed rough es-timate as to these sorts of matters. This doesn't mean that we ought simply to dismiss these statistics; it just means that we have to understand their limitations.

Statistics on the state of the economy are a case in point. Take the ones published by the federal government on business conditions in the United States. One of the major problems with these statistics is that their *margin of error* (not always provided) often is greater than the "significant" differences they report. This becomes evident when we consider that the government's later revisions of its own figures often reflect a change larger than the alleged margin of error.

In addition, problems arise from the need to use a base year in determining long-run trends. Those who want to show that a given year has had a high rate of growth can choose a low base year; those intent on proving a low rate of growth, a high base year. Meanwhile, the precisely true rate of growth may remain in doubt.

In the case of figures concerning the gross national product, we have several other reasons for being suspicious. One is that a good deal of commerce in the United States today is illegal. Think only of racketeering, gambling, drug traffic, prostitution, and the hiring of illegal aliens to do migrant farm labor or household cleaning and other low-paying, tedious, and often backbreaking jobs. Reliable statistics concerning illegal ac-tivities are by their nature hard to come by. Calculating, say, the commerce in illegal drugs has to be done indirectly, by reference to the sale of legal drug equipment, drug busts, and so on. Another reason for suspicion is that a good deal of otherwise legal com-merce is done "off the books," so that no taxes need to be paid or so that restrictive laws can be avoided. How are we to assess the value of goods when one kind is bartered for another?

Questionable statistics were fodder for both sides of the debate over the ban on semi-automatic weapons. When the decade-old bill came up for renewal in 2004, Senator Di-anne Feinstein, who authored the legislation, argued that assault weapon crimes had de-creased by two-thirds (from 3.57 percent in 1995 to 1.22 percent in 2002) since the bill was passed. Her statistics came from the Bureau of Alcohol, Tobacco and Firearms. But they were refuted by NRA board member, Senator Larry Craig, who had another set of statistics, this time from the Justice Department, showing no difference in the use of semi-automatic weapons before or after the ban—less than 2 percent in either case. Since authorities can't know for sure how many of the banned weapons were used in crimes, both supporters and opponents of the bill dredged up questionable statistics to bolster their claims.

The government's figures on unemployment also need to be viewed with a good deal of suspicion. These figures are calculated partly on the basis of information gathered via polls of "representative" individuals. How these people respond depends on the precise wording of the questions they are asked (a point soon to be discussed further), and this in part depends on what the government considers to be full-time, compared to part-time, employment and who is said to be seeking employment, compared to those who have given up the search. (It also depends on how truly representative the government's samples happen to be.) In 1998, for instance, President Clinton claimed that the unem-ployment rate was under 5 percent, yet these statistics left out anyone who hadn't looked for work that year or those who worked part-time but wanted full-time jobs. If these people had been included, the unemployment rate may well have more than doubled—to about 10 percent.[6] During the second President Bush's term in office, the unemployment rate rose steadily, but in July 2003, the Labor Department reported that it fell to 6.2 percent from 6.4 percent the previous month—despite continued job losses. This drop, however, failed to reflect the fact that over half a million workers left the labor force and were no longer officially counted as unemployed.

All of this certainly does not mean that government statistics on commerce and employment should be tossed into the nearest wastebasket. But it does mean that precise official figures should be taken for what they are: the best *approximations* we have of business activity—valuable primarily in showing very-long-term trends, but often calculated so as to serve short-term political interests.[7]

By way of contrast, consider a correctly cautious claim typical of those frequently made by scientists (*Science News,* January 19, 1991): Scientists using sophisticated techniques to determine the age of ancient cliff drawings in west Texas estimated that the drawings were painted "3,865 years ago, *give or take a century*" (italics added).

Finally, it's important to have some idea as to which sorts of statistics can be known, even in theory. Some statistics simply are unknowable, at least by human beings. How, for instance, could Dr. Dean Edell (whose TV and radio programs usually provide excellent information about health and medical matters) know that the average person tells 13 lies per week, as he stated on one of his programs? How could anyone know? Anyway, here is a letter one of the authors of this text received several years ago that contains examples of unknowable statistics it would be hard to top:

> Dear Friend: In the past 5,000 years men have fought in 14,523 wars. One out of four persons living during this time have been war casualties. A nuclear war would add 1,245,000,000 men, women, and children to this tragic list.

It's ludicrous to present such precise figures as facts. No one knows (or could know) the exact number of wars fought so far, to say nothing of the number of war casualties. (Does anyone even know the true casualty rates just for all of the wars that have occurred in the past ten years?) As for the numbers in a nuclear conflict, the casualty rate would depend on who fought such a war, and, in any event, it is a matter on which even so-called experts can only engage in the wildest sorts of speculations.

7. QUESTIONABLE USES OF GOOD STATISTICS

As we've just seen, statistics that are obviously questionable are a problem. But perfectly good statistics also can cause trouble—for two reasons. The first is the inability

---

[6]For more information, see *Real World Macro: A Macroeconomics Reader from Dollars and Sense* 1998).

[7]The 1996–1997 political battles over how the consumer price index (CPI) should be calculated are an interesting example. Because Social Security payments are tied to the CPI, those who wanted to balance the budget by reducing Social Security payments argued for a method that generally lowered the CPI; those who did not want to reduce Social Security payments fought to keep the old (in fact, more accurate) way of calculating.

of so many people to understand the significance of this statistic or that, made worse by the natural tendency in all of us to pay attention to statistics that support conclusions we already have drawn. The second is the ability of charlatans to bamboozle the rest of us via cleverly employed statistics. (That's the import of the old saying that figures don't lie, but liars figure.)

The ways in which we confuse ourselves seem to be limitless. HMO lobbyists helped us do this, for example, when they tried to dissuade members of Congress from regulating HMOs through patients' rights bills. They cited statistics from polls conducted by the American Association of Health Plans (AAHP)—the main HMO trade association—revealing that most Americans were satisfied with their managed care plans. In one sense, then, the AAHP and their lobbyists were right. A large majority of Americans have historically claimed to be satisfied with the health care they receive from their insurance providers, including HMOs.

But the AAHP suppressed all sorts of relevant facts that point to a different conclusion, including statistics from other polls. To start with, a 1999 CBS poll found that only 69 percent of those insured by HMOs were satisfied with their health care compared to 86 percent of those insured by more traditional "fee-for-services" plans. In addition, more specific surveys reveal far greater dissatisfaction with HMO care. A 1998 Kaiser Family Foundation/Harvard University poll found that 53 percent of the public said that, in general, HMOs made it harder than traditional plans to get care, as compared to only 29 percent who said it was easier, and that 62 percent claimed HMOs made it more difficult to see medical specialists, with only 23 percent saying it has become easier. Similarly, a 1998 CNN/*Time* poll found that 43 percent of those interviewed believe health care coverage had gotten worse during the previous five years (when HMOs made big inroads into the health care market), with only 18 percent saying it had improved. This poll also found that 64 percent of respondents believe health care costs have increased, only 11 percent that they have decreased.

We also need to notice that the AAHP lobbyists neglected the obvious thought that it isn't surprising a majority of Americans are satisfied with their health plans, given that at any particular time most of us are not experiencing serious health problems. A more relevant statistic would be one concerning what percentage of those who have had serious health problems are satisfied or dissatisfied with HMO coverage as compared to the more traditional fee-for-service plans still offered, say, by some Blue Cross/Blue Shield organizations. (Of course, as usual, those lacking relevant background information, even of the kind that might lead them to suspect that the AAHP might be concealing relevant facts, are fair game easily taken in by sharp operators.[8])

The misuse of statistics is just as common in economics as it is in medicine. For instance, a libertarian defending the current economy on a radio talk show claimed that less than 10 percent of Americans used to own stocks, but now up to 45 to 50 percent do. Thus, an ordinary wage earner who saves can take part in the increase in wealth the stock market provides. Although his figures are about right, he neglects two important points. First, the 45 to 50 percent includes retirement funds invested by companies, not individuals—the ordinary earner simply draws a pension from the invested fund.

---

[8]For more information on this topic, see, for instance, *The American Prospect,* December 20, 1999 issue.

Second, a tiny portion of stockholders own most of the stock and get rich. The large majority have less than $10,000 invested. The rich still have been getting richer, and the gap between the rich and the rest of us has been getting a good deal larger.

Going to another topic, an item in the famous *Harper's Index* (February 1994) indicated that the murder rate is twice as high in states that have a death penalty for major crimes as it is in other states. (The statistics have changed somewhat since 1994, but for our purposes here they are sufficiently similar today.) Those opposed to the death penalty on grounds that it does not deter took this to be evidence supporting that conclusion.

But sophisticated critical reasoners wondered whether doing so made them guilty of the fallacy *questionable cause* (or perhaps *hasty conclusion?*). For it very well may be that states with death penalties had a higher rate of murder to start with and that perhaps they opted for this harsh penalty to try to reduce the amount of serious crime. To prove their point, those opposed to the death penalty on these grounds would have to present statistics showing that serious crime remained the same, or increased, after a death penalty was imposed in particular states. Otherwise, the comparison is of apples and oranges. (Remember that the number of serious crimes tends to increase in hard economic times and decreases in good.)

It's often easy to prove a point simply by choosing statistics carefully, making sure not to cite the figures that are most relevant. Charlatans do this regularly, but everyone does so on occasion. The respected economist Robert J. Samuelson, for instance, did so when he argued that the American people "never had it so good," citing the fact that virtually all economic statistical indicators—concerning wages, family income, poverty, and so on—show a dramatic improvement now compared to 1945 at the end of World War II. What he neglected to mention (let's assume not with intent to deceive) is that nearly all of the improvements these figures demonstrate were made from 1945 to 1973. Since that time, the incomes of groups at the lower end of the economic pecking order have improved only very slightly or not at all—in some cases having actually declined —while the incomes of those higher up rose dramatically, thus widening the gap between the well-off and the poor.

8. POLLS: AN IMPORTANT SPECIAL CASE

A well-conceived and well-executed poll can be a fruitful way to find out all sorts of things, from the voter strength of a political candidate to Fido's preferences in dog food. Unfortunately, not all polls are created equal.

Statistics seem to baffle almost everyone. Several years ago, when 200 educators were asked what percentage of children read at grade level or below, 78 percent failed to provide the correct answer—50 percent. Even teachers have a hard time keeping straight on the difference between comparative and absolute scales.

Another comparative rating that causes confusion is the IQ rating: Half of those who take the test must be rated at 100 or below, given that 100 merely marks the halfway point in results.

Cartoon by Tom Meyer © *San Francisco Chronicle*. Reprinted by permission.

One problem is that the way in which a question is asked seriously influences the answers one can expect. It is extremely difficult, if not impossible, to word a question in a way that is completely neutral. At the height of the Watergate scandal, for instance, a Gallup poll asked the question

> Do you think President Nixon should be impeached and compelled to leave the presidency, or not?

Thirty percent said yes. But a Pat Caddell private poll asked the question this way:

> Do you think the President should be tried, and removed from office if found guilty?

Fifty-seven percent answered yes to that one. So 30 percent answered yes to the question worded one way, 57 percent when the same question was put another way.

This fact has not escaped those intent on skewing poll results one way or the other. Here, for example, are a couple of loaded questions in the "2000 Official NRA Gun Owners Survey":

Do you think gun owner names should be subject to surprise inspection by the Bureau of Alcohol Tobacco and Firearms (BATF)?

Do you think gun owners like you should be required to pay expensive liability insurance for every gun you own?

What gun owners in their right minds would answer *no* to these questions?

Of course, when it comes to slanted poll questions, the Democratic and Republican parties take a back seat to no one. Here is an example from the 1999 mailings conducted by the Democratic National Committee of the Democratic party:

> Should the projected budget surplus be used to support tax cuts that are weighed more heavily toward the rich?

What voters, other than the very rich, would answer yes to this question?

Polls also can be manipulated by means of the choice of questions asked or by the answers from which those polled are instructed to choose. Here is a *Washington Monthly* item (November 1989) that makes this point nicely:

> A friend who is a Harvard alumnus received a questionnaire from his alma mater asking him to choose "the three most important issues facing Harvard" from a list of nine. None of the nine mentioned the high cost of tuition.

But the biggest problem with polls no doubt is the difficulty of tapping a truly representative sample. The 1936 *Literary Digest* poll, based on names lifted from telephone directories and auto registration lists, is perhaps the most famous example of an extremely biased poll. It predicted that Alf Landon would defeat Franklin Roosevelt, while the actual result was a tremendous landslide for Roosevelt. The magazine (which went out of business shortly afterward—*questionable cause*?) failed to take into account the fact that few

---

Many surveys ask biased questions to make something seem more popular than in fact it is, because of the "bandwagon" effect of being popular (discussed in the next chapter). An egregious example surfaced during the antitrust trial in 1999 against Microsoft Corporation when the government accused the company of chicanery in Microsoft's attempt to make Bill Gates look good in a Senate hearing in 1998. A Microsoft witness, Richard Schmalansee, cited a survey of independent software vendors who overwhelmingly agreed that Microsoft should hard-wire its Web-browsing software directly into its Windows operating system. But the government's lead counsel, David Boies, brought out under cross-examination that the poll was the brainchild of Microsoft's top technologist, Nathan Myhrvold, in response to the following request from Bill Gates: "It would HELP ME IMMENSELY to have a survey showing that 90 percent of developers believe that putting the browser into the (operating system) makes sense" (February 14, 1998).

The next day Myhrvold replied by e-mail: "I think that it is crucial to make [sure] the statement we ask people about in the survey . . . is worded properly. Saying 'put the browser in the [Windows operating system]' is already a statement that is prejudicial to us. The name 'browser' suggests a separate thing." Instead, Myhrvold decided on "a more neutral question about how internet technology needs to merge with local computing." (The issue of integration is central to the charges brought against Microsoft by the Department of Justice and 19 states.) Had the survey questions not been manipulated to elicit the desired response, the software vendors might have answered differently.

people in the bottom half of the American population had telephones or autos in those days, so that their sample was completely unrepresentative of American voters.

Of course, the art of polling has come a long way since 1936, or even 1948, when polls predicted an easy victory for Thomas E. Dewey over Harry Truman. The *Chicago Tribune*—whose motto, incidentally, was and still is "The World's Greatest Newspaper"—was so sure Dewey would win that it grossly misinterpreted early returns and printed one of the most infamous headlines in newspaper history—"Dewey Defeats Truman"—which an exultant Truman held up to the crowd at his victory celebration.

But it still is difficult to get a representative sample of the voting population by polling only 1,500 or so potential voters—the standard practice today. In theory, a very carefully selected sample of roughly this size should be almost as reliable as one of 15,000 (a poll of this size would be much too expensive and is never conducted). But in practice, for all sorts of reasons, things frequently don't work as planned. This doesn't mean that we should not pay attention to polls. They often are the best or even the only way we have of testing the water. It just means we have to pay heed to them in an intelligent manner. A presidential election poll taken in September is of much less value, other things being equal, than one conducted in October; polls paid for by one side or the other are worth less than those conducted by truly independent organizations. But most important, we have to remember that even the best polls have a batting average well below 100 percent. In the 2004 presidential election, when voters were equally divided between Kerry and Bush, the polls' predictions flip-flopped between the two candidates and gave no true indication of who would win in the end. No one knew the outcome until early in the morning after the election when Bush won Ohio and nailed down the presidency.

Note, by the way, that there is no such thing as a "poll fallacy," even though, as just illustrated, polls do give rise to fallacies such as *questionable statistics* and *hasty conclusions*.

Finally, polls conducted during the 2000 and 2004 presidential elections provide good examples of another interesting feature of a great many polls: They often claim margins of error less than the difference of one poll from another. For example, the NBC/*Wall Street Journal* poll of August 13, 2000, showed George W. Bush favored by 44 percent of those polled to Al Gore's 41 percent, claiming a margin of error of 3.5 percent, while another poll showed Gore ahead by 4 percent, with a similar margin of error. An NBC/*Wall Street Journal* poll in mid-September had it 45 percent for Gore, 42 percent for Bush, margin of error 2.2 percent, while a CNN/*USA Today* poll at that time listed 41 percent for Bush and 38 percent for Gore, margin of error 3 percent. The same problem occurred in the polls conducted during the 2004 presidential election.

9. FALSE CHARGE OF FALLACY

It often is all too easy to charge others with fallacious reasoning. This is particularly true when people change their minds and embrace positions they previously denied. The temptation is to charge them with the fallacy of *inconsistency.* But making a given statement at one time and one that contradicts it at a later time does not necessarily indicate inconsistency; we may have, and express, good grounds for changing our minds.

Take the person who says, "I used to believe that women are not as creative as men, because most of the intellectually productive people I knew about were men; but I've changed my mind, because I believe now (as I didn't then) that environment (culture,

surroundings), not native ability, has been responsible for the preponderance of intellectual men." Surely, that person cannot be accused of the fallacy of *inconsistency,* since he
(or she!) has explained the change of mind.

Anyway, in good textbook style, let's say that those who falsely accuse others of fallacy are themselves guilty of making a **false charge of fallacy.**

Of course, falsely accusing someone of *inconsistency* is not the only way in which
someone might be guilty of *false charge of fallacy.* Recall, for example, the earlier discussion of the distinction between analogical reasoning and explanatory analogies;
clearly, we are guilty of making a *false charge of fallacy* if we accuse someone of per-
petrating a *questionable analogy* when his or her intent is not to prove something but
merely, via an analogy, to explain it.

We are also guilty of falsely charging someone with a fallacy when we take literally
an ironic jab at the opposition. In the following letter to the editor, for example, the
writer clearly intends to be ironic:

> Billions of dollars and two decades later, the War on Drugs has successfully
> eliminated illegal drugs from the face of America. The country is finally free
> of pot, coke and heroin. With this as a model, the War on Junk Guns is bound
> to be successful.

Claiming that the writer is guilty of *questionable premise* or *suppressed evidence* because the War on Drugs hasn't eradicated illegal drugs clearly constitutes a *false charge
of fallacy.* The letter writer just employs sarcasm to remind us ironically that the War on
Drugs has been a failure.

Note, by the way, that some of the alleged fallacies that have been discussed in logic
textbooks since time immemorial are not generally fallacious, at least according to the
criteria set up in this text. Take the fallacy called *appeal to force* (traditional name: *argumentum ad baculum*), committed, it is said, when a conclusion is accepted after a
threat of force of one kind or another. Lawmakers, for instance, sometimes are charged
with commission of this fallacy when they are convinced to vote a certain way by the
implied threats of lobbyists to stop the flow of campaign contributions.

---

*Exercise item from the second edition of a certain textbook on logic and contem-
porary rhetoric:*

Newspaper story: Thor Heyerdahl has done it again, crossing the Atlantic in a pa-
pyrus raft designed according to ancient Egyptian tomb carvings. Landing in the
Western Hemisphere on the island of Barbados, he was greeted by the Barbados
prime minister, Errol Barrow, who declared, "This has established Barbados was
the first landing place for man in the Western World."

---

*This was a very "un-PC" remark by Barrow, but that is not the point here. The
point is that the correct answer to this exercise item was supposed to be* hasty conclusion, *but a student from Barbados pointed out that the prime minister was
known for his sense of humor. Another false charge of fallacy, this time by the
(here nameless) author of the critical reasoning textbook in question.*

But legislators whose arms are twisted in this way generally are not guilty of a fallacy—the arm twisting doesn't convince them of the merits or demerits of particular legislation but rather of the personal (career) benefits to be gained by voting as lobbyists "suggest" they should. We need to know here, though, that self-interest frequently motivates people, lawmakers included, to believe what they otherwise would see to be false. More is said in Chapter 6 about the power of self-interest to influence beliefs.

Quibbling

When deciding whether someone has or has not committed a fallacy, we don't want to **quibble.** We don't want to take advantage, for instance, of the fact that life is short, and, in everyday life, we don't usually bother to spell out every detail. Some things can, and should, be taken for granted.

Consider the American Medical Association (AMA) ad that stated:

> 100,000 doctors have quit smoking.
> Maybe they know something you don't.

Students have called this ad fallacious because, among other reasons, it suppresses evidence as to what kind of doctors have quit. ("Maybe it was horse doctors." "They don't say if they were doctors of medicine.") But this sort of response amounts to nothing better than *quibbling*. It resembles the remark of a student who objected to Shakespeare's wonderful line "He jests at scars, that never felt a wound" (*Romeo and Juliet*), on grounds that *he* (the student) had felt a wound—a mere scratch—and still jested at scars. (Other students have objected to the line on the grounds that Shakespeare incorrectly used *that* instead of *who,* but they [the students!] were guilty of another, grammatical sort of quibbling—to say nothing of *hubris,* in having the temerity to "correct" the grammar of someone who may well be the greatest writer to ever work in the English language.)

This (finally!) concludes our discussion of fallacies, unfortunately restricted to just a few of the more common varieties that have been discussed in one place or another in the literature. While it is useful to become adept at aptly applying specific names to cases of fallacious reasoning, the point of acquiring this skill, after all, is to learn how to improve one's own reasoning and to be better able to spot the fallacious reasoning of others. Remember, though, that what counts is not the ability to apply a label to poor reasoning. Labels certainly are useful in getting adept at spotting bad arguments, but seeing that they are bad and understanding why they are bad is the name of the game.

In any case, we will soon see that spotting fallacies is only part of the larger enterprise of evaluating more complicated passages containing related arguments that are intended to form a coherent whole. *Extended arguments* of this kind—argumentative essays—are discussed in Chapters 8 and 9.

SUMMARY OF CHAPTER 5

1. *Hasty conclusion:* Accepting an argument on the basis of relevant but insufficient information or evidence. *Example:* Sherlock Holmes's conclusion that Dr. Watson was an army man just back from Afghanistan.

2. *Small sample:* Drawing conclusions about a population on the basis of a sample that is too small to be a reliable measure of that population. *Example:* Conclusions

drawn about primate mating habits based on a sample of three human couplings, a gibbon mating, and those of one troop of baboons.

3. *Unrepresentative sample:* Reasoning from a sample that is not representative (typical) of the population from which it was drawn. *Example:* The sample of primates just mentioned.

4. *Questionable cause:* Labeling *A* as the cause of *B* on evidence that is insufficient, negative, or unrepresentative or in serious conflict with well-established high-level theories. *Example:* Blaming President Bush for the downturn in the economy when other, more complex factors are at work.

5. *Questionable analogy:* Drawing an analogical conclusion when the cases compared are not relevantly alike. *Example:* Comparing Bush to Hussein in the prisoner abuse scandal at Abu Ghraib.

   Note, by the way, that the quality of statistics sometimes differs a great deal from time to time and place to place.

6. *Questionable statistics:* Employing statistics that are questionable without further support. *Example:* Accepting government statistics on short-term business trends as completely accurate rather than just educated approximations. *Extreme example:* Employing unknowable statistics about how many wars have been fought in the past 5,000 years and how many casualties there have been.

7. *Questionable uses of statistics:* Perfectly good statistics also sometimes are a problem—for two reasons. The first is the inability of so many people to understand the significance of this statistic or that, made worse by the natural tendency in all of us to see statistics as favoring conclusions we already have drawn. The second is the ability of charlatans to bamboozle the rest of us via cleverly employed statistics. *Example:* Accepting evidence that the murder rate in states that have adopted a death penalty for serious crimes is higher than in states that have not done so as proof that the death penalty does not deter crime, without further evidence that this statistical evidence has a causal foundation; it could well be, for example, that states adopting death penalties had even higher murder rates than other states and have adopted a death penalty in an attempt to do something about that unfortunate fact.

8. *Polls:* Although polls are an important source of information, they need to be dealt with cautiously. Polls can be misleading (1) because of the way in which questions are worded—often deliberately, to obtain the desired statistics; (2) because they ask the wrong questions; (3) because respondents don't want to appear ignorant, immoral, odd, or prejudiced; or (4) because they are based on a sample that is too small or unrepresentative. *Example:* The Harvard University poll that failed to list high tuition rates as one of the problems respondents could cite as most important.

9. *False charge of fallacy:* Erroneously accusing others of fallacious reasoning. *Example:* Accusing someone of fallacy who has changed his mind about the lack of creativity of women in the light of contrary evidence.

   Note that ironic rhetoric which, if taken literally, would be fallacious, may well not be. Note also that we don't want to be overly critical of the reasoning of others to the point that we are guilty of *quibbling*.

Some of the alleged fallacies that have been handed down to us in logic textbooks often are not fallacious. For example, legislators who vote so as to satisfy lobbyists are not usually guilty of the fallacy of *appeal to force:* They become convinced by the implied threats of the lobbyists to vote as "suggested" because of self-interest, not because they change their minds about the merits of the legislation. Sad.

EXERCISE 5-1

1. Here is a survey question taken from a Democratic party mailing during the recent presidential campaign:

   Do you believe that government has a right to make decisions about a woman's reproductive rights?

   a. What was the answer the survey makers wanted most people to give? What clues, perhaps plus background information, lead you to this answer?
   b. Construct an alternative question designed to elicit the opposite answer from respondents, and explain why you think they would be more likely to answer that way.

2. Comment on the following item, with respect to what was discussed in this chapter: A survey reported in *Psychology Today* (March 1990) of 657 randomly selected respondents, queried by telephone shortly before Christmas, revealed that 90 percent of the married respondents said they had never had extramarital affairs; almost two-thirds were "very happy" in their marriages; three-fourths still found their spouses physically attractive; and four-fifths would marry the same person again, if they had to do it all over.

3. Here is a paraphrase of a letter to the editor of the *Nutrition Action Health Letter* (November 1993):

   I am a diabetic who has found the artificial sweetener NutraSweet to be "a total nightmare." I thought it would be a good substitute for sugar [diabetics have to severely limit their intake of sugar]. But when I started using it, I began to have serious headaches that my doctor could not account for. So under my doctor's supervision, I stopped using NutraSweet and my headaches stopped. Going back onto NutraSweet was followed by a renewal of my headaches. I did this back and forth three times and the scenario was the same each time: "no NutraSweet, no headache; NutraSweet, headache."

   Do you agree with the unstated implication of this letter—that taking the NutraSweet was the cause of the headaches? Defend your answer against likely objections.

4. Comment on this quote (attributed to Rush Limbaugh) from an ad urging people to join the National Organization for Women. "What if a man claimed the right to rape using the same principle found in the theory that it is his body and he has the right to choose?"

false analogy

5. Earlier in this chapter, we questioned the use of *Harper's Index* statistics concerning the death penalty to show that that extreme form of punishment does not deter crime more than lesser penalties. What about the *Harper's Index* item indicating that the chances of a white teenager arrested on a drug charge being tried in adult court, rather than a juvenile court, are about 1 in 70, while for blacks the chances are 1 in 18? Is the implied conclusion that black teenage offenders are discriminated against compared to whites justified on the basis of this evidence?

*6. Comment on the following statistic listed in the November 2000 *Harper's Index:* Points by which the average SAT score of a home-schooled student exceeds that of other United States students—81.

EXERCISE 5-2

Determine which fallacies (if any) occur in the following short passages and justify your answers (as you did when working on Exercises 3-1 and 4-1). (Note again that some of these passages may also contain fallacies discussed in previous chapters and some *may* not contain fallacious reasoning.)

1. *Bangkok Post* (June 7, 1990): "In sweltering California, a Red Indian brave performed a water ceremony in Claremont in the middle of last month. Now everyone is raving about the fact that just nine days after he returned to his teepee, 'the skies opened up and a 2.54 cm deluge soaked the region.' Three Valleys Municipal Water District supremo Paul Stiglich insists there is a connection. 'The Indians came, they danced, it rained,' he said."

2. Candice Bergen, when queried about lending her name to a Spiegel summer catalog: "I felt it my civic duty to put together this collection of summer essentials for all my fellow Americans out there."

3. From a Bob Schwabach "On Computers" newspaper column: "There aren't just a couple of brands [of IBM-compatible computers] for those [very low] prices; there are dozens. Do they work? Someone I know has been running one continuously for five months, and it's never missed a beat."

4. A while back, the National Highway Traffic Safety Administration placed a value on human life, for purposes of assessing the costs to society of an accidental death, at $287,175.

5. Smoking pot definitely leads to heroin use. A report by the U.S. Commissioner of Narcotics on a study of 2,213 hard-core narcotics addicts in the Lexington (Kentucky) Federal Hospital shows that 70.4 percent smoked marijuana before taking heroin.

6. Susan Brownmiller, arguing against the legalization of pornography: "Pornography, like rape, is a male invention designed to dehumanize women, to reduce the female to an object of sexual access, not to free sensuality from moralistic or paternal inhibition."

7. From a student essay: "It is wrong to criticize advertisers for manipulating people through psychological ploys because that's what makes ads effective."

8. Overheard in a local bar: "You women are wrong to be for censoring pornography, even if it's true, and I'm pretty sure it isn't, that porno stuff makes a few men more likely to rape. Would you want to ban miniskirts, bikini outfits, low-cut dresses, and such—require women to wear Muslim-style outfits—if it's true that scanty clothes make some men more likely to rape?"

9. A *Wall Street Journal* headline (July 29, 2002):

Man's Lawsuit Claims Fast-Food Restaurants Caused His Obesity

The article went on to explain that Caesar Barber ". . . a 5-foot-10 maintenance worker who weighs 272 pounds had heart attacks in 1996 and 1999 and has diabetes, high blood pressure and high cholesterol. He said he ate fast food for decades, believing it was good for him until his doctor cautioned him otherwise. . . . His lawyer, Samuel Hirsch, said the restaurants should list ingredients on their menus. 'There's direct deception when someone omits telling people food digested is detrimental to their health.'"

10. The president of a college who shall go unnamed here justifying the reduction of salaries for adjunct (part-time) teachers who are paid only 75 percent of the rate paid to full-time staff per course: "I don't see the problem here. No other college in the state pays more than we do."

11. Comment in *Time* article (May 14, 2001) by Tom Green, a self-proclaimed fundamentalist Mormon, who was indicted in Utah on four counts of bigamy: "Mormons say polygamy is immoral and wrong, but the church was founded by polygamists. That is hypocrisy."

12. From a student paper arguing against national health care in the United States: "Think of how it fails in Russia, where you have to bribe doctors to get service."

*13. In February 1999, Larry King said on his program *Larry King Live* that since the Lewinsky story broke in January 1998, we'd had an excellent year: crime down, business up, unemployment lower. So he asked his guests, Wasn't Monicagate good for the country?

14. In a speech at the Naval Postgraduate School in Monterey, California, Albert Gonzales, the president's White House counsel, justified the second President Bush invading Iraq without a congressional declaration of war. When one officer asked how Bush could legally do this, Gonzales said that we had conducted 100 military actions in the past without a congressional declaration of war; furthermore, past presidents often declared war without a congressional declaration.

15. Bill Gates, commenting on the government's antitrust suit against Microsoft: "Forcing Microsoft to include Netscape's competing software in our operating system is like requiring Coca-Cola to include three cans of Pepsi in every six-pack it sells." In response, the chief of the Justice Department antitrust division, Joel Klein, said Microsoft's actions are similar to one company owning all the

supermarkets and refusing to carry any soda brand other than its own. In your opinion, who won this little to-and-fro, and why?

16. From a student essay: "The United States Department of Health states that only 3–5 percent of sexually transmitted diseases in this country are related to prostitution."

17. Paraphrase of part of a letter in a December 1990 "Ann Landers" advice column: "My parents didn't give me much guidance about social behavior, morals, or sex. But I read your column—you were one person I learned from. You said not to go for looks and popularity, but to pay attention to 'the quiet one in the corner.' So about nine years ago, I married an average-looking guy who is a 'great father and a good provider,' and have been very happy. Thanks very much for your excellent advice."

18. Paraphrase of part of a letter to the editor, *Marin* (California) *Independent Journal:* "When the first heart transplant was done by Dr. Christian Barnard, he was praised, not his scalpel. It was Cain, according to the Bible, not a rock, that killed Abel. Why, then, listen to the pseudoliberals and other nitwits when they blame crimes on guns rather than on people who use guns?"

*19. Wayne LaPierre, executive vice president, National Rifle Association: "I think that [the ban on assault weapons] has as much to do with crime control as making a wish while you blow the candles out on a birthday cake." He then provided reasons that he believed showed that such a ban would not reduce the crime rate.

20. Student paper: "According to U.S. Dept. of Justice statistics, between 1977 and 1990, only one female was executed, out of a total of 143 executions. Similar stat ratios apply since then [1990]. This shows the bias against males that exists in the U.S. contrary to PC [politically correct] claims."

    Another student's reply to this: "You might just as well argue that there is a bias against young males, say, those under 30, as compared to older males, since the vast majority of those convicted of murder are under 30, as are their victims."

    Which student was right, and why?

*21. Comment on the following *Associated Press* item, November 10, 1997: "Americans spent $57.3 billion on illegal drugs in 1995, a catastrophic amount but down from previous years, a report by the White House Office of National Control Policy says. The report . . . said [that] estimated spending on . . . illicit drugs compared with 57.5 billion in 1994 and continued a downward trend from 1988 . . . [when] drug sales were estimated at 91.4 billion."

22. Comment by Dr. James M. Orient, Executive Director of the Association of American Physicians and Surgeons, on President Clinton's February 2000 proposed $3,000 fine on tobacco manufacturers for each underage smoker:

    What's next? Fining auto makers for each speeding driver, nailing Hershey for every diabetic who eats a candy bar, or gouging MacDonald's for all obese people who order a Big Mac?

EXERCISE 5-3

Here are a few more short passages to be evaluated.

*1. A response to the criticism of the danger of the Cassini space mission because it contained 72.3 pounds of plutonium: "Would you decide not to drive a car because you might have an accident and harm others?"

*2. Although traditional Jewish practices forbid eating the meat of the pig, a large minority of Jews in Israel have developed a taste for bacon, pork, and the rest. This offended Orthodox Jews, who wanted to pass a law prohibiting the sale of these products. Explained Rabbi Avraham Shapira, a leader of Orthodox Jews (in the fall of 1985—a law concerning meat from the pig was passed in 1990): "Our law is not to forbid people to eat pork. We are very democratic here. What we want is people not to be able to sell pork. It hurts every religious man when he passes through a city in Israel and he sees a shop with pork in the window."

3. When Arnold Schwarzenegger announced his decision on the *Tonight Show* to run for governor in the 2003 California recall election, he vowed he would rid the government of special interest politics, implying that he was the ideal candidate to do so because he didn't "need to take money from anybody." In the weeks that followed, he received millions of dollars in campaign contributions from some of the largest corporations in the state.

4. Taken from a student's paper (paraphrased): "The prohibition amendment, which made drinking alcohol illegal early in this century, reduced consumption by 50 percent. When the amendment was repealed, the consumption of alcohol almost tripled. This shows that Americans take the law seriously; when something is illegal, they tend to stay away from it."

   Instructor's comment on the student's paper: "This must be why we have no drug problems today."

5. Item from Molly Ivins's column during the Democratic challenge to the Florida vote, November 2000: "George [W.] Bush claime[ed] throughout the campaign 'We trust the people,' then complain[ed] after the election: 'No way can you trust the people. What idiots are counting these votes?'"

6. Newspaper Association of America's spokesperson Paul Luthringer (quoted in *Extra!*, September/October 1995), responding to a survey that found only 19 percent of sources quoted or referred to on newspaper front pages were women: "The fact that women are quoted less than men has nothing to do with the state of journalism, but has more to do with who—male or female—is the first to return a reporter's call."

*7. From a *Science News* article:

   [Scientists] produced their map of the vegetation existing 18,000 years ago by sifting through published reports on ancient pollen and other plant remains in sediments from around the world. They then estimated how much carbon dioxide was locked within the plants, soil and peat in specific regions. Continental vegetation and soils contained far less carbon dioxide during the Ice Age than they do today, researchers report. . . . Carbon storage on the continents totaled 968.1 billion tons 18,000 years ago, compared with 2,319.4 billion tons now, an increase of 140 percent.

8. *New York Times* article: "When several women's groups protested the Pakistani law that accords the legal testimony of women half the weight of the testimony of men, Qazi Hussain Ahmed, leader of the Islamic party, said, 'These laws do not affect women adversely. Our system wants to protect women from unnecessary worry and save them the trouble of appearing in court.'"

*9. Item in *Science* 80 (November/December 1979): "The chief trouble with the word 'superstition' is that it always applies to the beliefs of someone else, not your own. The entire history of science shows that, in varying degrees, much that even the greatest scientists believed to be fact is today either false or else somewhat less than factual, perhaps even superstitious. It follows that what the best scientists today believe to be fact will suffer the same fate."

10. From *Slander*, by Ann Coulter: "The only reason Northeastern liberals such as Jeffords [Vermont senator who switched from Republican to Independent in 2001] call themselves Republicans in the first place is class snobbery. They disdain Democrats, whom they view as the dirty working class, and think being Republican should entail nothing more than thrashing the servants."

11. An item from the *New York Times* (June 13, 2001) reported that the Justice Department announced in June 2001 that violent crime had fallen 15 percent the previous year, the largest drop on record. The report, based on a survey of 160,000 crime victims nationwide indicated that "[s]imple assaults accounted for 61.5 percent of all violent crime . . . and because they declined by 14.4 percent in 2000 compared with 1999, they accounted for most of the drop in violent crime. . . ." Two weeks earlier, "the FBI reported that serious crime had remained stable in 2000, ending an eight year period of significant declines. . . . [It] measures only the most serious crimes . . . but does not include simple assaults like pushing and shoving."

12. A letter to the *San Francisco Examiner* from a physician argued that if juries award sums like $10.5 million to plaintiffs who have contracted toxic shock syndrome—even though that disease wasn't known to medical science when the damage took place—perhaps we can now expect lawsuits against pharmaceutical companies and physicians by the relatives of people who died of pneumonia before 1943, on the grounds that as-yet-undiscovered penicillin hadn't been prescribed.

*13. When it was pointed out to Stephen Schneider, a climatologist at Stanford's Institute for International Studies, that he was recommending action now even though he was only 90 percent sure that global warming was occurring because of atmospheric emissions, he replied, "Why do we need 99 percent certainty when nothing else is that certain? If there were only a 5 percent chance the chef slipped some poison in your dessert, would you eat it?"

14. Peter Singer in his book *Animal Liberation*: "The racist violates the principle of equality by giving greater weight to the interests of members of his own race when there is a clash between their interests and the interests of those of another

race. The sexist violates the principle of equality by favoring the interests of his own sex. Similarly, the speciesist allows the interests of his own species to override the greater interests of members of another species. The pattern is identical in each case."

15. In an article on projected tax cuts, Molly Ivins quotes Senate Majority Leader Trent Lott saying, "A 10 percent across-the-board tax cut, what could be fairer?"

    Her response: "What could be fairer than a tax cut that gives 62 percent of its benefits to the richest 10 percent of the people? A tax cut where the lowest 60 percent of income earners would get a tax cut averaging $99 while the 1 percent of the tax payers making more than $301,000 a year would receive a cut averaging around $20,700?"

    Who is guilty of fallacious or shady reasoning—Trent Lott or Molly Ivins?

16. Hitler's version of Darwin's theory of evolution by natural selection (from *Mein Kampf*): "No more than Nature desires the mating of weaker and stronger individuals, even less does she desire the blending of a higher with a lower race, since if she did her whole work of higher breeding over perhaps hundreds of thousands of years, might be ruined with one blow."

17. In defending one of the Menendez brothers charged with murdering their parents, the lawyer, Leslie Abramson, argued, "What they did is not the issue. It's why they did it. These boys were not responsible for who they turned out to be. They were just little children being molded."

18. Part of a political column by George Weigel (November 29, 1992), in which he argued against the *Roe v. Wade* Supreme Court decision: "The hard sociological fact is that abortion on demand (the regime established by *Roe*) has been the greatest deal for irresponsible or predatory men in American history. Why? Because whatever else is said, *Roe* frees men from responsibility for the sexual conduct they consensually enter. *Roe* is alleged to have empowered women; in fact, *Roe* legally disempowered women from holding men accountable for their sexual behavior where that behavior had unplanned results."

*19. From an article in the January/February 1994 issue of *Quill* magazine about the claim by Dr. John Pierce (University of California–San Diego) that the Joe Camel cigarette ads were responsible for "a sharp increase in teen smoking": "His study shows that first-time smokers among Californians from the ages of 16 to 18 had steadily declined from 12.5 percent in 1975 to 6.2 percent in 1988, but then began sharply increasing again. Joe Camel, a cool-looking, cartoonish character, was introduced as the Camel symbol in 1988. Teenage smoking immediately began increasing by 0.7 percent a year, through 1990. In 1992, Pierce conducted another study that showed Joe Camel was as familiar a character as Mickey Mouse to children as young as six."

    The *Quill* article also indicated that because of his research, Dr. Pierce stated that he believes we should ban all tobacco advertising. When asked whether this wasn't censorship contrary to the Constitution's First Amendment, he replied, "There is no free speech [issue] here. The issue is to protect our children from being influenced into an addiction that will cause cancer."

*20. Since the 55-mile-per-hour speed limit was introduced by President Carter, traffic fatalities in the United States have dropped almost in half. So now that the Republican Congress (in 1995) has repealed the 55-mph limit we can expect traffic fatalities to go back to where they were—almost double what they are now. (Note: We now have the advantage of hindsight, since we can find out whether the repeal did or did not go back to where they were or significantly increased. But do this exercise item without resort to later information of this kind. By the way, did traffic fatalities significantly increase?)

21. Paraphrase of part of a letter to the editor in the *Honolulu Advertiser,* July 17, 1999, disagreeing with the Supreme Court ruling that flag burning was protected as free speech: "Rights entail responsibilities. Since you can't yell fire in a crowded theater and can't utter racial slurs in a schoolroom, you shouldn't be allowed to burn the flag. There should be limits to speech that is hateful or that harms people."

*22. Taken from an item in *Extra!* (December 2003): "Fox News anchor Brit Hume . . . argued (August 26, 2003) that U.S. soldiers were better off than Californians. 'Two hundred seventy-seven U.S. soldiers have now died in Iraq, which means that statistically speaking U.S. soldiers have less of a chance of dying from all causes in Iraq than citizens have of being murdered in California, which is roughly the same geographical size. The most recent statistics indicate California has more than 2,300 homicides each year, which means about 6.6 murders each day. Meanwhile, U.S. troops have been in Iraq for 160 days, which means they're incurring about 1.7 deaths including illness and accidents each day.' "

EXERCISE 5-4

*A letter to the editor of *Free Inquiry* (Winter 1999/00) argues against hanging copies of the Ten Commandments in public schools on the grounds that it may promote church attendance, which may well be harmful. As evidence, the writer cites statistics from two different issues of *Scientific American.* The first (July 1999) notes the percentage of adults in the United States and in European countries who attended church at least once a month in the 1990s. The second (August 1999) lists the criminal population per hundred thousand behind bars during that period. Evaluate these statistics and explain why you think they do or don't support the claim that churchgoing may be harmful.

40 Percent or More Attending Church

Country	Percentage Attending Church	Number in Jail per 100,000
Ireland	88	55
Poland	74	170
U.S.	55	668
Italy	47	85
Canada	40	115
Mean	61	219

Under 20 Percent Attending Church

France	17	95
Norway	13	55
Sweden	11	65
Finland	11	60
Iceland	9	40
Mean	12	63

EXERCISE 5-5

A customer, call her Mrs. Smith, signs a contract to purchase a new car for cash but is then offered the following deal (typical of deals described in a Jane Bryant Quinn article that appeared in many newspapers on March 24, 1990):

> The cost of her new car is $11,434. Instead of paying cash, it is suggested that she can save money by taking out a loan, the current auto loan rate being 12.75 percent. Mrs. Smith earns 8.5 percent on her bank deposits. It is explained to her that by leaving the $11,434 in the bank at 8.5 percent, instead of paying cash for the car, she will net $6,029 over the five-year period of a car loan, money she won't earn if she pays cash. During that five-year period, she is told, the interest on a loan at 12.75 percent will amount to $4,153 (given that this interest will be paid on the "declining balance" of money owed on the loan—declining because the amount owed decreases with every monthly payment). So Mrs. Smith is told she will come out ahead $1,876 ($6,029 minus $4,153) by putting the money in the bank and taking out a loan on the car.

There were other advantages claimed for taking out a loan as compared to paying cash, but your job is just to evaluate the alleged advantage described above. Will Mrs. Smith be ahead of the game by $1,876 if she takes out a loan instead of paying cash for the car? (The example is typical of deals offered by many car dealers in recent years. The exact figures have changed because of changes in interest rates, but the idea remains the same. In answering this question, assume the interest rates cited in the article.)

EXERCISE 5-6

*The ACLU has been severely criticized by many for opposing a ban on commercial advertising of cigarette companies while taking large contributions from those companies (for example, from Phillip Morris since 1987 to the tune of $500,000 and similar large quantities from R. J. Reynolds). But the ACLU claims that it has opposed bans on commercial ads on First Amendment grounds for more than 50 years. If true, are the opponents guilty of *questionable cause*? Do some research. (See, for example, *Public Citizen's Health Letter,* April 1999, or *The Progressive,* February 1999.)

EXERCISE 5-7

Find several fallacy examples of your own, perhaps gleaned from newspapers, magazines, television programs, textbooks (hopefully not this one, but anything is fair game), or what have you, provide a name in each case if you can, and carefully explain why the passage is fallacious.

Calvin & Hobbes © Watterson. Reprinted with permission of Universal Press Syndicate. All rights reserved.

Memory says, "I did that." Pride replies, "I could not have done that." Eventually, memory yields.

        —Nietzsche

Every dogma has its day.

        —Abraham Rotstein

Think with your head, not your guts.

        — Old saying

Populus vult decipi. *(The people want to be deceived.)*

        —Ancient Roman saying

Nothing is so firmly believed as what we least know.

        —Montaigne

How strange it is to see with how much passion
People see things only in their own fashion.

        —Molière

I wouldn't have seen it if I hadn't believed it.

        —Insightful takeoff on an old saying

Chapter

6

PSYCHOLOGICAL IMPEDIMENTS TO COGENT REASONING: SHOOTING OURSELVES IN THE FOOT

Good reasoning is a matter of character as well as brain power. If human beings were completely rational animals, learning how to reason well would be a relatively easy task. We would simply learn which patterns of reasoning are good and which bad, and then make all of our reasoning conform to good patterns while avoiding the bad. Even if we started out with poor background beliefs, repeated use of valid deductive and inductive inferences, based on all of what we have experienced so far, would soon set things straight.

Unfortunately, human beings are not completely rational, although rationality is an important part of our makeup. This chapter is concerned with that other part of human nature—the nonrational, emotional component that prevents us from being perfect reasoners. While no one can completely eliminate these nonrational impediments to cogent reasoning, any more than a leopard can change its spots, understanding how they work can help us to reduce the harm they do to our attempts at completely rational thought.

1. Loyalty, Provincialism, and the Herd Instinct

Throughout history, individual chances for success at most things—getting enough food, attracting and holding a mate, successfully raising children—have depended on two fundamental factors. The first is the success of the groups we belong to in their competitions with other groups. Members of primary in-groups (nations, tribes, cultures) defeated by competing out-groups generally suffer serious harm to their chances of having a good life or any life at all. That is why we all feel a tug of **loyalty** to our own in-group; a society that has too many disloyal people has little chance against other, more cohesive groups. (Note, however, that the strength of this tug differs greatly from person to person.)

But being a member of a successful in-group is of little value if others in the group do not allow us reasonable chances for success in whatever it is we want to do. That is an important reason why we all are so anxious to get along with the other members of the groups to which we owe loyalty. The person who is completely out of step with everyone else is not likely to be successful, even if the group as a whole thrives and multiplies.[1] Enter the **herd instinct** that tends to keep our beliefs, and thus our actions, within the bounds of what society as a whole will accept. Finding ourselves in a culture in which everyone covers certain parts of the body, we feel uncomfortable leaving those parts naked. Those belonging to Moslem or Orthodox Jewish groups find eating parts of the pig abhorrent. In Western societies, virtually everyone avoids eating the meat of horses and dogs; in China, dog meat is a delicacy.

Of course, there is no harm in feeling embarrassed if caught in public with the wrong attire or in finding shellfish repugnant. But the herd instinct sometimes leads people to do horrendous things, as they do when mobs carry out "vigilante justice" or when whole nations acquiesce to unfair practices. Refraining from eating the flesh of the cow is one thing; branding some of one's compatriots as "untouchables" is another.

The point is that it is part of human nature to find it easy and natural to believe what everyone else in our society believes and foolish to believe what others find foolish. This is no doubt one reason for what sociologists call *cultural lag,* the tendency of practices and beliefs to persist long after whatever conditions made them useful or sensible have disappeared.

We all desire to have at least a minimal status in the groups that we belong to, for the reasons just mentioned. But the higher our status, the better our chances. That's why most of us have such a strong desire to make a better than minimally good appearance when in public. We want to look intelligent, informed, and decisive—to shine compared

[1] For more on this way of looking at the human repertoire, see Howard Kahane, *Contract Ethics: Evolutionary Biology and the Moral Sentiments* (Lanham, Md.: Rowman & Littlefield, 1995), and James Q. Wilson, *The Moral Sense* (New York: Free Press, 1993).

> Man is a social animal; only in the herd is he happy. It is all one to him whether it is the profoundest nonsense or the greatest villainy—he feels completely at ease with it—so long as it is the view of the herd, and he is able to join the herd.
> —Søren Kierkegaard

to others. And that is why, for instance, millions of Americans who had never heard of Osama bin Laden before the devastating terrorist attack on the World Trade Center, who had no idea what the Taliban was until it gave refuge to bin Laden, and who knew next to nothing about Islam and the Muslim religion, let alone the meaning of *jihad,* formed almost instant opinions on the invasion of Afghanistan and later Iraq. After the two-pronged war began, newspapers across the country were filled with letters to editors expressing demands for this action or that. The need to be in the swim, to talk "intelligently" about topics of the day, leads us to form and broadcast these quick opinions based on superficial evidence. And once we have pronounced them, the need to avoid appearing to have been wrong in public leads us to hang onto those beliefs, often in the face of conflicting evidence. The underlying psychological mechanism is the desire to gain, and retain, the status in the eyes of others in our group that is vital to success in everyday life.[2]

It also should be noted that hardly any of the large societies common in today's world are completely cohesive. Nations such as the United States, Canada, India, and Russia are composed of all sorts of diverse subgroups, the United States being one of the two most diverse cultures in history. (The other was the Soviet Union before its disintegration.) Most people are completely loyal to their own nation but also have a special interest in the fates of subgroups. They therefore tend to see things not just from the point of view of the mainstream culture but also from that of smaller groups within the primary culture. We see the results of this in current political rhetoric designed to appeal to "special interest" groups such as religious fundamentalists, African Americans, Latinos, Jews, and so on. (Note, by the way, that we all have a very special interest in the welfare of members of our own families.)

Provincialism stems in large part from this natural tendency to identify with the ideas, interests, and kinds of behavior favored by those in groups with which we identify. That is why blacks are more likely to notice injustices perpetrated against blacks, Jews against Jews, and women against women. (Think only of polls that showed a majority of black Americans agreed with the verdict in the O. J. Simpson murder trial, while the reverse was true of white Americans, even though both groups were exposed to the same evidence.)

Of particular importance is the fact that we tend to see things from the point of view and interests of our primary culture—our primary in-group—especially when there is conflict with other groups. The result is a kind of belief provincialism operating at various levels—leading Americans, for example, to pay relatively little attention to what happens to the peoples of the rest of the world and to misconstrue what is happening there. That is why, although the United States was founded on the principles of democ-

---

[2]Erving Goffman's fascinating book *The Presentation of Self in Everyday Life* (New York: Doubleday, 1959; Penguin, 1969) still is an excellent source of information on these matters.

racy and fair play, a great many Americans have failed to notice that since World War II the United States government has helped to overturn several democratically elected governments around the world (for instance, in Chile) and attempted to murder Cuba's Fidel Castro. It is difficult to swallow unpleasant truths when loyalty and the herd instinct reinforce what others in our group vehemently assert, and when provincialism narrows our range of interests and tends to make us see everything in terms of the interests of our own primary group.[3]

2. PREJUDICE, STEREOTYPES, SCAPEGOATS, AND PARTISAN MIND-SETS

Loyalty and provincialism often lead to **prejudice,** including prejudice against all or almost all members of other groups, and to thinking in terms of unverified **stereotypes** that support prejudicial beliefs. But being prejudiced against others is quite different from simply having a bad opinion of them. We are prejudiced only when our nasty beliefs about others are not justified by sufficient evidence. So prejudice can be defined as thinking ill of others without sufficient warrant.

Of course, no group of any size is composed of people who resemble each other as do peas in a pod, so it is foolish to be prejudiced against every member of such a group. It's just silly to think that the French all are great lovers, that all Jews and Scots are unusually frugal, or that all women are more emotional than men.

It *is* true, though, that people in a given large social group generally are different in many ways from those in other groups. The French as a group are modestly different from Germans, as are Iranians from Pakistanis, something anyone can notice simply by going from one of these countries to the other. The trouble with stereotypical thinking is rather that, even when accurate with respect to groups as a whole (and they often are not), it fails to take account of the differences between individual members.

The flip side of prejudice and intolerance directed against members of other groups is overtolerance of, even blindness to, the defects and foibles of our own group and its members. Loyalty tends to make us see our own leaders as a good deal more intelligent, informed, and honest than in fact they are (or than it would be reasonable to expect the leaders of any society to be) and to regard the general run of our compatriots as better on average than the people in other societies. People are particularly prone to loyalty to the government in times of war, as was evident during the early months of the war in Iraq, when the media were so uniformly patriotic that it was considered taboo for journalists to break rank and criticize the government—this, despite the fact that unprecedented protests were occurring throughout the world. (More discussion on this is in Chapter 11.) Clear thinkers need to overcome this reverse prejudice in favor of people in their own in-groups, especially of in-group leaders (an important reason for the inclusion in this text of so many examples illustrating the clay feet of quite a few elected officials).

---

[3]Another reason for this difficulty is that public school textbooks and the mass media generally play down or try to justify these kinds of breaches of professed ethical ideals. See Chapters 11 and 12 for more on this topic.

Prejudice against members of other groups, particularly of minorities within a larger culture, often is reinforced by the need to find **scapegoats**—others we can blame for the ills of the world—when in fact we ourselves may bear a large measure of responsibility. That a group being trashed cannot possibly have produced the troubles it is charged with rarely makes a difference.

This tendency to put the blame elsewhere is captured with chilling effect by Shirley Jackson in "The Lottery," her classic story of scapegoating. The residents of a small village gather in the town square for the annual lottery, an archaic ritual performed for so many years that the people have forgotten its original purpose. They know that one of them must draw the fateful lot, but beyond that they only remember how to use the pile of stones that figures prominently in the story. Until the lot is drawn, the villagers behave in a decent, kindly manner to each other, but once the "winner" is known, they grab stones from the pile and pelt her viciously, driven by the herd instinct to satisfy a barbaric practice of scapegoating whose purpose they no longer understand. The story is an allegory for practices that have unfortunately prevailed for centuries.

The classic scapegoat in the Christian world has always been the Jews. In days of old, when Christian theology was interpreted to say that lending money at interest constituted usury (a sin), Jews therefore became important moneylenders. Blaming them for calamities then sometimes at least had the practical motive of serving as an excuse for the repudiation of outstanding loans. But at most times, the primary point of anti-Semitism has been simply to place the blame for ills elsewhere.

Everyone nowadays is familiar with the way in which the Nazis used the Jews as scapegoats and with their attempt to exterminate all European Jews. So it might be supposed that picking on the Jews would have little appeal these days. Yet anti-Semitism is still very common in many places. In Russia, to take one example, Jews are commonly held responsible for the ills produced by 70 years of Soviet communism. (The thin thread of truth behind this ridiculous idea—note that Stalin was not Jewish—is that a very few of the high officials in the Communist party and in the Soviet government were Jews.) In other Eastern European countries, Jews were similarly often held responsible for the problems generated by Soviet domination. This was true even in Poland, where only about 10,000 out of more than 3 million Jews survived the German attempt at genocide and still resided in Poland.

One might suppose that the murder of millions of Jews in Europe during World War II, and the still existing anti-Semitism just described, would make Jews, of all people, the least likely to relegate others to second-class citizenship. And yet, in Israel, the first primarily Jewish state in about 2,000 years, Israeli Arabs do not have the same status as Israeli Jews, and Arab lands in the West Bank have been taken from them and given to Jewish "settlers." Not that the Arabs have been paragons of virtue—think only of the stated objective of several surrounding Arab countries to destroy Israel.

And then there are the genocidal tribal battles going on in Africa, the recent mass destruction and murder in the former Yugoslavia, hostilities between Hindus and Moslems, and so on. In every case, those on both sides in these ethnic battles feel justified in their vindictive hatred and prejudice against the "enemy."

Prejudice and scapegoating, of course, also occur in the United States. As usual, small or less powerful groups tend to be the ones picked on, including people of African or Asian descent, Latinos, Native Americans (American Indians), and, naturally, Jews. Since the attack on the World Trade Center, an irrational prejudice against Middle Easterners has sprung up in this country. Yet almost all Middle Easterners in the United States are peaceful, productive members of society who are just as horrified at the terrorist attacks as everyone else. Only a handful are involved in terrorist activities.

Thinking in terms of unverified stereotypes and scapegoats often results from a **partisan mind-set** that leads people to perceive evidence and to judge arguments via an "us against them" or a "my right view against your wrong view" attitude. We all are tempted to arrange facts to fit our side of an issue and tend to be blind to the import of evidence supporting any other side. Good reasoners fight this tendency in all of us to favor ideas already held and automatically to see our side as right and the other guy's as wrong. Those with a partisan mind-set give in to this all too human tendency, generally without being aware that they have done so. This is true, for example, of some individuals who are vigorously engaged in the social or political arenas. That is why it can be so maddening to discuss touchy issues with some very committed people—they tend to be deaf to counterevidence and counterarguments. (Another reason, of course, is that we ourselves may be "hearing impaired" when it comes to their reasons and arguments.)

Consider, for example, the student in a critical thinking class some time back who complained vigorously about the required textbook—an earlier edition of this one— pointing out that in one place it said that the Soviets under Stalin had murdered millions of their own citizens and then a few pages later claimed that these same Soviets, not the Americans or British, had done the principal fighting and defeating of the Germans in World War II. "Which side is the text's author on, here?" the student wanted to know. He was genuinely confused. He couldn't grasp the idea that the author's intent was neither to champion communism nor to root for "our side" but rather in order to present the facts of the matter in order to make a completely different point (about how history is distorted in public school textbooks).

A really good critical reasoner has a mind-set that is completely different from those who see everything from a partisan point of view. This does not mean that good reasoners lack a sense of loyalty! It means simply that they have an open mind rather than a mind that sees everything from the point of view that "our side always is right and the other side always wrong"—a mind open to the truth, wherever it may lie.

3. SUPERSTITIOUS BELIEFS

Prejudice against members of other groups at least has group loyalty going for it. That can't be said about **superstitions.** It is true, though, that superstitions often are based on some small scrap of evidence or other. Bad things obviously do occasionally happen after a mirror is broken. Coincidences do happen. And even newspaper astrology columns are moderately accurate once every blue moon.

The difference between superstitious and sensible beliefs is that sensible beliefs are based on sufficient evidence that justifies those beliefs, not on carefully chosen scraps of support. Superstitious beliefs are generally based on biased evidence or on small or unrepresentative samples (discussed in Chapter 5)—evidence from which all negative cases have been removed. Bad things do happen on Friday the 13th, but so do lots of good things. And bad things happen on other days also, so that there is nothing remarkable about the fact that they happen on Friday the 13th. Superstitious people ignore facts of this sort and pay attention just to the evidence supporting their superstitious convictions.

The foolishness of the superstitious beliefs of peoples in other societies is much easier to see than the irrational nature of our own. Superstition and provincialism go hand in hand. Here are two examples of superstitious beliefs common in Hong Kong today:

The word for fish in some Chinese dialects looks very much like the word for surplus. So on the Chinese New Year, lots of businessmen eat fish in order to generate assurances of profit (surplus).

   The number 8 is thought to be extremely lucky. The auto license plate bearing just that number was auctioned off recently for 5 million Hong Kong dollars (a bit over 640,000 U.S. dollars).

These superstitious beliefs are rather harmless, but others have bad, even terrible consequences. For instance, women born in the year of the horse, which occurs every 12th year, are believed by many Asians to be smart, active, impatient, and argumentative. Women who exhibit these qualities are not considered desirable mates by most Korean men. Women born in the year of the white horse, which comes around every 60 years, are believed to be particularly "bad" in these ways, so superstitious men, a large percentage of the population, shy away from marriage to women born in such a year. To save potential offspring from spinsterhood, when the year of the white horse rolled around in 1990, lots of pregnant women in Korea consulted obstetricians to find out whether they were carrying male or female fetuses, and abortions of female fetuses reached epidemic proportions.

The odd thing about superstitious beliefs is that their complete irrationality doesn't seem to stop even the most brilliant people from having them. Chess grand masters, for example, display amazing intelligence and insight when playing that great intellectual game, not to mention incredible memories. (The "grand old man of chess," George Koltanowsky, several times played more than 40 games simultaneously—blindfolded.) Yet a recent world chess champion, Garry Kasparov, thinks the number 13 is his lucky number (he was born on April 13—well, he's Aries, so that explains his great ability— and he was the 13th world chess champion). The previous champion, Anatoly Karpov, changes his suit every time he loses a game.

4. WISHFUL THINKING AND SELF-DECEPTION

As we have just seen, loyalty, prejudice, stereotypical thinking, the herd instinct, and superstition tend to give us beliefs that do not square with reality. Beliefs acquired in these nonrational ways often result from **wishful thinking**—believing what we would like to be true, no matter what the evidence—or from **self-deception**—consciously believing what at a deeper level we know to be dubious. It is a very human trait indeed to believe

In Chapter 4, we presented the first of four "causes of the utterance of fallacies" that Jeremy Bentham described in his famous book The Handbook of Political Fallacies. *Here is an excerpt from the second of the four, which happens to be relevant to the topics discussed in this chapter:*

Second Cause: Interest-Begotten Prejudice

If every act of the will and hence every act of the hand is produced by interest, that is, by a motive of one sort or another, the same must be true, directly or indirectly, of every act of the intellectual faculty, although the influence of interest upon the latter is neither as direct or as perceptible as that upon the will.

But how, it may be asked, is it possible that the motive by which a man is actuated can be secret to himself? Nothing, actually, is easier; nothing is more frequent. Indeed, the rare case is not that of a man's not knowing, but that of his knowing. . . .

When two persons have lived together in a state of intimacy, it happens not infrequently that either or each of them may possess a more correct and complete view of the motives by which the mind of the other is governed, than of those which control his own behavior. Many a woman has had in this way a more correct and complete acquaintance with the internal causes by which the conduct of her husband has been determined, than he has had himself. The reason for this is easily pointed out. By interest, a man is continually prompted to make himself as correctly and completely acquainted as possible with the springs of action which determine the conduct of those upon whom he is more or less dependent for the comfort of his life. But by interest he is at the same time diverted from any close examination into the springs by which his own conduct is determined. From such knowledge he would be more likely to find mortification than satisfaction.

When he looks at other men, he finds mentioned as a matter of praise the prevalence of . . . social motives. . . . It is by the supposed prevalence of these amiable motives that he finds reputation raised, and that respect and goodwill enhanced to which every man is obliged to look for so large a proportion of the comforts of his life. . . .

But the more closely he looks into the mechanism of his own mind, the less able he is to refer any of the mass of effects produced there to any of these amiable and delightful causes. He finds nothing, therefore, to attract him towards this self-study; he finds much to repel him from it. . . .

Perhaps he is a man in whom a large proportion of the self-regarding motives may be mixed with a slight tincture of the social motives operating upon the private scale. In that case, what will he do? In investigating the source of a given action, he will in the first instance set down the whole of it to the account of the amiable and conciliatory motives, in a word, the social ones. This, in any study of his own mental physiology, will always be his first step; and it will commonly be his last also. Why should he look any further? Why take in hand the painful probe? Why undeceive himself, and substitute the whole truth, which would mortify him, for a half-truth which flatters him?

that which we would like to be true and to deny those things we find unpalatable (or, as in the case of our own eventual death, extremely hard to accept).

An extreme example in literature is Jay Gatsby's idealization of Daisy Buchanan in *The Great Gatsby,* by F. Scott Fitzgerald. Gatsby persists in deceiving himself about her character despite mounting evidence that she not only is self-centered, irresponsible, and fickle but also has let him take the blame for a crime she has committed. His self-deception is so great it could be called a **delusion**—one that leads tragically to his own death. Gatsby's adoration of Daisy is an exaggerated example of what many people feel in the early stages of love. We commonly indulge in wishful thinking about our lovers and deceive ourselves about their imperfections despite evidence to the contrary (hopefully imperfections of much less magnitude than Daisy's).

When the stakes are high, we have a natural tendency to deceive ourselves rather than face reality. This tendency is just as prevalent in world leaders as it is in the average person. A classic case is British Prime Minister Neville Chamberlain's decision to sign an agreement with Hitler in 1938 to achieve, in his words, "peace in our time." Chamberlain was so conscious of the horror another world war would bring, and so desperately anxious to spare his nation and the civilized world from such a disaster, that his judgment was destroyed and he failed to see Hitler's intent in spite of all sorts of evidence that many others, including Winston Churchill, perceived for what it was.[4]

The difficulty is in catching ourselves in the act of believing what we want to believe rather than accepting what the evidence indicates to be the reality. Of course, most of us, luckily, have no opportunity to make mistakes of the kind that Chamberlain committed. Our self-deceptions tend to result in less global evils, although they still may have catastrophic consequences for ourselves or friends. Think of the large number of people who drink and then drive. Or consider the significant percentage of adults in every industrial country who still smoke cigarettes or chew tobacco in the face of overwhelming evidence linking tobacco to all sorts of fatal illnesses, including heart disease, various kinds of cancer, and emphysema. Millions of people everywhere continue to puff or chew away, undeterred even by warning labels on tobacco products like this one:

> SURGEON GENERAL'S WARNING: Smoking Causes Lung Cancer, Heart Disease, Emphysema, And May Complicate Pregnancy.

5. RATIONALIZATION AND PROCRASTINATION

Perhaps the most common form of self-deception is **rationalization.** We engage in this kind of psychological ploy when we ignore or deny unpleasant evidence so as to feel justified in doing what we want to do or in believing what we find comfortable to believe. Rationalization is nicely illustrated by the old joke about the psychiatrist and a delusional patient who believes he is dead. To prove to the patient that he is alive, the psychiatrist first gets him to agree that dead men don't bleed and then makes a cut in the

---

[4] In fairness to Chamberlain, note that a very few historians claim, on rather sparse evidence, that Chamberlain knew chances for peace were not great and wanted to gain time for Britain to rearm.

man's arm, which, of course, bleeds. Smiling, the psychiatrist tilts his chair back and waits. "Well," says the dismayed patient, "I guess I was wrong. Dead men do bleed." He thus manages to sustain his delusion by rationalizing away undeniable proof to the contrary.

Another example, from the play *Cabaret:* A credulous German is reading the latest Nazi propaganda. Scowling he says, "The Jews own all the banks. And they're behind an international communist conspiracy too." Whereupon his clearer-thinking companion observes, "But bankers are capitalists and communists are opposed to capitalism. How can Jews be both?" The first man pauses, then nods knowingly and rationalizes: "They're very crafty."

Questionable activities in the business world are commonly rationalized to make them acceptable to the public. When promotional literature for Pfizer, a pharmaceutical giant, claimed that advertising prescription drugs in the mass media benefited consumers because it "destigmatizes diseases . . . and helps consumers better communicate with doctors," the drug company was rationalizing the real reason for direct-to-consumer advertising—to make money. (See Chapter 10 for the downside of this practice.) A

Here is a short excerpt from Jane Austen's celebrated novel, Sense and Sensibility, *that nicely reveals a kind of rationalization all too common in real life. The excerpt (from Chapter 2) starts with John Dashwood explaining to his wife, Fanny, why he intends to give his stepmother and half sisters 3,000 pounds from his very comfortable inheritance:*

"It was my father's last request to me, . . . that I should assist his widow and daughters."

"He did not know what he was talking of, I dare say; ten to one but he was light-headed at the time. Had he been in his right senses, he could not have thought of such a thing as begging you to give away half your fortune from your child." [In fact, it was very much less.]

"He did not stipulate any particular sum, my dear Fanny; he only requested me, in general terms, to assist them, and make their situation more comfortable than it was in his power to do. . . ."

"Well, then, *let* something be done for them; but *that* something need not be three thousand pounds. . . . [W]hen the money is once parted with, it never can return. Your sisters will marry, and it will be gone forever. If, indeed, it could ever be restored to our poor little boy—"

"Perhaps then, it would be better for all parties if the sum were diminished by one half—five hundred pounds [each] would be a prodigious increase in their fortunes!"

"Oh! beyond anything great! What brother on earth would do half so much for his sisters, even if *really* his sisters! And as it is—only half blood! . . ."

". . . As it is, without any addition of mine, they will each have above three thousand pounds on their mother's death—a very comfortable fortune for any young woman."

spokeswoman for the firm conceded that the ads were also selling the product, but "there's got to be some benefit to the company for doing this advertising." Another rationalization.

Rationalization often leads to **procrastination**—to putting off for "tomorrow" what common sense tells us needs to be done today. Young smokers often tell themselves that they'll quit a few years down the pike before any serious harm is done; students are famous for delaying work on term papers until the day before they're due. (Recall the old song about how "Mañana is good enough for me" and the Hispanic saying "Mañana será otro día," "Tomorrow will be another day.") It is an all-too-human tendency to favor immediate gratification at the risk of possible long-term harm. In general, the more likely or more serious the long-term harm, the less likely that an intelligent person will choose immediate gratification. The trouble is that most of us tend to weigh long-term harms or losses too lightly when compared with short-run gains.

The unwillingness of human beings to face unpleasant reality often is revealed strikingly in important works of fiction. In his novel *Heart of Darkness,* for example, Joseph-Conrad describes the way in which Europeans who invade Africa in the 19th century

---

"To be sure it is: and, indeed, strikes me that they can want no addition at all. . . ."

"That is very true, and, therefore, I do not know whether, upon the whole, it would not be more advisable to do something for their mother while she lives rather than for them. . . . A hundred a year would make them all perfectly comfortable." . . .

"[I]t is better than parting with fifteen hundred pounds at once. But then if Mrs. Dashwood should live fifteen years, we shall be completely taken in. . . . [P]eople always live forever when there is an annuity to be paid them. . . ."

"I believe you are right, my love; it will be better that there should be no annuity in the case. . . . A present of fifty pounds now and then will prevent their ever being distressed for money, and will, I think, be amply discharging my promise to my father."

"To be sure it will. . . . I am convinced within myself that your father had no idea of your giving them any money at all. . . . Altogether they will have five hundred a-year amongst them, and what on earth can four women want for more than that?—They will live so cheap! Their housekeeping will be nothing at all. They will have no carriage, no horses, and hardly any servants; they will keep no company and can have no expenses of any kind! Only conceive how comfortable they will be! . . . They will be much more able to give *you* something!"

And so, the wealthy Dashwoods not only manage to rationalize their way out of helping John's stepmother and half sisters but convince themselves that their much poorer relatives are better able to give something to them!

Reprinted by permission of Paul Miller.

rationalize their exploitation and degradation of native populations. He thus chronicles a case of self-deception and rationalization engaged in by a whole group of people over an extended period of time. In his novel, set in the Belgian Congo at the turn of the century, European invaders claim that their aim is to enlighten and civilize the African natives—to "wean those ignorant millions from their horrid ways." But it becomes evident as the story develops that the colonial traders have only one mission—to plunder the land for ivory.

Although a work of fiction, *Heart of Darkness* was based on the true conditions that existed in the Belgian Congo at the turn of the century. In 1876, when the Belgians began their colonization of the Congo, their monarch, King Leopold, who literally took personal ownership of the Congo, described his intent as "to open to civilization the only part of our globe where Christianity has not yet penetrated and to pierce the darkness which envelops the entire population." But in fact the king was a tyrant; the colonials, profiteers; and the Congolese, virtual slaves. When news of the atrocities committed against African natives reached Europe, a vague uneasiness rippled across the continent, but Europeans managed to deal with these reports by rationalization. If the natives rebelled, the sentries had to defend themselves, didn't they? Weren't some natives bound to die in the civilizing process in any case? Et cetera.

In *Heart of Darkness,* Conrad punctured European rationalizations about what they were doing in Africa in a graphic way by concentrating on a few characters whose development revealed the underlying truth that the European claim to be bringing civilization to the Africans was a smokescreen whose consequence (and unconscious intent?) was not to deceive the natives but rather to deceive the Europeans themselves.

Anyone who dismisses the *Heart of Darkness* portrayal of mass self-deception as just fiction—a story—or thinks that this sort of thing only happened a long time ago might reflect on the present-day confiscation of native lands in Brazil, Indonesia, and elsewhere, where the destruction of indigenous ways of life and peoples is justified in the name of "the integration of native populations into modern life" or "maximal uses of resources."

Cartoon by Beattie. Reprinted by permission of Copley News Service.

Instant Denial

6. OTHER DEFENSE MECHANISMS

When we rationalize or procrastinate, we usually are consciously aware of our actions. But there are a number of psychological strategies (defense mechanisms) that we generally are not consciously aware of using to avoid negative emotional feelings. Because they involve distortion of reality, these defense mechanisms can seriously undermine our ability to think critically.

In **suppression,** we avoid thoughts that are stressful by either not thinking about them or, more commonly, by thinking nonstressful thoughts. In this way we manage to avoid the anxiety associated with the stress-provoking situation. Although suppression may reduce stress in the short run, it often has negative consequences later on. For instance, a student failing a statistics course may block his anxiety by thinking about happier events—his new girlfriend, an upcoming dance, a sports event—or anything else that will suppress his deep-seated fear of failure. Yet in the long run he'd be better off to face the problem, get help, and work to improve his grade.

Denial involves some suppression, but instead of replacing the stressful thoughts with more benign ones, we change our interpretation of the situation to perceive it as less threatening. When a love relationship goes bad, we may remain in denial until our partner walks out on us—even though the signs of discontent are apparent to other people. Instead of paying attention to these signs, we may reinterpret our partner's negative behavior by making excuses for it, or blaming ourselves, or ignoring it. Our need to protect ourselves against separation and loss may prevent us from facing the problems in our relationships and, perhaps, finding solutions.

Albert Camus created an extreme case of denial and suppression in his existentialist novel *The Stranger*. The protagonist, Meursault, kills an Arab on an Algerian beach for no apparent reason and remains in denial about his own motivation, blaming it on the scorching heat of the sun instead. Thus, he reinterprets the situation to diminish his own responsibility and the psychological threat it entails. Later, in jail, he suppresses the anxiety one would expect him to feel about the upcoming trial and thinks instead about his bedroom at home. He spends literally hours recalling every crack in the wall, every chip in the paint, every item in the room—and successfully manages to avoid stress-provoking thoughts. Suppression and denial prevent him from devising his own best defense—that he shot the man in self-defense—a claim for which there is some evidence in the novel, but that, of course, would undermine the existential theme.

7. THE BENEFITS OF SELF-DECEPTION, WISHFUL THINKING, AND DENIAL

Our account of human beings as self-deceivers, as well as rational agents, has been objected to on several grounds, perhaps the most important being that such a harmful device could not have evolved and, if it did, would long since have been weeded out by natural selection.[5] There are at least two important responses to this objection. First, whatever any theory may say, it seems clear that human beings do in fact deceive themselves and do engage in wishful thinking that sometimes results in harmful behavior. Those who accept a theory of evolution and natural selection have to make their theory conform to this fact—they cannot deny the fact because of their theory. (One of the great virtues of science is that scientists are not permitted to engage in this kind of monkey business.)

The second response is that self-deception and wishful thinking do in fact provide important survival benefits as well as harms; it thus makes sense to conclude that they evolved because of these beneficial effects. Although these benefits are not yet clearly understood, we now are beginning to grasp how this side of human nature works.

One important function of self-deception is to reduce anxiety or stress, giving us greater ability to make decisions and to act when delay might bring on disaster. One of the authors of this text, for example, was in a serious auto accident a few years ago during which he felt no fear whatsoever. He thus was able to control his car during the crucial moments in a way that would have been impossible had he been paralyzed by conscious fear. (After the accident was over, of course, he pretty much fell apart.) Psychologists would say that his fear was repressed during the crucial moments.

Anxiety reduction also is crucial with respect to long-term dangers and potential failures. Scientists are beginning to understand the biological effects of long-term anxiety on the body, and they are not good, to say the least. Stress is related to reduced effectiveness of the immune system and perhaps also to problems with other important body

---

[5] That the rational, intelligent side of our nature should have evolved seems quite natural, given its immense value in solving life's problems, and this idea was held even in the 19th century, for instance, by Charles Darwin and Charles Peirce, among many others.

Andy Capp by Reggie Smith. © 1976 Daily Mirror Newspapers Ltd.
Dist. Field Newspaper Syndicate. Reprinted with permission.

Self-deception at work.

systems.[6] The relationship between anxiety or stress and belief systems is still not very well understood by psychologists, but this much seems to be true: Doubt, particularly doubt about important matters, produces anxiety in most people. Settling doubt and coming to some belief or other thus reduces anxiety and makes us feel better. So it isn't only the need to act, to do something, that sometimes leads us to premature or unwarranted beliefs. Even when there is nothing to be done right now, doubt may produce ongoing anxiety (sometimes referred to as *"generalized anxiety"*), and wishful thinking that eliminates this doubt may reduce the anxiety.

Perhaps the classic case in which self-deception helps people to feel better and to act more effectively occurs when, in spite of medical evidence, the terminally ill deny the proximity of death, thus reducing the numbing effect of terrible fear. We all need defenses against the knowledge of the certainty of death; those close to it much more than the rest of us. Similarly, it may be useful to be able to deny the seriousness of ailments that are not life-threatening, as it was for Franklin D. Roosevelt, whose denial for some time of the permanence and debilitating nature of his paralysis may well have been an important reason that he was able to persevere and become president of the United States.

Self-deception also plays a positive role in life for those who tend to relive in memory the good experiences life has afforded them while tending to forget the bad ones. Why, years later, dwell on the bad? Why drag ourselves down in this way? (It's important, of course, to remember the mistakes one has made in order to make sure not to repeat them. The point is that nothing useful is accomplished by dwelling on them needlessly, as so many depressed people do.)

In some cases, however, there may be a serious difference of opinion concerning the benefits of the denial that death lurks nearby. It is notorious, for example, that most

---

[6]For an excellent and very readable account of the relationship of self-deception to anxiety reduction and of how the unconscious mind selects what comes into consciousness, see Daniel Goleman's *Vital Lies, Simple Truths* (New York: Simon & Schuster, 1985). For a short account of one theory concerning the relationship between stress and the immune and endocrine systems, see the May 1987 *Scientific American,* pp. 68B–68D.

young men who find themselves in the lethal killing zones typical of modern wars are able to function even though terrified in a way that most of the rest of us can hardly imagine. They can fight (those who can—many cannot) in large part because they tend to see the flying bullets and exploding shells hitting the other guy, not themselves. Soldiers tell stories of the extreme surprise some individuals show when they realize that they have been hit and are dying. The people who send young men into battle rely on this ability of the young to deny consciously what in some sense they know all too well—that they may be the next one to get it. The obviously good function of this kind of self-deception is that it enables soldiers to fight for their country when outside forces threaten its existence. The not entirely good consequence is that tyrants and other megalomaniacal leaders find it easier to get the young to risk their lives in immoral or foolish endeavors.

8. THE PULL OF PSEUDOSCIENCE AND THE PARANORMAL

That scientists, particularly those in the "hard sciences," generally know what they're talking about is vouchsafed by the everyday miracles that science makes possible, from computers to automobiles, TV sets, electric lightbulbs, nylon, toilet paper, eyeglasses, insulin, and clean water, hot or cold, flowing out of kitchen faucets. **Pseudoscientific theories** continue to be accepted by a significant number of people in spite of the fact that they produce no positive results whatsoever. Why is that?

A 2001 Gallup Poll update on belief in the "paranormal" showed that a half or more Americans believe in psychic or spiritual healing, and a third or more believe in such things as ghosts, haunted houses, possession by the devil, telepathy, and so on. This is a significant increase over the past decade in the number of people who believe these phenomena. Why are they all so gullible?

The answer lies in the strength of the various psychological mechanisms that we have been discussing in this chapter. Although science produces results, it doesn't always provide easy or satisfying answers to our problems. Instead, it often confirms what we would like very much to deny, including, unfortunately, the fact that we are not entirely rational animals; that the virtuous are not always rewarded, nor the guilty punished; that hard work is the fate of most of us; and that in the end we all die. (It also says nothing one way or the other about the possibility of life after death.)

Pseudoscience, on the other hand, while it often titillates with predictions of disasters others will experience, generally has rosy things to tell us about our own futures. It sometimes allays fears that it itself has generated—for instance, by transforming the fear that extraterrestrials lurk about by making them into benign cuddly creatures. It tends to be comforting, uplifting, optimistic. It often provides relatively easy solutions to our problems. Astrologers tell us that we, too, can be successful in business, provided, of course, that we schedule economic transactions on the "right" days. Fortune-tellers predict success in romance and marriage. Mediums claim to put us into contact with departed loved ones (implying the happy thought, by the way, that we too will survive death). One astrologer told Nancy Reagan which days were safe for her president husband to do his business (Mrs. Reagan apparently insisted that the president alter his schedule accordingly).

Nevertheless, it is bound to seem odd that pseudosciences are so widely believed, given that they are regularly proved worthless. Astrology, for example, has been disproved countless times over the centuries. Pliny the Elder (Roman scholar and naturalist, 23–79 A.D.), for instance, stated a simple yet devastating objection to astrology way back then when he said, "If a man's destiny is caused by the star under which he is born, then all men born under that star should have the same fortune. But masters and slaves and kings and beggars all are born under the same star." Can wishful thinking alone generate the considerable acceptance so many pseudosciences enjoy in the face of constant refutation? Whatever the answer to that question, it is clear that a pseudoscience like astrology retains much of its appeal in spite of crushing objections in part because charlatans have devised ways to make it seem plausible to the very suggestive (most of us in weak moments).

One weapon in the con artist's arsenal is what some psychologists call the "Barnum effect," after 19th-century circus magnate P. T. Barnum. Barnum is deservedly famous for remarking that "There's a sucker born every minute," but he also maintained that the secret of his immense success was in providing a little something for everyone. Con artists disguised as astrologers follow this advice very carefully. They word their horoscopes ambiguously, so that virtually everybody who wants to can see themselves in the descriptions under their sign. Here is part of a "typical Barnum profile":

> You have a great need for other people to like you and admire you. You have
> a tendency to be critical of yourself. You have a great deal of unused capacity
> which you have not used to your advantage. While you have some personality
> weaknesses, you are generally able to compensate for them. . . . You pride your-
> self on being an independent thinker and do not accept others' statements with-
> out satisfactory proof.

In fact, this description fits relatively few people, but it does fit how most of us think of ourselves — or want to think of ourselves.

However, not all statements in horoscope columns are of the Barnum type. The typical "Aries" is generally said to be "bold, energetic, assertive, selfish, insensitive, and aggressive." Only some of these characteristics are highly thought of. Typical horoscopes mix statements listing these kinds of character traits with statements of a general

---

Belief in astrology is a worldwide phenomenon. Here, for instance, is an excerpt from a Skeptical Inquirer *article (Spring 1990) on this point:*

While France [a predominantly Catholic country] has fewer than 36,000 Roman Catholic clergy, there are more than 40,000 [!] professional astrologers who declare their income to tax authorities—which says nothing of the undoubtedly far greater number of moonstruck stargazers, faith healers, mediums, necromancers, and fortune tellers of every imaginable stripe who choose not to declare their income. . . . Large and established companies turn to graphologists, birthdate interpreters, and plain old astrologers before hiring job candidates. A leading computer company only hires people after a tarot card reading. A big insurance company uses a swinging pendulum [!!] to judge whether a candidate is honest.

Well, at least trial by fire has gone out of style.

Barnum nature. "People tend to be impressed by the specific details that appear to fit (and pay less attention to those that do not), while the general Barnum-type statements provide readily acceptable 'padding'."[7]

Extrasensory perception (telepathy, clairvoyance, precognition, etc.) is another form of pseudoscience widely believed by the public. According to a Gallup poll, half the people in the United States believe in ESP (including 67 percent of those who are college educated!). Gulled by sensational press reports about "scientific" studies, they accept as evidence of psychic powers such flawed studies as the tests on Uri Geller performed at the Stanford Research Institute (definitely not affiliated with Stanford University!). Geller, by the way, has been exposed as a fraud countless times; the way in which he appears to bend spoons "psychically"—the trick for which he is most famous—has been demonstrated on several TV magic shows and can be learned by anyone sufficiently motivated to practice a bit.

In fact, over a century of research fails to confirm the existence of ESP in any of its

---

Con artists like Jeane Dixon and Uri Geller are pikers in the great sweep of things. They titillate, comfort, and do a small amount of harm, and that's about it. But the great mesmerizers, the Benito Mussolinis and Ruholla Khomeinis, who sell whole nations a bill of goods, are another matter. Here are a few pronouncements about mass propaganda by Adolf Hitler, an intuitive master at the game (culled from his writings by the Secular Humanist Bulletin, *March 1988):*

> All propaganda must be popular and its intellectual level must be adjusted to the most limited intelligence among those it is addressed to.
>
> All effective propaganda must be limited to a very few points and must harp on these slogans until the last member of the public understands what you want him to understand by your slogan. . . . [T]he masses are slow-moving, and they require a certain time before they are ready even to notice a thing, and only after the simplest ideas are repeated thousands of times will the masses finally remember them.
>
> *Propaganda's effect . . . must be aimed at the emotions and only to a very limited degree at the so-called intellect.* [Italics added.]
>
> The very first axiom of all propagandist activity: to wit, the basically subjective and one-sided attitude it must take toward every question it deals with. The function of propaganda is . . . not to weigh and ponder the rights of different people, but exclusively to emphasize the one right that it has set out to argue for. Its task is not to make an objective study of the truth, . . . its task is to serve our own right, always and unflinchingly.

Does this sound like the formula to which most political rhetoric in the United States today is tailored?

---

[7]Taken from a fascinating article by Christopher C. French, Mandy Fowler, Katy McCarthy, and Debbie Peers entitled "Belief in Astrology: A Test of the Barnum Effect," *Skeptical Inquirer* (Winter 1991).

alleged forms. After reviewing a large body of research in this area for the National Research Council, a scientific committee concluded that "despite a 130-year record of scientific research on such matters our committee could find no scientific justification for the existence of phenomena such as extrasensory perception, mental telepathy, or 'mind over matter' exercises. . . . Evaluation of the large body of the best available evidence simply does not support the contention that these phenomena exist.[8]

In the face of such findings, why do people continue to believe in ESP? We mentioned a few reasons a few pages back, but Thomas Gilovich, a cognitive psychologist at Cornell University, concludes (from surveys asking people to explain the origin of their beliefs) that personal experience also plays an important role. When by chance or coincidence people experience a run of good or bad luck they often attribute it to some special power. Gamblers who have streaks of luck at blackjack or roulette have trouble accepting the fact that the theory of probability predicts that streaks of luck are likely to occur every once in a while. They often become convinced that some special power is at work—that unseen forces are on their side—rather than accept the fact that coincidences are bound to happen now and then.

Premonitions fall into the same category. A premonition is really a coincidence that occurs between someone's thoughts and actual events in the real world. A young man dreams about his ex-girlfriend, and lo and behold, she calls him the next day. If he thinks his dream is a premonition, he has forgotten for the moment the many times he has dreamed about her when she didn't call. After all, people frequently dream about ex-lovers, but rarely do they telephone the next day. When they do, it's coincidental. This element of chance applies as well to extraordinary premonitions that foretell an important event that really does occur. A woman has a dream that a TWA DC 6 will crash in the Florida Everglades—and it does! Of what significance is this? The question to ask is whether such events occur more often than we would expect them to by chance. People have an unfortunate tendency to believe premonitions that come true and to forget those that don't. This, by the way, nicely illustrates the difference between pseudoscience and science. Pseudoscience pays attention to successes and ignores failures; science never ignores failures. It puts its hypotheses to severe tests, requiring independent repetition of observations and experiments rather than relying simply on coincidence and anecdote.

9. LACK OF A GOOD SENSE OF PROPORTION

The kinds of irrationality catalogued in this chapter so far—provincialism, self-deception, and so on—seem to have evolved primarily because they are advantageous in certain kinds of circumstances. Self-deception, as mentioned before, may reduce stress, and provincialism tends to increase group cohesiveness. But explanations as to why so many of us lack a good **sense of proportion** are much harder to come by.[9] In any

---

[8]*American Psychological Association Monitor,* January 1988—more recent evaluations come to the same conclusion.

[9]Part of the explanation lies, no doubt, in the benefits of the psychological mechanisms already discussed. But perhaps another part lies in two important facts about human evolution. The first is that behavior guided by intelligence is a later arrival on the scene than responses motivated purely

case, there can be no doubt that on occasion we all lack a good sense of proportion when we make decisions and come to conclusions in everyday life. The trick is to learn how to minimize this natural impediment to cogent reasoning.

Prudence is one of the chief components of a good sense of proportion. In the sense intended here, prudence consists in being provident—of tempering what we do today to maximize our overall, long-run interests. Of course, being prudent does not mean becoming a drudge, or a workaholic. It doesn't mean always putting off until tomorrow pleasures that could have been had today. But it does mean carefully weighing today's pleasures against long-term interests.

Note, though, that imprudence frequently is not a factor when people lack a sense of proportion. The impediments to cogent reasoning already discussed certainly play an important role here. A sense of loyalty, for example, sometimes clouds the perspective of even the most level-headed among us, leading us to exaggerate the wonders of our own society while neglecting its defects. And wishful thinking certainly plays an important role. People play state lotteries not just because they have little understanding of what it means to say the odds are a million or a hundred thousand to one against winning the big prize but also because of wishful thinking. ("This is my lucky day," or "I was born on 1/23/45, so 12345 is my lucky number.")

But there are plenty of cases, some of a much more serious nature, in which wishful thinking or self-deception plays little or no role. After the attack on the World Trade Center, for instance, Americans stopped flying just about everywhere. While this reaction was understandable, given the terrifying nature of the event, the odds against being killed in this way were millions to one. (Again, driving to work every day is much more life-threatening.) Many Americans refuse to fly commercial airplanes from one city to another even though driving is many times more dangerous. In fact, flying commercial airlines is just about the safest way to travel ever invented, yet lots of people, including one of the authors of this chapter on pseudoreasoning, have serious bouts with fear every time they fly.[10]

In fact, failure to see things in proper perspective is one of the most serious errors in reasoning that most of us are guilty of. This is true in particular concerning value judgments. For example, when *60 Minutes* aired a segment in January 1993 on animal re-

---

by desires and emotions (something that is confirmed by what is known about the development of the brains of vertebrate animals—in particular, mammals). Strong emotions that appropriately guided behavior at much earlier times now sometimes skew rational thought and motivate responses that are less than optimal. The second relevant fact is that until quite recently, very little was known about what philosophers used to call the "secret powers" that move things, and a great deal that was "known" has turned out to be false. (Think only of medicine until about 150 years ago, when practices such as bloodletting were common.) If we go back, say, just 10,000 or 20,000 years in human history—an eye blink on the evolutionary time scale—we are back to a time when exceedingly few accurate general beliefs about cause-and-effect relationships can have been known. So it is only recently in the great sweep of things that it has slowly become increasingly beneficial to moderate the urges of immediate desire and strong emotions in terms of what intelligence can learn from experience. Perhaps, then, the lack of a better sense of proportion is partly explained as being due to a kind of "evolutionary lag."

[10] In some of these cases, psychologists understand the mechanisms leading to the poor sense of proportion—for example, a fear of unfamiliar threats as compared to the familiar and, in the case of airline flying, a lack of personal control of the plane (similar to fear felt when sitting in the back seat of a car). But they don't understand why people are prone to these kinds of irrationality.

> It often is difficult to know whether someone is irrationally self-deceived, or perhaps imprudent, rather than being completely rational. Take the case of professional boxers and football players. Do they deceive themselves about the likelihood of permanent and serious damage to their bodies? Are they being extremely imprudent? Or do they so value their professional life (and its financial rewards) that to them it is worth the pain and suffering likely at a later date? Some retired professional football players, for instance, say that they were foolish to take the pounding week after week that has left them walking wounded; others say it was worth it. Are the latter still deceiving themselves?

search and another on the ill treatment of women, they received many more letters of complaint about cruelty to animals than to women. (We assume that most people, even "animal liberationists," value human welfare over that of other animals.) Another example: In a restaurant conversation overheard recently, someone defended a friend who had bilked an elderly couple of their life savings by pointing out the truth that we all break the law from time to time.

As might be expected, politicians frequently (one might say continually) take advantage of the failure of so many people to see things in a proper perspective. They know that people can be diverted from important issues and problems by being provided with "bread and circuses" and that, for instance, the best time to announce unpopular measures is when the minds of masses of people are riveted on the private lives of celebrities such as Leonardo Di Caprio or Julia Roberts. It also is one reason that the mass media so frequently stretch the "human interest" angles to stories way out of proportion to their importance. (A good deal more on these topics is included in later chapters.)

But before going on to other matters, perhaps it needs to be made clear that our having chosen most of our examples here from the scene in the United States does not mean that lacking a good sense of proportion is common primarily in this country. Right after the 2000 U.S. presidential election, for instance, the media in Spain, Britain, and other European countries, even including Italy (!), had a field day gloating about how the United States had so often criticized elections in other countries (Chile, Nigeria, Burma, and so on) for fraud and other "irregularities" and now was in the same boat—fighting over dimpled and hanging chads, disqualification of black voters, and having the U.S. Supreme Court arbitrarily step in, halting recounts and declaring George W. Bush the winner.

But this American electoral glitch was tiny compared to what so often has gone on in other countries that the United States has criticized. Did Europeans who had fun laughing at the United States fail to exercise a good sense of proportion?

SUMMARY OF CHAPTER 6

Human beings are not completely rational animals. There also is a nonrational component to our makeup that often interferes with our ability to argue or reason cogently.

1. Our reasoning sometimes is skewed from the truth because of *loyalty,* which inclines us to see our own society and its beliefs in a more favorable light than the

evidence may warrant; because of *provincialism,* which tends to narrow our interests and knowledge of what goes on in the world; and because of the *herd instinct,* which makes it easy and natural for us to believe what most others in our society believe. *Example:* failing to notice the undemocratic and nasty things our own government does on the international scene.

2. Loyalty and provincialism are related to *prejudice*—in particular, to prejudice against members of other groups, and to thinking in terms of unverified stereotypes. *Example:* the stereotype that was common in the United States until about the late 1950s, which pictured African Americans as foot-shuffling, obsequious children. But believing bad things about others constitutes prejudice only when not justified by sufficient evidence.

   Prejudice against others often is conjoined with an overtolerance of the defects and foibles of one's own group and its members, and it may be reinforced by the need to find *scapegoats*—others who can be blamed for our own troubles and mistakes. *Example:* blaming the Jews for the transgressions of others.

   Thinking in terms of stereotypes and scapegoats often stems from a *partisan mind-set*—viewing everything in terms of "us against them" or "my right opinions against your wrong ones." Good reasoners, by way of contrast, have minds open to the truth, wherever it may lead.

3. *Superstitions* often are supported by a small amount of evidence. What makes them superstitions is that we believe them on the basis of insufficient and, frequently, biased samples from which all negative evidence has been eliminated. *Example:* overlooking the fact that good things sometimes happen on Friday the 13th and bad things on other days.

4. Beliefs acquired in the irrational ways just described generally result from *wishful thinking*—believing what we want to believe, no matter what the evidence— or from its variant, called *self-deception*—consciously believing what, at some deeper level, we know to be dubious. *Example:* British Prime Minister Neville Chamberlain wishfully believing that the Munich agreement with Hitler had assured "peace in our time."

5. Two other important ways to cut the wishful thinking pie are *rationalization, suppression,* and *denial. Example:* smoking cigarettes after being exposed to all sorts of evidence that they're bad for one's health. Rationalization often supports *procrastination*—putting off until tomorrow what ought to be done today. *Example:* starting to write a term paper the day before it's due.

6. While we can't yet be sure why nonrational mechanisms have evolved, scientists are beginning to understand some of their beneficial effects. Loyalty and provincialism increase group cohesiveness when there is competition or strife with other groups. The herd instinct helps individuals to work well with others in their group. And self-deception frequently aids in the reduction of anxiety and stress, both of which can be harmful to health. Prolonged doubt about serious matters tends to produce stress and anxiety; coming to firm beliefs about these matters tends to combat depression and thus be good for one's physical well-being. *Example:* denying the seriousness of a terminal illness, thereby reducing grief at the end of one's life.

7. *Pseudoscientific beliefs* are adopted, and endure, in spite of their failure to help us deal successfully with everyday problems, because of wishful thinking, self-deception, and similar psychological mechanisms. *Pseudoscience* is comforting and upbeat concerning our own welfare and the satisfaction of our deepest desires. *Example:* seances that practitioners claim can put us into contact with deceased friends and relatives.

But pseudosciences also gain widespread acceptance because charlatans have learned how to manipulate us in our unguarded or weak moments. *Example:* alleged astrologers papering over the phoniness of their forecasts by larding them with "Barnum" profiles that tend to fit everybody. Note that the con artists who play on our weaknesses in this way are two-bit operators compared to such great political mesmerizers as Adolf Hitler, who expertly manipulate masses of their compatriots by clever and sophisticated appeals to the irrational side of the human psyche.

8. On occasion, most of us lack a good *sense of proportion,* a defect in reasoning that critical reasoners try to minimize. *Example:* being persuaded by political rhetoric to pay more attention to relatively unimportant matters than to those that are more serious. Being *prudent,* in the sense of provident—acting so as to maximize long-run interests—is an important component of a good sense of proportion that we often lack. *Example:* weighing today's small pleasure more highly than the long-run benefits of doing well on a final exam, thus not preparing until the last minute. But people often fail to see things in proper perspective for other reasons; for example, because of group loyalty or wishful thinking or because of other emotional interferences with cogent reasoning. *Example:* being more afraid of small risks than of much bigger ones.

EXERCISE 6-1

1. How, if at all, do the following items taken from the *Harper's Index* (March 1996) illustrate matters that were discussed in this chapter?

Percentage of Americans earning less than $30,000 a year who believe "the meek shall inherit the earth": 61

Percentage earning more than $60,000 who believe this: 36

2. How about this Luann cartoon?

Luann reprinted by permission of United Features Syndicate, Inc.

3. When France defied the United States and came out against the Iraq War in 2003, the same sort of stereotypes surfaced among some Americans as did at the end of World War II when the GIs liberated Paris: The French don't bathe, they're cowardly collaborators, their women are loose, and the like. Explain the psychological impediments involved and compare the political climates that gave rise to these attitudes.

4. Explain how this conversation between a student and a teacher (not quite verbatim) relates to topics discussed in this chapter:

   Student: I've come to your office to see about getting a B in this course.
   Teacher: But you're doing C work, the semester ends next week, and you missed two assignments. What makes you think you can get a B?
   Student: Well, I need to get a B to get into Berkeley [University of California at Berkeley] next fall.
   Teacher: But why didn't you come in sooner and talk to me about this and perhaps get help to do better work?
   Student: Yes. But I really need to get that B or I can't get into Berkeley.

5. Explain how this conversation between two students (again not quite verbatim, with names changed to protect the guilty) relates to topics discussed in this chapter:

   Smith: Loan me 20 bucks. I'm strapped and have a heavy date with you-know-who.
   Jones: You're always asking me for favors, but you never do any for me. I always do the favors you ask of me; you regularly turn me down. Sorry, Charlie.
   Smith: Hey! What about last year when I got you a date with Charlene? You never got me a date with anyone. So how about it?

6. Do you believe that loyalty really does skew people's beliefs away from what the evidence will support? If so, support your belief with at least one example not mentioned in the text. If not, show that the examples given in the text are somehow mistaken.

7. Do human beings really have a herd instinct, or is that just true of cows and such? Defend your answer.

8. How does the text use the expression "belief provincialism"? Give some examples, other than those mentioned in the text, and explain why they are examples.

9. According to the text, what is wrong with categorizing, say, the French as great lovers, Germans as obedient automatons, and so on? After all, doesn't experience show that the members of a given group tend to be different from the members of other groups, as Greeks are different from Pakistanis and Mexicans from Nigerians?

10. Give at least two examples of other people engaging in self-deception or wishful thinking, and explain why you think their actions fit the relevant descrip-

tions provided in the text. Do you ever engage in this sort of funny business? Explain and defend your answer. (Hint: You do.)

11. What are some of the good consequences of wishful thinking and self-deception that are mentioned in the text? Explain. Can you think of others?

12. Critically evaluate the following argument. (Does it contain a correct use of induction?) "Several of my friends have been very lucky in life so far, and I've read of quite a few other lucky souls. So when I say that my lucky friends will continue to have good luck, I'm basing my conclusion on experience, not wishful thinking."

13. If you had been interviewed for the Gallup poll discussed on page 134, would you have been among those expressing belief in at least one of the claims asked about by that poll? If so, explain. If not, you get a free ride on this question. (Note the temptation for those who would have been among the ones with the appropriate beliefs to engage in a tiny sort of "lie of silent assertion" by simply passing over this question!)

14. Carefully explain the so-called Barnum effect. How did the typical Barnum profile reprinted in this chapter fit you?

15. The box on page 136 lists some of the principles underlying Adolf Hitler's propaganda technique. Find at least two examples from the speeches of American presidents, members of the U.S. Congress, or Supreme Court justices that seem to be in accordance with these principles. Explain and defend your choices. (It's cheating to use examples that appear in this text.)

16. We all suffer to some extent from the impediments to rational thinking described in this chapter, the authors of this text not being exceptions. (Actually, one of us is an exception, but the other isn't.) Doesn't this textbook, for example, reflect the provincialism of its authors in some ways? If so, how? If not, why might some readers think otherwise? What about any other ways in which you think the text could be construed so as to indicate rational failures—of the kind discussed in this chapter—on the part of its authors? (Be brief!)

An important art of politicians is to find new names for institutions which under old names have become odious to the public.

—Talleyrand

*If concepts are not clear, words do not
fit. If words do not fit, the day's work
cannot be accomplished, morals and art
do not flourish. If morals and art do not
flourish, punishments are not just. If
punishments are not just, the people do
not know where to put hand or foot.*
                    —Confucius, *Analects,* XIII: 3

*When an idea is wanting, a word can
always be found to take its place.*
                                                —Goethe

*He who defines the terms wins the
argument.*
                            —Chinese proverb

*Beware of and eschew pompous
prolixity.*
                        —Charles A. Beardsley

Chapter

7

LANGUAGE

Language is the indispensable tool used in formulating arguments. We all are familiar (or should be!) with the power of language when it is employed by fine writers of fiction—Shakespeare, Fielding, Austen, Conrad (to name just a few who wrote in the English language)—the list is very long. The principal point of literature classes is precisely to make this apparent. But good writing can be equally effective when used in the construction of argumentative essays and other argumentative passages. The trouble is that language also can be used effectively in the service of fallacious as well as cogent arguments, deceiving the unwary or unknowing into accepting arguments they should reject.

1. COGNITIVE AND EMOTIVE MEANINGS

If the purpose of a sentence is to inform or to state a fact, some of its words must refer to things, events, or properties of one kind or another. These words must thus have what is commonly called **cognitive meaning.** (The sentences they compose also are said to have cognitive meaning.)

But most words also have **emotive meaning,** which means that they have positive or negative overtones. The emotive charges of some words are obvious. Think of the terms *wop, kike, nigger,* and *fag,* or the so-called four-letter words that rarely appear in textbooks, even in this permissive age.

The words just mentioned have negative emotive charges. But lots of words have positive overtones. Examples are *freedom, love, democracy, springtime,* and *peace.* And plenty of others have either neutral or mixed emotive force. *Pencil, run,* and *river* tend to be neutral words. *Socialism, politician,* and *whiskey* get mixed reviews.

In fact, almost any word that is emotively positive for some people or in some contexts may be just the opposite for others. One person's meat often is indeed another's poison. Perhaps the paradigm case is the word *God,* which has one kind of overtone for true believers, another for agnostics, and still another for strident atheists. To the average person, the word *student* has positive connotations, but not to a landlord or landlady.

Terms that on first glance may appear to be emotively neutral often turn out to have at least modest emotive overtones. The terms *bureaucrat, government official,* and *public servant,* for instance, all refer to the same group of people and thus have approximately the same cognitive import, but their emotive meanings are quite different. Of the three, only *government official* comes close to being neutral in tone.

2. Emotive Meanings and Persuasive Uses of Language

The fact that expressions have emotive as well as cognitive meanings has not escaped the notice of con artists, advertisers, politicians, and others whose stock in trade is the manipulation of attitudes, desires, and beliefs. Over the years, they have learned how to use the emotive side of language to further their own ends, whether benevolent or self-serving.

One common way in which the emotive force of language can be used to con, as Talleyrand observed some time ago, is to mask the odious nature of an institution or practice by giving it a nice name rather than a more accurate, nasty one. Why call the Chinese dictatorship by an accurate name when it can be called the *People's Republic of China*? When Saddam Hussein took control of Iraq, why should he have fiddled with the increasingly inaccurate name *Republic of Iraq*? The ruling clique in Myanmar (formerly Burma) surely has no reason to call its thugs who engage in mass murder and other kinds of nasty business anything other than the *State Peace and Development Council.* In a slightly different vein, why call diluted beer *watered-down beer* when you can call it *lite*? Why should a minority political group call itself *The Moral Minority,* when it can puff itself up into *The Moral Majority*? (Note, by the way, the implication that the individuals in this group are more moral than other people.) And doesn't *Department of Defense* have a much sweeter ring to it than the original and more accurate name *War Department*? And how about the *Clear Skies Initiative,* Bushspeak for the new set of pollution laws that dumb down the *Clean Air Act*?

I am firm, you are obstinate, he is pigheaded.
> —Bertrand Russell's example of words having similar
> cognitive meanings but much different emotive senses

In recent years, manipulative uses of language have been given a spate of emotively negative names, each with a slightly different connotation, including *doublespeak* (deliberately ambiguous or evasive language), *bureaucratese* (governmental doublespeak), *newspeak* (media doublespeak), *academese* (the academic variety), *legalese* (lawyer talk), *gobbledygook, bafflegab,* and *jargon.*

Take *militaryese.* The military at all times and places has devised expressions intended as much as possible to hide the fact that war is, to put it mildly, unvarnished hell. Here are a few examples:

Comfort women	Women of conquered countries forced to work as prostitutes "servicing" soldiers (term used by the Japanese during World War II)
Battle fatigue	Insanity suffered as a result of the unbearable horrors and strains of battle
Collateral damage	People who are inadvertently killed or property that is inadvertently destroyed in warfare
Ethnic cleansing	Driving out unwanted citizens of a country, burning their houses, and killing some along the way (as in Kosovo, 1999)
Friendly fire	Shelling friendly villages or troops by mistake
Servicing a target or visiting a site	Bombing a place flat (used during the Gulf War)
Pacification center	Concentration camp (itself originally doublespeak)
Termination	Killing (also used by the CIA, where *termination with prejudice* means *assassination*)
Selective ordinance	Napalm (used to kill by incineration)
The Final Solution	Plan of the Nazis to murder all European Jews

During World War II—one of the most awful of all wars—the expression *dehousing industrial workers* was used by the British and Americans to mean killing civilians, including women and children via *saturation* air raids. The indescribably horrible massive air raids on Germany and Japan that created incredible firestorms were said to result in *self-energized dislocation,* not widespread death by either incineration or asphyxiation. The term *war* itself has been euphemized into *conflict* or *operation.* Bush the elder waged "Operation Desert Shield"; Bush the younger, "Operation Iraqi Freedom." In the latter conflict the term *war* was used to describe the War on Terrorism or the War for Peace (!), but not the Iraq War, which is what it really was. During that war, both sides manipulated terminology to suit their own bias. In the United States the networks used the term "coalition forces" for what the Arab media called "occupation forces." And when CNN reported that 16 "insurgents" were killed in an Iraqi uprising (May 7, 2004), the Arab media described them as "resistance fighters."

Then there is *legalese,* a hybrid of French, English, and Latin that baffles the average person. In plain English a *writ* is a claim form, and a *plaintiff* is someone who makes a complaint against another party. Meetings with the judge *in camera* are just private meetings behind closed doors. Why all this turgid terminology? The principal reason is to ensure certainty, to protect clients by using phrases defined by statutes or case law. Using different expressions may raise doubts as to precisely what is meant. But why can't plain English accomplish the same thing? Another justification is that it's cheaper and less trouble to use archaic language than to rewrite everything. Maybe, but then again, lawyers might have to charge lower fees if legal documents were clear.

Of course, bureaucratese, governmentese, and politicalese (we all can play at this game) don't exactly suffer from a paucity of examples. In Philadelphia, the jail for juvenile "offenders" is called the "Youth Study Center." Florida chain gangs, for a short time, were called "restricted labor squads." The two young high school students who murdered 15 people in a Littleton, Colorado high school in 1999 had earlier been enrolled in a "diversion program" in lieu of jail for burglary. Their "disease" is now sometimes labeled "intermittent explosive disorder," for which they would get "cognitive behavioral therapy" instead of counseling.

These examples illustrate the use of *euphemistic language*—locutions from which as much negative emotive content as possible has been removed—and the replacement of accurate names with more high-flown locutions. The point generally is to conceal or to mislead, which could be one reason that this kind of talk has become so popular with government officials, lawyers, military officers, doctors, and (alas!) a large number of academics. (Is this one reason why so many other[!] textbooks are so dull?)

In recent years, however, it's possible that doublespeak in the business world has managed to surpass even that of militaryese in its deviousness. Well, maybe not. But consider these examples of euphemisms used when someone is fired:

> *bumped, decruited, dehired, deselected, destaffed, discontinued, disemployed, dislocated, downsized, excessed, involuntarily separated, nonretained, nonrenewed, severed, surplussed, transitioned, vocationally relocated* [1]

Everyone knows that politics is fertile ground for doublespeak. One euphemistic evasion in particular has gained currency in the past few years. Nowadays politicians don't admit to being wrong when they are wrong—instead, they "misspeak." For example, during the Iraq War, Paul Wolfowitz, then Deputy Defense Secretary, contended on ABC's *Good Morning America* (September 11, 2003) that Iraq under Hussein had been in league with terrorists, particularly Al Qaeda, and ". . . a great many of bin Laden's key lieutenants are now trying to organize in cooperation with old loyalists from the Saddam regime to attack in Iraq." The implication was that a dangerous new terrorist force threatened the military in postwar Iraq. The next day, in an interview with the Associated Press (AP), Wolfowitz said he had "misspoken," and that he was referring to one bin Laden supporter, not many key lieutenants (a correction that slipped under the radar, since it was buried in the news section of most papers). This reduced the implied threat to U.S. forces considerably, but somehow "misspeaking" made it seem less reprehensible than getting it wrong and misleading the audience.

---

[1] New York Times Service (March 8, 1996); mentioned in the July 1996 issue of the *Quarterly Review of Doublespeak.*

TOLES © *The Buffalo News*. Reprinted with permission
of Universal Press Syndicate. All rights reserved.

*A play on words that distorts paying off the national debt to mean paying down the debt
that the G. W. Bush character owes to his campaign contributors.*

Firing large numbers of workers is *corporate rightsizing,* by the way, and the place
where you get *downsized* is sometimes called the *outplacement office.*

Most large companies these days desperately want to avoid use of the *f*-word—*fired*
—but at Bill Gates's Microsoft outfit, it's the *b*-word—*bug*—that is the no-no. Employees are required instead to speak of *undocumented behavior* or of a *design side
effect, known issue,* or *intermittent issue.*

This euphemistic trend in the business world is often satirized in the media. For instance, in a *Doonesbury* cartoon (November 20, 1999) satirizing the owners of start-up
companies that earn no money but make millions from IPOs (initial public offerings of
stock), one character says, "We'll probably walk away with a fortune. It's only the small
investors who get burned. It's called socializing the risk while privatizing the profit."

Interestingly, class differences have always been mirrored euphemistically. Average
people *rent* apartments; the rich *lease* them. The nonrich talk of *social climbers;* social
climbers like to think of themselves as *upwardly mobile* or (more recently) *changing
course,* and not as *pushy* but rather as *emphatic.* The wealthy don't earn a *salary,* they
receive *compensation* or have an *income.*

In the field of education euphemisms abound (and why should we be different?). One
college gives placement tests in *Student Success Workshops,* presumably to soften the
blow to the many students who place in remedial (uh, developmental) classes. Teachers
no longer *teach* but *facilitate* in *comfort zones* where *collaborative learning* occurs.

The deliberate use of euphemistic language has been going on at least since the beginning of recorded history, but it seems to have increased dramatically in recent years, perhaps because of the professionalization of most trades. Titled professionals want to sound objective and authoritative, not opinionated or biased. Also, controversial topics can be toned down when dressed in euphemistic language. For instance, to lessen its negative connotation, the term *abortion* comes in many guises nowadays: *effecting fetal demise, planned cessation of gestation, interrupted pregnancy, termination,* and *selective reduction.*

It's true that euphemisms can and often do serve useful, nonmanipulative functions. Circumlocutions used to replace offensive four-letter words are good examples. Using expressions like *put to sleep, passed gas,* and *for the mature figure* often is just a matter of politeness. Why shock or offend when we don't have to? Nevertheless, all too often euphemisms are used to further Machiavellian purposes. Indeed, the nastier something is, the greater the need to clothe it in neutral garb.

Doublespeak is especially deadly when it comes in whole sentences or runs on for whole paragraphs. Academese illustrates this nicely. Here, for example, is a tiny snippet from Zellig Harris's well-known text *Structural Linguistics* that makes a simple idea seem more profound:

> Another consideration is the availability of simultaneity, in addition to successivity as a relation among linguistic elements.

This seems to mean (there is a certain amount of vagueness here) that we can do two things at once, like gesture while we talk. (You didn't know that, did you?)

Now that appetites have been whetted, how about a sampling of truly impenetrable prose?

> Indeed dialectical critical realism may be seen under the aspect of Foucauldian strategic reversal—of the unholy trinity of Parmenidean /Platonic/Aristotelian

---

The popularity of the writings of George Orwell is an important reason that doublespeak has received more than a usual amount of attention in recent years. In this excerpt from his 1948 classic, "Politics and the English Language," he explains one reason why politicians favor this less-than-straightforward kind of rhetoric:

In our time, political speech and writing are largely the defence of the indefensible. . . . Thus political language has to consist largely of euphemism, question begging, and sheer cloudy vagueness. Defenceless villages are bombarded from the air, the inhabitants driven out into the countryside, the cattle machine-gunned, the huts set on fire with incendiary bullets: This is called *pacification*. Millions of peasants are robbed of their farms and sent trudging along the roads with no more than they can carry: This is called *transfer of population* or *rectification of frontiers.* . . .

The inflated style is itself a kind of euphemism. A mass of Latin words falls upon the facts like soft snow, blurring the outlines and covering up all the details. *The great enemy of clear language is insincerity. When there is a gap between one's real and one's declared aims, one turns as it were instinctively to long words and exhausted idioms, like a cuttlefish squirting out ink.* [These italics added.]

provenance; of the Cartesian-Lockean-Humean-Kantian paradigm, of founda-
tionalism . . . new and old alike; of the primordial failing of western philosophy,
ontological monovalence, and its close ally, the epistemic fallacy with its ontic
dual. (*New York Times,* February 27, 1999, report of a Modern Language Association [MLA] speech)

This little gem earned the author, Roy Bhaskar, first prize for bad writing by "serious"
scholars, awarded by the New Zealand–based *Journal of Philosophy and Literature.*

Both these examples of academese are badly written in one way or another (actually
several). They use inflated or obscure language and, of special note, are full of *jargon.*
There are several senses of this term, one being nonsensical, incoherent, or meaningless
talk; another the specialized language used by professionals when talking (or writing) to
each other. The trouble is that jargon intended in the professional sense can and often
does turn out to be jargon in the meaningless or incoherent sense, making vacuous or
otherwise simple and easily understood remarks appear to be profound. The MLA item
quoted here may well illustrate the incoherent variety (who can be sure?); the Harris remark exemplifies the obvious made to seem important.

Note the connection here, by the way, with what we said in Chapter 3 in the discussion of appeals to authorities about not being intimidated by professional lingo. Telling
patients that they have a *malignant melanoma,* for example, may leave them ignorant of
the fact that they have a form of skin cancer which, if untreated, quickly leads to death.

We need to remember, though, that technical terms used by professional people generally do have an important function—namely, to ensure precision when it counts. Lawyers want contracts to be airtight. Doctors need to be sure they understand each other
when they talk about patient illnesses. It may be adequate for a layperson to talk, say,
about rapid or irregular heartbeats, but cardiologists need a more precise way of distinguishing the various kinds—distinguishing, for example, *supra ventricular tachycardia*
from *atrial fibrillation* or from the immediately life-threatening *ventricular fibrillation.*
Use of these technical expressions quickly conveys rather precise and absolutely vital
information from one doctor to another. Technical jargon used by people in the same
field is an essential form of communication, but when it deteriorates into incoherent or
meaningless verbiage, it is puzzling at best and incomprehensible at worst.

As the world changes, language inevitably changes with it. New words come into
common use for things and procedures that didn't exist just a few years ago; old
words take on new meanings. The computer age illustrates this nicely. We now
talk glibly of an inanimate variety of *mouse,* clipless *clipboards,* nonedible
menus, floppy and *hard* discs, *RAM, ROM, bytes* and even *megabytes,* and glass-
less *windows.* We *cut* and *paste* without scissors or glue, and not only *delete* but
also *unerase.* We *surf* the (dry) *'Net* and zero in on spiderless *Web* sites, *navigat-
ing* with a *cursor.*

Initially, these new locutions were used and understood primarily by computer
nerds and functioned, as professionalese generally does, to exclude the uniniti-
ated. But they quickly worked their way into the vocabularies of everyone who
uses computers, even though much of what we do with them is word processing
or game playing, not mathematical computation. So it goes.

Unfortunately, human nature being what it is, even medicalese sometimes is used to conceal. For example, in March 1995, the *New York Times* reported that when Dr. Mark Siegler conducted a study of surgical errors, he discovered that he was not supposed to use the words *error* or *mistake,* because they "distressed the surgeons" and were "fraught with meaning." Instead, the term *E.R.E. (eyebrow-raising episode)* was substituted. So much for the slip of a knife or a twitch of the laser beam. (In defense of the surgeons, we might remember that when they make honest mistakes, as being human they occasionally must, they become open to unfair malpractice suits.)

Another common feature of jargon, by the way, is *padding*—adding significant-sounding sentences here and there that in fact say little or nothing. Here is an example typical of a common variety in psychological writings: "Although the effects of mental attitudes on bodily disease should not be exaggerated, neither should they be minimized." True. And here is an example of another type: "As soon as there are behaviors you can't generate, then there are responses you can't elicit." Yes. And another: "In order to achieve products, outputs, and outcomes through processes, inputs are required." Absolutely.

Evasive language is just as common in other countries as it is in our own. Now that the European Union is firmly established in Brussels, *Eurobabble* is flourishing. Buses are *intermodal transport systems,* gums are *mucous membranes* of the oral cavities, bulls are *male bovine animals,* and to some Eurocrats, sheep are *grain-eating units!* Doublespeak knows no geographic boundaries. (For more, see *Quarterly Review of Doublespeak,* April 1999.)

3. OTHER COMMON RHETORICAL DEVICES

Let's now look at a few of the many other rhetorical devices that are frequently used to manipulate the unwary or less knowledgeable. (This does not mean that these devices cannot be used in the services of truth and justice!)

Tone

Good writers or speakers try to choose the **tone** best suited to their audience, as students are taught to do in writing classes. Tone expresses attitudes or feelings—of compassion, anger, levity, humility, congeniality, and so on—and can be quite powerful when employed properly in argumentative passages. Using the proper tone, even though doing so clearly plays to emotions, isn't like arguing fallaciously or from premises known to be false, but rather is just a matter of common sense; arguments aren't won by unnecessarily ruffling the other guy's feathers.

But tone can be employed for nefarious purposes, not just virtuous ones. Lawyers addressing juries are masters of the art, as are politicians addressing constituents. Success in politics requires knowing how to use the tone of "Mom and apple pie" rhetoric when addressing, say, families of soldiers returning from overseas duty and humor when dealing with matters of a lighter nature. Here, for instance, is an excerpt from the veto by Adlai Stevenson, then governor of Illinois, of a bill to protect birds by restraining the roaming of cats:

> It is in the nature of cats to do a certain amount of unescorted roaming. . . . That cats destroy some birds, I well know, but I believe this legislation would further but little the worthy cause to which its proponents give such unselfish effort. The problem of the cat versus the bird is as old as time. If we attempt to resolve it by legislation who knows but what we may be called upon to take sides as well in the age-old problem of dog versus cat, bird versus bird, or even bird versus worm. In my opinion, the state of Illinois . . . already has enough to do without trying to control feline delinquency.

Just the right touch to put the quash on a bill that members of the legislature cared little about anyway. By using elevated language to explain his decision on a rather minor matter, and by carrying the consequences of the vetoed bill's logic to ridiculous lengths, Stevenson managed to undermine the opposition with gentle humor and without offending anyone. (Stevenson, by the way, was rightly famous for his ironic humor; witness his remark when accused of being an "egghead": "Eggheads of the world unite; all we have to lose are our yolks.")

Contrast the tone of the Stevenson veto with the following excerpt from the best-known speech by Winston Churchill, a master at the trade. It is taken from the end of an address to the British parliament in the summer of 1940, during the darkest days of World War II, when the British expected to be invaded by German armies flush with

Farley by Phil Frank; *San Francisco Chronicle,* April 22, 1998. © Phil Frank. Used by permission.

The double meaning of the expression Piggy Bank nicely makes the suggestion that a big dose of good old greed might be the motive for lots of today's megamergers.

recent and spectacular victories in France—a time when most observers believed Britain was about to be crushed by German military power:

> We shall not flag nor fail. We shall go on to the end. We shall fight . . . on the seas and oceans; we shall fight with growing confidence and growing strength in the air. We shall defend our island whatever the cost may be; we shall fight on beaches, landing grounds, in fields, in streets and on the hills. We shall never surrender and even if, which I do not for the moment believe, this island or a large part of it were subjugated and starving, then our empire beyond the seas, armed and guarded by the British fleet, will carry on the struggle until in God's good time the New World, with all its power and might, sets forth to the liberation and rescue of the Old.

The point of Churchill's rhetoric was to buck up the courage of the British people—to stiffen their resolve to fight in the face of terrible odds—and the tone of his speech, not to mention its content, accomplished exactly that. (Incidentally, Churchill's address was not recorded; the recording frequently heard of this momentous speech is by someone else, later.)

Slanting

Slanting is a form of misrepresentation. In one version, a true statement is made so as to imply or suggest something else (usually either false or not known to be true). For example, a defense lawyer may try to blunt damaging testimony by stating, "All this proves

---

Monroe C. Beardsley was one of the first to write a textbook dealing strictly with critical reasoning (as opposed to formal logic). In this excerpt from his book Thinking Straight, *he explains an example of* suggestion:

On November 30, 1968, the *New York Times* reported on the construction site for a new jetport in the Everglades, 40 miles from Miami:

> Populated now by deer, alligators, wild turkeys, and a tribe of Indians who annually perform a rite known as the Green Corn Dance, the tract could someday accommodate a super jetport twice the size of Kennedy International in New York and still have a one-mile buffer on every side to minimize intrusion in the lives of any eventual residents.

A more horrible example of suggestion could hardly be found. First, note that by putting the Indians in a list with deer, alligators, and wild turkeys, the writer suggests that they belong in the same category as these subhuman species. This impression is reinforced by the allusion to the "Green Corn Dance," which (since it is irrelevant to the rest of the story) can only suggest that this kind of silly superstitious activity sums up their lives. And the impression is driven home sharply at the end when we get to the need to "minimize intrusions on the lives of any eventual residents"—the Indians, of course, can hardly be counted as real residents.
—*Thinking Straight,* 4th edition (Englewood Cliffs, N.J.: Prentice Hall, 1975)

is that . . . " or "Since we willingly admit that . . . ," implying that the testimony is of little importance when in fact it is quite damaging. Or an advertisement may say, "Try our best-quality knife, *only* $9.95," implying that the price is very low when in fact it may be just the ordinary price. Punctuation also can be used to make a point. In this headline from the *New York Times* (June 22, 1999)—"In Principle, A Case For More 'Sweatshops'"—the quotation marks around the term "sweatshops" create doubt that such things as sweatshops exist in the United States. (Alas! They do.)

Slanting creeps into objective news reports, as in this example from a *Washington Post* article (February 23, 2001) of a federal probe into whether outgoing President Clinton's commutation of the fraud sentences of four Hassidic Jewish leaders was "payback" for his wife's Senate campaign. ". . . [This] is bad news for the newly-minted senator, whose campaign also benefited from the largess of Rich's [ex]wife, Denise Rich." The quote implies that the "newly-minted senator" was elected because of Rich's "largess," and thus the president's pardon of Marc Rich was a quid pro quo. Another example: In a *San Francisco Chronicle* article (October 29, 2003) about a White House press conference on the rebuilding of Iraq, the comment "Much of Bush's black-and-white view of the war persists" implies that the president habitually ignored not only the complexity of postwar problems in Iraq but of all other issues he faced as well.

Slanting also can be accomplished by a careful selection of facts. (So slanting often invites the fallacy of *suppressed evidence,* discussed in Chapter 3.) For example, the authors of most United States history texts used in public schools select facts so as to sanitize American history as much as they can (given the general stricture against wandering too far from the straight and narrow). The point of public school history texts, after all, is not to produce disaffected citizens. (More is said on this topic in Chapter 12.)

It's no secret that political parties slant information to favor their political bias. Under the second President Bush, for example, health information on government Web sites was subtly changed to reflect the administration's ideology. On the National Cancer Institute Web site, the statement that there was "no association between abortion and breast cancer" was changed to "the evidence is inconclusive." And the Web site for the Center for Disease Control and Prevention used to explain that condoms could protect people effectively from HIV infection, but the revision claimed that "more research is needed."

Slanting sometimes goes under the name *suggestion* or, in some cases, the more pejorative name *innuendo.* The latter term might well be applied to the politician who responded to a statement by then Vice President Dan Quayle, "Well, I admit he wasn't lying *this time.*" The nice thing about slanting, so far as practitioners of the art are concerned, is that you can always deny that you implied or suggested what you in fact have implied or suggested.

Weasel Words

Weasel words (or phrases) are locutions that appear to make little or no change in the content of a statement while in fact sucking out all or most of its content.[2] Typical is the

---

[2] Weasels often suck out the content of eggs without breaking their shells. The expression, by the way, was first used by Theodore Roosevelt.

use of the terms *may* or *may be,* as in this example from a student paper: "Economic success *may be* the explanation of male dominance over females" (italics added). Using the expression *may be* instead of the straightforward verb *is* protected the student from error by reducing the content of her statement close to zero. What she said is consistent with the economic success of males *not* being the reason for male dominance. By the way, note the assumption that males do dominate females in the last analysis, a contention some males (and females!) would deny.

The term *arguably* is another weasel word frequently employed to spruce up weak arguments. The student quoted here might just as well have protected herself by stating that "Economic success *arguably* is the explanation for male dominance over females."

Fine-Print Disclaimers

Another common trick is to take back unobtrusively in the (usually) unread fine print what is claimed in the most easily read part of a document. Schlock insurance policies are notorious for their use of this device. They tout wonderful coverage in large type while taking it away in the fine print. When private property is damaged by earthquakes, tornadoes, or hurricanes, for instance, people usually think they are sufficiently insured against damage from natural disasters, but they often discover to their chagrin that upfront promises of replacement cash are severely limited in the fine print of their insurance policies.

Advertisers regularly use very small asterisks to direct readers to the bottom of ads, where they find out, say, that to get the "low-low" airline fare, tickets must be purchased 21 days in advance and cover a stay over at least one Saturday and also learn that "other restrictions may apply" (note the weasel word *may,* hiding the fact that they do).

Fine-print disclaimers have become so odious that advertisers have begun to play on the fact with a bit of humor, announcing (as some Lexus auto commercials did) that their lawyers have gone into paroxysms of joy while writing the fine print that is then scrolled across the TV screen (very quickly, so it can't be read—but that's part of the humor).

A variation of the fine-print disclaimer is the sneaky stipulation buried in contracts. A blatant example of this fine-print finagling occurred in the case of a fellow named Jim Turner, who rented a car in Connecticut, but discovered when he returned it to the car rental company that he had been charged $450 because of a stipulation in the contract that "fined" the driver $150 every time the speed exceeded 79 miles per hour. His car had been tracked by satellite over seven states! Alas, poor Mr. Turner didn't read the fine print in the contract when the agent asked him to sign his initials by the X.

Another variation on the fine-print disclaimer gambit is the *reinterpretation ploy.* Having said what turns out to be unpopular, or perhaps offensive, the best strategy for a politician often is just to reinterpret the ill-advised remark. On one of the tapes released by Gennifer Flowers, Bill Clinton is heard making a remark that clearly implies he thought Mario Cuomo (then governor of New York) acted like a mafioso. When the tapes became public, an embarrassed Clinton apologized, which is the right thing to do when caught with . . . uh . . . one's pants down, but also stated that "I meant simply to imply that Governor Cuomo is a tough, worthy competitor," which was a clever, but somewhat shady, reinterpretation of his remarks.

Blending Value Claims into Factual Assertions

One way to get value judgments across to others without justifying them is to slip them in with factual statements and hope they won't be noticed. The fewer the words used to do this, the better. Here is an interesting example from a 1994 CBS radio report (italicized emphasis added) in which only one even mildly value-tinged word is used and yet the point gets across:

> *Leftist* state [of California] Senator Tom Hayden of Chicago Seven and Jane Fonda fame has announced his intention to run for governor of California.

Anyone who knows about either the Chicago Seven or Jane Fonda's reputation because of her anti–Vietnam War stance will get the suggestion that Hayden is a bad guy. Jane Fonda's name continues to crop up in election campaigns. In 2004, John Kerry's name was linked to hers in an attempt to discredit him for protesting the Vietnam War. (A digitally manipulated photo even appeared, faking his appearance next to her at an anti-war rally.)

Or how about this somewhat more straightforward newspaper snippet: "*Self-appointed* consumer advocate Ralph Nader . . ." (italics added).

Obfuscation

Dictionaries tell us that to *obfuscate* is "to be so confused or opaque as to be difficult to perceive or understand" or "to render indistinct or dim." George W. Bush wins a prize for opacity in his response to the question "Do you support affirmative action?"

> What I am against is quotas. I am against hard quotas, quotas they basically delineate based upon whatever. However they delineate, quotas, I think, vulcanize society. So I don't know how that fits into what everybody else is saying, their relative positions, but that's my position.

Since *vulcanization* is the process of treating rubbery material with chemicals, one wonders what mischief those quirky quotas will do to society—not to mention what Bush's position is on the issue.

Let's stretch the definition of *obfuscation* a bit here to cover cases in which an issue or question has been *evaded* by *wandering from the point* or by snowing one's audience with an immense amount of detail in the hope that they either won't notice or at least won't press the point. Here, for example, is conservative political pundit William Kristol, when asked what he meant by "within its proper sphere" in his remark that "Conservatives do of course favor an energetic government within its proper sphere":

> What's most striking today is when there's a problem—spouse abuse, you name it—right away someone stands up and introduces federal legislation. There is something crazy about politics of this sort. It creates a politics that is so driven by the crisis of the day or the week that it's awfully hard to have a sensible debate about anything.

There certainly is some truth in this answer, but what there isn't is an answer to the question as to what Kristol meant by "proper sphere." What constitutes the proper sphere of government is, after all, an exceedingly difficult question—one might even call it "the mother of all political questions" (thank you, Saddam Hussein). Kristol took a tiny stab at it (he implied that spousal abuse is not a concern of government) and then retreated to the safety of evasion via obfuscation by wandering from the point while appearing to answer.

In this example, it isn't clear whether Kristol was being wise—deliberately evading a hard question—or just being what political pundits often are—long-winded and overly fond of their own voices. In some cases, however, the intent to evade an issue is fairly obvious. In others cases—*academese* provides plenty of examples—we can be reasonably sure that there is no intent to obfuscate.

By the way, it needs to be said that not all wandering from the point constitutes obfuscation. We have to say this here because the many asides in this textbook ("Interestingly, . . ." and "By the way, . . . ," for example) definitely are not intended as obfuscations but merely as remarks about related or secondary matters that it is hoped the reader will find either interesting or informative.

4. LANGUAGE MANIPULATORS

People manipulate language for all sorts of reasons: to flatter, to impress, to persuade, to obfuscate, and to distort the truth—to name a few. Sometimes language manipulation is benign, but when it is done to benefit those in power, it can undermine the rights of others. Often the point of redefining language is to circumvent legal stipulations or to justify inequities—as noted below.

When the torture scandal at Abu Ghraib hit the news, officials in the Bush administration claimed it was the work of a few bad apples, but skeptics dug deeper and came up with the Justice Department's interpretation of existing laws banning torture abroad (posted on the *Washington Post* Web site, June 14, 2004). In Section 2340 of the U.S. Criminal Code, torture is defined as any act "specifically intended to inflict severe physical or mental pain or suffering . . . upon another person within his custody or physical control." The Justice Department's legalistic explanation (written in June 2002) was that "mere" pain wasn't enough. "Physical pain amounting to torture must be equivalent in intensity to the pain accompanying serious physical injury, such as organ failure, impairment of bodily function, or even death."[3] This interpretation seems to make torture legal, unless it is extreme.

As for the fate of interrogators "who might arguably cross the line drawn in Section 2340" and be charged with torture—not to worry: They could claim they acted out of "necessity" or "self-defense," pleas that "would potentially alleviate criminal liability." In other words, they could get off the hook.

Those Who Control the Definitions . . .

Calling something by just the right name is crucial when you want to bend the law in your favor, influence public opinion, or justify funny business of one kind or another. For example, employers who want to pay employees less than the legal minimum wage or escape contractual obligations to provide health and other benefits to employees need only categorize them as *subcontractors* and arrange paperwork accordingly. Minimum

---

[3] Taken from "Small Comfort," in the *Washington Post,* June 15, 2004.

wage laws in the United States apply to employees but not to subcontractors; union-brokered agreements concerning employee health insurance don't cover subcontractors.[4] Attempts at this kind of chicanery via definition occasionally have been overturned by the courts, but often they are successful. However, since the number of independent contractors has mushroomed over the past decade, lawsuits and union protests demanding job reclassification are expected to increase.

The food industry is plagued with misleading labels initiated by special interest groups who change the meaning of words used to describe food. For example, in 2003 the House and Senate passed a huge federal spending bill with the last-minute provision that meat, poultry, and dairy products could be labeled "organic" even if the animals were fed partly or entirely nonorganic feed. This rider was added to the bill on behalf of Fieldale farms, which complained about the supply of organic feed (though organic farmers say that what is really at issue is the price, not the supply—which is sufficient). So when does organic mean organic?

Closer to home, college administrators manage to cope with shrinking budgets by hiring lots of cheap labor, often referred to as *adjunct faculty* to distinguish them from "tenure-line" professors. Teachers hired as adjunct faculty earn a good deal less per course than do their tenured colleagues, receive many fewer, if any, fringe benefits, and

---

Presidential Doublespeak: Clintonese

*In a spoof of Bill Clinton's carefully phrased responses to accusations of wrongdoing, columnist Art Hoppe explains how the former president told the "absolute" truth without getting into trouble (*San Francisco Chronicle, *February 11, 1998):*

His first known use of Clintonese came during his initial presidential campaign. You remember: When asked if he had ever smoked marijuana he nobly replied, "I have never broken the laws of the United States." This was absolutely true because, as it turned out later, he had smoked marijuana in England.

He then added that even so, he didn't inhale. This means that either (1) he didn't inhale while swimming underwater or (2) he was the first person in history to smoke pot for the flavor. . . .

When first asked about Monica Lewinsky, Mr. Clinton said flatly: "There is no improper relationship." But the pundits were growing wary, and at least a half dozen pondered suspiciously: Maybe there *is* none, but maybe there *was* one. . . .

And why did the FBI find no evidence in Ms. Lewinsky's closet? The absolute truth is that Ms. Lewinsky was coming home on the bus from the cleaners. She placed her garment bag on the seat next to her, and a sailor inadvertently sat on it. This, of course, was what she meant when she told her friend, Linda Tripp, that there was a "seaman on my dress."

---

[4] While billionaire Bill Gates was becoming the richest person in the world, his Microsoft Corporation was using the subcontractor ploy to stiff over a thousand of his employees out of several perks other employees were entitled to. At one time or another, Microsoft has been embroiled in court battles over classification since 1990.

don't enjoy similar job security. This division of labor can be thought of as an academic analogue to the "downsizing" that goes on in the business world.

On a worldwide level, rich nations manage to undercut the labor force of poor ones by manipulating the language of international agreements to their advantage. Farm subsidies unfairly undercut the agricultural industry of developing countries, particularly in Africa, where most farmers are desperately poor, partly because they cannot compete with the subsidized products from the United States and European Union (EU). A world trade agreement was drawn up to prevent this situation from occurring, but the United States and the European Union managed to slide out of it by simply using different language for export subsidies. For instance, instead of violating the agreement with "trade-distorting" subsidies by paying farmers according to the amount they produce, the European Union gives them direct grants that have almost the same effect on the price of these crops as before but are now called "non-distorting" because grants are determined by the amount of land a farmer owns and how much the land produced in the past.[5] Thus the EU is able to undercut the labor force of developing countries without breaking the trade agreement.

Although the United States Constitution grants Congress the sole right to declare war, this has rarely deterred American presidents from waging war without obtaining any such declaration. As we noted earlier in the chapter, they have simply renamed their escapades or declared them not to be wars. Assuming the December 1990 congressional measure allowing President Bush (the elder) to carry out United Nations resolutions did indeed constitute a declaration of war, even though it didn't actually say we were declaring war, then the Gulf conflict is very likely the only legal war out of at least five fought by the United States since World War II.

In 2002 Congress gave President Bush (the younger) authorization to use the Armed Forces as he considered necessary to defend our country's national security against the threat of Iraq and to enforce the United Nations Security Council resolutions with regard to Iraq. Thus Congress gave Bush the authority to wage war on Iraq but managed to avoid a congressional declaration of war. This equivocation enabled Congress to pass the buck and avoid criticism if the war went badly.[6]

In the war in Afghanistan, the Bush administration classified as "enemy combatants" hundreds of suspected Al Qaeda and Taliban fighters detained by the United States at Guantanamo Bay Naval Base. Had they been called "prisoners of war," they would have been entitled to release when the war was over, but as "enemy combatants," not only could they be detained indefinitely for questioning without charge, they couldn't challenge their imprisonment in court, nor were they entitled to any other constitutional rights.

On a less vital note, here is a provocative job reclassification:

> When the Swiss government determined that women who sold sexual favors practiced a *therapeutic trade,* they were exempt from taxes. Now known as prostitutes, the same women must pay a 65% value-added tax.[7]

---

[5] For more on this see the (London) *Guardian,* June 3, 2003.
[6] See "Is the War on Iraq Lawful?" by Michael C. Dorf, March 19, 2003. writ.findlaw.com/dorf.
[7] Taken from the October 1995 *Quarterly Review of Doublespeak,* which credited the January 1995 *Playboy.* (Well, that figures. Note that because the authors of this text wouldn't stoop so low as actually to read stuff like *Playboy,* they had to get this item secondhand. Let's be clear on this.)

© 1996 Don Wright, Inc.

Not all attempts at victory via definition are successful. In the Microsoft antitrust case, the Justice Department wasn't persuaded by Microsoft's claim that its Internet Explorer was an integral part of its Windows operating system, "not an add-on, like a flash on a camera or a car radio," but an integral part of Windows, like "a shutter on a camera or a car's transmission." The point was crucial to whether bundling Internet Explorer into Windows was a violation of antitrust laws and thus unfair to competition, chiefly Netscape and its Internet browser. But the analogies didn't convince the Justice Department. (By the way, why shouldn't it have?)

Of course, Americans did not invent the practice of victory through definition. It has been employed frequently elsewhere and throughout history. Back in the 1970s, for example, in Muslim Saudi Arabia, where the commandment not to make graven images is taken very seriously, photography, therefore, was forbidden. But aerial photography was such a boon to oil exploration that something had to be done. The result:

> King Ibn Saud convened the Ulema [a group of Muslim theologians who have great power over public morals] and eventually prevailed over them with the argument that photography was actually good because it was not an image, but a combination of light and shadow that depicted Allah's creations without violating them.[8]

The obvious reasons this sort of chicanery is so frequently gotten away with are self-interest and lack of careful attention. But a less obvious reason is that it isn't always easy to determine whether there is indeed some sort of sleight of hand going on. For years, the psychologist Thomas Szasz has been campaigning against the use of the expression

---

[8] Peter A. Iseman, "The Arabian Ethos," *Harper's* (February 1978).

> *Conservative, n.* A statesman who is enamored of existing evils, as distinguished from the Liberal, who wishes to replace them with others.
>
> —Ambrose Bierce (*The Devil's Dictionary*)

mental illness, on grounds that there is no such thing as *mental* illness. Declaring John Hinkley "not guilty by reason of insanity" after his attempt to assassinate President Reagan was for Szasz just an extreme example of what happens when we take the analogy between physical illness and alleged mental illness seriously. (He does believe, however, that sometimes what is thought of as mental illness really is physical dysfunction.)

But Szasz is in the minority on this point, with the result, he claims, that various kinds of serious abuses of civil rights occur. One is that close relatives of the "mentally ill" often are able to have them "hospitalized for treatment" against their will. Forcing people into institutions in this way is a practice some see as not unlike the one that used to be common in the Soviet Union of confining political opponents in "mental institutions." In a similar vein, Szasz argues, "we call self-starvation either *anorexia nervosa,* a *hunger strike,* a *suicide attempt,* or some other name, depending on how we want to respond."

Well, then, is Szasz right about this? A number of psychologists find his position modestly persuasive, while the majority do not. The reason for this split of opinion is that good arguments can be made on both sides of the issue, making it difficult to choose one over the other. Which choice we should make may well depend, as Szasz notes, on how we wish to deal with whatever circumstances our decisions affect. (Philosophy students might note the connection of this sort of case to the age-old conundrum about whether, when every part of an old ship has been replaced over the years by a new part, it is still the same ship; the answer, at least half of this writing team believes, is that it depends on who we wish to have title to ships repaired in this way, not on any truth written in the sky.)

This does not mean clear-cut cases are not clear-cut. We did blockade Iraq before starting the Gulf War, thus engaging in warlike actions against that country without a congressional declaration. Calling our action an "interdiction" cannot change that fact. But it does mean that there are no easy or definite answers in every case.

5. LANGUAGE REVISION

Languages aren't artificial products constructed by "linguistic experts" in some laboratory or "think tank." They are living, changing products of human intelligence designed to perform various functions, including not just communicating ideas from one person to another but also issuing commands, asking questions, and certifying relationships and bargains (as in wedding ceremonies). This being the case, languages tend to mirror the foibles, aspirations, loyalties, and (alas!) prejudices of those who speak them. English is no exception. Like all languages, English undergoes revision on a regular basis.

The Reform of Sexist Language

In the past 20 or 30 years, a minor revolution has taken place in the United States, as well as many other countries, in the attitudes of most people toward members of minority groups and women. Inevitably, this revolution has been mirrored in the linguistic practices of those caught up in it. The pejorative terms mentioned at the beginning of this chapter are not often heard in polite circles these days, and expressions like "free, white, and 21," common until about 40 years ago, are now as outdated as "23 skidoo."

But the most extensive linguistic changes of this kind have been those reflecting the changing attitudes of most people concerning relationships between men and women and the roles played by women in society. A large majority of previously common sexist locutions have disappeared from everyday speech. This linguistic change has occurred very quickly, as these things go, no doubt in part because of the persistent demands of women's rights advocates. But it also has happened quickly because of the swiftness with which attitudes toward women and their roles in society have changed and because of the speed with which women have entered fields previously reserved primarily for men.

Not so long ago, when the overwhelming majority of those in high offices were men, it may have made some sense to refer to these people as business*men* and congress*men*. But in this day and age, with increasing numbers of women taking on these roles, it makes much less sense. In addition, there is a general realization that these sexist terms imply not just that those holding these offices always are male but also, and wrongly, that only males are supposed to, or are competent to, fill them. The old sexist language implies in subtle but persuasive ways that positions of power should be *manned,* not *personed* or *womaned,* and this in turn implies that only men are capable of holding these important positions. Thus, substituting nonsexist words for the old sexist terms puts women on an equal linguistic footing with men that not only reflects their growing equality but also helps make it possible. Our thoughts about the world—how it works and how it should work—always are framed in language; sexist locutions tend to introduce sexist thoughts into our minds.

So today, people who head committees or departments are generally called *chairs,* not *chairmen* ("I would like to address the chair about . . . " or "The chair has ruled that . . . "). Similarly, people who deliver the mail tend to get called *letter carriers,* not *mailmen.* We say *firefighter* instead of *fireman* and *police officer* rather than *policeman.* The term *man* and its many derivatives now often are replaced by *people, person,* and the like. Publishers don't cotton to manuscripts that contain locutions like "Of course, a *man* might be described as taking a . . . " when it would be more accurate to say "*Someone* might be described as taking a . . . " or to phrases like "even if *he* is willing to allow . . . ," when what is meant is *he or she.*[9]

One of the more interesting language changes accompanying the feminist revolution has been the widespread use of the term *Ms.,* intended to serve when the marriage status of a woman is not considered relevant. The point of this change was to foster equal treatment of the sexes. Men, whether married or single, have always been referred to by the same term, *Mr.,* whereas women have had to be called either *Miss* or *Mrs.,* depending on their marital status. In magazine and newspaper articles the trend is to drop the title entirely and simply refer to women by their last names—the way men always have been. A similar, and perhaps much more significant change, is the fact that women nowadays don't always take on the last name of their mates, although, interestingly, they still usually do (while men rarely do). But even when women do adopt their husbands'

---

[9] Both of these examples are taken, alas, from a journal article coauthored back in the bad old days by the male coauthor of this text.

last names, they often also hang onto their own, so that, for example, ex-President Clinton's wife is referred to as Hillary *Rodham* Clinton, not just Hillary Clinton.

But an even more important language change may be the elimination of locutions like this one, once typical of the language encountered in all sorts of places, including public school history textbooks: "Pioneers moved west, taking their wives and children with them." That made all of the pioneers into men, while women and children were just accessories. A text written today would get it right and say something like "Pioneer families moved west."

On the other hand, things can get carried too far. It would be unnecessary, wouldn't it, for Germans to stop referring to their homeland as the *Fatherland,* or Englishmen — that is, citizens of England — to their *mother tongue*? What purpose would be served by replacing *Uncle Sam* with *Aunt Sarah*? And why worry about using the term *manhole* when talking about those round excisions in streets and avenues, as did the Public Works Departments of several American cities? (Would it be wrong to change biblical references to God from the *He* employed in the original versions to some more neutral term?) The term *humankind* seems an apt substitute for *mankind,* but somehow the "era of ordinary people" doesn't have the same ring as the "century of the common man."

In any case, the changes in linguistic style brought on by the feminist revolution have also raised questions of aesthetic taste — of what sounds right or wrong rolling off the

---

The Los Angeles Times, *one of America's best newspapers, now has a guideline concerning "Ethnic, Racial, Sexual and Other Identification" that prohibits the use, among others, of the following words when describing individuals:*

Co-ed, deaf, deaf-mute, biddy, bra-burner, crazy, divorcee, gal, ghetto, gypped, handicapped person, hillbilly, Hispanic, holy rollers, Indians, inner city, lame, male nurse, normal, pow-wow, queer, WASP, welsher.

Commenting on the Times' *guidelines, syndicated columnist Robert Novak had this to say:*

The *Times* forbids reporters to write about a "Dutch treat" because this phrase is allegedly insulting to the Dutch. Nor can one report that a person "welshed on a bet" because that would be insulting to the Welsh. . . . I asked one of the *Los Angeles Times* editors, "How do you refer to Indian summer? Is it now Native American summer?" He replied that he would substitute "unseasonably warm weather late in the year." This is what political correctness can do to language; it destroys meaning. It also demeans the ethnic groups it supposedly protects. Do we really think that these groups are so unintelligent as to be unable to distinguish between conventional idioms and genuine prejudice? Is their identity so fragile that it must depend on censorship?

Well, then, is Novak right about his thoughts concerning what he sees as overzealous PC?

tongue or when reading a book. The expression *her or his,* to take one example, rings false, perhaps because it calls attention to the avoidance of *his* (used to mean *his* or *her*) or of *his or her,* and thus detracts from what is being said. Good taste sometimes dictates other sorts of moves, for instance, employing plural rather than singular pronouns, thus saying things like, "when students read their textbooks . . ." rather than "when a student reads his textbook . . . ." (That's one reason for the plethora of plural expressions that occur in this textbook. Note, by the way, that the term *congressperson* nowhere appears on these pages, although *member of Congress* is used quite often.)

Interestingly, no one seems overwrought by the fact that Liberty always is portrayed as a woman. (Think, for instance, of the Statue of Liberty in New York harbor.) Note also that, although there are lots of complaints about sexist terms like *waitress* and *actress,* no one seems bothered by the equally sexist term *widower.* Women still receive an award each year for best *actress.* And freshmen still are called *freshmen.* Ah, well.

PC (Politically Correct) Terminology

The revolution concerning gender rhetoric is part of a larger movement that also has dramatically changed the ways in which we speak of minorities. As attitudes have changed, language, inevitably, has followed suit.

Robert Hughes, an Australian who lived in Europe before settling in the United States, is an iconoclastic commentator of the American scene. He has this to say about what he perceives to be an excess of PC in this country:

. . . There are certainly worse things in American society than the ongoing vogue for politically correct language, whether of the left or the right. But there are few things more absurd and, in the end, self-defeating.

We want to create a sort of linguistic Lourdes, where evil and misfortune are dispelled by a dip in the waters of euphemism. Does the cripple rise from his wheelchair, or feel better about being stuck in it, because someone in the days of the Carter administration decided that, for official purposes, he was "physically challenged"?

. . . The notion that you change a situation by finding a newer and nicer word for it emerges from the old American habit of euphemism, circumlocution, and desperate confusion about etiquette, produced by fear that the concrete will give offense. And it is a particularly American habit. The call for politically correct language . . . has virtually no resonance in Europe. In France, nobody has thought of renaming the Frankish King Pepin le Bref, Pepin le Verticalement Defie. . . .

. . . When the waters of PC recede—as they presently will, leaving the predictable scum of dead words on the social beach—it will be, in part, because young people get turned off by all the carping of verbal proprieties on campus. The radical impulses of youth are generous, romantic, and instinctive, and are easily chilled by the atmosphere of prim, obsessive correction.

—Robert Hughes, *Culture of Complaint* (New York: Oxford University Press, 1993), 18–24.

The result is that certain locutions have become "in," while others are "out." Some
are *politically correct,* some politically incorrect. Careers have been wrecked by publicly using expressions like "fat Jap" and "Nigra." It would be political suicide today to
say publicly, as someone did in the 1970s, when then Governor Tribbitt (Delaware) hired
a woman as his press secretary at $20,000 a year, "If he wants to pay $10,000 a mam-
mary, that's his business." We aren't supposed to use phrases like *admitted homosexual*
(because it implies that being a homosexual is bad) or *tidal wave of immigrants* (because
of its negative implication concerning immigrants).

On the whole, of course, changes of this nature are all to the good and are applauded
by just about everybody. But problems do arise, and it is quite possible that an excess of
zeal causes some of them. One of the authors of this textbook, for example, received letters from students and teachers accusing him of race prejudice, or at least insensitivity,
for having used the term *black* in the sixth edition of this textbook, on the grounds that
the politically correct, nondenigrating, term for the minority in question is *African
American.*[10] But when the sixth edition was published, the politically correct term happened to be *black,* which earlier had replaced the term *Negro* (which, of course, happens
to mean black in several romance languages).

Anyway, the academic world is particularly fertile ground for PC talk. For example,
the University of Cincinnati Student Senate has declared their higher institution of
learning "a Columbus-myth-free campus." (The allusion, in case you missed it, is to
the fact that Columbus could not possibly have "discovered" America—Native Americans having been here for at least 10,000 years before Columbus was born.) At Stanford
University students can be punished for violating speech codes designed to suppress
racist, sexist, and homophobic speech that carries no legal penalty in the "real" world.
An administrator at the University of California, Santa Cruz, was even wary of phrases
like a "nip in the air" and "a chink in one's armor" because certain of these words could
be construed as racial slurs in other contexts.

Sometimes the attempt to be PC defies all logic. The reading passages of the New
York State Regents English exam were edited to delete anything that might make "any

---

[10] Whether this is or isn't the PC term, many members of the group—for example, African American politicians on television and students in many college classes—often refer to themselves as
black. (Interestingly, both of these terms conceal the fact that most of the people so labeled also
are genetically part Caucasian—indeed, often primarily Caucasian—or part Asian. The point is
that both of these labels are social/political, not scientific, referring to class, not race.)

student feel ill at ease when taking the test." For example, all references to Judaism were cut from an excerpt from a work by Isaac Bashevis Singer about Jewish life in Europe! In one revision, for instance, "most Jewish women" was changed to "most women." For this PC passage, the New York State Regents were given the NCTE Doublespeak award for 2002.

Are we getting a bit overzealous in our, shall we say, *linguistic cleansing*? It no doubt is a good idea, now that the children of unwed parents are not looked down upon, to refer to them as *nonmarital children* rather than *bastards,* thus getting rid of the unfair opprobrium of that nasty term. And why not change the name of the Italian Welfare Agency to the *Italian-American Community Service Agency*?

But is there anything wrong with calling "mixed-breed" dogs *mongrels,* "visually impaired" people *blind,* or the "psychologically impacted" *insane*? Don't those who call the *Sports Illustrated* swimsuit issue *pornographic* rob that word of its legitimate meaning? (Is there a risk here that the door will be opened to wrongheaded legislation?) Was Newt Gingrich just being polite when he said President Clinton was "factually challenged" instead of calling him a liar? (Was he just trying to be cute, snide, or clever?) Anyway, was the First Amendment bruised when the University of Michigan punished students for having uttered "hate speech" when they aired their belief that homosexuality is a disease in classroom discussions? And didn't certain Native Americans make some kind of mistake when they demonstrated during the 1995 World Series against the "demeaning symbols" used by the beloved Cleveland Indians and the Atlanta Braves?

SUMMARY OF CHAPTER 7

1. Most words have emotive meanings (in addition to cognitive meanings). Words like *oppression, kike,* and *bitch* have more or less negative (con) emotive overtones; words like *spring, free,* and *satisfaction* have positive (pro) emotive overtones; and words like *socialism, marijuana,* and *God* have mixed overtones.

2. Con artists use the emotive side of language (1) to mask cognitive meaning by whipping up emotions so that reason is overlooked and (2) to dull the force of language so as to make acceptable what otherwise might not be. The latter purpose often is accomplished by means of *euphemisms* (less offensive or duller expressions used in place of more offensive or emotively charged locutions).

3. Common rhetorical devices often are used in a slippery manner. *Examples: Slanting* words and expressions ("All this proves is that . . ."); *weasel words* that suck out all or part of the meaning of a sentence ("Economic success may be . . ."); *fine-print disclaimers* that take back part of what was originally asserted ("Tickets must be purchased 30 days in advance, subject to availability . . ."); *obfuscation* that, for example, may mask failure to respond to questions (William Kristol wandering from the point of the question about what he meant by "proper sphere" of government). Other devices include making unsupported value judgments that are inserted into primarily factual assertions ("*Self-appointed* consumer advocate Ralph Nader . . ."). Note that employing the right tone can be used to mask lack of cogent reasoning or content or to sway audiences via emotional appeals.

4. The meanings of words and expressions sometimes are changed so as either to get around or to take advantage of laws, rules, or customs. *Example:* Calling an employee a *subcontractor* to avoid paying a minimum wage or Social Security taxes. But it isn't always easy to determine whether terms have been used rightly or wrongly. *Example:* Psychologists disagree about whether it makes good sense to use the expression *mental illness,* because they disagree about whether the implied analogy to physical illness is useful or accurate.

5. The recent social revolution that changed the roles played by women in society, as well as the attitudes of most Americans concerning male-female relationships, has resulted in matching linguistic changes. *Examples:* Replacing expressions in which the term *man* is used to refer to people in general by more neutral words such as *person;* using *Ms.* in some cases instead of *Miss* or *Mrs.;* not repeatedly using *his* to mean *his* or *her;* or switching to the plural form to avoid this use of *his.* (Note that when use of dechauvinized language may ring a bit false—*her or his* can sound somewhat forced—there always are aesthetically acceptable ways to avoid sexist locutions.) But do we go a bit too far when we start talking, say, about *personhole* covers?

6. The linguistic revolution that has replaced sexist language with locutions that are more congenial with today's attitudes and beliefs also has changed many of the ways in which we refer to members of minorities and other groups, as well as to activities in several important areas of life. Using current lingo, we can say that some ways of speaking are *politically correct* (PC), others not. *Examples:* The terms *Native American, physically challenged,* and *Latino* are "in"; *Indian, crippled* (or *handicapped*), and *Hispanic* (used to refer, say, to Mexican Americans) are "out." In some cases, the PC revolution may have gone a bit too far. *Examples:* Referring to women as *people of gender;* objecting to the use of Indian symbols by baseball teams.

EXERCISE 7-1

1. Louisiana license plates feature the motto "Sportsman's Paradise." Is this sexist? Defend your answer.

2. Over the past decade, the term *illegal alien* has been euphemized as "undocumented worker" or even "guest without status." What is the point of these euphemisms and who would be most likely to use them?

*3. Translate the following statement, found on the back of a Hallmark greeting card, into everyday lingo:

Printed on recycled paper. Contains a minimum of 10% post-consumer and 40% pre-consumer material.

Aside from the euphemistic use of language in this statement, is there something a bit sneaky going on here?

4. Here is a passage from a thankfully out-of-print edition of the United States history textbook *America: Its People and Values:*

A friendly Indian named Squanto helped the colonists. He showed them how to plant corn and how to live in the wilderness. A soldier, Captain Miles Standish, taught the Pilgrims how to defend themselves against unfriendly Indians.

How is language used to slant this account? In what other ways is it slanted? Rewrite the passage from the point of view of the "unfriendly Indians" (that is, Native Americans) in question.

5. Explain in plain English Annette Koloday's "reconceptualization" of the term *family* in this quote from her book *Failing the Future: A Dean Looks at Higher Education in the Twenty-First Century.* (This passage was nominated for the Doublespeak Award, *Quarterly Review of Doublespeak,* January 2002.)

To conceptualize what I am calling the "family-friendly campus" means reconceptualizing what we include in the term family. The family in the twenty-first century will no longer be identified by blood ties, by legalized affiliations, by cohabitation, or by heterosexual arrangements.

How, then, would you define *family?*

*6. Translate into plain English the following remark by Admiral Isaac C. Kidd when he was chief of Navy matériel:

We have gone with teams of competent contract people from Washington to outlying field activities to look over their books with them . . . to see in what areas there is susceptibility to improved capability to commit funds.

7. During the 2000 presidential campaign and thereafter, Republicans high up in government started referring to the federal tax hitherto known as the *inheritance tax* as the *death tax.*
   a. Does *death tax* more accurately describe the tax in question than *inheritance tax?*
   b. Why do you suppose Republican big wigs continually use the locution *death tax* intead of the older, traditional name of this tax?

8. An animal rights organization wants to replace the term *pet owner* in San Francisco laws with the expression *pet guardian* because the term *owner* implies that animals are property. Defend or challenge their view on this.

9. Several groups opposed to legal abortions, as well as a few state legislatures in recently enacted laws, refer to a fetus as an *intact child,* a *partially born infant,* or an *unborn child* (see, for example, the March–April 2000 edition of *Extra!*).
   a. What is the point of their use of these locutions instead of the medical term *fetus?*
   b. To which sections or topics of this chapter is this example relevant?

EXERCISE 7-2

1. Find at least one good example of an inappropriate name (for example, *subcontractor*) that is applied so that the law, a custom, or whatever deals with them differently, and explain the chicanery. (No, you aren't supposed to "find" the example in this textbook.)

2. Check your local newspaper, magazines, television programs, the Internet, or some such; find at least two examples of doublespeak or jargon, and translate them back into plain English.

3. Do the same with a particularly obtuse use (as opposed to a "mention") of academese from one of your textbooks (*definitely* not from this one!).

4. Do the same with respect to sexist locutions, but this time translate into PC language.

EXERCISE 7-3

1. Reread Robert Hughes's criticism of politically correct language. Do you agree or disagree with him that Americans have gone overboard in their use of PC? Defend you answer and give examples.

*2. Each chapter in this text starts out with a few (hopefully) apt quotes. But doesn't one of the quotes that starts this language chapter use one of the devices railed against in this chapter? Which one might this be? If it doesn't, why doesn't it? If it does, wasn't it a mistake to use this quotation? Explain. (By the way, does a different one of these quotes commit the fallacy *slippery slope*?)

3. Previous editions of this text have been criticized by some for implying that in some cases the recent linguistic revolution has gone a bit overboard. This edition contains the question "Why worry about using the term *manhole* when talking about those round excisions in streets and avenues, as did the Public Works Departments of several American cities?" Should we worry? Why, or why not?

4. Do you think universities should develop speech codes designed to suppress racist, sexist, and homophobic speech on campus? Write an argument for or against this policy.

5. The writer of a letter to the editor of the *New Republic* (November 8, 1993) disagreed with the insistence of Native Americans that they be called *Native Americans* and not *American Indians,* stating that it is an "affront" to "the millions of native Americans of European, African and Asian descent." Is this writer on target? Defend your answer.

6. Explain what you think (and why, of course) of the following explanation (in Robert J. Ringer's irreverent—and fascinating—book *Looking Out for Number One*) of President Kennedy's famous remark in his inauguration address "And so, my fellow Americans, ask not what your country can do for you; ask what you can do for your country":

Ask what you can do for your country? Does this mean asking each of the more than 200 million individuals what you can do for him? No, individuals are not what Kennedy or any other politician has ever had in mind when using the word *country*. A country is an abstract entity, but in politicalese, it translates into "those in power." Restated in translated form, then, it becomes: "Ask not what those in power can do for you; ask what you can do for those in power."

EXERCISE 7-4

1. One good way to figure out the tone of a passage is to underline and then categorize its emotively charged words. In the Churchill excerpt cited earlier, for example, he uses several charged words suggesting combat: *fight* is employed (several times); as are *defend, struggle, armed,* and *guarded.* He also favors phrases of cautious optimism: *growing confidence, growing strength, never surrender,* and *liberation.* The determination to carry on until victory is emphasized also by the effective use of parallel construction (a device used by virtually all great speech writers): "We shall not flag. . . . We shall go on. . . . We shall fight. . . . We shall defend. . . . We shall never surrender. . . ."

    Churchill's tone was forceful and expressed confidence and determination, thus furthering his aim, which was to buck up flagging confidence during one of the darkest moments in British history. Get a copy of Abraham Lincoln's Gettysburg Address and explain the tone of this famous speech and what sorts of linguistic devices were used to convey that tone.

2. Do the same with respect to the following excerpts from President Kennedy's famous 1961 inaugural address:

    Let every nation know, whether it wishes us well or ill, that we shall pay any price, bear any burden, meet any hardship, support any friend, oppose any foe to assure the survival and the success of liberty.

    This much we pledge—and more. . . .

    So let us begin anew—remembering on both sides that civility is not a sign of weakness, and sincerity is always subject to proof. Let us never negotiate out of fear. But let us never fear to negotiate. . . .

    In the long history of the world, only a few generations have been granted the role of defending freedom in its hour of maximum danger. I do not shrink from this responsibility—I welcome it. I do not believe that any of us would exchange places with any other people or any other generation. The energy, the faith, the devotion which we bring to this endeavor will light our country and all who serve it—and the glow from that fire can truly light the world.

    And so, my fellow Americans, ask not what your country can do for you; ask what you can do for your country.

    My fellow citizens of the world, ask not what Americans will do for you, but what together we can do for the freedom of man.

    (Do politicians these days even occasionally inspire us with political rhetoric of this caliber?)

Chapter

8

EVALUATING EXTENDED ARGUMENTS

Our principal topic in this chapter is the evaluation of extended passages, or **essays,** that argue to a conclusion. Up to this point, we've considered mainly short arguments, and these primarily to illustrate fallacious reasoning or manipulative uses of language. But in daily life, we frequently encounter longer passages, generally containing several related arguments, offered in support of a **thesis**—the overall conclusion of the passage.

We should recall, however, that there are other kinds of persuasive essays in addition to the argumentative variety. Even simple **description** or **narration** often is used for this purpose. For example, in his essay "A Hanging," George Orwell argues with some force against capital punishment simply by graphically describing a hanging and one person's gut-wrenching response to it. (The ongoing abortion debate is studded with detailed descriptions of aborted fetuses.) And just explaining something may effectively persuade others to our point of view. An article on chlorofluorocarbons, for instance, may simply describe how these chemicals deplete the ozone layer, thus increasing our chances of getting skin cancer, and yet convince readers of the implied conclusion that the use of Freon in refrigerators and other modern equipment should be stopped.

But our main concern in this chapter will be rhetoric in which there is an attempt to present reasons for conclusions. We need to remember, however, that a conclusion can be argued for in various ways. We may, for example, weigh the merits and demerits of a possible course of action, instead of just presenting favorable reasons. A **pro and con argument** of this kind can be very effective because it tends to answer questions or objections the reader or listener may have about the thesis being argued for. This also is why essays often provide a **refutation to counterarguments,** as in the case of politicians who, after arguing for their position, may then go on to say, "Now my opponent will no doubt respond _____; but I say _____," and then attempt to refute their opponent's objections. An essay may also argue for a course of action by showing that likely alternatives are less desirable, which means arguing by a **comparison of alternatives.**

Note, by the way, that a legitimate appeal to experts in a field may count as a reason for accepting their conclusions, even in the absence of an account of their reasoning processes. During World War II, for example, President Roosevelt accepted the conclusion of physicists Leo Szilard and Albert Einstein (conveyed to the president in a famous letter) that it was possible to build an atomic bomb, even though Roosevelt, like every other lay person, would have been unable to comprehend the reasoning behind their conclusion (which, no doubt, is why the two scientists didn't bother to provide it).

Finally, note that essay writers frequently employ more than one of the methods just mentioned. They first may argue, for instance, by a general comparison of alternatives and then, finding the alternative that seems to be the most attractive, zero in on it for a more careful analysis. Or they may provide reasons that support the essay's thesis and are in turn supported by expert opinion.

1. The Basic Tasks of Essay Evaluation

There are almost as many ways to evaluate extended passages as there are evaluators. What works best for one person may not work so well for others. And time and interest always need to be taken into account. Even so, there are guidelines that most people find of value, in particular, those who initially have a bit of trouble handling lengthy or complicated passages. (Most of the discussion that follows will deal with written passages, but applies also to those that are verbal.)

The next few sections of this chapter describe a method for evaluating essays when the topic being dealt with is of great importance and we have the time necessary to do a thorough job. In daily life, of course, these two conditions are not often met. But getting good at a method like the one described here is a good way to become adept at the quicker kinds of evaluations that we do frequently have to make in everyday life.

Find the Thesis and Keep It in Mind

The most important thing, obviously, is to *locate the thesis*—the main conclusion of the argument. The thesis isn't always obvious because the passage may be poorly written, or because the thesis may be implied but not explicitly stated, or simply because the author may build up to it and reveal it only near the end of the work. The thesis is the point of an essay, so you have to keep it in mind to determine whether sufficient **reasons** are provided for accepting it. In many sports, the trick is to keep your eye on the ball; in evaluating extended passages, the trick is to keep your mind's eye on the thesis, so that you can better judge whether the reasons do, or don't, adequately support it.

Find the Reasons That Support the Thesis

Obviously, then, the next task after locating the thesis is to *find the reasons*—the *premises*—that are provided in support of the thesis. Again, this will be hard or easy depending on the author's style and competence. But it may also be hard because the reasons themselves are supported by reasons, so that the sheer complexity of an extended passage makes analysis difficult.

Typically, however, it isn't all that hard to see what the thesis of an essay is and to discover the principal reasons offered in its support. For example, a newspaper columnist arguing for the thesis that cigarettes should be made illegal supported his conclusion by pointing out that cigarette smoking kills millions of people; then supported that claim by presenting statistics concerning smoking and heart disease, cancer, and emphysema; and then claimed that anything so bad for us should be illegal. The logical structure of his essay thus was something like this:

> *Thesis:* Cigarettes should be made illegal.
> *Reasons:* 1. Cigarette smoking is deadly.
>   2. Anything so deadly should be illegal.
> *Support for 1:* Statistical proof linking smoking cigarettes with heart disease, cancer, and emphysema.

The columnist assumed (wrongly) that most people would accept his second reason without further justification.

Identify the Evidence

Effective extended arguments usually provide evidence, or support, for the reasons they present. That is, they provide reasons for believing their reasons. In the cigarette example, statistical evidence was cited in support of the claim that cigarette smoking is deadly. But many other sorts of evidence may be appealed to, including authoritative pronouncements, examples, personal experiences, generally accepted facts or common knowledge, and so on. In the Szilard/Einstein letter mentioned before, the evidence for the conclusion that an atomic bomb could be built was just the authority of the letter's authors. Someone might defend the claim that cigarette smoking is deadly simply by appealing to what by now is common knowledge—that it causes lung cancer, heart disease, and so on. A powerful argument against war might well contain specific examples of wars—for example, World War I—that produced incredible misery with little else to show for them.

In a sense, of course, all reasons or premises offered in support of a thesis constitute evidence in its favor. The important point here is that reasons themselves often need, and receive, supporting evidence. Indeed, good essay writers always support reasons in this way except when confident that readers will accept them without further argument.

Identify Responses to Likely Objections or Counterarguments

The sample essay concerning cigarette smoking did not discuss likely objections or counterarguments, but essays often do. The cigarette essay, for instance, might have raised and argued against the objection that we have a right to risk shortening our lives

by smoking, or taking other sorts of risks, if we want to. If this objection had been included in the essay, then it would have been important to note and take account of it.

Skip Whatever Doesn't Argue for (or against) the Thesis

People write essays to persuade other people. So they sometimes include irrelevant material if they think it will help them to persuade others. This kind of "flavoring" material
makes reading more fun, but it shouldn't influence the assessment of an argument.

Add Relevant Information or Reasons

Everything needed to prove a thesis is *never* included in an essay, no matter how long it
may be. There is no point in trying to prove things that are obvious or generally accepted. Good writers try to provide just the information their audiences will need in
order to see the merit of the writer's point of view. For instance, someone writing about
education for an audience of teachers doesn't need to prove that plenty of students graduate from high school today without having developed sufficient ability in reading, writing, and basic arithmetic. Every teacher knows that.

Of course, writers, being human, often fail to do the best job of supporting their
theses. They often overlook important evidence, or they reason incorrectly to a conclusion that can be supported by better logic. Good critical thinkers try to evaluate the best
version of an argument, adding material that its author may have neglected. By the same
token, of course, good reasoners also bring to bear whatever negative evidence or reasons they may know about.

Consider Tone and Emotive Language

Although tone and emotive language are not part of the formal elements of argument,
they are subtle manipulators that deserve attention, particularly when considering a
strongly emotive topic or one that uses irony or humor to persuade. When Adlai Stevenson argued against a state senate bill to restrain cats (quoted in Chapter 7), his droll exaggeration of the consequences was part of the persuasive power. The idea that the senate might be "called upon to take sides in the age-old problem of dog versus cat, cat
versus bird, or even bird versus worm" made the bill seem just plain silly and thus not
worth passing.

One way to identify these hidden persuaders is to underline or circle the emotive
words or humorous phrases and then see how they nudge the reader into agreeing with
the writer's thesis. Becoming aware of these expressions helps us guard against their un-
due influence.

Come to an Evaluation

While evaluation is logically the last thing we need to do when dealing with an argumentative passage, good critical thinkers start evaluating from the word go. They keep
in mind questions such as, Do I already accept this thesis? Does it fit well with what
I already know and believe? If not, in what way is the argument fallacious and why?
What sort of reasons or evidence might change my mind? And they continue to evalu-

ate as they go along, bearing in mind questions such as, Is this reason acceptable without further justification? Does that reason really defend the thesis at hand? Do the facts alleged seem plausible, given my background beliefs? Has the writer forgotten a serious counterargument or omitted important counterevidence? Is the use of tone and emotive language unduly persuasive? It's true that a completely confident judgment about a work can't be reached until an essay has been thoroughly examined, but it still is useful to make provisional evaluations right from the start.

Successfully bringing relevant background information to bear clearly is the key to good evaluations, but other relevant thoughts often play an important role. We often simply don't know enough to come to a confident evaluation but still may be able to speculate intelligently by thinking about the right questions that need to be raised either for or against a particular thesis. For example, one of the important reasons often given in favor of laws requiring capital punishment for heinous crimes is that these laws will act as a deterrent—criminals may think more carefully before committing murder if they know conviction means death. This sounds like a very plausible reason given the strength of the urge most of us have to stay alive. But does it in fact work this way? Not knowing the answer may be a good reason for withholding judgment, or for seeking further information, or for at least only *provisionally* assuming that the threat of death deters criminals more than do lesser penalties. The point here is that coming to a justified evaluation requires us to think of what it would be useful to know that we don't as yet know —it requires us to raise the right sorts of questions. (Raising questions of this kind, of course, also serves as a guide to research that might have to be undertaken.)

When the entire structure of an extended argument has been figured out, its relevant passages will divide into those that are argued for within the essay and those that are not. The latter are the writer's basic *assumptions—starting points*—assumed without being justified. When evaluating an extended passage, you need to ask and answer three vital questions, corresponding to the three basic requirements of cogent reasoning (discussed in Chapter 1):

1. Are the writer's assumptions and stated reasons justified by what you already believe?
2. Do you know other relevant reasons or arguments? (If so, then you need to add them before coming to a final conclusion as to the essay's cogency.)
3. Do the reasons (plus any relevant material you may have added) justify acceptance of the thesis—that is, is the reasoning valid?

If an assumption or reason is not supported by your background beliefs, if you know of relevant information that refutes or casts doubt on the thesis, or if the reasoning is not completely valid (taking into account material you may have added), then clearly you should not be convinced by that particular extended argument. It may be, of course, that your background beliefs neither support nor conflict with an argument's assumptions or reasons, in which case you can't either accept or reject the argument's thesis; you need to withhold judgment or delve further into the matter.

A note of caution: It is common for some of the subsidiary arguments in a long essay to be cogent, while others are fallacious. When this is the case, reason dictates accepting only the untainted portions of the overall argument. But it would be wrong to automatically toss out the whole extended argument—wrong to reject the thesis of the essay—if that thesis can stand on the basis of the legitimate portions of the essay (along with relevant material you may have added from your background beliefs). This point often is characterized as one of *charity*—of being fair to the other side on an issue— but it also is an important requirement of good critical reasoning.

Exercise 8-1

Here are several short passages (taken from longer works). Reveal the structure of each passage, including reasons that support the thesis, reasons for the reasons, counterarguments, extraneous material, and so on, as in this simple example. (Remember, sometimes a reason or thesis may be implied.)

Example

Original passage (from an essay by Baruch Brody on the abortion issue): "There is a continuity of development from the moment of conception on. There are constant changes in the foetal condition; the foetus is constantly acquiring new structure and characteristics, but there is no one state which is radically different from any other. Since this is so, there is no one stage in the process of foetal development after the moment of conception which could plausibly be picked out as the moment at which the foetus becomes a living human being. The moment of conception is, however, different in this respect. It marks the beginning of this continuous process of development and introduces something new which is radically discontinuous with what has come before it. Therefore, the moment of conception, and only it, is a plausible candidate for being that moment at which the foetus becomes a living human being."

Rewritten Passage

Reason (premise): After the moment of conception, there is a continuous development of the human fetus, with no one state being much different from the next.

Conclusion: No moment after conception can be selected as the moment the fetus becomes a human being. (This conclusion then becomes a reason [premise] in the larger argument.)

Reason (premise): But the moment of conception introduces something radically different from what came before.

Conclusion (thesis): The moment of conception is the only plausible moment when the fetus becomes a human being.

1. Excerpt from a speech by then President Reagan to the Congress: "As many of you know, our administration has . . . strongly backed an amendment that will permit school children to hold prayer in our schools. [Applause] We believe that school children deserve the same protection, the same constitutional consensus that permits prayer in the House of Congress, chaplains in our armed services, and the motto on our coinage that says, 'In God We Trust.' [Applause] I grant you, possibly, we can make a case that prayer is needed more in Congress than in our schools, but . . . ." [Laughter, applause]

2. Excerpt from "The Case for Censorship," by Roger Kimball, the *Wall Street Journal* (October 8, 2000):

   . . . What's wrong with a little censorship? Until quite recently all sorts of things were censored in American society. There were very strict rules about what you could show on television and in movies, what you could describe in books and what you could reproduce in magazines. Were we worse off then?

. . . There are plenty of reasons to support government censorship when it comes to depictions of sex and violence. For one thing, it would encourage the entertainment industry to turn out material that is richer erotically. . . . Another reason . . . is that it would help temper the extraordinary brutality of popular culture.

. . . [Society] has an interest in protecting the moral sensibility of its citizens, especially the young. Freedom without morality degenerates into the servitude of libertinage. Which is why judicious government censorship is not the enemy of freedom but its guarantor.

*3. Thomas Paine, in his classic *The Age of Reason:* "Revelation is a communication of something which the person to whom that thing is revealed did not know before. For if I have done a thing, or seen it done, it needs no revelation to tell me I have done it or seen it, nor to enable me to tell it or to write it. Revelation, therefore, cannot be applied to anything done upon earth, of which man himself is the actor or the witness; and consequently, all the historical and anecdotal parts of the Bible, which is almost the whole of it, is not within the meaning and compass of the word 'revelation,' and therefore, is not the word of God."

4. Argument implied in this excerpt from the *International Herald Tribune* (July 3, 2003): "The federal appeals court in Atlanta has ordered the chief justice of the Alabama Supreme Court to remove a monument engraved with the Ten Commandments from the rotunda of his courthouse. The 11th U.S. Circuit Court of Appeals concluded the monument violates the First Amendment's prohibition on government establishment of religion. In its ruling Tuesday, the court was unusually blunt in responding to the assertion by Chief Justice Roy Moore in court papers in the case that he did not recognize the authority of the federal court in this matter. The appeals court compared Moore to those Southern governors [George Wallace and Ross Barnett] who attempted to defy court orders during an earlier era."

5. Philosopher John Locke, in his classic *The Second Treatise on Government:* "Though the earth and all inferior creatures be common to all men, yet every man has a property in his own person; this nobody has any right to but himself. The labor of his body and the work of his hands, we may say, are properly his. Whatsoever then he removes out of the state that nature has provided and left it in, he has mixed his labor with, and joined to it something that is his own, and thereby makes it his property. It being by him removed from the common state nature has placed it in, it has by this labor something annexed to it that excluded the common right of other men. For this labor being the unquestionable property of the laborer, no man but he can have a right to what that is once joined to, at least where there is enough and as good left in common for others."

6. Abstract of an article by Joyce Neu, "The United States Should Seek Alternatives to Military Action":

Americans are justifiably angry at the terrorists behind the September 11 attacks. Many call for military reprisals. However, war has failed to deter terrorism and inevitably kills innocent bystanders and civilians. The United States should reject calls for war and revenge and instead seek out alternative ways of bringing the terrorists to justice and work to remove the underlying causes of terrorism. By responding with restraint and magnanimity, America can help prevent terrorism in the future.

7. From an article on genetically engineered foods, by John B. Fagan:[1]

Giant transnational companies are carrying out a dangerous global experiment by attempting to introduce large numbers of genetically engineered foods widely into our food supply. Because genetic manipulations can generate unanticipated harmful side-effects, and because genetically engineered foods are not tested sufficiently to eliminate those that are dangerous, this experiment not only jeopardizes the health of individuals, but could also lead to national health threats. . . . Tampering with the genetic code of food is reckless and poses a serious threat to life. It could easily upset the delicate balance between our physiology and the foods that we eat. There is already ample scientific justification for an immediate ban on genetically modified foods in order to safeguard our health.

8. Philosopher Sidney Hook, on recovering from a near-fatal stroke:

A few years ago, I lay at the point of death [following the stroke]. . . . At one point my heart stopped beating; just as I lost consciousness, it was thumped back into action again. In one of my lucid intervals during those days of agony, I asked my physician to discontinue all life-supporting services or show me how to do it. He refused. . . .

A month later I was discharged from the hospital. In six months I regained the use of my limbs [and voice]. . . . My experience . . . has been cited as an argument against honoring requests of stricken patients to be gently eased out of their pain and life. I cannot agree. . . . As an octogenarian, there is a reasonable likelihood that I may suffer another "cardiovascular accident" or worse. . . . It seems to me that I have already paid my dues to death—indeed . . . I suffered enough to warrant dying several times over. Why run the risk of more?

Secondly, I dread imposing on my family and friends another grim round of misery similar to the one my first attack occasioned. My wife and children endured enough for one lifetime. . . .

EXERCISE 8-2

In general, we do not read poetry with the intent of constructing a summary and then evaluating for cogency. We read out of love for effective poetic expression. Nevertheless, it is a fact that poems often argue for a conclusion. Andrew Marvell's wonderful (one might say "Marvell-ous") poem "To His Coy Mistress" is a case in point. Clearly, there would be no point in constructing a detailed summary of this, or perhaps any, poem, citing every bit of support given for the reasons provided for its thesis. So in this

---

[1] From "Genetically Engineered Food: A Serious Health Risk," posted on the World Wide Web, February 26, 1997, at www.natural-law.org/issues/genetic/gehazards.html.

case, after first reading the poem for the enjoyment of the experience, simply state in a general way and in your own words the poem's thesis; the reason, or reasons, provided in its support; and a rough idea of the support provided for the reason or reasons.

To His Coy Mistress

Had we but world enough, and time,
This coyness, Lady, were no crime.
We would sit down and think which way
To walk and pass our long love's day.
Thou by the Indian Ganges' side
Shouldst rubies find: I by the tide
Of Humber would complain. I would
Love you ten years before the Flood,
And you should, if you please, refuse
Till the conversion of the Jews.
My vegetable love would grow
Vaster than empires and more slow;
An hundred years would go to praise
Thine eyes and on thy forehead gaze;
Two hundred to adore each breast,
But thirty thousand to the rest;
An age at least to every part,
And the last age should show your heart.
For, Lady, you deserve this state,
Nor would I love at lower rate.

But at my back I always hear
Time's winged chariot hurrying near;
And yonder all before us lie
Deserts of vast eternity,
Thy beauty shall no more be found,
Nor, in thy marble vault, shall sound
My echoing song; then worms shall try
That long preserved virginity,
And your quaint honor turn to dust,
And into ashes all my lust;
The grave's a fine and private place,
But none, I think, do there embrace.

Now therefore, while the youthful hue
Sits on thy skin like morning dew,
And while thy willing soul transpires
At every pore with instant fires,
Now let us sport us while we may,
And now, like amorous birds of prey,
Rather at once our time devour
Than languish in his slow-chapped power.
Let us roll all our strength and all
Our sweetness up into one ball,
And tear our pleasures with rough strife
Through the iron gate of life,
Thus, though we cannot make our sun
Stand still, yet we will make him run.

EXERCISE 8-3

The Declaration of Independence contains a thesis and reasons supporting that thesis. Get a copy of that important document, and (1) determine what its thesis is and (2) list the reasons provided in defense of that thesis. Is the argument inductive or deductive? What is the worldview?

2. THE MARGIN NOTE AND SUMMARY METHOD

The **margin note and summary method** is a good method to use when an evaluation has to be right. The idea behind this method is that a summary can be more easily worked with than the longer work from which it is drawn, provided the summary is *accurate*. (Making a summary helps us to remember things better and thus is a good study technique — one, in fact, that instructors often use when preparing class material.)

The margin note and summary method has four basic steps:

1. Read the material to be summarized.
2. Read it through again, this time marking the important passages with an indication of their content written in the margin. (The point of the first reading is to

enable you to spot the important passages more accurately when you read through the material a second time. First readings often don't catch the drift.) Margin notes need not be full sentences or grammatically correct. They may contain abbreviations or whatever shorthand notes you care to employ.

3. Use the margin notes to construct a summary of the passage, indicating which statements are premises (reasons) and which conclusions, so that the structure of the passage's argument is laid bare.

4. Evaluate the essay by evaluating your summary, checking back and forth to be sure there are no significant differences between the essay and your summary.

Two things need to be remembered about the margin note and summary method. First, when we skip portions of a passage, we make a judgment that the passed-over material is relatively unimportant. It takes practice and skill to know what to include and what to omit, and even those with a good deal of experience may differ on such matters. (This does not mean, however, that anything goes!) Second, margin notes and summaries are shorthand devices; they should be briefer than the passages they summarize — if possible, a good deal briefer. The risk in this process, obviously, is falsification. We don't want to commit the *straw man* fallacy by making judgments about the shortened version that would not be valid for the original.

Evaluation

A summary restates the position of the author of an essay. The evaluation contains the reader's appraisal. Here is an example showing how the margin note and summary method can be used to evaluate an essay:

How McDonald's Caved in to Environmental Yuppies

After building its colossus by feeding ordinary folks, the McDonald's restaurant chain has unaccountably allowed itself to be pressured by elitist yuppies of the Environmental Defense Fund.

Statement of fact: EDF has pressured McDonald's into replacing polystyrene hamburger cartons with coated-paper ones.

In the process, it has done serious harm to its customers and suppliers and, ironically, increased its net contribution to pollution. The incident, instead of building environmental credibility, heightens the growing perception of green silliness.

On November 1, McDonald's decided to abandon its recycling program on polystyrene foam hamburger cartons (clamshells) and replace them with coated paperboard containers. The three network anchors immediately saluted this decision as "good news for the environment." In fact, every scientist will tell you that the decision was, on balance, bad news for ecology.

Thesis: This was an ecological mistake.

Indeed, one of the main reasons that McDonald's chose to expand polystyrene foam for its hamburger packs was a nonpartisan 1975 Stanford Research Institute study, which said: "There appears to be no supportable basis for any claim that paper-related products are superior from an en-

Premise: Polystyrene is ecologically superior to paper.

vironmental standpoint to plastic-related ones, including polystyrene. The weight of existing evidence indicates that the favorable true environmental balance, if any, would be in the direction of the plastic-related product."

Reasons in support:

Or as scientist Jan Beyea of the National Audubon Society explained: "Using a lot more paper means a lot more pollution."

The reasons are obvious to any scientist or engineer. First, and most obvious, polystyrene is easily recyclable, while coated paper is not.

1. Polystyrene easily recycled, but not coated paper.

Second, comparable paper packaging requires on average 40 percent to 50 percent more energy, in part because the paperboard weighs more and consumes three times its weight in raw wood per pound of production—and that assumes no recycling of either product. That incidentally includes the energy value of the petrochemicals consumed in polystyrene manufacture.

2. Paper uses 40–50% more energy to make.

Third, the atmospheric emissions involved in producing paper are at least two to three times those for producing polystyrene, and the waterborne wastes and effluents are at least 70 percent higher.

3. Paper manuf. produces more air & water pollution.

Finally, coated paper is only slightly more biodegradable than polystyrene. While polystyrene takes up 50 percent more space in landfills than its paper substitutes, it still constitutes less than 0.4 percent of total landfill waste. Even a modestly successful polystyrene recycling program kills coated paper's advantage.

4. Although paper slightly more biodegradable, polyst. recycling kills coated paper's advantage.

(Repeat)

This means that the McDonald's decision to expand polystyrene use in 1975 was not only sound economically, but it was by far the most environmentally sensible approach. The decision to reverse course is not sound science, but ill-informed yuppie-ism.

The recent McDonald's decision is one more reason why serious scientists and economists now have almost universal contempt for the environmental advocacy movement and what Senator Daniel Patrick Moynihan called its "middle-class enthusiasms."

(Extraneous)

Dumb, McDonald's, really dumb.[2]

Now here is a summary of the Brookes essay taken primarily from the margin notes:

> The EDF has pressured McDonald's into replacing polystyrene containers with coated-paper ones.
>
> *Thesis:* This was an ecological mistake.

---

[2]From Warren T. Brookes, "How McDonald's Caved in to Environmental Yuppies." © 1990 by Creators Syndicate. Reprinted by permission of Jane S. Brookes and Creators Syndicate.

Premise: Polystyrene is ecologically superior to paper.

Evidence 1 (supporting this premise): Polystyrene is easily recycled; paper is not.

Evidence 2: Making paper requires 40 to 50 percent more energy than does polystyrene. (The implied premise here is that increased uses of energy in the modern world are a threat to stable air and water temperatures, contribute to a greenhouse effect, and so on.)

Evidence 3: Making paper products pollutes the air more than does manufacturing polystyrene. (Brookes clearly meant in ways other than merely by increasing air and water temperature.)

Evidence 4: Although coated paper is slightly more biodegradable than polystyrene, a "modestly successful polystyrene recycling program kills coated paper's advantage."

Here is a brief evaluation of Brookes's argument:

Brookes presents no reasons in support of his claims that McDonald's switched from polystyrene to coated paper and that they did so because of pressure from environmental groups. But it was common knowledge at the time (well known, for instance, to the authors of this text) that this was true.

Doing a modest bit of research indicates that polystyrene foam is indeed ecologically superior to coated paper, according to experts in the field, and for pretty much the reasons Brookes cites. Readers are invited to do their own research on this question. (Note, however, that uncoated-paper products, which McDonald's could use instead of coated-paper containers, can be recycled! It's true, though, that they aren't as sturdy and don't hold in heat or moisture as well as the coated variety, making them more difficult and dangerous to use.) So Brookes's thesis seems on target.

It's worth noting that in trying to fight the good ecological fight, groups such as the EDF sometimes become overzealous or, as in this case, act on the basis of inaccurate, unscientific information (as movement enthusiasts often do—one of the authors of this text having often been a case in point . . . in the distant past, of course). But Brookes's denigration of his opponents as "elitist yuppies" and his characterization of the environmentalist movement as "green silliness" are extremely unfair and uncalled for. The EDF and other environmentalist groups are trying to combat the callous disregard, in the absence of outside pressure, of corporate America (as of industry everywhere) of the environmental effects of their activities.

EXERCISE 8-4

Using the margin note and summary method, construct a summary of the following Gore Vidal essay (written in 1970 but still relevant), making sure to label premises (reasons) and conclusions, including the grand conclusion that constitutes the passage's thesis. Then write a quick evaluation of the essay:

Drugs

It is possible to stop most drug addiction in the United States within a very
short time. Simply make all drugs available and sell them at cost. Label each
drug with a precise description of what effect—good and bad—the drug will
have on the taker. This will require heroic honesty. Don't say that marijuana is
addictive or dangerous when it is neither, as millions of people know—unlike
"speed," which kills most unpleasantly, or heroin, which is addictive and difficult to kick.

For the record, I have tried—once—almost every drug and liked none, dis-
proving the popular Fu Manchu theory that a single whiff of opium will en-
slave the mind. Nevertheless, many drugs are bad for certain people to take and
they should be told why in a sensible way.

Along with exhortation and warning, it might be good for our citizens to
recall (or learn for the first time) that the United States was the creation of men
who believed that each man has the right to do what he wants with his own life
as long as he does not interfere with his neighbor's pursuit of happiness (that
his neighbor's idea of happiness is persecuting others does confuse matters
a bit).

This is a startling notion to the current generation of Americans. They
reflect a system of public education which has made the Bill of Rights, literally, unacceptable to a majority of high school graduates (see the annual
Purdue reports) who now form the "silent majority"—a phrase which that
underestimated wit Richard Nixon took from Homer who used it to describe
the dead.

Now one can hear the warning rumble begin: if everyone is allowed to take
drugs, everyone will and the GNP will decrease, the Commies will stop us
from making everyone free, and we shall end up a race of zombies, passively
murmuring "groovy" to one another. Alarming thought. Yet it seems most unlikely that any reasonably sane person will become a drug addict if he knows
in advance what addiction is going to be like.

Is everyone reasonably sane? Some people will always become drug addicts
just as some people will always become alcoholics, and it is just too bad. Every
man, however, has the power (and should have the legal right) to kill himself if
he chooses. But since most men don't, they won't be mainliners either. Nevertheless, forbidding people things they like or think they might enjoy only
makes them want those things all the more. This psychological insight is, for
some mysterious reason, perennially denied our governors.

It is a lucky thing for the American moralist that our country has always existed in a kind of time-vacuum: we have no public memory of anything that
happened before last Tuesday. No one in Washington today recalls what happened during the years alcohol was forbidden to the people by a Congress that
thought it had a divine mission to stamp out Demon Rum—launching, in the
process, the greatest crime wave in the country's history, causing thousands
of deaths from bad alcohol, and creating a general (and persisting) contempt
among the citizenry for the laws of the United States.

The same thing is happening today. But the government has learned nothing
from past attempts at prohibition, not to mention repression.

Last year when the supply of Mexican marijuana was slightly curtailed by the Feds, the pushers got the kids hooked on heroin and deaths increased dramatically, particularly in New York. Whose fault? Evil men like the Mafiosi? Permissive Dr. Spock? Wild-eyed Dr. Leary? No.

The Government of the United States was responsible for those deaths. The bureaucratic machine has a vested interest in playing cops and robbers. Both the Bureau of Narcotics and the Mafia want strong laws against the sale and use of drugs because if drugs are sold at cost there would be no money in it for anyone.

If there was no money in it for the Mafia, there would be no friendly playground pushers, and addicts would not commit crimes to pay for the next fix. Finally, if there was no money in it, the Bureau of Narcotics would wither away, something they are not about to do without a struggle.

Will anything sensible be done? Of course not. The American people are as devoted to the idea of sin and its punishment as they are to making money—and fighting drugs is nearly as big a business as pushing them. Since the combination of sin and money is irresistible (particularly to the professional politician), the situation will only grow worse.[3]

3. Extended Evaluation of an Argument

An extended evaluation examines an argument in more detail, using the critical thinking tools covered throughout this text. The first step is to identify the thesis and reasons and to summarize the main points of the argument. Then the task is to determine whether the argument is convincing. Do the reasons really defend the thesis or are they fallacious? Is the evidence plausible? Has the writer included important counterarguments? Is the use of emotive language persuasive or manipulative? Is the worldview convincing? These are some of the questions to consider when evaluating arguments.

It is important to keep in mind that there is no such thing as a perfectly reasoned, totally convincing argument (though there are plenty of really bad ones out there). Even brilliant thinkers slip up once in a while or get carried away with their own rhetoric. A good analysis determines what is convincing and what is not, then comes to an overall evaluation of the argument.

Here is a condensed version of an argument on capital punishment by probably the most famous trial lawyer of the 20th century, Clarence Darrow, followed by an evaluation. One of Darrow's most celebrated cases was his defense of Richard Loeb and Nathan Leopold, two teenagers who pled guilty to kidnapping and murdering a 14-year-old boy. The prosecution was determined to hang the killers, but Darrow's brilliant 12-hour summation, an eloquent attack on the death penalty, was so effective that the presiding judge wept at its conclusion and gave Leopold and Loeb a life sentence instead of the death penalty. (An interesting footnote on Darrow is that no client of his was ever executed.) The following essay was published a few years after the trial. Although written in the first half of the 20th century, the arguments Darrow made are still used by abolitionists today. Given his legendary prowess in a court of law, one might think his ar-

---

[3] © 1970 by Gore Vidal. Originally published in the *New York Times*.

guments were airtight, but even the great Darrow lapsed into fallacious reasoning and used rhetorical tricks to persuade.

The Futility of the Death Penalty[4]

. . . It is my purpose in this article to prove, first, that capital punishment is no deterrent to crime; and second, that the state continues to kill its victims, not so much to defend society against them—for it could do that equally well by imprisonment—but to appease the mob's emotions of hatred and revenge. . . .

Behind the idea of capital punishment lie false training and crude views of human conduct. People do evil things, say the judges, lawyers, and preachers, because of depraved hearts. . . .

If crime were really the result of willful depravity, we should be ready to concede that capital punishment may serve as a deterrent to the criminally inclined. But it is hardly probable that the great majority of people refrain from killing their neighbors because they are afraid; they refrain because they never had the inclination. Human beings are creatures of habit; and, as a rule, they are not in the habit of killing. The circumstances that lead to killings are manifold, but in a particular individual the inducing cause is not easily found. In one case, homicide may have been induced by indigestion in the killer; in another, it may be traceable to some weakness inherited from a remote ancestor; but that it results from *something* tangible and understandable, if all the facts were known, must be plain to everyone who believes in cause and effect.

Of course, no one will be converted to this point of view by statistics of crime. In the first place, it is impossible to obtain reliable ones, and in the second place, the conditions to which they apply are never the same. But if one cares to analyze the figures, such as we have, it is easy to trace the more frequent causes of homicide. The greatest number of killings occur during attempted burglaries and robberies. The robber knows that penalties for burglary do not average more than five years in prison. He also knows that the penalty for murder is death or imprisonment. Faced with this alternative, what does the burglar do when he is detected and threatened with arrest? He shoots to kill. He deliberately takes the chance of death to save himself from a five-year term in prison. It is therefore as obvious as anything can be that fear of death has no effect in diminishing homicides of this kind, which are more numerous than any other type.

The next largest number of homicides may be classed as "sex murders." Quarrels between husbands and wives, disappointed love, or love too much requited cause many killings. They are the result of primal emotions so deep that the fear of death has not the slightest effect in preventing them. Spontaneous feelings overflow in criminal acts, and consequences do not count.

Then there are cases of sudden anger, uncontrollable rage. The fear of death never enters into such cases; if the anger is strong enough, consequences are not considered until too late. The old-fashioned stories of men deliberately plotting and committing murder in cold blood have little foundation in real life. Such

---

[4] From Clarence Darrow, "The Futility of the Death Penalty," in *Verdicts Out of Control,* edited by Arthur and Lila Weinberg (Chicago: Quadrangle Books, 1963), pp. 225–234. This essay first appeared in *The Forum,* September 1928.

killings are so rare that they need not concern us here. The point to be emphasized is that practically all homicides are manifestations of well-recognized
human emotions, and it is perfectly plain that the fear of excessive punishment
does not enter into them.

In addition to these personal forces which overwhelm weak men and lead
them to commit murder, there are also many social and economic forces which
must be listed among the causes of homicides, and human beings have even less
control over these than over their own emotions. . . . the United States has gathered together people of every color from every nation in the world. Racial differences intensify social, religious, and industrial problems, and the confusion
which attends this indiscriminate mixing of races and nationalities is one of the
most fertile sources or crime.

Will capital punishment remedy these conditions? Of course it won't; but its
advocates argue that the fear of this extreme penalty will hold the victims of adverse conditions in check. To this piece of sophistry, the continuance and increase of crime in our large cities is a sufficient answer. No, the plea that capital
punishment acts as a deterrent to crime will not stand. The real reason why this
barbarous practice persists in a so-called civilized world is that people still hold
the primitive belief that the taking of one human life can be atoned for by taking
another. It is the age-old obsession with punishment that keeps the official
headsman busy plying his trade.

And it is precisely upon this point that I would build my case against capital
punishment. Even if one grants that the idea of punishment is sound, crime calls
for something more—for careful study, for an understanding of causes, for
proper remedies. To attempt to abolish crime by killing the criminal is the easy
and foolish way out of a serious situation. Unless a remedy deals with the conditions which foster crime, criminals will breed faster than the hangman can
spring his trap. Capital punishment ignores the causes of crime and, like the
methods of the witch doctor, it is not only ineffective as a remedy, but is posi-
tively vicious in at least two ways. In the first place, the spectacle of state executions feeds the basest passions of the mob. And in the second place, so long as
the state rests content to deal with crime in this barbaric and futile manner, society will be lulled by a false sense of security, and effective methods of dealing
with crime will be discouraged. . . .

. . . while capital punishment panders to the passions of the mob, no one takes
the pains to understand the meaning of crime. People speak of crime or criminals as if the world were divided into the good and the bad. This is not true. . . .

Human conduct is by no means so simple as our moralists have led us to
believe. There is no sharp line separating good actions from bad. The greed
for money, the display of wealth, the despair of those who witness the display,
the poverty, oppression, and hopelessness of the unfortunate—all these are factors which enter into human conduct and of which the world takes no account.
Many people have learned no other profession but robbery and burglary. The
processions moving steadily through our prisons to the gallows are in the main
made up of these unfortunates. And how do we dare to consider ourselves civilized creatures when, ignoring the causes of crime, we rest content to mete out
harsh punishments to the victims of conditions over which they have no
control? . . .

Even now, are not all imaginative and humane people shocked at the spectacle of a killing by the state? . . . How can the state censure the cruelty of
the man who—moved by strong passions, or acting to save his freedom, or
influenced by weakness or fear—takes human life, when everyone knows
that the state itself, after long premeditation and settled hatred, not only kills,
but first tortures and bedevils its victims for weeks with the impending
doom?

For the last hundred years the world has shown a gradual tendency to mitigate
punishment. We are slowly learning that this way of controlling human beings is
both cruel and ineffective. . . . There is no doubt whatever that the world is growing more humane and more sensitive and more understanding. The time will
come when all people will view with horror the light way in which society and
its courts of law now take human life; and when that time comes, the way will
be clear to devise some better method of dealing with poverty and ignorance and
their frequent byproducts, which we call crime.

Analysis

In "The Futility of the Death Penalty," Clarence Darrow argues against capital punishment because it is "no deterrent to crime" and it is the state's attempt "to appease the
mob's emotions of hatred and revenge." His overall argument is valid and often persuasive, but he sometimes reasons fallaciously, and though he uses language effectively, he
also uses it cleverly, to manipulate the reader. He is at his best, however, when he urges
us to consider the humane world view at the heart of his argument.

Darrow's first premise, that capital punishment is no deterrent to crime, is hypothetical, based on common sense and his own background experience as a defense lawyer.
Darrow himself concedes that "no one will be converted to this point of view by statistics of crime" partly because "it is impossible to obtain reliable ones." Although recent
studies seem to provide some statistical corroboration that the death penalty is a deterrent, Darrow's reservations about crime statistics are just as relevant today as they were
then. The *New York Times* published a survey in September 2000 revealing that the
homicide rate in states with the death penalty has been 48% to 111% higher over the past
20 years than in states without the death penalty. However, these findings suggest the fallacy of questionable cause, since the states cited may have had a higher rate of murder
to start with and may have instituted the death penalty to reduce the number of homicides.

Instead of using questionable statistics to make his point, Darrow reasons that most
killers are not deterred by the death penalty when they kill in the heat of the moment—
during attempted burglaries, in sex-related quarrels, or in cases of uncontrollable rage.
Our own background beliefs would probably confirm his assumption that people aren't
likely to think of the consequences under these circumstances. But he is guilty of suppressing evidence when he dismisses the idea of premeditation in his claim that "men
deliberately plotting and committing murder in cold blood have little foundation in real
life." Countless examples of premeditated murder could be used to refute this claim, but
the most obvious in Darrow's case is the gruesome crime committed by his own clients,
Leopold and Loeb, who systematically planned to commit the perfect crime to kidnap
and murder their 14-year-old victim. His argument that a "great majority of people refrain from killing their neighbors . . . because they never had the inclination" probably

applies to most people but doesn't take into account those who *do* have the inclination to kill and who *are* deterred by the fear of punishment.

There is some truth to his second premise that the state continues to kill its victims to appease the mob's emotions of hatred and revenge. Politicians do, indeed, pay attention to the attitudes their constituents have about capital punishment. In Texas, for instance, candidates who take a stand against the death penalty would have a hard time getting elected. But Darrow relies more on provocative rhetoric than reasoning to make his point. He argues that those who favor the death penalty are a " mob," incited by "hatred and revenge," and the state is a murderer in the questionable premise that "the state itself, after long premeditation and settled hatred, not only kills but first tortures and bedevils its victims for weeks with the impending doom." By presenting the criminal as the "victim," he transforms the entire legal process—from the interrogation, to the trial, sentencing, and appeals—into torturous treatment of the murderer, all of which evade the issue that a real victim is dead at the hands of a killer.

Darrow's argument is driven by highly emotive, often persuasive language, used to engage the reader in his crusade. His tone is characterized by compassion for the hapless killer and moral outrage at the harsh retribution exacted by the state. Capital punishment is condemned as a "barbarous practice," the "easy and foolish way out of a serious situation." Those who favor it are "moralists" with "crude" notions of human conduct, people with the "primitive belief" that executing the killer will atone for the murder. To counter these uncivilized tendencies in human nature, Darrow describes right-thinking people as "imaginative and humane," "shocked at the spectacle of killing by the state." This is an effective ploy to jar the reader into seeing the state in a different light—as a killer not far removed from the murderer it condemns. Less persuasive is the linguistic sleight-of-hand he reserves for the criminals, whom he repeatedly refers to as "victims"—of social forces, emotional drives, or biological quirks—implying that they commit crime through no fault of their own because of the questionable premise that their behavior is the result of "conditions over which they have no control."

Perhaps more than anything else, his argument stands or falls on his worldview, which encompasses his attitude toward the criminal class and the responsibility of society in dealing with it. Darrow's philosophy of determinism is evident throughout when he claims that homicides may be "traceable to some weakness inherited from a remote ancestor" or "the result of primal emotions" or "uncontrollable rage," or that criminals are "victims of conditions over which they have no control." Although it is true that we have no control over the environment we are born into or the genes we inherit, most of us believe that we not only can but should control our actions, despite the problems inherent in our background. A more compelling reason for abolishing capital punishment is rooted in his humane worldview that a civilized society should not sink to the level of the criminal, that it should resist the primitive urge to exact retribution, and that it should deal with criminals in a humane manner, by mitigating punishment and trying to remedy the conditions that foster crime. In this way he appeals to our better natures and presents his most convincing argument.

EXERCISE 8-5

1. The above analysis of Darrow's argument is one person's evaluation and may not agree with your own. In what ways would you agree or disagree with it? Analyze

the premises, reasoning, language, and worldview of Darrow's argument and come up with your own evaluation.

2. Find a 2- to 3-page argument in a magazine or on the Internet and evaluate it, using the critical thinking tools covered in the text.

4. Dealing with Value Claims

By now, it should have become clear how often the reasons presented in favor of a thesis are at least in part about values, not facts. It is a *fact,* for example, that sugar sweetens coffee; it is a *value judgment* that sweetened coffee tastes better than unsweetened. It is a fact that the Earth goes around the sun once every 365 days or so; it is a value judgment that, other things being equal, those who give to the poor are better people than the Scrooges who don't. (Note the slanting word used in the previous sentence.)

When someone argues, say, that vacations are better taken in the spring, because spring is the best time of the year, that person uses a value judgment as a reason (premise) supporting the conclusion that vacations are best taken in the spring. (Note, by the way, that this conclusion is itself in part a value judgment, as are all conclusions that depend on at least one reason that is a value judgment.)

Value judgments typically are justified, or defended, in ways that are different from judgments about facts. Someone who claims, for example, that gold does not rust can support that claim by citing the fact that nothing made of gold has ever been observed to rust and that all attempts to rust gold have failed. But the person who says that gold makes beautiful jewelry has to cite a different sort of evidence—for example, that people generally like the look of gold jewelry. That is why many philosophers say that value judgments concern matters that are **subjective,** while judgments about alleged facts deal with matters that are **objective.**

The idea that values are subjective is captured nicely by the saying that beauty is in the eyes of the beholder and by the old precept that there is no disputing about taste. According to these maxims, the fact that some people like string beans, or Bach fugues, while others don't doesn't make those who do or those who don't wrong. By way of contrast, those who make a nonvalue, factual claim—for instance, that the Earth is flat (so-called "flat earthers")—are wrong; the rest of us who believe that it is spherical (well, extremely close to being spherical) are right. (Yes, there are people who still, in this day and age, believe that the Earth is flat. Recall the discussion of self-deception in Chapter 6.) Merely believing that something is a fact doesn't make it a fact; nor is such a belief justified in the absence of evidence (experience about something relevant) to support that belief.

It's true, of course, that lots of philosophers would argue against the idea that value judgments are by their nature subjective. Some would say, for example, that beauty is in the object, not just in the eyes of the beholder, so that the person who doesn't see the beauty in beautiful objects is like someone who is color-blind. (One of the points of a philosophy course in which value judgments are discussed is precisely to deal with disagreements of this kind.)

Fortunately, when the value judgments relevant to an argument are about beauty, or taste, or other aesthetic matters, we generally can come to an evaluation without having to deal with underlying philosophical issues like the one about objectivity versus subjectivity. Suppose, for example, that some people in a community want to make un-covered auto junkyards illegal, on the grounds that they constitute an "eyesore." Voters don't need to decide whether being an eyesore is an objective or a subjective property to figure out how to vote. They can just find out whether most people find them to be ugly, or at least whether they themselves see junkyards as a good deal less than attractive. (There may, of course, be good reasons against banning open auto graveyards, but that is another matter.) The point is that, in these cases, we can appeal to something subjec-tive—namely, whether we see junkyards as ugly or not—without answering the under-lying questions about whether the ugliness of something is in the thing itself or merely in the eyes of the beholder.

But other sorts of value cases are more problematic, the prime case being **moral val-ues.** If it is true that moral values are subjective, then claims about them can be justified simply by appealing to evidence that most people hold these values. Enslaving people and working them to death then become morally wrong just because virtually everyone finds this sort of behavior wrong or unfair. But if moral values are objective, judgments about them cannot be defended in this way. Subjective feelings become irrelevant if moral principles are objective—if there is something outside us, be it biblical com-mandments, natural rights, the greatest good for the greatest number, or whatever, that determines which actions are right and which wrong.[5] Thus, those who hold that moral standards are objective need to think carefully as to what sorts of justifications—appeal to cultural norms, natural rights, religious principles, or something else—they believe should count in assessing moral claims and whether these allegedly objective standards in turn can be justified without appeal to subjective values or standards.

The point here, however, is that when someone makes a moral value claim in an ar-gument, it may be crucially important to find out what makes that person hold the value in question. Those who argue against legal abortions, for example, often present as their principal reason the claim that taking a human life is morally wrong; but if their justi-fication is the biblical commandment "Thou shalt not kill," then those who do not accept the Bible as the ultimate authority on moral matters have not been given a persuasive rea-son for accepting this claim about the immorality of taking a human life.[6] Similarly, those who argue in favor of legalizing prostitution often claim that a woman has a right to use her body in any way that she sees fit; but if their justification is a theory of objec-tive natural rights, then those who reject the idea of objective rights have not been given a satisfactory reason for being in favor of legal prostitution.

In any case, good critical reasoners accept premises that contain moral value judg-ments only if those judgments conform to their own moral standards. Socialists, for in-

---

[5]All of these, and many other allegedly objective factors, have been argued for, and against, by philosophers and theologians.

[6]Note that appeals to documents such as the Bible can be tricky. With respect to the abortion case, for instance, it has been argued that the original Hebrew has been mistranslated and that what the commandment says is better translated as "Thou shalt not *murder,*" so that the question remains as to whether abortion is murder—immoral killing. There also is the problem that most who deny the legitimacy of abortion believe certain kinds of killing are justified—for instance, in wartime or in self-defense; those who believe this would have to show why killing fetuses is not also some-times justified.

stance, sometimes argue that it is not just impractical but also immoral to allow some workers in a community to earn thousands of times more than others (as is currently the case in the United States and some other industrial countries), and they use this claim as a reason for overturning, or at least modifying, the free enterprise system now in place in most industrial countries. Good critical reasoners accept or reject moral claims of this sort by seeing how they fit with the moral principles they already accept.

This does not mean, of course, that moral standards and values are exempt from challenge. Those who believe, say, that it always is morally wrong to violate legally enacted legislation may see the matter differently if laws are enacted forbidding the practice of their own religion or forcing acceptance of another faith.

It also needs to be noted that there often are no simple principles—say, those like the Ten Commandments—to apply in determining moral right and wrong. It seems morally right to many people that income should be proportionate to what one produces, a standard encapsulated in the idea that one should reap what one sows. According to this *principle of just desserts,* the fruits of a cooperative effort ought to be distributed according to the relative contributions of the various parties, whether in labor, capital, or whatever. But even supposing this idea is accepted, how are just desserts to be determined in actual cases? How do we compare, for instance, the efforts of a corporate chief executive officer who oversees the successful introduction of a new product with the engineers who designed and perfected that product, or with workers on the line who actually produce the goods? How do we compare the contributions of those who put up the money (stockholders) with those of company executive or production line employees?[7]

Finally, it is important to remember that those who go through life without carefully examining and questioning their moral principles run the same risk of mistake as do those who fail to acquire accurate factual beliefs about how things work in this complicated world of ours. This is true even if the subjectivist view of moral right and wrong is correct, for it still could well be that a person's unexamined feelings about this or that moral issue will fail to agree with how that individual might see the matter after giving it careful thought or after bringing to bear relevant background information. The first thought that virtually all of us have about infanticide, to take an interesting case, is that it always and everywhere is the worst sort of murder; but thinking carefully about the hard choices life presents to some parents has changed the minds of more than a few thinking and even compassionate individuals.[8]

EXERCISE 8-6

A while back (Exercise 8-1, number 5), you were asked to summarize excerpts from the writings of philosopher John Locke.

---

[7] For more on this topic, see Howard Kahane, *Contract Ethics: Evolutionary Biology and the Moral Sentiments* (Lanham, Md.: Rowman & Littlefield, 1995).

[8] It sometimes happens that the only alternatives open to parents in poor societies, or societies in the throes of famine, are to do away with a newborn child so as to be able to keep their other children alive or else to see all of their offspring slowly starve to death.

1. Indicate which of his assertions, if any, in his essay concern values, moral or nonmoral.

2. Use the summary of the article that you constructed before, along with your beliefs about any value statements the essay in question may contain, to come to an evaluation of Locke's view on the matter, indicating where you think his argument is weak, where strong, and what your overall evaluation is, making sure, of course, to explain why you think so.

EXERCISE 8-7

Follow the instructions for Exercise 8-6 for the following excerpt from "On Date Rape," by Camille Paglia:

> Dating is a very recent phenomenon in world history. Throughout history women have been chaperoned. As late as 1964, when I arrived in college, we had strict rules. We had to be in the dorm under lock and key by 11 o'clock. My generation was the one that broke these rules. We said, "We want freedom—no more double standard!" When I went to stay at a male friend's apartment in New York, my aunts flew into a frenzy: "You can't do that, it's dangerous!" Still, we understood in the '60s that we were taking a risk.
>
> Today these young women want the freedoms that we won, but they don't want to acknowledge the risk. That's the problem. The minute you go out with a man, the minute you go to a bar to have a drink, there is a risk. You have to accept the fact that part of the sizzle of sex comes from the danger of sex. You can be overpowered.
>
> So it is women's personal responsibility to be aware of the dangers of the world. But these young feminists today are deluded. They come from a protected, white, middle-class world, and they expect everything to be safe. Notice it's not black or Hispanic women who are making a fuss about this—they come from cultures that are fully sexual and they are fully realistic about sex. But these other women are sexually repressed girls, coming out of pampered homes, and when they arrive at these colleges and suddenly hit male lust, they go, "Oh, no!"
>
> These girls say, "Well, I should be able to get drunk at a fraternity party and go upstairs to a guy's room without anything happening." And I say, "Oh, really? And when you drive your car to New York City, do you leave your keys on the hood?" My point is that if your car is stolen after you do something like that, yes, the police should pursue the thief and he should be punished. But at the same time, the police—and I—have the right to say to you, "You stupid idiot, what the hell were you thinking?"
>
> I mean, wake up to reality. This is male sex. Guess what, it's hot. Male sex is hot. There's an attraction between the sexes that we're not totally in control of. The idea that we can regulate it by passing campus grievance committee rules is madness. My kind of feminism stresses personal responsibility. I've never been raped, but I've been very vigilant—I'm constantly reading the signals. If I ever got into a dating situation where I was overpowered and raped,

I would say, "Oh well, I misread the signals." But I don't think I would ever press charges. . . .[9]

EXERCISE 8-8

In the fall of 2003, Californians were asked to vote on Proposition 54, a measure that prohibits state and local governments from classifying any person by race, ethnicity, color, or national origin. Your task is too evaluate the argument for Proposition 54 and decide whether you would vote for or against it.

Argument in Favor of Proposition 54

"'What is your race?'"

African-American? Mexican-American? Asian-American? White? Native American? Or, the mysterious 'other?'

If you're like most Californians, you're getting tired of that question.

Californians are the most racially and ethnically diverse people in the world—and we are proud of it. We are also among the most independent; and we resent being classified, categorized, divided and subdivided based on our skin color and the origin of our ancestors.

When you're asked to check a government form with row after row of these rigid and silly little 'race' boxes, have you ever just wanted to say, "None of your business; now leave me alone?' Proposition 54 seeks to eliminate racial categorization, by the government, in all areas except medicine, health care and law enforcement.

The advocates of racial categorization maintain that you have no right to privacy concerning your ancestry and racial background. They see no problem if your employer or school officials label you AGAINST YOUR WILL often without telling you—or charge you with 'racial fraud' if their 'racial' definitions are different from yours.

Dare we forget the lessons of history?

Classification systems were invented to keep certain groups 'in their place' and to deny them full rights. These schemes were not invented by the Civil Rights movement! They were anathema to it. In fact, former Supreme Court Justice Thurgood Marshall once said, "Distinctions by race are so evil, so arbitrary and invidious that a state bound to defend the equal protection of the laws must not involve them in any public sphere."

Throughout history, government-imposed racial classifications have been used to divide people. They have been used to set people against each other. The slave owners and segregationists of the American past knew it when they labeled European Jews a separate and inferior 'race'; American judges knew it when they had to determine if Asians or part-Asians were white or non-white for the purposes of naturalization. Now, the advocates of racial categorization tell us that government-imposed racial categories will somehow yield the

---

[9] From Camille Paglia, "On Date Rape," *San Francisco Examiner,* July 7, 1991. Copyright © 1991. Reprinted by permission of the *San Francisco Examiner.*

very opposite of what they were originally intended to do! They insult our intelligence!

The unrelenting daily racial categorization of people by the government is one of the most divisive forces in American society. It is constantly emphasizing our minor differences, in opposition to our better instincts that tell us to seek our common interests and common values.

It's time for a change!

The government should stop categorizing its citizens by color and ancestry, and create a society in which our children and grandchildren can just think of themselves as Americans and individuals.

The colorblind ideal—judging others by the content of their character rather than the color of their skin—is more than a dream in California; it is central to the definition of who we are as a people, because, in California, we don't just dream; we do what others dream of doing.

Vote 'YES' on Proposition 54 (*www.racialprivacy.org*)!

Ward Connerly, *University of California Regent*
Martha Montelongo Myers, *Columnist*
Joe Hicks, *Human Relations Consultant*

1. Using the margin note and summary method, or whatever method works best for you, construct a summary of the excerpt, and then identify the thesis and the main premises.

2. Critically evaluate the article, using your summary as your guide, making sure that your evaluation accurately reflects the excerpt itself, as well as your summary.

3. Drawing on your background knowledge and beliefs, decide how you would vote on this issue and defend your decision.

5. EVALUATING IRONIC WORKS

Jonathan Swift, author of *Gulliver's Travels,* wrote a famous satire called "A Modest Proposal" in which he suggested that the Irish should raise babies to be eaten in order to solve the myriad problems confronting that famine-stricken land back in the 18th century.

But the point of his essay, of course, was completely other than that people should literally carry out the plan he proposed. He was, to be plain, writing in an **ironic** vein, saying one thing but meaning something entirely different. So when evaluating ironic works it is a mistake to take them literally; you need to evaluate them in terms of their underlying message. Swift's point was to force his British audience to face the mass starvation and misery in Ireland that British policies had produced; his ironic suggestions were intended to shock his audience into a recognition of what they were doing in Ireland.

Irony often is combined with humor or exaggeration to form a potent weapon in the hands of a master at the trade. Telling us what is true in a funny or exaggerated way makes it harder to deny than if it is put to us in a straightforward, serious manner. Ironic writing is particularly effective in penetrating the kinds of self-serving psychological defenses—denial, rationalization, and so on—that were discussed in Chapter 6.

Exercise 8-9

Here is the beginning of an ironic essay, "What Radio Reports Are Coming to," published way back in 1926 in the now long-defunct *New York Sun:*

> This, ladies and gentlemen, is the annual Yale-Harvard game, sponsored by the Wiggins Vegetable Soup Company, makers of fine vegetable soups. The great bowl is crowded, and the scene, courtesy of the R. & J. H. Schwartz Salad Company, is a most impressive one.
>
> The officials are conferring with the two team captains at midfield under the auspices of the Ypsilanti Garter company of North America. They are ready for the kickoff. There it goes! Captain Boggs kicked off for Yale by courtesy of the Waddingham Player Piano Company, which invites you to inspect its wonderful showrooms. "Tex" Schmidt recovers the ball, by arrangement with the Minneapolis Oil Furnace Company, Inc., and runs it back twenty-three yards courtesy of Grodz, Grodz, & Grodz, manufacturers of . . . .

1. What is the point of this item—its unstated thesis?

2. Clearly, things have changed a good deal since 1926. In your opinion, is the point of this ironic snippet relevant to what goes on today? Explain.

3. Does it make you take account of something that you already knew or that you hadn't paid sufficient attention to or appreciated the significance of? If so, explain. If not, why not?

Exercise 8-10

Today, political columnists such as Russell Baker and Maureen Dowd use a combination of irony and humor to make points about the current social/political scene. Here is an example, written in 1999 by the late and sadly missed Arthur (Art) Hoppe, believed by some critics and by the authors of this text to have been the very best in the 20th century at this game:

Our Deserving Rich

Let us pray that not a hand is laid on the $792 billion tax cut passed by the House when the Senate takes it up today. Never has a piece of legislation been so pure in its concept, so efficient in its means, so right on the mark.

As you may have read, the Republican measure passed by the House proposes giving 79 percent of the income-tax reductions to the richest one-fifth of our citizens and .03 percent to the poorest. The richest's take would average $4,592, while the poorest would haul in $15.

It is high time we recognized the tremendous contributions the rich have made to this great land of ours. Hitherto, we have punished them for their well-earned money. The harder they labor and the more they make, the more we penalize them financially. What sort of a message does this send to every little tad in the land?

At the same time, we have rewarded the poor for their inability to find well-paying jobs. The less money they make, the more we subsidize them with

Before I pronounce you man and wife, a brief word from Archer Daniels Midland.

Irony and exaggeration work well not only in written works but also in drawings and cartoons.

our taxpayer dollars. There can be no doubt that they take far more from us than they give.

Let's ask ourselves: What has poverty ever done for America? The answer is absolutely nothing. Do the poor endow the symphonies and operas that flood our souls with musical grandeur? Of course not. Do they build the museums that increase our knowledge of the world or the galleries where hang the masterpieces of human creativity? Do they donate vast acreages of untouched land as a heritage for generations yet unborn? Don't be silly.

How many poor people have adopted a highway or saved a baby harp seal? Their commitment to the environment is infinitesimal at best. Indeed, rather than devoting themselves to improving our surroundings, they go out of their way to make our cities and towns far less inviting.

Their ghetto tenements, their sleazy housing projects and their skid row hotels are a blight on the landscape. Generally speaking, their wardrobes are tasteless, if not downright appalling. And those who live in the country have a penchant for littering their yards with unsightly collectibles such as broken-down washing machines and rusted-out cars.

Contrast this utter disregard for our sensibilities with the care the rich lavish on their surroundings. How pleasant it is to stroll through a wealthy neighborhood, graced with high flower-bedecked walls, verdant hedges and stately cast-iron fences.

How pleasing to the eye is the sight of an immaculately tuxedoed man and his bejeweled wife in her haute couture gown stepping from a limousine to attend a culture-improving function. Never could a poor person hope to equal their gratifying splendor.

Yes, as we would say in the rosy Ronald Reagan days, "It's morning in Palm Beach."

So hail the Republicans! Let us take comfort in the adage that the rich will always be with us—at least as long as the Republicans are in power. As for the Democrats, they would foolishly squander our hard-won budget surplus on Social Security, Medicare and other give-aways to the less successful members of our society.

Let's admit that the Democrats were not totally defeated. In what was obviously a last minute compromise, the Republicans agreed to give the poor families that $15. I can't for the life of me think why. It will only encourage them.[10]

1. What is Hoppe's point—his unstated thesis?

2. Why does Hoppe bash the poor and praise the rich? What is the point of such questions as "What has poverty ever done for America?" or "Do the poor endow symphonies and operas that flood our souls with musical grandeur?"

3. In your opinion, is he on target or not? Explain.

4. Does he make you take account of something that you already knew or that you hadn't paid sufficient attention to or appreciated the significance of? If so, explain. If not, why not?

---

[10] From Art Hoppe, "Our Deserving Rich," *San Francisco Chronicle,* July 28, 1999. © *San Francisco Chronicle.* Reprinted by permission.

SUMMARY OF CHAPTER 8

Chapter 8 concerns the evaluation of extended arguments—essays.

1. Most types of essays are straightforwardly argumentative, but some—for instance, descriptive or explanatory essays—may mask their theses in one way or another. *Example:* Orwell's essay, "A Hanging."

   Essays may argue by considering reasons *pro and con* a thesis, by providing a *refutation to counterarguments,* or by making a *comparison of alternatives,* as well as simply by presenting *reasons (premises)* in support of a *thesis.*

   There are several guidelines to use in evaluating argumentative passages: (1) Find the thesis and keep it in mind as you read; (2) find the reasons (premises) that support the thesis, and (when there are any) the reasons for the reasons, and so on, taking into account the evidence presented; (3) identify responses to likely objections or counterarguments; (4) skip whatever doesn't support (or argue against) the thesis; (5) add relevant information, pro or con, that you may know of; (6) consider the tone and emotive language; and (7) come to an evaluation.

   Coming to an evaluation consists primarily in asking and answering three questions, corresponding to the three basic requirements of cogent reasoning introduced in Chapter 1: (1) Are the writer's (or speaker's) assumptions and stated reasons justified by what you already believe? (2) Do you know other relevant reasons or arguments? (If so, they need to be added to the mix.) (3) Do the reasons (plus any added material) justify acceptance of the thesis—that is, is the argument then valid?

2. The *margin note and summary method* is a useful way to clarify the main ideas of an essay before analyzing it. This method has four steps: (1) Read the material carefully, (2) read it again and add margin notes at the relevant spots in the essay, (3) construct a summary from the margin notes, and (4) evaluate the summary, making sure to bring relevant information to bear.

3. Reasons offered in support of a thesis may be about *facts* or about *values.* Claims about values typically are justified differently than those about facts.

   It often is said that facts are *objective,* values *subjective.* On this view, the shape of a gold ring, for example, is an objective fact about the ring itself; the beauty of the ring is "in the eye of the beholder." A contrary view is that values inhere in the valuable objects themselves, so that they too are objective.

   Among value claims, those about *moral* matters tend to be both controversial and important. If moral values are subjective, then moral claims can be justified by evidence that the writer or speaker, or most or even all people hold that value. But if moral right and wrong are objective facts, then how people feel about them is irrelevant, and something outside our feelings—for example, biblical commandments—need to be appealed to in order to justify a particular moral claim. So when one is evaluating arguments containing moral claims, it often is important to try to find out what makes the writer or speaker make such a claim and to then assess the claims in view of one's own moral standards, however one has arrived at them. Of course, one's own moral standards should not be exempt from challenge and improvement (for example, in subtlety). Those who accept, say, the Ten Commandments need to see that they do not automatically answer all questions—they don't answer all economic ones, for example—and thus are in need at the very least of interpretation and perhaps also augmentation. Careful consideration of a standard may lead to a change of mind, say, about abortion or infanticide in view of the dire situations some people find themselves in.

4. Ironic essays argue for a point indirectly and thus are not to be taken literally. (For example, Swift did not espouse the eating of Irish babies.) The point in irony is not to present reasons for a conclusion so much as to get readers to see something clearly that they may have overlooked, or not paid sufficient attention to, or defended against by some sort of self-serving self-deception. An honest evaluation of ironic writing requires us to determine whether, as implicitly claimed, we have overlooked or denied something important.

There are no dull subjects. There are
only dull writers.

     —H. L. Mencken

Learn as much by writing as by
reading.

      —Lord Acton

He can compress the most words into
the smallest idea of any man I ever met.

    —Abraham Lincoln

A deluge of words and a drop of sense.

      —John Ray

Chapter

9

WRITING COGENT
(AND PERSUASIVE) ESSAYS

The discussion in Chapter 8 should make clear the essential contents of an argumentative essay: a thesis (grand conclusion) and reasons (premises) supporting the thesis. It also should be clear that in most cases the reasons themselves need to be supported by evidence or secondary reasons and that it often is useful to consider and refute likely objections.

But it should quickly become evident that writing a cogent and effective essay is much more difficult than summarizing and evaluating someone else's effort. Writing is character forming; it does indeed make evident the truth that writing is nature's way of letting us know how sloppy our initial thoughts on a topic often are. There are three reasons for writing essays, and one is without doubt that it is the very best way to sharpen sloppy thoughts into ideas that are clear, sensible, and well supported by good reasons and evidence. (The other two are to convince others and—obviously—to satisfy course or other requirements.)

1. THE WRITING PROCESS

Experienced writers tend to keep their basic goals firmly in mind as they write and, indeed, as they prepare to write. They usually develop a plan of attack designed to meet their goals, but they don't generally move relentlessly from one idea to the next. Rather, they frequently revise their original plans in the light of new evidence or ideas or in the face of unexpected difficulties. One task often interrupts another. (Interestingly, editing seems to have a higher priority with most experienced writers than any other writing task and tends to interrupt others at any time. Having used an inaccurate word, for example, writers tend to put aside whatever they are doing and search for one that is more precise.) The point is that for most people essay writing is a convoluted process, not a straightforward, linear one.[1] Skilled writers constantly rework their ideas as they plan and then write. The process itself leads to discovery, including, alas, the discovery of the inadequacy of our previous thoughts.

2. Preparing to Write

Students generally are asked to write short argumentative essays on specific topics—for instance, literacy in the United States or legalizing marijuana. Suppose your assignment is to write an essay on the topic of regulating the possession of firearms.

The first task is to determine what the precise thesis of your essay will be. Gun regulation might involve restricting the carrying of handguns to specific places or perhaps only to specified individuals. Your thesis might be for, or against, the legal possession of automatic, quick-firing weapons, or it might focus just on handguns such as pistols.

Once you have provisionally decided on a thesis, your research and greater thought on the matter may well urge a change of mind, perhaps even a switch from pro to con, or vice versa. Unless a precise thesis is forced on you, say, by your instructor, the very process of thinking about the topic and investigating the evidence and the reasonings of others is likely to motivate you to revise your thesis in one way or another. Poor thinkers often decide on a thesis and hang on to it no matter what the evidence seems to indicate, as though changing one's mind indicates failure. Good thinkers realize that changing one's mind *for good reason* is the hallmark of intelligent thought. In the case of laws concerning firearms, for instance, evidence about the incredible destructive firepower of handheld automatic weapons such as Uzis might convince you to argue for the banning of these weapons.

After you have provisionally selected a thesis and have developed reasons and evidence in its favor, it often is useful to construct an outline of the essay that is to be the finished product. It's true, of course, that we all are different. Some people do better just starting out writing, doing research, and even altering their thesis as they go along rather than following the order suggested here. (Recall the earlier remark about writing being a convoluted process.) But most writers, in particular those with little experience, find it useful to do a good deal of preparation, including the construction of an outline, before starting to write the essay itself. (That is an important reason why essays written the night before they're due seldom get good grades—the fact that they are "off the top of the head" is obvious to instructors.) At the very least, an outline should include a provisional thesis and the principal reasons and supporting evidence expected to be presented

---

[1] There have been a very few exceptions to this rule, the philosopher Bertrand Russell, interestingly, being a case in point. His handwritten first drafts, with extremely few changes here and there, often were used by publishers to set final type. We ordinary writers can only examine these drafts with a sense of awe, not with the intent to acquire the knack ourselves.

in its favor. Outlines need not be written in grammatically correct or even whole sentences. Phrases and key words often are sufficient. But it is a good idea for inexperienced writers to state the thesis and principal reasons in complete sentences.

Calvin (of the Calvin and Hobbes duo) found it overly tedious having both to write an essay about bats and to do research on the topic, but research—diligent research—usually is essential. When doing research, take notes (including citations!) of pertinent evidence—statistics, examples, the opinions of experts, and so on. Regularly review what you have discovered in the light of your thoughts on the topic to see how the evidence supports, or undermines, your thesis or important reasons. If research undermines your thesis, it obviously needs revision (making the thesis narrower, perhaps) or a significant change in the reasons you intend to offer in its support. *Never simply ignore counterarguments or reasons!*

Some reasons involve legal matters that require us to review the law and interpretations of it. For instance, many arguments address issues that involve constitutional law (such as abortion, gun control, pornography, and so on). Because the Constitution often is used to support either side of an argument, it needs careful interpretation to be persuasive. For this reason, it's a good idea to research judicial opinion (the majority and dissenting opinions of high-court judges) in court cases addressing the issue you are writing about. Consulting expert opinion will help you understand the kind of careful deliberation needed in arguing complex legal matters.

Of course, you don't want to snow readers with a mountain of reasons or evidence. Plan to stick to your best reasons—those that reflect your most convincing evidence. Remember, though, that not all reasons are based on factual research or evidence. When relevant, moral convictions and standards, or beliefs about aesthetic or other values, constitute very good reasons indeed. For instance, the belief that taking the life of animals solely for our own purposes—for food or for furs—is morally wrong certainly is relevant to issues concerning the treatment of animals.

Finally, before starting to write an essay, make sure that its thesis follows logically from the reasons (premises) you intend to offer in its support. After all, validity—deductive or inductive—is an absolutely necessary condition of cogent argument. And reasons that do not genuinely support a thesis are useless.

3. Writing the Essay

Argumentative essays typically divide into three parts: an introduction (usually including the essay's thesis), the body of the essay, and a conclusion. Each part helps to develop, organize, and support the argument.

The Introduction

A good introduction engages the reader's attention and lays the groundwork for an essay's thesis, which usually is stated toward the end of the introduction but may be placed right at the beginning. The point of the introduction is to start persuading readers to accept your thesis, perhaps before it is even stated. (Remember, you have two goals in mind. One is to write an essay that is cogent. The other is to persuade readers to accept

Reprinted by permission of the *Detroit Free Press*.

your thesis. A perfectly cogent essay that is not well written may very well not convince many readers.)

An essay can be started in all sorts of ways, a good one being to quote from an authoritative source. For instance, an essay on the need for greater adult literacy might begin with the following statistics:

> According to the National Adult Literacy Survey, 40 to 44 million adults are functionally illiterate, a number that is increasing by about $2\frac{1}{4}$ million a year. Fifty million adults recognize so few printed words that they read on a fourth- or fifth-grade level.

The essay might then tie this quote into the rest of the introduction:

> These alarming statistics suggest that there is something drastically wrong with a system of education that turns out so many poorly prepared adults. . . .

After a few more introductory remarks, provide readers with a clear statement of the essay's thesis, followed by an enunciation of the three major reasons that are offered in its support:

> We, as a country, must do what is necessary to ensure that our people are literate [thesis], not only to improve the lot of those who suffer from illiteracy [reason 1], though that is reason enough, but to reduce the economic burden on society [reason 2] and to strength our democracy with an informed citizenry [reason 3].

Starting the essay in this way prepares the audience to read the body of the essay intelligently. Although it isn't necessary to include the main reasons after the thesis, doing so helps to keep both the writer and the reader on track.

The Body of an Essay

The body of an essay develops the reasons and evidence offered in support of the essay's thesis. How much support is needed depends on how resistant the intended audience is likely to be (or on how much space is available to make your case). You don't want to hit people over the head with what they already believe or know. The body of the essay on illiteracy might contain two subsidiary reasons offered in defense of the first major reason that illiterate individuals suffer personally. The first might be this one:

> The humane argument for a completely literate population is quite simply that illiterate people suffer a great deal from their affliction—both on a psychological and a practical level. Consider the man who is so embarrassed at being unable to read that he *pretends* to read so as to conceal his ignorance. . . .

Note the use of an example to illustrate the first subsidiary reason.

After providing several examples that make the point about the psychological problems facing the illiterate, the essay might then describe other problems that the functionally illiterate face in everyday life:

> Personal humiliation, however, is only one consequence of illiteracy. Perhaps even more important are the ways in which the lives of functional illiterates are severely restricted. Imagine, for instance, how difficult perfectly ordinary, everyday tasks become for those unable to read product labels, telephone books, ...

The stage has now been nicely set for the essay's second major reason—that society as a whole suffers when many of its citizens are illiterate, stated perhaps in a way that at the same time counters a likely objection to the essay's thesis that America should act to greatly reduce its rate of illiteracy:

> It may be argued that the expense of tracking down and stamping out illiteracy is more than our pocketbooks can bear. But that argument fails to take into account how much we, as a society, have to pay for the illiteracy of a third of our people. . . .

At this point, after providing examples of how illiteracy is an economic drain on society as a whole, the essay might continue in this way:

> Even more important, though, literate citizens are more likely to strengthen our democracy because they have the ability to be well informed. For example, ...

The Conclusion

The conclusion of an argumentative essay often restates the thesis—perhaps with emphasis. If the essay is rather long or complicated, the main points may need to be summarized. Here, for instance, is part of what would make a good conclusion to the illiteracy essay:

> In sum, everyone will benefit from the eradication of functional illiteracy. Certainly the illiterate one-third of our adult population has a great deal to gain by learning to read. They will be better able to cope with such simple practical tasks as . . . . Those of us who enjoy the advantages of literacy will also benefit because . . . .

Here, now, is what the entire essay on illiteracy might look like. It is rather short as essays go, intended primarily to serve as an example, but it nevertheless does a satisfactory job of clearly presenting and defending an important thesis:

> According to the National Adult Literacy Survey,[1] 40 to 44 million adults are functionally illiterate, a number that is increasing by about $2\frac{1}{4}$ million a year.

Fifty million adults recognize so few printed words that they read on a fourth- or fifth-grade level. These alarming statistics suggest that there is something drastically wrong with a system of education that turns out so many poorly prepared adults. Those with rudimentary skills have trouble functioning effectively in society, finding employment or training for new jobs. Yet fewer than 10 percent of those needing help are being reached.[2]

The National Committee on Education was right in claiming that we are "a nation at risk." We, as a country, must do what is necessary to ensure that our adult population is literate, not only to improve the lot of those who suffer from illiteracy, though that is reason enough, but to reduce the economic burden on society, and to strengthen our democracy with an informed citizenry. The humane argument for a literate population is quite simply that people who cannot read suffer a great deal from their affliction—both on a psychological and practical level. Consider the man so embarrassed by his illiteracy that he *pretends* to read books on buses and in restaurants, just to save face, or the woman who can't read street signs and is ashamed to ask someone to read them for her. The functionally illiterate regularly suffer embarrassment because of their affliction. I once knew a young man who, to avoid ridicule, went to great lengths to hide the fact that he could not read. Although in constant fear of discovery—by friends, his boss, even his relatives—he sometimes was forced to accept help, for instance, when filling out simple forms—much to his mortification.

Personal humiliation, however, is only one consequence of illiteracy. Perhaps even more important are the ways in which the lives of functional illiterates are severely restricted. Imagine, for instance, how difficult perfectly ordinary, everyday tasks become for those unable to read product labels, telephone books, prescriptions, or even bills or letters from friends. Think of how illiteracy prevents them from getting any but the most menial jobs. At the turn of the century, when the economy was more dependent on factory and farm workers, nonreaders might have been able to support themselves reasonably well, but in this age of technology, where computers dominate the workplace, employees *must* be literate. These days it is a rare job that doesn't require reading ability.

It may be argued that the expense of tracking down and stamping out illiteracy is more than our pocketbooks can bear. But that argument fails to take into account how much we, as a society, have to pay for the illiteracy of a third of our people. The functionally illiterate are disproportionately on welfare rolls, or in jail.[3] Unable to earn good incomes and often ignorant of simple preventive health or birth control measures, they increase the cost of programs such as Medicaid. Taxpayers, already heavily burdened by high taxes, can ill afford the additional expense of an illiterate population.

The business sector of the economy suffers as well. The U.S. Department of Labor estimates that illiteracy costs businesses up to $225 billion a year in lost productivity. "The costs stem from employee mistakes . . . absenteeism, tardiness, missed opportunities, and other problems associated with illiteracy."[4] The illiterate are much more likely to be injured on the job, costing employers several billion dollars every year in workmen's compensation and other insurance premiums and in the expense of replacing damaged equipment. These losses are ultimately passed on to us, the consumers.

Even more important, though, literate citizens are more likely to strengthen our democracy because they have the ability to be well informed, unlike the illiterate one-third of the nation. They need not rely on television, as most illiterates do, for watered-down versions of the news, but can read about issues in greater depth and make informed decisions at the polls. (Note that the illiterate even have trouble following voting instructions when they go to the polls, let alone make informed decisions.) They are less likely to be manipulated by demagogues and charlatans and more likely to reason critically about matters of national importance. Democracy guarantees freedom to discuss issues and allows for the uncensored distribution of news and critical commentary—rights that can be practiced effectively only by a literate citizenry.

In sum, everyone will benefit from the eradication of illiteracy. Certainly those who are illiterate have a great deal to gain by learning to read. They will be better equipped to find decent employment, to function well in everyday life and thus to feel better about themselves. Those of us who enjoy the advantages of literacy will also benefit because the expense of supporting illiterates will be considerably reduced and we will have a more reliable, more efficient workforce. Above all, a literate, informed citizenry is more likely to benefit our democracy as a whole. We thus have everything to gain and nothing to lose by helping everyone to become literate.

NOTES

1. Compiled by the United States Department of Labor, 1993.
2. The Scope of Illiteracy in This Country," Adult Literacy Service, accessed August 10, 2000, <http://www.indian-river.fl.us/livingservices/als/facts.html>
3. Jonathan Kozol, *Illiterate America* (New York: Anchor Books/Doubleday, 1985).
4. Shelly Reese, "Illiteracy at Work." *American Demographics* (April 1996), accessed August 12, 2000, <http://www.demographics.com/publications/ad/9604AB02htm>

4. Supporting Reasons Effectively

Perhaps the most difficult part of writing an argument is to provide convincing evidence. It's not enough to have sensible reasons to begin with. You need to convince the reader that those reasons are worth believing. Here are a few guidelines.

Provide Concrete Evidence

When possible, provide evidence that is specific. Use examples, cite statistics, compare or contrast relevant material, and draw on factual information. Reasons are more likely to be convincing when they can be verified by specific information than when they are explained in terms of generalities. Statistics reported in the National Adult Literacy Survey are a case in point. The fact that 40 to 44 million adults are functionally illiterate and 50 million more read on a fourth- or fifth-grade level is persuasive evidence for the need to reduce illiteracy in our country.

Specific information of this kind is usually drawn from these three sources:

1. *Personal experiences:* Suppose your thesis is that the food served at school should be improved. In this instance you, yourself, have had personal experiences that can be used to support your position. Every time you have eaten lunch in the cafeteria, the food has been terrible: the bread is hard as a rock, and the spaghetti tastes like rubber. Citing these personal experiences provides good support for your reasons, though usually other kinds of evidence are needed as well.

2. *The experiences of others:* When using this type of evidence, you need to make sure that their information is accurate. You know what your own experiences are, but judgment is required in evaluating what others claim has happened to them. (Sad, but true.)

3. *Authoritative sources:* These include such sources as reference books, journals, and people who have extensive knowledge about a subject—experts. But here, too, judgment must be used. Reputable encyclopedias, dictionaries, and handbooks on specific subjects can usually be relied on with respect to bare facts or matters that are not politically controversial. You have to be more careful with magazines, newspapers, television programs, and particularly the Internet because people can put anything on-line they want to and claim to be authorities when they aren't.

Note this important point: *Authoritative sources must always be credited,* either in a footnote or in the text itself. And direct quotations must always be indicated by the use of quotation marks. Using someone else's material without acknowledging the source constitutes **plagiarism,** an extremely serious offense.

Provide Transitions

A good essay obviously has to have a logical structure, but you also want to write so that one thought flows into another—so that the logical structure of your essays is easy to follow. Transition terms and expressions highlight the flow of an essay, helping readers to know what to expect next—to know which expressions serve as reasons and which as conclusions and, in general, how things hang together. Note the use in the illiteracy essay of the words *but, thus, however, consider, although, yet,* and so on, and the expressions *think how, for instance, above all, it may be argued that,* and *in sum.*

Think Your Position through Carefully

Having to write so as to convince others—much more than speaking extemporaneously—is an excellent way to get clear in your own mind as to where the truth lies. Writing a good argumentative essay requires mental discipline—the ability to see through

The plural of anecdote is not evidence.

—Bill Lockyer, attorney general of California

Block Those Metaphors!

Metaphor is a time-honored linguistic device. In the hands of careful writers, it often can express ideas swiftly and more effectively than more literal language. The trouble is that writers often go overboard in their enthusiasm for this linguistic tool. Here is an example from the writings of Guy Gugliotta in the Washington Post *(carried as one of the* New Yorker's *occasional metaphoric overkill items):*

There was no time, Acting Chairman Matthew F. McHugh (D-N.Y.) said last week, and the committee was tired of stoking public outrage with fortnightly gobbets of scandal. It decided to publish everything it had left, warts and all.

Now everyone is tarred with the same ugly brush, and the myth that forever simmers in the public consciousness—that the House shelters 435 parasitic, fat-cat deadbeats—has received another shot of adrenalin.

This little snippet also illustrates another writing no-no: the use of obscure words few readers can be expected to understand. Or did you know what gobbet means without having to look it up?

the natural tendency to hang on to opinions once formed, even in the light of their inadequacy—to root out inconsistencies and fuzzy beliefs, and to arrange thoughts into a coherent whole.

Consider Your Audience

Writers who seriously intend to influence others have to keep their audience firmly in mind. It's all too easy to forget the audience as we sit alone at a desk scribbling away (well, these days also tapping away). But experienced writers learn that they must always write with the intended readers in mind. Past failures—having had manuscripts rejected, severely criticized, or simply passed over by others—motivate them to figure out who they are writing for and how best to engage the interest of that particular audience.

One way to develop a sense of audience is to have one immediately at hand. Much has been written about the importance of writing with an audience in mind, but this advice needs to be augmented by actually having others respond to your work. In college, papers are usually directed to an audience of one—the teacher who evaluates your work and provides valuable advice intended to improve your writing ability.

However, what do you do in the hazy prewriting stage when you have the glimmer of an idea but aren't sure whether it will work, or when you have thought of a thesis and reasons but don't know whether they are convincing? In this stage of the writing process, it is helpful to try your ideas out on other people. Their feedback will give you a sense of audience response. Some teachers divide their classes into response groups so that students can discuss their ideas and read drafts aloud to each other. Some schools have

Reprinted by permission of Paul Miller.

tutors who can act as an audience. The point is to use whatever resources happen to be available so as to become accustomed to addressing a real audience.

Here are some questions to ask about the audience:

1. What is your intended audience?

2. What are their worldviews and background beliefs?

3. What tone is appropriate?

Think of how different your approach would be if you were arguing for gun control either to a group of mothers or to a local gun owners' organization. Most likely their worldviews and background beliefs would differ considerably, and undoubtedly the gun owners would be harder to convince than the mothers. Once you have the audience firmly in mind, you can begin to see what reasoning and evidence would be most likely to persuade and what tone would be appropriate.

Rewrite! Rewrite! Rewrite!

The difficulty of arranging thoughts coherently is an important reason why rewriting almost always is necessary. When writing a critical essay, we often realize that our thoughts aren't as focused or penetrating as we supposed. The writing process itself constitutes an important part of the reasoning process.

That's why most writers, definitely including the authors of this text, construct the first draft of an essay as a learning, or thinking, device. They do the best job they can on the first draft and then critically evaluate it as they would an opponent's essay. The next draft then can take account of what has been learned, perhaps by introducing new reasons and arguments that aren't open to the criticisms made of the first draft.

But one thing is clear. Only a few of the very best writers can construct a really good critical essay in one draft. Writers like philosopher Bertrand Russell (recall that his manuscripts often showed only a word or two changed here and there to mark the transition

Good Writers Respect Their Audience

F. L. Lucas, once fellow and lecturer at King's College, Cambridge University, stressed the writer's obligation to readers in his essay "What Is Style?" from which this excerpt is drawn: *

The writer should respect his readers; therefore [he should behave with] courtesy. . . . From this follow several other basic principles of style. Clarity is one. For it is boorish to make your reader rack his brains to understand. One should aim at being impossible to misunderstand—though men's capacity for misunderstanding approaches infinity. Hence Molière and Po Chu-i tried their work on their cooks; and Swift on his men-servants—"which, if they did not comprehend, he would alter and amend, until they understood it perfectly." Our bureaucrats and pundits, unfortunately, are less considerate.

Brevity is another basic principle. For it is boorish, also, to waste your reader's time. People who would not dream of stealing a penny of one's money turn not a hair at stealing hours of one's life. But that does not make them less exasperating. Therefore, there is no excuse for the sort of writer who takes as long as a marching army corps to pass a certain point. Besides, brevity is often more effective; . . . And because one is particularly apt to waste words on preambles before coming to the substance, there was sense in the Scots professor who always asked his pupils—"Did ye remember to tear up that fir-r-st page?"

**Holiday* magazine, March 1960

from first to final draft) are extremely rare in this world. The rest of us have to write at least two drafts, usually more, to get our thoughts into good order and to express them so they can be easily understood by others. And you shouldn't be surprised to find out that learning to do this well takes . . . practice, practice, practice. (The good news here is that computers, those marvelous "word processors," make the task of seemingly endless revision a good deal easier for many—but not all!—writers.)

If the need to practice, practice, practice has been mentioned, can lots of exercise chores be far behind? Here are a whole bunch of exercises—just how many you will need to sweat over is up to your instructor.

EXERCISE 9-1

One good way to get practice in writing well is to critique poor writing. Here is a tiny (142 words) tongue-in-cheek essay from the delightful book *Ordinary Money* by Louis B. Jones (New York: Viking, 1990). For many years, Jones was a reader for freshmen English and other college writing courses. As a warm-up exercise, explain the various writing bloopers, of the kind that might move your instructor to make negative margin comments—blunders that Jones constructed into his little "student-written" essay

Student Essay Bon Mots

Here are a few extreme examples from student essays to serve as a reminder that good writing requires care and—yes—extensive revision.

The elementary school I first attended was racial towards minorities.
   (Poorly expressed thought.)
Women have sat on the back burner long enough.
   (Unfortunate figure of speech.)
She was a rabid typist.
   (Malapropism.)
Secondly, the American school system is more loose, thus encouraging students to be creative rather than Japanese.
   (Faulty comparison.)
Every day at 4:00 thousands of people evacuate on their jobs.
   (Poor choice of words and construction.)
The question of how a Sephardic language school in France and a privately owned airport in Texas benefits the economy as a whole boogles the mind.
   (Subject-verb disagreement plus lack of care in spelling.)
Little towns seem to start out as little towns.
   (First quick draft became final draft.)
He usually settled arguments with fist-de-cuffs.
   (Overly clever—or display of ignorance?)
The octopus of communism spread its testacles over the continent.
   (Really!)
Do punctual errors count?
   (Yes, they do.)
He resorts to name calling and puts himself on a peddle stool.
   (What a motor-mouth.)
A broader view also prevents the student from charging blindly into a brick wall of unconceptuality.
   (Block that metaphor!)
I have a fool-time job.
   (Freudian slip?)
The vowels we made at the alter.
   (Double display of ignorance.)
I am in favor of capital punishment particularly in cases of murder and rape and aggravated napping, child or otherwise.
   (Unintended humor.)

Ah, well, everyone can't go to the head of the class in this doggy dog world. But at least we all can have self-of-steam. (Our thanks to Fresh Person English students at Knownayme College.)

(described by one of the book's characters as "complete bull___, but Ohrbach [the instructor] never notices"):

> The comparison/contrast of the Greeks and Romans is a very important comparison/contrast. Since the beginning of time, people have pondered this question. In the hustle-bustle world of today, the comparison/contrast of the Greeks and Romans is very important and relevant. For example, the Romans were after the Greeks and therefore they had a more technology-oriented advancement. For example, they had plumbing and flush toilets and they had lead in the pipes which made everybody gradually insane. For example, Caligula, which caused the Decline and Fall of the Roman Empire. Another comparison/contrast of the Greeks and Romans is, the Greeks were very sane. For example, Plato and other world-famous philosophers pondered the greatest question of all time. Plato believed that everything was ideal. This is still true today. . . .

EXERCISE 9-2

Here are many issues that should be of some interest to college students. Select one and, bearing in mind the writing suggestions just discussed, write an essay (about 1,000 to 1,500 words), taking one side or the other of the issue. Then write a critical analysis in reply to your own essay (as though you were a competent—and fair!—opponent attacking your position). And then rewrite your original essay to try to take account of your own criticisms. Think of your fellow students, not your instructor, as your audience. Pick a topic that will let you show how well you can reason about a complicated issue. Do not pick an issue that you think has an obviously right solution to it. For example, do not select number 12 if all you are going to say is that of course we ought to provide sex education in high school, because we all have a right to know the reproductive facts of life. Every issue is more complicated than that, and there always are serious pros and cons to consider. This is a difficult and very important assignment; it absolutely cannot be done satisfactorily the night before it is due—if for no other reason than that a certain amount of research very likely is in order. (Your instructor definitely and without doubt will quickly tell when reading your essay if it's a last-minute concoction.)

1. Should all college students be required to take at least basic introductory courses in math and science? In a foreign language?

2. Should we have a military draft?

3. Should people be allowed to download music from the Internet for free?

4. Should affirmative action with respect to the education or employment of women and minorities be the law of the land? (If you write on this topic, you must carefully explain what you mean by "affirmative action," and you should restrict your topic either to education or to employment.)

5. Should colleges and universities support big-time football and basketball teams?

6. Should speech codes be instituted in colleges and universities to fight racism on campus?

7. Should Congress raise fuel-economy standards for SUVs and other light trucks?

8. Are the salaries paid to movie stars and sports stars too high? If so, what should be done about this? If not, rebut those who would argue otherwise. In either case, support the side of the issue that you chose.

9. Should stem cells from embryos be used in medical research?

10. Should we require every adult to be tested for the AIDS virus?

11. Is banning indecent material on the Internet unconstitutional?

12. Should sex education be taught in high school?

13. Should homosexuals have the legal right to marry and enjoy the same benefits as other married couples?

14. Should we legalize marijuana for medical use?

15. Should we abolish the electoral college?

16. Recent studies have found that children who watch entertainment violence are more likely to exhibit aggressive attitudes and behavior in childhood and later in adulthood. Now that videogames have become more lifelike and involve the players in killing police officers, running over pedestrians, and committing other heinous acts of violence, should the government prohibit the sale of graphically violent, shooter videogames to minors?

17. As of spring 2001, discoverers of human genes are allowed to patent their discoveries, so that, for instance, certain tests for a propensity to breast cancer cannot be conducted on your genes without paying a royalty to the patent holder. The principal argument in favor of gene patenting is that allowing it dramatically increases the incentive to discover such genes. Should we allow human genes to be patented?

18. Most scientists believe that increased use of fossil fuels (coal, oil, and so on) is leading to increases in global warming that will have adverse effects such as raised sea levels and the inundation of low-lying coastal areas. But some scientists deny this is true, and a very few argue that the good effects of global warming will outweigh the bad ones. Take sides in this debate.

EXERCISE 9-3

1. Supreme Court Justice Antonin Scalia has become famous for dissenting opinions based on his belief that judges should not, by their decisions, become "illicit legislators" who substitute currently popular ideas or their own opinions for laws legally and democratically enacted. For instance, he refused to join the other Supreme Court justices in their decision that the state-supported and (at that time) male-only Virginia Military Institute (VMI) could not reject students on grounds

of sex. (The majority view was that doing so violated a woman's right to "equal protection of the law.") Scalia wrote that a democratic system "is destroyed if the smug assurances of each age are removed from the democratic process and written into the Constitution." He believed that the Fourteenth Amendment requirement of equal protection did not overrule the decision of a properly elected legislature making a single-sex institution permissible. The Constitution, he said, "takes no sides in this educational debate." He saw what the majority of the court did in the VMI case as "not the interpretation of a constitution but the creation of one."

Write a paper either defending or attacking Scalia's opinion. (You might want to actually get and read a copy of his whole dissenting opinion.)

2. A Florida technology company has developed a computer ID chip that could be implanted inside the body. The implant, about the size of a grain of rice, can be encoded with a wide range of information—everything from secret codes to sensitive medical data. Such a device would be invaluable to the medical community for giving emergency workers access to an unconscious patient's medical history, but it raises questions about privacy rights. Lee Tren, a senior attorney for a privacy advocacy group, cautioned that ". . . you always have to think about what the device will be used for tomorrow. . . . At first a device is used for applications we all agree are good, but then it slowly is used for more than it was intended."

Write an argument either defending or rejecting the use of embedded ID chips.

3. Here are brief arguments for and against public colleges and universities soliciting private funding from corporations and wealthy benefactors. Take a stand on this issue and write an argument defending your position. Good sources of information might be professors, department chairs, and deans in your own school.

An argument for soliciting private dollars is that state and federal budget cuts have been so severe in the past decade that public schools have had to look to the private sector for funding in order to ensure a high-quality education, to do cutting edge research, to replace outdated equipment, and to upgrade deteriorating buildings.

The opposition argues that private funding transforms public schools into appendages of private industry, preoccupies the faculty with fund-raising instead of teaching, pits one department against another, and undermines the curriculum through corporate influence.

EXERCISE 9-4

Here are excerpts from Adolf Hitler's *Mein Kampf,* a book in which he explained his philosophy and his goals for a "Thousand Year Reich."

a. Construct a summary of Hitler's arguments.
*b. Write an essay in which you critically evaluate these arguments. (In this case, the friendly authors of this text provide a summary in the answer section at the back of the book but not a critical evaluation. You should, of course, construct your

own summary first and then compare it with the authors' summary at the back of the book.)

Nation and Race
There are some truths which are so obvious that for this very reason they are not seen or at least not recognized by ordinary people. They sometimes pass by such truisms as though blind and are most astonished when someone suddenly discovers what everyone really ought to know. Columbus's eggs lie around by the hundreds of thousands, but Columbuses are met with less frequently.

Thus men without exception wander about in the garden of Nature; they imagine that they know practically everything and with few exceptions pass blindly by one of the most patent principles of Nature's rule: the inner segregation of the species of all living beings on this earth.

Even the most superficial observation shows that Nature's restricted form of propagation and increase is an almost rigid basic law of all the innumerable forms of expression of her vital urge. Every animal mates only with a member of the same species. The titmouse seeks the titmouse, the finch the finch, the stork the stork, the field mouse the field mouse, the dormouse the dormouse, the wolf the she-wolf, etc. . . .

Any crossing of two beings not at exactly the same level produces a medium between the level of the two parents. This means: the offspring will probably stand higher than the racially lower parent, but not as high as the higher one. Consequently, it will later succumb in the struggle against the higher level. Such mating is contrary to the will of Nature for a higher breeding of all life. The precondition for this does not lie in associating superior and inferior, but in the total victory of the former. The stronger must dominate and not blend with the weaker, thus sacrificing his own greatness. Only the born weakling can view this as cruel, but he after all is only a weak and limited man; for if this law did not prevail, any conceivable higher development of organic living beings would be unthinkable. The consequence of this urge toward racial purity, universally valid in Nature, is not only the sharp outward delimitation of the various races, but their uniform character in themselves. The fox is always a fox, the goose a goose, the tiger a tiger, etc., and the difference can lie at most in the varying measure of force, strength, intelligence, dexterity, endurance, etc., of the individual specimens. But you will never find a fox who in his inner attitude might, for example, show humanitarian tendencies toward geese, as similarly there is no cat with a friendly inclination toward mice.

Therefore, here, too, the struggle among themselves arises less from inner aversion than from hunger and love. In both cases, Nature looks on calmly, with satisfaction, in fact. In the struggle for daily bread all those who are weak and sickly or less determined succumb, while the struggle of the males for the female grants the right or opportunity to propagate only to the healthiest. And the struggle is always a means for improving a species' health and power of resistance and, therefore, a cause of its higher development. . . .

No more than Nature desires the mating of weaker with stronger individuals, even less does she desire the blending of a higher with a lower race, since, if she did, her whole work of higher breeding, over perhaps hundreds of thousands of years, might be ruined with one blow.

Historical experience offers countless proofs of this. It shows with terrifying clarity that in every mingling of Aryan blood with that of lower peoples the result was the end of the cultured people. North America, whose population consists in by far the largest part of Germanic elements [Hitler classified the English as Germanic] who mixed but little with the lower colored peoples, shows a different humanity and culture from Central and South America, where the predominantly Latin immigrants often mixed with the aborigines on a large scale. By this one example, we can clearly and distinctly recognize the effect of racial mixture. The Germanic inhabitant of the American continent, who has remained racially pure and unmixed, rose to be master of the continent; he will remain the master as long as he does not fall a victim to defilement of the blood.[2]

EXERCISE 9-5

Here are two essays arguing opposing points of view on the value of computers in the classroom. Write an essay taking one side or the other or arguing for a modified use of computers in education. As supporting evidence use your own experiences as well as research on the topic.

Computerized Lessons Help Motivate Kids
Need a stock tip? Ask one of Mark Neal's fourth-graders.

Students researched, "bought," and tracked stocks in their portfolios via Yahoo. Then, they developed final profit/loss reports for their shareholders that included spreadsheet-generated graphs of stock values during the project.

Look out Wall Street—here they come! Students in Rick Needham's and Joanne Zachariades' seventh-grade science classes simulated forming their own engineering companies to build bridges. Student companies designed the bridges and purchased materials with class "money." Company accountants kept checking account balances on spreadsheets, and workers built the bridges as the group's architect scanned plans into digital form for multimedia presentations. . . .

What was life like for a runaway slave in the South? If you could just talk to one. Well, you can—through Colonial Williamsburg interactive electronic field trips. Students in Patsy Lockhart's eighth-grade language arts/social studies class took a virtual trip back in time to Colonial Williamsburg. Via satellite broadcast, they watched three live re-enactments in the life of a runaway slave. After each segment, students' call-in questions were answered by the actors and on-site historians in real time. Students interacting with history—what an experience! . . .

---

[2] From Ralph Manheim's translation of *Mein Kampf* (Boston: Houghton Mifflin, 1971), 284–287. Copyright 1943 and renewed 1971 by Houghton Mifflin Company. Reprinted by permission of Houghton Mifflin Company and The Random Century Group Ltd.

These are just a few examples of the technology-integrated instruction that is taking place in classrooms in the New Haven Unified School District in Union City.

Computers, video, video conferencing, virtual field trips, multimedia and—motivation. Technology motivates students to do the everyday basics they often dread. The key is integration, not stand-alone technology for its own sake. As shown in the examples above, when technology is integrated into instruction, students still do the basics—reading, writing and math. The technology provides access to information, simulations, publishing tools, creative extensions and real-world connections.

Technology also helps provide students with instruction based on their needs—not a one-size-fits-all model that loses the struggling students and bores the others.

When teachers divide classes into groups based on the needs of their students, they can work with smaller rotating groups and focus on instruction. But what are the other students doing during these groups? They learn through a variety of independent activities. From skills practice to research to creative extensions, technology can provide activities that allow teachers to focus directly on instruction.

So what do we give up to put technology in schools? If the technology is integrated into instruction, very little. What's to be gained? Motivation, access to the basics, focused instruction, creative extensions and real-world connections. Technology is already thoroughly integrated into everyday life—from cell phones and checkout scanners at stores to dot-coms and Internet purchasing. We owe it to our students to join the real world and integrate technology in our classrooms.[3]

Computers Dumb Down Education
Thinking about buying a computer for your kids? Everyone else is. Indeed, our children are being sold down the river of technology. Throngs of educators, lemminglike, line up to wire schools. Parents grin as they plunk down credit cards to buy electronic machines for their children, anticipating an educational jump-start or quick fix. Meanwhile, English teachers cope with semiliterate students who are itching to play with computers but can't read a book.

Computer literacy doesn't demand the same level of instruction as English, American history or physics. It doesn't require the same amount of effort, either. Today, practically all office workers know word processing. Most learned it late in life.

But some subjects, while easy for a child to learn, are impossible for adults, like languages, for instance. The earlier you start, the easier it is to become fluent. The same with playing a musical instrument. Or drawing. Or public speaking.

---

[3] From Stephen W. Politzer, "Computerized Lessons Help Motivate Kids," *San Francisco Chronicle,* August 14, 2000, Copyright 2000. Reprinted by permission of the author.

Which gives you more advantages in business: having a long history of computer experiences going back to programming Logo or fluency in Japanese, German, French or Chinese? Which is more likely to lead to a rich, happy life: a childhood of Nintendo and PlayStations or a childhood of hikes and bikes?

Probably because computers are so easy for students to learn, educators love to teach computer techniques. But what are their students prepared for? A lifetime of poking at a keyboard for eight hours a day. It's one more way to dumb down the school, giving the appearance of teaching futuristic subjects while dodging truly challenging topics. . . .

Plenty of job skills get bypassed in our rush to get online. Today in the [San Francisco] Bay Area, Web programmers get $40 or $50 an hour—pretty good wages. Yet plumbers charge twice as much. How come? One reason plumbers charge so much is that almost every Bay Area school teaches computing. Almost none teach the trades: auto mechanics, carpentry or plumbing. When every student—good and bad—is pressed to become a computer maven, and only the incompetents are allowed to become plumbers, neither our programs nor our pipes will hold water.

Computers aren't compatible with the clay, dirt and cookie crumbs of a 5-year-old's life. Kids mustn't pour sand into the keyboard or smear peanut butter on the monitor. . . .

In Columbus, Ohio, Dana Elementary School installed three Compaq Presario computers in its kindergarten class, despite the kindergarten teacher telling the principal that computers were superfluous. Nevertheless, the technicians lugged in the equipment, only to haul out the sandbox and block table. There wasn't enough room for both. . . .

There's plenty wrong with our schools—lack of discipline, low interest in scholarship, leaky roofs, big classes, politically inspired curricula. But more computers and video monitors won't improve this. Do the politicians who promote wiring our schools really believe that Internet access will develop a love for mathematics, physics, history, reading or playing the violin?

So what computer should you buy your kids? Save your money and go hiking with them on Friday afternoons. Rather than checking into some science Web site, go to the kitchen and experiment with ice cubes sprinkled with salt, sugar and baking soda. Rather than a virtual online trip to the Louvre, bicycle over to the deYoung Museum and see real Asian art. Instead of a copy of *Reader Rabbit,* spend a half-hour every night reading stories.[4]

EXERCISE 9-6

The Patriot Act, passed by Congress after the September 11, 2001, terrorist attack on the World Trade Center and the Pentagon, gave federal authorities the power, in cases involving national security, to get an order from a secret court giving them permission

---

[4] From *San Francisco Chronicle,* August 14, 2000. Reprinted by permission of Cliff Stoll.

to obtain various records relevant to an investigation—including medical files, library records, and business documents. Groups like the American Library Association and civil rights advocates have opposed the legislation because of the far-reaching, invasive powers it gives the government. Advocates of the Patriot Act have countered that the Justice Department must have the authority to examine the records in question in order to identify terrorists dangerous to our country.

Do some research and examine both sides of the issue. Then write an argument defending your position.

EXERCISE 9-7

The opinions written by high-court judges constitute a good source for essay topics because they often are written on matters of general concern and tend to be logical, or at least somewhat intelligent. Here are four short excerpts from opinions of judges of the U.S. Court of Appeals concerning suits challenging state laws against assisted suicides. Write an essay in which you evaluate the statements made in these excerpts, being sure to consider whether at least two remarks in them that might be thought to commit fallacies discussed earlier in this text in fact do so.

> *Judge Stephen Reinhardt, Ninth Circuit:* Those who believe strongly that death must come without physician assistance are free to follow that creed, be they doctors or patients. They are not free, however, to force their views, their religious convictions or their philosophies on all the other members of a democratic society, and to compel those whose values differ with theirs to die painful, protracted, and agonizing deaths.

> *Judge Roger Miner, Second Circuit:* Physicians do not fulfill the role of "killers" by prescribing drugs to hasten death any more than they do by disconnecting life-support systems.

> *Judge Andrew Kleinfeld, Ninth Circuit:* It is very difficult to judge what ought to be allowed in the care of terminally ill patients. The Constitution does not speak to the issue. People of varying views, including people with terrible illnesses and their relatives, physicians and clergy, can, through democratic institutions, obtain enlightened compromises of the complex and conflicting considerations. They can do so at least as well as we judges can.

> *Judge Robert Beezer, Ninth Circuit:* If physician-assisted suicide for mentally competent, terminally ill adults is made a constitutional right, voluntary euthanasia for weaker patients, unable to self-terminate, will soon follow. After voluntary euthanasia, it is but a short step to a "substituted judgment" or "best interest" analysis for terminally ill patients who have not yet expressed their constitutionally sanctioned desire to be dispatched from this world.

EXERCISE 9-8

Here is an excerpt from an essay that is interesting because it argues for a more or less anti-PC thesis—that is, it defends a currently frowned-on side of an issue.

1. Construct a short summary.

2. Write an essay either attacking or defending the thesis, being sure to take account of what is said in the work in question, as well as in other writings that occur in this text. (Again, note that there is no law against doing outside research.)

Demystifying Multiculturalism

If you believe the multiculturalists' propaganda, whites are on the verge of becoming a minority in the United States. The multiculturalists predict that this demographic shift will fundamentally change American culture—indeed destroy the very idea that America has a single, unified culture. . . . But has America truly become a multicultural nation? And if not, will those who capitulate to these demands create a self-fulfilling prophecy?

At the heart of the argument is the assumption that the white population is rapidly declining in relation to the non-white population. . . .

In fact, white males will still constitute about 45 per cent—a plurality—of the workforce in the year 2000. The proportion of white men in the workforce is declining—it was nearly 51 per cent in 1980—but primarily because the proportion of white women is growing. They will make up 39 per cent of the workforce within ten years, according to government projections, up from 36 per cent in 1980. Together, white men and women will account for 84 per cent of all workers by 2000—hardly a minority share.

But the business world is behaving as if a demographic tidal wave is about to hit. A whole new industry of "diversity professionals" has emerged to help managers cope with the expected deluge of non-white workers. These consultants . . . train managers to "value diversity." [But what] precisely does valuing diversity mean? The underlying assumptions seem to be that non-whites are so different from whites that employers must make major changes to accommodate them, and that white workers will be naturally resistant to including non-whites in their ranks. Public-opinion polls don't bear out the latter. They show that support among whites for equal job opportunity for blacks is extraordinarily high, exceeding 90 per cent as early as 1975. As for accommodating different cultures, the problem is not culture—or race, or ethnicity—but education. Many young people, in particular, are poorly prepared for work, and the problem is most severe among those who attended inner-city schools, most of them blacks and Hispanics.

Nevertheless, multiculturalists insist on treating race and ethnicity as if they were synonymous with culture. They presume that skin color and national origin, which are immutable traits, determine values, mores, language, and other cultural attributes, which, of course, are learned. In the multiculturalists' world view, African-Americans, Puerto Ricans, or Chinese-Americans living in New York City have more in common with persons of their ancestral group living in Lagos or San Juan or Hong Kong than they do with other New Yorkers who are white. Culture becomes a fixed entity, transmitted . . . in the genes, rather than through experience. Thus, "Afrocentricity," a variant of multiculturalism, is "a way of being," its exponents claim. According to a leader of the Afrocentric education movement, Molefi Kete Asante, there is "one African Cultural System manifested in diversities," whether one speaks of Afro-Brazilians, Cubans, or Nigerians (or, presumably, African-Americans). Exactly how this differs from the traditional racist notion that all blacks (Jews, Mexicans, Chinese, etc.) think alike is unclear. What is clear is that the multiculturalists have abandoned the ideal that all persons should be judged by the content of their character, not the color of their skin. Indeed, the multiculturalists seem to believe that a person's character is determined by the color of his skin and by his ancestry.

Such convictions lead multiculturalists to conclude that, again in the words of Asante, "[T]here is no common American culture." The logic is simple, but wrong-headed: Since Americans (or more often, their forebears) hail from many different places, each of which has its own specific culture, the argument goes, America must be multicultural. And it is becoming more so every day as new immigrants bring their cultures with them. . . .

The urge to assimilate has traditionally been overpowering in the United States, especially among the children of immigrants. Only groups that maintain strict rules against intermarriage with persons outside the group, such as Orthodox Jews and the Amish, have ever succeeded in preserving distinct, full-blown cultures within American society. (It is interesting to note that religion seems to be a more effective deterrent to full assimilation than the secular elements of culture, including language.) Although many Americans worry that Hispanic immigrants, for example, are not learning English and will therefore fail to assimilate into the American mainstream, little evidence supports the case. By the third generation in the United States, a majority of Hispanics, like other ethnic groups, speak only English and are closer to other Americans on most measures of social and economic status than they are to Hispanic immigrants. On one of the most rigorous gauges of assimilation—intermarriage—Hispanics rank high. About one-third of young third-generation Hispanics marry non-Hispanic whites, a pattern similar to that of young Asians. Even for blacks, exogamy rates, which have been quite low historically, are going up; about 3 per cent of blacks now marry outside their group. . . .

Affirmative-action programs make less and less sense as discrimination diminishes in this society—which it indisputably has—and as minorities improve their economic status. Racial and ethnic identity, too, might wane if there weren't such aggressive efforts to ensure that this not happen. . . .

Multiculturalism is not a grassroots movement. It was created, nurtured, and expanded through government policy. Without the expenditure of vast sums of public money, it would wither away and die. That is not to say that ethnic communities would disappear from the American scene or that groups would not retain some attachment to their ancestral roots. American assimilation has always entailed some give and take, and American culture has been enriched by what individual groups brought to it. The distinguishing characteristic of American culture is its ability to incorporate so many disparate groups, creating a new whole from the many parts. What could be more American, for example, than jazz and film, two distinctive art forms created, respectively, by blacks and immigrant Jews but which all Americans think of as their own? But in the past, government—especially public schools—saw it as a duty to try to bring newcomers into the fold by teaching them English, by introducing them to the great American heroes as their own, by instilling respect for American institutions. Lately, we have nearly reversed course, treating each group, new and old, as if what is most important is to preserve its separate identity and space.

It is easy to blame the ideologues and radicals who are pushing the disuniting of America, to use Arthur Schlesinger's phrase, but the real culprits are those who provide multiculturalists the money and the access to press their cause. Without the acquiescence of policy-makers and ordinary citizens, multiculturalism would be no threat. Unfortunately, most major institutions have little stomach for resisting the multicultural impulse—and many seem eager to comply with whatever demands the multiculturalists make. Americans should have learned by now that policy matters. We have only to look at the failure of our welfare and crime policies to know that providing perverse incentives can change the way individuals behave—for the worse. Who is to say that if we pour enough money into dividing Americans we won't succeed?[5]

EXERCISE 9-9

In a very well-known, often reprinted lecture, "The Idea of a University," Cardinal John Henry Newman (1801–1890) argued that the principal work of the university is to provide a liberal education, not merely, or even primarily, professional training. He said that a liberal education

> gives a man a clear conscious view of his own opinions and judgments, a truth in developing them, an eloquence in expressing them, and a force in urging them. . . . it prepares him to fill any post with credit and to master any subject with civility.

Do you agree with Cardinal Newman's assessment of a liberal education and agree that the primary job of a university (or college) is to provide such an education? Write an essay defending your opinion.

EXERCISE 9-10

High-tech cheating has increased dramatically now that almost all students have access to the Internet. Some examples: 78 students at Dartmouth College were caught copying on-line answers to homework assignments; 150 students from two classes at the University of California, Berkeley, were caught plagiarizing papers from the Internet; and 30 engineering students at Northeastern University were caught gaining access to each other's on-line homework assignments.

---

[5] By Linda Chavez. © 1994 by National Review, Inc., 150 E. 35th Street, New York, NY 10016. Reprinted by permission.

It has been suggested that this new wave of cheating is due in part to there being a relatively low risk of detection and even more to the lenient nature of punishments when caught. In view of this and the fact that cheaters do harm to those who do not cheat, would you approve expulsion from college for first-time proven cheaters? Or flunking the course? Or suspension for one semester? Defend your answer.[6]

SUMMARY OF CHAPTER 9

The essential contents of an argumentative essay are a *thesis* and *reasons (premises)* supporting the thesis. Usually, reasons need to be supported in turn by evidence or secondary reasons.

1. Experienced writers tend to keep their basic goals in mind as they prepare to write, developing a plan of attack to meet those goals, revising their original plans in the light of new evidence or unexpected difficulties. But they don't generally write in a linear fashion; writing tends to be a convoluted process.

2. The first task when preparing to write is to determine precisely what your thesis will be. Later, of course, you may change your mind, perhaps by narrowing the topic or zeroing in on it more carefully. While preparing to write and during the writing process itself, changing one's mind for good reasons is the hallmark of intelligent thought.

   After selecting a thesis and developing your principal reasons in its support, you may find it useful to construct an outline of the proposed finished product. When doing the generally inevitable research, be sure to take notes, including reference citations. If research undermines your thesis, or reasons in its support, you must revise. Never simply ignore counterarguments or reasons. Before starting to write, make sure your thesis follows logically from the reasons you intend to offer in its support.

3. Argumentative essays typically divide into three parts. The *introduction* generally states and lays the groundwork for the thesis, either before or after stating it explicitly. The *body* of the essay should contain the reasons and evidence, perhaps also reasons in support of the reasons. It is likely to be more convincing if it contains examples. If counterarguments are to be discussed, the right time to do so is in the body of an essay; and similarly for comparing or contrasting with other ideas. The *conclusion* of your essay may restate the thesis or perhaps provide a short summary of the essay's most important points.

4. The point of writing an argumentative essay is to persuade readers to accept your thesis. To do so, effective writers provide convincing reasons and supporting evidence. They also keep the reader firmly in mind by considering the background beliefs of their audience and the appropriate tone to take given that audience.

---

[6] See the article by Ted Wallach, *San Francisco Chronicle,* August 14, 2000.

Good writers also try to achieve a natural flow by providing readers with transition words and expressions such as *but, although, for instance,* and *nevertheless.*

But (note the transition word), however well planned an essay may be, rewriting almost certainly will be necessary. A first draft may thus serve as a learning device, so that later drafts can take account of what has been learned.

The ads of our times are the richest and most faithful daily reflection that any society ever made of its entire range of activities.

—Marshall McLuhan

Advertising is legalized lying.

—H. G. Wells

Doing business without advertising is like winking at a girl in the dark. You know what you are doing, but nobody else does.

—Stuart Henderson Britt

Would you persuade, speak of interest, not reason.

—Ben Franklin

Advertising persuades people to buy things that they don't need with money they ain't got.

—Will Rogers

Advertising is what you do when you can't go see somebody. That's all it is.

—Fairfax Cone (ad executive)

Chapter

10

ADVERTISING:
SELLING THE PRODUCT

Advertising is so obviously useful that it's surprising it has such a bad name. Ads tell us what is new and what is available, where, when, and for how much. They tell us about a product's (alleged) quality and specifications. All for free, except for the effort of reading or paying attention.

Yet there are legitimate gripes about advertising. Ads don't tell us about product defects. They often mislead, either via exaggeration or, occasionally, downright lies. And because some products are advertised more heavily or more effectively than others, ads tend to skew our choices in unreasonable ways.

It also has been argued that advertising increases the costs of goods to consumers. It isn't uncommon for a quarter, or even a third, of the price of an item to be due to advertising costs, and critics have argued that this constitutes a tremendous waste.

But this charge is misleading. Advertising does cost a great deal of money, and this expense has to be factored into the costs of finished goods. Nevertheless, advertising greatly reduces the prices of those goods in the marketplace compared to what they would cost were advertising abolished or greatly restricted. It does so because it lowers production costs by making mass production profitable, thus enabling producers to obtain a mass market. In short, advertisers advertise because it reduces the costs of *selling goods*. It is not an accident that virtually all businesses advertise; they do so because they don't know of a better or cheaper way to sell their products. Those who argue otherwise generally forget that if a company doesn't advertise, it will have to increase other selling costs, especially sales commissions. (Advertising also has been objected to on the grounds that it gives an unfair advantage to large organizations when they compete against smaller ones, but objections of this kind raise large issues best left unexplored here—for example, about the desirability of large versus small businesses.)

In any case, it is worth noting that advertising has become an important part of our lives in a way separate from its informative aspect. Ads become part of the common experience and knowledge of a culture, taking their place alongside myth and well-known stories. In every generation, ad slogans ("Where's the beef?" and "You're in the Pepsi generation") are instantly recognizable by virtually everyone.

1. PROMISE AND IDENTIFICATION ADVERTISEMENTS

Virtually all ads are one or another (or both) of two basic kinds. **Promise advertisements** promise to satisfy desires or allay fears. All you have to do is buy the product advertised (remove bad body odor by using Old Spice deodorant; enjoy life more by driving a Ford Explorer). Most promise ads provide "reasons why" the product will do the job or do it better than competitors (Kleenex tissues are softer; a bowl of Total cereal has more vitamins and minerals).

Identification advertisements sell the product by getting us to identify with the product. They are a kind of promise ad, since they promise that somehow or other you will be better off using the product. But the promise is made indirectly through identification with respected institutions or individuals (or occasionally simply by fostering identification with the product directly, as in the case of some Pepsi commercials). We all tend to identify with our own group and with those whom we respect—people who are famous, rich, accomplished, unusually brave, or powerful. Identification ads take advantage of this very human trait. Celebrity ads work precisely because we identify with the famous people they feature and thus with the products they tout; we become like them in some small way by using Chanel No. 5 (Nicole Kidman), by playing golf with Nike golf balls (Tiger Woods), or by reading a good book (Oprah Winfrey).

Identification ads—indeed, all ads—work for another interesting reason. When people shop, say, in a supermarket, they tend to purchase products whose brand names are familiar to them. Few of us, for example, will buy a brand of toothpaste we have

---

Promise, large promise, is the soul of advertising.

—Samuel Johnson

Many advertising executives subscribe to the idea, mentioned before, that there are just two ways to influence people: via promises and identification. This Marine Corps advertisement invites young men to identify with the Marines pictured handsomely decked out in fancy dress uniforms. It was so successful that it spawned several even more successful TV commercials, one showing a piece of steel being made into a sword that was then nicely placed into its scabbard by a handsome Marine in dress uniform, while the voiceover intoned, "We're looking for a few good men—with the mettle to be Marines!" An absolutely brilliant ad series.

never heard of or never seen advertised; we buy a brand we recognize even though we know no other "reason why" we should buy that brand and not a competing one. (When was the last time you chose an unadvertised product rather than an advertised competing product?)

Among identification ad campaigns, those tailored to group identification are particularly interesting. Magazines often are chosen for these campaigns because they tend to tap specific markets. *Examples:* The Virginia Slims cigarette ads, built around the slogan "You've come a long way, baby!" featured dolled-up, foxy, white ladies in most magazines but pictured dolled-up, foxy, *black* ladies in publications with primarily African American readers such as *Essence;* the National Rifle Association (NRA) campaign that featured the slogan "I'm the NRA" and showed a macho state trooper in hunting magazines and a pediatrician and father in women's periodicals. An ad for Swanson's Hungry Man XXL made fun of men who ate quiche and sprouts instead of Backyard Barbecue, a hefty meal of barbequed chicken patties, pork patties, and mashed potatoes. The tagline on the back of some Hungry Man meals, "I know what I like and I like a lot of it," emphasized the macho image.

Occasionally these ads border on the nauseating. A disturbing trend features violence and death in ads. Example: An ad for a hair product shows a dead woman on a bed with the tagline "Great hair never dies." Another, for Bitch skateboards (of all things) shows a cartoon man pointing a gun at a cartoon woman under the bold-faced heading "BITCH." Men are sometimes targets as well: An ad for motorcycle clothing features an angry African American woman with the tagline "Where women are women and men are road kill." Even more troubling is the increasing sexualization of children in ads. Little girls are made up like women and posed seductively, and boys are depicted as sexually precocious, ogling sexy women, for instance, or looking up a woman's skirt. If ads influence consumer behavior, we're in for trouble.[1]

2. THINGS TO WATCH OUT FOR IN ADVERTISEMENTS

The good news about advertising, you will recall, is that it often provides true and useful information about products and entertains us with humor, storytelling, or just nice scenes or sentiments. Time enjoyably spent is time not completely wasted. *Examples:* The Budweiser Christmas TV commercials featuring their magnificent Clydesdales in winter scenes; Black and Decker's: "You don't have to be crazy to buy a Black and Decker cordless screwdriver. You just have to have a screw loose." Or the Billy Graham billboard ad:

> You're born.
> You suffer.
> You die.
> Fortunately, there's a loophole.

The bad news about advertising stems from the increasing ability of advertising geniuses—and some of them, alas, *are* geniuses—to manipulate audiences via sophisticated psychological ploys. Everyone realizes how others are conned by advertising, but

---

How Visuals Distort Reality

This excerpt from "The Archenemy of Flavor," by David Harris, appeared in Harpers *magazine (May 1999).*

The equation of beauty and taste is a false one, for nothing ever tastes as good as it looks in advertisements or food magazines. It is widely known that the fantastical foods in glossies such as *Gourmet* and *Bon Appétit* are actually inedible, that the voluptuous centerfolds of these gastronomical *Playboys* and *Penthouses* have communicable diseases, that those "willowy wonton strips gracing the salad" are the equivalent of prosthetic food, toxic concoctions of varnish, hair spray, and shoe polish. Wedges of cheese have been swabbed with rubbing alcohol to bring out their color, piping hot sauces are actually ice-cold so that they won't congeal, the grill marks on chicken have been drawn in with Magic Marker, and desserts made of gelatin have been so fortified with artificial thickeners that they are as indestructible as hockey pucks and are often tossed around among the staff, who exhibit the macabre sense of humor of medical students in the morgue.

---

[1] For more on these disturbing trends see *Deadly Persuasion: Why Women and Girls Must Fight the Addictive Power of Advertising,* by Jean Kilbourne, Simon and Schuster, 1999.

most of us think that we somehow are exceptions. Young people, including college students, often deny that they are influenced by advertising. They typically say that they don't wear designer jeans or Adidas shoes because of advertising but rather that they just "like" these products, self-deceptively ignoring the effect of advertising on their preferences. In fact, *no one* is immune to the influence of advertisements. (A Madison Avenue bigwig owned up to this when he said, "Even I fall for the stuff.") So we all are faced with the problem of how best to use advertising without being used. One way is to become familiar with the advertising devices and gimmicks used to appeal to our weaknesses, prejudices, and emotions unguided by intelligence. No doubt we'll still get taken now and then, but perhaps less often and with less seriously harmful consequences.

Ads Invite Us to Reason Fallaciously

We've already noted that ads often feature celebrity endorsements to manipulate us into buying the product. They thus invite us to commit the fallacy *appeal to authority*. We don't stop to think whether Britney Spears really does prefer Pepsi to Coca-Cola or whether she just gets paid to say she does. Anyway, what difference would it make to you if she didn't drink soft drinks at all? (*Consumer Reports* taste tests, by the way, show hardly anyone can distinguish between Pepsi and Coke. Can Britney Spears? Can you? Hint: In several actual classroom tests conducted by one of the authors of this text over a period of years, students consistently failed to distinguish their favorite brands of beer from competing brands.)

In the case of Britney Spears advertising Pepsi, it seems obvious that she is no authority on the taste of soft drinks, which, anyway, certainly are a matter of individual preference. But some celebrity ads are different, sports endorsements being a case in point. In recent years, Tiger Woods has dominated the golf scene, many professional golfers stand in awe of his accomplishments at that game, and he is often said to be the greatest golfer in the history of that sport. So his endorsement of Nike's "Tour Accuracy" golf balls carries great weight with golf duffers intent on improving their scores. But in fact Woods doesn't use these ordinary golf balls in tournaments. Instead, he hits custom-made balls not available to the general public (as do, by the way, some other pro golfers who endorse other brands). (Why millionaire actors and professional athletes feel that they need to make extra money by touting products they don't use is one of those mysteries of human nature that, perhaps fortunately, is not our topic here.)

Anyway, moving on to a related topic, it should be clear by now that ads generally are designed to invite us to overlook their *suppression of evidence*. They tell us the good features of products but always hide their product's warts. (Why should they do otherwise?) *Examples:* Ads for brand-name painkillers such as Tylenol acetaminophen tablets, St. Joseph aspirin, and Advil ibuprofen don't mention the fact that drugstore and supermarket brands sell for much less and are pharmaceutically identical. Bayer aspirin ads correctly point out that taking Bayer aspirin may save your life if you have a heart attack, but they direct attention away from the fact that every other brand of aspirin has the same good feature.

Advertising audiences also are invited to make *faulty* or *invidious comparisons*. *Examples:* Pizza Hut ads that compared their delivery service with dingbat pizza parlors that don't deliver at all, ignoring their true competitors, such as Domino's Pizza, that do;

> There is an art to making whole lies out of half truths.
>
> —Christy Mathewson (baseball hall of fame
> pitcher who was paid to endorse Tuxedo
> pipe tobacco)

Wisk ads that claim their product is more powerful than Tide, so you need to use less, making it seem that it costs less to use Wisk than Tide, which is not true (figure out why).

Some ads, though, use fallacious reasoning humorously and aren't meant to be taken seriously. A good example is this BMW ad: "Doctors say increased activity slows the aging process. Coincidentally, BMW drivers are ten years younger than other luxury car drivers." This humorous use of cause and effect was not an example of *questionable cause* because it was not intended to be taken literally. (But it nevertheless definitely was intended to manipulate prospective customers into buying a BMW.)

Advertisements Pound Home Slogans and Meaningless Jargon

In fact, ads run through the entire range of fallacies, challenging theorists to invent pigeonholes into which to put them all. How, for instance, should we categorize the fallacious reasoning that leads people to be swayed by endlessly repeated, mostly empty slogans? *Examples:* "Brut. Men are back." (Were they somewhere else?) "Nobody beats Midas. Nobody." "The World's Greatest Newspaper" (that's the *Chicago Tribune,* in case Chicago area readers didn't recognize it—well, we should mention that the *Chicago Tribune* is one of the better newspapers around these days). "I love what you do for me, Toyota." And so on, *ad* infinitum (heh, heh).

Slogans run the range from the modestly informative ("Miller Light: Great taste, less filling.") to the somewhat suggestive ("Chevrolet. Like a rock.") to the completely irrelevant ("Nike: Just do it."). In general, they work because they are repeated endlessly, so that they become ingrained in our minds. In the days before television, which is primarily a visual medium, singing commercials did the job on radio. There can be very few people over 60, for example, who could not at the drop of a hat sing the Rinso soap flakes jingle they heard belted out on radio countless times lo these many years ago: "Rinso white, Rinso bright; happy little washday song!"

Slogans that tout products as "the official" something or other are an interesting special case. In 2004, for example, Tylenol advertised itself as "The official supplier of pain relief products for the 2004 U.S. Olympic team" (accompanied by pictures of athletes with massive, rippling muscles, presumably injury prone). Puffs of this kind generally imply something that is false. The Tylenol slogan implied that Olympic athletes pre-

> The most brilliant propaganda must confine itself to a few points and repeat them over and over.
>
> —Adolf Hitler

ferred this brand to others or that Tylenol was better than any other painkiller. But you can bet your life that if they were in real pain, they would take something stronger, like Vicodin. In fact, becoming official whatever merely means paying for the privilege of being identified with a name. Tylenol paid through the nose to be identified with the Olympic Games, as did other official Olympic sponsors, like Coca Cola, Chevrolet, and Budweiser. Another wrinkle on the "official" gambit is the naming of sports arenas and stadiums after companies that buy this privilege (Coors, 3Com, Enron, and so on).

Ads Play on Weaknesses, Emotions, Prejudices, and Fears

Particular kinds of advertisements sell some products more easily than they do others. Those that play on weaknesses or fears are a case in point, one reason so many TV commercials are of this nature. *Examples:* The "ring around the collar" commercials; ads for mouthwashes, hair restorers, and hair colorers; "roach motels"; and so on. Some of these ads do have the virtue of being informative (Grecian Formula does darken gray hair), but in many cases the product doesn't do the job advertised (Listerine does very little if anything for bad breath, since most bad breath originates elsewhere; it does, though, kill some mouth bacteria). In many other cases, the advertised product doesn't do the job any better than competing products (Mylanta isn't any better at counteracting stomach acidity than Maalox, Gelusil, or several other brands; Energizer and Duracell batteries are equally good).

Ads Draw on Trendy Issues in the News

Issues that grip the country are fertile ground for advertisers, who use them to play on our fears and desires. For instance, mounting concerns over the obesity epidemic has inspired a glut of low-fat, low-sugar, low-salt, low-carb products. McDonald's is pushing McVeggie Burgers and McGriddles (cheese, eggs, and meat wrapped in pancakes). Kraft Foods is marketing a new version of Lunchables called Fun Fuels made with fruit, meat, grain, and dairy products. And Hershey's has launched sugar-free chocolates with slogans like "Your recommended daily allowance of indulgence."

Weight-loss ads aimed at fat-conscious consumers have been making such exaggerated claims lately that the Federal Trade Commission released a guide in 2003 to help

consumers spot deceptive ads for phony weight-loss products. You'd think people would
be skeptical of slogans like "lose weight without diet or exercise," but apparently not.
P. T. Barnum got it right when he said there's a sucker born every minute.

Ads Employ Sneaky Rhetoric

In particular, **weasel words** are quite common in advertising. When an ad says the product *"fights* bad breath," it's wise to assume it doesn't *cure* bad breath, because if it did,
the ad would make this stronger, less weasely claim. Similar remarks apply to claims
such as *"helps* control dandruff with regular use," "gets dishes *virtually* spotless," and
so on.

We also need to watch out for sneaky uses of *comparative* and *evaluative* terms, like
good, better, and (best of all) *best.* The term *best* at best translates into "tied for first with
all other leading brands." The "lowest fare to Europe" may turn out to be the standard
fare every airline charges. And when an ad says "No one sells ___ for less," you can be
pretty sure others sell for the same price. And then there is that wonderful term, *free,* itself perfectly unsneaky, but so often used to lure the gullible (all of us in weak moments)
into thinking they're getting something for nothing.

But these kinds of ads aren't as sneaky as the "official sweepstakes" notifications that
arrive regularly in the mail. Their fine-print disclaimers have reached a high art, as the
one recently received from *Time,* Inc., that featured very large type showing through a
transparent window in the envelope stating:

**THE RESULTS ARE NOW IN: HOWARD KAHANE
HAS WON ONE OF OUR TWO $1,666,675.00 PRIZES!**

Deliberate deception: A Charles Schwab commercial shows a satisfied couple
talking about their successful investments with the brokerage firm. Then a three-second statement appears on the screen with about ten lines of print, starting with
the information that the people telling their story were real customers of Schwab.
But only a speed reader could get to the end fast enough to read the sentence revealing that the customers were paid for their testimonials.

Above this, on one line and in very tiny and easily overlooked type, came the fine-print disclaimer:

> "Be it henceforth known that if you have and return the grand prize winning entry, we will be pleased to announce that . . . ."

All of which means that if H. K. happened to have been assigned the perhaps-one-chance-in-ten-million winning number, he would win the big bucks by returning the grand prize entry. (H. K. didn't waste time or a stamp finding out.) See the appendix for more on the topic of chances—probabilities—in general.

Here's another ad with fine print disclaimers—this time for a Web site.

> "Today at 12:00 noon, GO.COM WILL LAUNCH THE WORLD'S FIRST ON LINE AUCTION SITE.*"

This deceptively clear claim is immediately contradicted in the footnote: "[The Web site is the first on-line] since e-bay, amazon.com, yahoo, and a few others. But it is the first designed with better architecture, so it's more reliable . . . there's a better auction at go.com." In other words, it wasn't the first on-line auction site.

Ads Play to Patriotism and Loyalty

If appeals to fears and prejudices can sell the product, why not patriotism and loyalty to one's country? At least that was what advertisers thought after September 11, when patriotic fervor was at its highest pitch since World War II. Everything from cars to the stock market to sports clubs was wrapped in the flag and sold to the public. Ford pledged to "Help America Move Forward" in zero financing ads and GM used the controversial tagline "Keep America Rolling." The New York Stock Exchange urged Americans to invest in the market with the slogan "Let Freedom Ring," and the New York Sports Clubs offered reduced initiation fees under the tagline "Keep America Strong." Images of the flag popped up everywhere—on sheets and underwear, on napkins and sweatshirts—but the trend was short lived. Consumers criticized many ads as tasteless, coming so soon after a national tragedy, and focus groups sent marketers the message that using patriotism to sell products was a turnoff.

Some ads were understandable, perhaps. Given the drastic drop in air travel after the terrorist attack, United Airlines had good reason to launch a major ad campaign. The documentary style ads featured interviews with United employees making patriotic

Boondocks © Aaron McGruder. Reprinted with permission of Universal Press Syndicate. All rights reserved.

All of us come from someplace else.

Just once, you should walk down the same street your great-grandfather walked.

Picture this if you will.

A man who's spent all his life in the United States gets on a plane, crosses a great ocean, lands.

He walks the same streets his family walked centuries ago.

He sees his name, which is rare in America, filling three pages in a phone book.

He speaks haltingly the language he wishes he had learned better as a child.

As America's airline to the world, Pan Am does a lot of things.

We help business travelers make meetings on the other side of the world. Our planes take goods to and from six continents. We take vacationers just about anywhere they want to go.

But nothing we do seems to have as much meaning as when we help somebody discover the second heritage that every American has.

America's airline to the world.

See your travel agent.

Courtesy of Pan American World Airways, Inc.

Advertising tends to concentrate on marginal needs, desires, and fears at the expense of many more important ones. Indeed, a frequently heard charge against advertising is that it increases the already strong tendency of people in industrial countries to become pre-occupied with buying and consuming goods. (Note the humorous bumper sticker WHEN THE GOING GETS TOUGH, THE TOUGH GO SHOPPING.) *Occasionally, however, an ad comes along that reminds us of what (for most of us) are much more important values, even though we tend to forget them in the hustle and bustle of everyday life. This Pan Am ad is one of those rare ads that tend to push us in the right direction. Yes! If we can afford it (and more of us could if we spent less on lesser needs), just once, we should walk down the same street our great-grandfather walked. (Pan Am went belly-up in the early 1990s, but for other reasons.)*

comments like "We're Americans and this is not gonna beat us down" and "We took the blow but we're gonna get up." The ads received mixed reviews, and though they might have boosted United's image, they didn't sell tickets—air travel was down for two years after the attack.

Puffery Is Legal, But Not Deceptive Advertising

Finally, it's worth noting that what is called "puffery"—generalized, vague, or exaggerated claims, particularly when asserted humorously—is legal. *Example:* The claim by BMW to be "The Ultimate Driving Machine." (Litigation does very occasionally arise concerning borderline cases.) However, ads can overstep legal boundaries and make fraudulent claims. The cigarette industry, in particular, has come under fire for deceptive advertising. For example, in spring 2003, Philip Morris was found guilty of consumer fraud in its ads for "light" cigarettes. Judge Nicholas Byron ruled that the company intentionally misled the public into thinking that Marlboro Lights and Cambridge Lights were "less harmful or safer than their regular counterparts" and ordered the company to pay $10.8 billion to the plaintiffs. This case is one of several lawsuits brought against cigarette companies in recent years.

EXERCISE 10-1

Here are several advertising snippets (usually including the main ploy). Evaluate each of them for honesty, cogency, and the like, and point out uses of the various kinds of gimmicks and devices (humor, jargon, etc.) discussed in the text.

1. Woman in a cigarette ad: "Until I find a real man, I'll settle for a real smoke."

*2. Burger King sign: "10 FREE French Fry Certificates for only $1.00."

3. Theme line in a French Government Tourist Office brochure touting the advantages of European travel originating in France: "The only European country that borders on six *other* countries, France brings you into the heart of Europe."

4. Calvert Gin ad: "Dry, Drier, Driest, Crisp."

5. "Just as you can depend on the sun to rise, you can count on Metropolitan [Life Insurance Co.]."

6. Ad for a car: "You can love it without getting your heart broken."

7. "Ford Mustang: It is what it was, and more."

8. Mail-order ad: "Special collector's edition. Priceless recordings. $6.98 per album."

*9. Part of a Nike commercial: "You don't win silver; you lose gold."

*10. Commercial for Dean Witter (investment brokers): "We must plan for our client's future as if it were our own. . . . We measure success one investor at a time."

11. Ad for Swiss Mocha: "Drift into a Chocolate Daydream."

12. Budweiser commercial: A rooster very carefully crosses the road and then goes into a tavern where they serve Budweiser. A guy watching this then says to his buddy, "Well, I guess that answers that question." (Hint: This ad is a particular favorite of at least one of the authors of this text.)

*13. The principal part of a newspaper ad sponsored by the U.S. Council for Coconut Research/Information featuring a photo of Martin Agronsky: "The truth told by a famous U.S. television personality: Whoever says coconut oil's 'poisoning' America isn't supported by facts. . . . In fact, an on-going medical study in a Boston hospital has turned out some strong evidence that the 'fatty acids' of coconut oil could be beneficial to human health. America's intake of coconut oil fats is a lot less than what you think. The FDA [Food and Drug Administration] commissioner testified recently before the U.S. Congress that less than 1.5% of U.S. total fat intake is made up of coconut oil. . . ."

14. Newspaper ad for the Massachusetts State Lottery: "There's a good chance you could win the Numbers Game today. Just ask the 12,000 people who won yesterday. . . . The only thing that's hard to do is lose. When this many people win, how can you lose?"

15. Notice on the package of Elizabeth Arden Ceramide Time Complex Capsules: "Take your skin back in time to the future of a younger tomorrow."

EXERCISE 10-2

1. What is your opinion of the Nike commercial showing a woman struggling as she ran to the tape with the voiceover "If you don't lose consciousness in the end, you could have run faster. FASTER! Nike Air."

2. How about the following excerpts (paraphrased) from a *Wall Street Journal* commercial:

   Twenty-five years ago, two very similar young men graduated from the same college and started work at the same company. Returning to college for their 25th reunion, they still were much alike—happily married, three children, and so on—but one was manager of a small department in the company, the other was the company's president.
       The difference that made the difference was in what each of these two men knew and how they made use of that knowledge: one read the *Wall Street Journal;* the other did not.

*3. Here is a United Airlines TV commercial (used by permission of Leo Burnett Co.):

   Ben (the boss, addressing his sales force): I got a phone call this morning from one of our oldest customers. He fired us. After 20 years. He fired us. He said he didn't know us anymore. I think I know why. We used to do business with a handshake—face to face. Now it's a phone call and a fax—get back to you later. With another fax probably. Well folks, something's gotta change. That's why we're gonna get out with a little face-to-face chat with every customer we have.

Salesman: But Ben, that's gotta be over 200 cities.

Ben: I don't care. Edward, Ryan, Nicholas, ...

Voiceover: If you're the kind of business that still believes personal service deserves a lot more than lip service, . . . welcome to United. That's the way we've been doing business for over 60 years.

Salesman: Ben, where're you going?

Ben: To visit that old friend who fired us this morning.

Voiceover: United. Come fly the friendly skies.

Do you think this was a successful commercial? Why, or why not? Is this primarily a promise or an identification ad?

4. A letter from a travel company included this note on the envelope. "Lowest Fare Advertised on Holland America Guaranteed." Assume, as is likely, that this ad for Holland America (a large cruise ship company) is true. Is there something about this blurb that should make you suspect that the rates quoted are not the lowest you can get? Explain.

5. One of the classic ads in the Pepsi-Coke advertising competition is set some time in the distant future and shows a teacher taking his students to an archeological site containing artifacts from the late twentieth century. He explains the various objects while his students drink cans of Pepsi. One of them holds up a bedraggled Coke bottle and asks the teacher what it is, to which the teacher responds, after much puzzled thought, "I've no idea." A great commercial (why? what is its pulling power?), it brings to mind the way in which ordinary items from a time and place can reveal a great deal to discerning investigators (doing the archeological equivalent of reading between the lines).

Advertisements, if you can believe Marshall McLuhan, contain a treasure trove of clues about our times. If you were an investigator who came across records containing most of today's advertisements a thousand years hence, what might you learn from them about life in the latter part of the twentieth and early twenty-first centuries? Explain.

EXERCISE 10-3

1. Create a magazine ad for a product: (1) Decide which product it will be, (2) decide on an intended audience for your ad, and (3) design the picture and the copy. Use the ad to make a sales pitch to the class. Then ask students why they would or wouldn't buy the product, based on your ad, and analyze the ad's appeal, or lack of same. (Doing this will make you better appreciate the creative ability of professionals in the advertising business.)

2. Compare two ads for the same or similar products in magazines with very different audiences (for instance, *Vogue* and *Time* magazine or *Sports Illustrated*). Explain how the intended audience influenced the ad design and sales pitch.

3. The Upside of Ads

Although most ads hawk consumer goods, a few actually attempt to educate us or warn us against harmful activities. In recent years Partnership for a Drug-Free America has aired a series of ads aimed at combating drug use in this country. The ads, targeting young people as well as parents, focus on the harmful effects of drugs ranging from Ecstasy to marijuana to alcohol. For example, one set of TV spots focuses on embarrassing or disturbing moments that teen drug users experience as a result of their habit. One ad shows a girl trying to conceal a drug-induced nosebleed that starts suddenly in class. Another features a boy inadvertently dropping a drug packet on the counter of a fast-food restaurant. A more shocking series of ads appeals to the vanity of teens by running photographs of young adults who are long-term users in fashionable but grotesque poses that highlight the disfiguring effects of methamphetamines. For instance, under the caption "Body by Crystal Meth" a young man stands, hand on hips, revealing a skeletal body ravaged by drugs. Ads aimed at parents urge them to monitor their kids' activities and social life. They feature parents asking questions like "Where are you going after school?" or "What are your plans after soccer?" Companion ads show older, grateful teens who realize in hindsight that all those irritating questions their parents asked managed to deter them from using drugs. Clearly the message is that parents should be involved in their kids' lives by asking questions and by knowing what they do, whom they hang out with, and where they go. We can only hope that all the advertising devices and gimmicks used so effectively to market goods and services will be just as successful at discouraging drug use among teens.

4. Trends in Marketing

Although the advertising professionals are exceedingly good at their business, they are forced by increasing competition between advertisers, coupled with increased consumer sophistication, to do a good deal of market research. That is why, these days, there is an immense amount of research behind every successful advertising campaign. One way for consumers to defend themselves against the ad campaigns that result from sophisticated market research is to become familiar with some of the recent developments in the field.

Eric Clark notes, in *The Want Makers,*[2] that "virtually nothing appears from a major advertiser or agency until it has been opinion-polled, test-marketed or copy-tested, submitted on the way to panels of consumers whose words have been turned into statistical tables or analyzed by psychologists." Most large agencies have research staffs of their own, in addition to using specialist agencies such as the A. C. Nielsen Company.

Types of research vary, depending on the method in favor at any given time, but roughly they can be divided into *qualitative research*—getting into people's heads to find out their thoughts and feelings—and *quantitative research*—gathering information by observation, experimentation, and surveys.

Qualitative research grew out of Freud's theory that unconscious motivations often influence behavior. The underlying assumption, already stressed here, is that people make many decisions irrationally and often are not even aware of their reasons for making them. So researchers try to figure out how people really feel about products, not just

---

[2] Some of what follows is summarized from this fascinating book.

how one might suppose they would feel. For example, on the basis of interviews with 300 mothers about how they fed their babies, researchers concluded the mothers were more concerned that feedings should be convenient and enjoyable for *themselves* rather than for their children, even though the mothers themselves said their baby's satisfaction was paramount. The resulting successful marketing ploy was merely to mention that babies would enjoy being fed the food but to stress that feeding time would be shortened.

Since all of us are motivated by unconscious desires at some time or other, these marketing techniques make it more difficult for us to make rational decisions about the products we buy (including political products, to be discussed shortly). We need to be more careful about what we buy and ask ourselves some commonsense questions before plunking down our money. Do we really need the product? Can we afford it? How does it compare with other similar products? Are we being conned—perhaps overly motivated—by advertising?

The quantitative approach to research has come a long way since the days when researchers asked people on the street what brand of soap or cereal they preferred. When you buy goods at most stores these days, the bar codes that are read at the checkout counter provide the retailer with a good deal of information concerning price, item purchased, and so on, that can be stored in computers; market researchers are now tapping into this information to find out what products people actually buy, not what they say they will buy. They are keeping track of the purchases made by carefully selected families, linking this information with further data concerning family income, number of children, and TV programs watched, including special test commercials. The result is that these marketing gurus can identify the ads that effectively sold the targeted products and plan large-scale ad campaigns accordingly. The currently popular "shopping cards" that claim to give discounts to customers on certain products are really intended to provide information on customer shopping habits that is analyzed and then sold to marketing companies. In many stores, sales clerks ask shoppers for their ZIP codes, which are fed into a marketing program (called PRIZM) that gathers consumer information. This program is advertised to marketers in *Advertising Age* as "the targeting tool that turns

---

Two electronic advertising ploys have raised a good bit of commotion because they raise serious political questions. The first is so-called dynamic pricing on e-commerce Web sites—setting different prices on items for different customers, depending on their personal "profile," based on electronically stored information concerning purchasing habits, and so on. (When accused of this practice, Amazon.com claimed its video sales price differences were completely random, simply a way to test the market.)

The other serious issue resulting from the electronic collection of information has to do with insurance policies, especially health insurance policies. Having access to a person's medical records, for example, could enable HMOs to deny coverage to those at great risk of serious illness, perhaps for genetic reasons.

It is unclear how these two problems will be worked out. What is clear is the threat the ability to electronically collect all sorts of information on virtually everyone poses, a new wrinkle indeed, but to a very old problem.

birds of a feather into sitting ducks." Perhaps an appropriate slogan these days would be that eternal vigilance is the price of economic solvency.

The object of all this research is not necessarily the low-income consumer but the more affluent. As Michael Schudson points out in *Advertising: The Uneasy Persuasion,* marketers are more interested in people with $100,000 to spend on nonessential goods than those with $1,000. The consequence is that consumer choices are often top-heavy in luxury items. Schudson argues that this tendency sometimes works to reduce the spectrum of goods available to people with modest incomes. The example he gives is the transformation of the automobile. "More and more extras become standard equipment in automobiles and other products, and the low income consumer has no choice but to go deeper into debt to pay for the simplest model, now weighted with superfluous 'standard' equipment." (In fairness, we need to note that used cars do cost less than new ones, although prices for used, ah . . . , "pre-owned" cars, also reflect the fancy equipment — electric windows and doors and the like — that they, too, are loaded with.)

There are psychological consequences to targeting the affluent as well. Fed a steady diet of ads for upscale goods, low-income consumers begin to crave luxuries beyond their wallets. How many people can afford a Rolex watch, a BMW 525i, or diamonds from Tiffany? But they can fantasize about luxury items in classy ads — and maybe then max out their credit cards.

Even the best targeted ads, however (fortunately?), often miss their mark because people have become more adept at tuning them out. Increasingly sophisticated technology allows just about everyone to zap commercials with remote controls. Bob Goldstein, once the president of Proctor and Gamble, estimated that his company was losing 25 percent of its audiences for commercials through zapping alone. And it's no news to anyone that the favorite time for a kitchen or bathroom break is during commercials. (Recall the Budweiser ad that tried to make hay out of this practice, saying that they heartily approved of this practice, while showing TV viewers going to their fridges to get Budweisers.)

To offset audience apathy and devices used to block regular commercials, advertisers are coming up with insidious ways to market their products. Increasingly, characters on TV shows use brand-name products, like Kleenex for crying women on *Days of Our Lives* or Nokia cell phones on *Alias.* Revlon paid millions for the writers of *All My Children* to incorporate the company name into the plotline of the soap opera that unfolded over several months. Hyundi bought a segment of the talk show *The Other Half,* featuring a Hyundi representative who gave tips on shopping for cars. Even *Playboy* magazine got into the act with a centerfold of a BMW on its June 2002 issue.[3] We can expect to see more "product placement" as conventional ads become less effective.

Advertisers also have to contend with the growing popularity of less well advertised generic products, and with the escalation of price wars that squeeze profit margins and advertising budgets. In response to this trend, advertisers regularly try new strategies. For the past decade, marketing money has shifted away from conventional media and into nonmedia sectors, such as sales promotions, public relations, direct mail, catalog marketing, and trade promotions. Think for instance of the avalanche of junk mail just about everybody gets these days. At least consumers inundated by telemarketing sales pitches can now block the calls by entering their names in the do-not-call registry.

---

[3] See "Ads Gone Mad," in *Extra!,* September/October 2002, for ads that cross the line between commercials and content.

Databased marketing is another of the current advertising concepts. As Stan Rapp and Thomas L. Collins point out in their book *Beyond Maxi Marketing,* advertisers are reducing their concentration on mass marketing in favor of more focused, less wasteful, individualized marketing strategies, using precisely targeted database programs. For example, a Tennessee department store chain's database identified 1,400 customers who purchased clothes by high-fashion designers such as Anne Klein and Liz Claiborne only when they were on sale and then notified these customers when designer clothes went on sale, increasing two-day sale receipts on these items by 97 percent. Personalized marketing is much more likely to appeal to consumers than is mass marketing, making it harder to resist.

Drug manufacturers have come up with a new marketing ploy in recent years that has physicians and the FDA worried. Instead of advertising prescription drugs to doctors only, as has been the practice in the past, drug companies are marketing directly to consumers. Probably the most widely hyped product is Viagra, but all manner of drugs are hawked to the public for treating everything from depression to heart disease. It comes as no surprise that patients are now insisting that doctors prescribe the pills advertised on TV and are often unwilling to consider alternative treatments. One unfortunate consequence, noted in the *New England Journal of Medicine,* is that "demand by patients is the most common reason offered by physicians for inappropriate prescribing."

Another troubling wrinkle in marketing is the way brand-name consumer products have begun to appear in schools and textbooks. Schoolchildren are considered prime targets by corporations convinced that brand loyalty begins at an early age. This trend began in 1989 when schools across the country took advantage of Channel One's offer of free television sets with the agreement that they would show current affairs programs. The hitch was that these programs included a raft of commercials aimed at children. By the mid-1990s, ads were plastered on school buses and scoreboards and were creeping into textbooks in the form of examples that grounded lessons in real-life situations. For example, the 1995 edition of *Mathematics: Applications and Connections,* by McGraw-Hill, Inc., includes this word problem, accompanied by a full-color picture of a pair of Nikes: "Will is saving his allowance to buy a pair of Nike shoes that cost $68.25. If Will earns $3.25 per week, how many weeks will Will need to save?" Although the intent of these "ads" seems to be to turn abstract problems into concrete situations that students can relate to, critics argue that they push specific consumer products onto unsophisticated schoolchildren. The 1995 and 1999 editions of this McGraw-Hill math text were so drenched in product references (everything from Barbie dolls to Cocoa Frosted Flakes to Sony PlayStations) that a California Assemblywoman, Kerry Mazzoni (D-Novato), was prompted to sponsor a state bill banning commercial references and logos in school textbooks. (See Chapter 12 for more on the topic of classroom advertising.) On the whole, though, the United States has done little to protect children from the onslaught of ads they face daily. Many other industrialized countries (Belgium, Denmark, and Sweden, to name a few) have banned ads from radio and television that target children.

The Shape of Things to Come

The days when the Internet was exclusively, or even primarily, noncommercial are now long-since over. A growing number of businesses are advertising their products on home pages on the World Wide Web. Users can click on to a commercial and read about and order the product in one fell swoop. Quick, easy, and tempting.

But Internet advertising is not always under this sort of user control. As explained on *60 Minutes* (November 29, 1999), advertising networks now use tracking devices that allow them to record, *without our knowledge,* where we surf the 'Net, thereby collecting data concerning our interests, shopping tastes, and even our medical concerns. With this information they develop a profile of us that enables them to personalize ads that come up on our screen. The more data we give them, the more complete their profile. To entice users to give personal information, Internet ad companies such as Double Click offer an array of personalized services. For instance, when we tell them our travel plans, they can let us know whether our plane is delayed or give us the weather forecast or provide an entertainment guide for the city we are visiting.

Perhaps the most questionable feature of this kind of practice is that the information we give Internet companies can be, and often is, shared with "off-line" companies as well and can be obtained by employers or insurance companies doing background checks. So far there are no regulations governing the Internet. Savvy users give fake names and information to guard against invasion of privacy, but most people surfing the 'Net do not.

E-mail marketing has increased dramatically in recent years. In just two years (2001–2003) spam went from 8 percent to 45 percent of e-mail—two-thirds of which includes fraudulent offers, according to a Federal Trade Commission estimate. In December 2003, the president signed the CAN-SPAM Act banning commercial e-mail from using false headers and requiring U.S. businesses to include opt-out instructions. But this legislation is unlikely to rein in the spam stampede, since it is a worldwide phenomenon that is increasingly driven by Internet service providers abroad. Also, the new law overrides stricter state laws, like California's anti-spam legislation that was due to go into effect in 2004.

On a more postive note, computers are becoming a kind of television set, allowing users to do things like switch from on-line programs to television, to films, to game playing. In a few places today, viewers using remote-control pads can play along with video quiz shows, select camera angles for sports events, and access detailed information about advertised products. These sophisticated telecomputers open up a whole new world for the advertising industry. Consumers can scroll through a mail-order catalogue, order products instantaneously from the already-popular shopping channels, and access detailed information about the car they want to buy or the HMO they want to join. Which of these new marvels will turn out to be the wave of the future remains to be seen; billions are being spent by various competing parties intent on getting their feet in the doors they hope will be the right ones. But however these battles turn out, the danger is that lots of us will be pushed even more into the "consumer mode" and become even more likely to be talked into buying products it would be prudent for us to pass over.

EXERCISE 10-4

1. Find an ad that has strong emotional appeal for you and try to figure out why you find it so engaging. Once you have done so, decide whether you would purchase the product, and explain your decision. (Be honest. Think carefully about it. No off-the-top-of-the-head goody-goody.)

2. Go through a bunch of ads on some kind of product that interests you—cars, cosmetics, sports gear, whatever—and choose the one you would like to buy based on what you are told in these ads. Then do some research in *Consumer Reports, Consumers Digest,* or any one of several publications that specialize in product comparisons. On the basis of your research, decide whether you would still purchase the item you selected. Explain your decision.

3. Here is part of a comment made by John Kasson: "Advertising . . . has become . . . a way of telling us not just what we should buy but how we should live, how we should associate the advertised objects with ourselves."

   Is Kasson right? Or do ads primarily appeal to already-existing desires and lifestyles? It is obvious, for example, that we cannot have a desire to play computer games like Nintendo before they exist, but do most ads touting products merely tell us about new ways to satisfy old desires, or do they create new ones, or perhaps just strengthen existing desires so that we spend more on them than we should? Do ads, say, for designer jeans and other fashion clothes just reinforce existing preferences? (Defend your answer.)

4. In his book *Business Civilization in Decline,* Robert Heilbroner claims that advertising is "the single most value-destroying activity of a business civilization." Would you agree or disagree with this statement? Write an argument defending your position.

5. Imagine that you live in another country (or on another planet, for that matter) and know nothing about the United States except what you see in ads. What values and attitudes do you think Americans might have? Support your response by using ads as evidence.

5. POLITICAL ADVERTISING

By now, just about everybody knows that political candidates and issues are marketed in pretty much the same way as breakfast foods and laundry detergents. This means that appeals to reason tend to be scarce, while devices designed to move emotions preempt the field.

In the very old days, only candidates for local office could reach more than a tiny fraction of their prospective constituents—via "whistle stop" campaigns in which they made speeches before small audiences and "pressed the flesh." Billboards, lawn signs, newspaper ads, posters, patriotic bunting, and that sort of thing were extremely important parts of any successful campaign.

But the average voter never heard the actual voices of candidates running for high office or, except for some presidential candidates, ever saw their pictures or photographs. Political parties and platforms thus loomed much larger than they do today. Charisma didn't travel very widely.

Things began to change early in the twentieth century with the introduction of electronic and other scientific devices, starting with methods for printing pictures in newspapers and continuing with the widespread ownership of radios. Franklin Roosevelt was the first president to fully understand and gain significant political advantage from the miracle of radio; his "fireside chats" were an immensely successful public relations instrument, and his voice was instantly recognized by virtually everyone in America in those days.

But the changes in political rhetoric and tactics that came after World War II dwarfed those that preceded it. A large increase in the number of primary elections reduced the power of political parties and party "bosses" and, much more important, television brought candidates and their pitches into living rooms across the nation. Political campaigns were changed forever (as was pretty much everything else—but remember the saying that "The more things change, the more they remain the same"). Within a few years, image makers, which means advertising experts, reigned supreme. Names such as Roger Ailes became familiar to careful viewers of the political scene.

The first presidential candidate to make full and effective use of the new medium was Dwight D. Eisenhower. His successful 1952 campaign against Adlai Stevenson featured short television commercials like the following example, part of a series of TV spots in which General Eisenhower read from letters sent in by "citizens" asking questions that Eisenhower then "answered":

> *Citizen:* Mr. Eisenhower, what about the high cost of living?
> *General Eisenhower:* My wife, Mamie, worries about the same thing. I tell her it's our job to change that on November 14.[4]

No need for Eisenhower to tell viewers *how* he planned to change it.

Of course, Eisenhower conveyed an almost perfect image—war hero and father figure—and most people therefore strongly identified with him. War heroes, father figures, and candidates with charisma, John Kennedy being perhaps the best example, are very hard to beat. When Kennedy ran for office, his father, whose connections in Hollywood dated back to the 1920s, hired film professionals experienced in using effective film production techniques, to hype the candidate as a symbolic role model—a strong, courageous hero—and to capitalize on his undoubted glamorous appeal. Nowadays, candidates who project a less appealing image can, and frequently do, overcome their handicaps by hiring image makers to attractively tailor their campaigns *and their personalities.*

Eisenhower's TV spots were very effective, but image makers have honed their craft a great deal since then. They have learned, for example, that negative ads attacking one's opponent can be dynamite. Mudslinging isn't new, of course. John Adams was labeled a closet monarchist, Thomas Jefferson was derided because he didn't enlist in 1775 (!), and Abe Lincoln was dubbed "Honest Ape." But television brought mudslinging to a far wider audience, and thus it was more effective. One of the first TV spots to use this tech-

---

Orthodontics and the hair dryer have become vital to the achievement of political power.

—Len Deighton

---

[4]David Ogilvy, in his classic book on advertising *Confessions of an Advertising Man* (New York: Atheneum, 1963). Ogilvy quotes Eisenhower as moaning between takes, "To think that an old soldier should come to this." Note that the device used is a promise to satisfy a strong desire (for lower prices) without providing a single reason for believing that the promise would be kept.

nique to full effect—the 1964 "Daisy/Girl/Peace" spot—also is probably the most famous of all political TV commercials. It ran just once as a paid advertisement but received so much comment that it was broadcast several times as a news item. (It was once believed that this commercial was never run again because of a public outcry against it, but in fact the original plan was to run it just once and then to garner free repeat TV coverage, which is exactly what happened.)

The spot starts by showing a very young girl picking petals from a daisy while counting, "1, 2, 3, 4, 5, 7, 6, 6, 8, 9, 9," at which point there is the voiceover of a man counting, "10, 9, 8, 7, 6, 5, 4, 3, 2, 1, 0," followed by the blast of an atomic bomb on the screen and the voice of President Lyndon Johnson saying, "These are the stakes—to make a world in which all God's children can live—or to go into the dark. We must either love each other or we must die." Then another voiceover: "Vote President Johnson on November 3rd. The stakes are too high for you to stay home."

The point of this commercial was to picture Johnson's opponent, Republican senator Barry Goldwater, as an extreme hawk all too willing to push the button, while Johnson is portrayed as a responsible "peace" candidate. Is it an accident that this best-known of all political spots also is one of the most vicious, inaccurate, and unfair?[5]

Everyone assumed that this infamous ad had sunk into the quagmire of history, where it belonged, but MoveOn.org resurrected it in the weeks preceding the Iraq War. The ad began with scenes of escalating violence—from military invasions to burning oil fields, wounded soldiers, and chaotic anti-war protests—climaxing in a mushroom cloud followed by a black screen and the warning that war with Iraq might lead to the unthinkable. Finally the countdown began "10 . . . 9 . . . 8 . . . 7 . . ." with the message "Maybe that's why the overwhelming majority of Americans say to President Bush: let the inspections work."

Nowadays, particularly in the final weeks of a close election, negative ads have become the staple of campaigns. Candidates have had to face the reality that, however much they may find it odious to slam opponents in this way, victory often depends on doing so. In particular, a candidate far behind in the polls may feel compelled to resort to a bit of mud slinging. When two candidates are running neck and neck, as John Kerry and George Bush were in 2004, the negative ads start early and heat up as election day approaches. In March 2004, the Bush campaign launched ads claiming Kerry was "Wrong on taxes. Wrong on defense." (Campaign aides came up with the implausible euphemism "contrast" ads for these commercials and refused to characterize them as

---

Hitler's henchman, Joseph Goebbels, summed up the Nazi position on negative advertising: "The propaganda which produces the desired results is good and all other propaganda is bad. . . . Therefore, it is beside the point to say your propaganda is too crude, too mean, too brutal, or too unfair, for all this does not matter. Propaganda is always a means to an end."

---

[5]For more on this and other classic TV spots, see *A Viewer's Guide,* by David Beiler, a companion pamphlet to the fascinating videotape documentary *The Classics of Political Television Advertising* (Washington, D.C.: Campaigns & Elections, 1986), which contains a copy of the Daisy/Girl/Peace spot.

"negative.") It didn't take Kerry long to counter with ads claiming that Bush was "misleading America," and so it went, escalating in intensity to the end. Both sides were dissuaded from releasing really nasty ads, though, because of the new legal regulations under the McCain-Feingold law that require candidates to give their approval of TV ads in their own voice, with their picture displayed on the screen. The harshest attacks came from other media or independent organizations (known as 527s) that weren't covered by the disclosure rule. For example, "Swift Boat Veterans for Truth" mounted a barrage of ads smearing Kerry's military record, and Texans for Truth countered with ads that Bush failed to fulfill his National Guard duties.

Although negative ads have proliferated in recent years, attacking one's opponent via barbed humor has always been an acceptable part of the political process (going back, in fact, to the time of the ancient Greek democracy in Athens, where comic plays regularly made fun of well-known figures in all walks of life). Here is a rather appealing low blow delivered by ex-president Gerald Ford at the 1996 Republican National Convention: "When I was in the White House, I said I was a Ford, not a Lincoln. Today, what we have in the White House is neither a Ford or [sic] a Lincoln. What we have is a Dodge." During the 1990 California gubernatorial campaign, Dianne Feinstein came up with a humorous quip aimed at her opponent, Pete Wilson, that paid off politically quite nicely. Taking clever advantage of Wilson's change of mind on the abortion issue, she remarked, "My opponent isn't pro-choice: he's multiple choice." But perhaps Ronald Reagan's put-down of candidate Bill Clinton at the 1992 Republican convention was the best quip of the decade. "This fellow [Clinton] they've nominated claims he's the new Thomas Jefferson. Well, let me tell you something, I knew Thomas Jefferson. Thomas Jefferson was a friend of mine. And Governor, you're no Thomas Jefferson." (This was a takeoff on Lloyd Bentsen's famous putdown in the 1988 vice-presidential debates of Dan Quayle's attempt to identify himself with Jack Kennedy.) Rick Lazio's Senate campaign against Hillary Clinton in 2000 featured a nicely humorous way of reminding New York state voters that Clinton was a newcomer to that state: it featured several babies in diapers, noting that these new additions to the state's citizenry had been residents longer than Clinton had been. More recently there was an anti-Bush ad showing an Asian factory with the voiceover explaining that Bush created a lot of new jobs—in China.

Negative ads rejected by networks sometimes get more publicity than if they are aired. A good case in point is the "Child's Pay" ad generated by MoveOn.org, showing children doing adult work with the tagline "Guess who's going to pay off President Bush's $1 trillion deficit?" When CBS rejected the ad for airing during the 2003 Super Bowl, it got widespread publicity in the press. (The ad was later picked up by CNN.) This tactic is used increasingly by groups with advocacy ads that will certainly be re-

---

Most people are eternally taken in by the myth and rhetoric of democracy. . . . What we have now is an increasingly uneducated public—especially in what used to be called civics—dealing with evermore complex issues with which they are unequipped to knowledgeably deal. . . . We have a population ripe for manipulation by powerful public relation firms and political consultants who are expert in sound bites and seductive imagery.

—Gray Brechin, *Imperial San Francisco:*
Urban Power, Earthly Ruin

jected. By issuing press releases and other protests to the media, these groups generate free publicity for their causes.

When celebrities turn against candidates, they can create a media blitz of negative publicity that sometimes reaches a far wider audience than traditional ads. After the FCC cracked down on radio host Howard Stern for alleged indecent comments and fined Clear Channel $1.75 million, Stern launched an anti-Bush campaign that reached 8–10 million people daily—one-third of whom were independent voters and thus critical in the tight 2004 election. Another case in point is Michael Moore and his Bush-bashing documentary *Fahrenheit 9/11,* an overnight sensation that reached an audience of millions.

Of course, not all campaign advertisements feature mud slung at one's opponent. Tearing down the other guy is important, but propping up your own candidate is equally important. One way to do this is via image building and *identification.* During both the 1992 and 1996 campaigns, for example, Al Gore was portrayed as a "rural youth" from Tennessee (thus suppressing the fact that he was brought up the son of a rich United States senator and throughout his life lived in very comfortable circumstances in such places as Washington, D.C.). When he ran for the presidency in 2000, he still wanted the image of a Tennessean, but the media caught on to the fact that he was really a Washington insider. (Nevertheless, the film shown at the Democratic National Convention pictured Gore as a Tennessee down-home kind of guy. There was a good deal more truth to the Bush film run at the Republican National Convention showing him as a good-old-boy Texan, born and raised in that state.)

During the 2004 campaign, as the war in Iraq dragged on, John Kerry ran bio ads touting his military service. They began with his birth in Fitzsimmons Army Hospital where his father was an Army pilot, then panned to his combat years in Vietnam, with testimonials from fellow soldiers about his heroic rescues and savvy decisions that saved the lives of troops—all of which earned him multiple medals. These ads, of course were intended to establish him as a military leader, in contrast, to the second George Bush, who remained in the reserves during the Vietnam War.

As must be evident by now, political campaigns are becoming indistinguishable from advertising campaigns. One of the most important ploys in marketing candidates is image making, and one of the most effective formats for candidates to sharpen their image is presidential debates. The presidential debates provide candidates with the largest audiences they will be able to advertise to during a whole election campaign. (Nowadays, of course, a tradition has been established so that candidates pretty much are forced to debate or lose face.) Political debates are hardly a new idea—think of the famous debates between Abraham Lincoln and Stephen Douglas. But the first presidential debates, between Richard Nixon and John Kennedy, did not take place until 1960. (Interestingly, these debates are still the most vividly remembered.) Kennedy is generally seen as the winner

---

I'm not an old hand at politics. But I am now seasoned enough to have learned that the hardest thing about any political campaign is how to win without proving that you are unworthy of winning.

—Adlai Stevenson (1956)

What one candidate learned from two (failed) runs at the presidency.

because he exhibited "vigor" and youth and exuded great charisma, whereas Nixon appeared to be overcautious and a bit sneaky. (Nixon later complained that his makeup was incorrectly applied—a very important point.) The debates generally are credited with being the crucial factor in Kennedy's extremely narrow victory (we pass over the controversy concerning alleged chicanery in counting votes in Texas and Illinois), but not because his proposals and comments were any better than those of Nixon.

In all of the presidential debates so far, just as in the Nixon-Kennedy debates, it has been *image,* not reasoning or displays of intelligence or character, that has determined the winners. (More will be said shortly on the topic of image building.) The 1988 debates between the first George Bush and Michael Dukakis illustrate this nicely. When Dukakis failed to respond with instant outrage to CNN commentator Bernard Shaw's famous question about what Dukakis would do if his wife were raped, his chances of winning the election pretty much flew out the window.

Oh, yes, the debates between George W. Bush and John Kerry. Bush was widely seen as losing the first debate, not so much because of what he said, but because of the image he projected. His frequent scowls and obvious impatience with Kerry's remarks seemed to turn viewers off. Kerry, on the other hand, appeared self-assured, well informed, and presidential. (Interestingly, radio listeners didn't think the debate was that lopsided.) In the last two debates Bush managed to control his facial expressions, but to no avail— the vote was close but Kerry still won (winning all three debates didn't help him win the election, though). For voters willing to look beyond the image, the debates provided a good deal of substance, unlike the campaign ads that hyped the candidates and had no substance whatsoever.

Election Polls—A Special Case

Finally, no account of campaign rhetoric could be complete without mention of the role of polls in elections. No serious candidates for high office these days would open their mouths without having first tested the wind via polls. Whatever may be the case after they have won, when running for election, smart candidates make their pitches conform to what the polls indicate about voter sentiments and prejudices. During campaigns, at any rate, successful politicians generally are followers, not leaders. They waffle because they have to in order to get elected. It's always better to tell voters what they want to hear, not what the candidate genuinely intends to do if elected.

Of course, smart candidates also tailor their pitches to particular targeted audiences, often those who are undecided or already inclined to vote for them. Computer data on voter preferences make this information much more available than it was in the days when campaign aides thumbed through voter registration files to figure out likely supporters. Nowadays, software programs like Calipers Political Maptitude access files on census data, voter registration, and other pertinent records. Databases provide informa-

---

If politicians all told the truth, we'd be out of business.
               —Talk show host Jay Leno (on Larry King Live)

---

[6]For more on this matter see "Where the Voters Are," by Holly Bailey, *Newsweek,* March 29, 2004.

tion on voters' magazine subscriptions, car purchases, charitable contributions, and consumer preferences that give both political parties the information to "microtarget" likely supporters and market their candidates and issues.[6] For example, direct mail ads for health care initiatives can be tailored to seniors and sent to AARP subscribers, issue advertising against tax cuts to the rich can be targeted to labor union members, and phone solicitations to boost voter turnout can be made to party supporters.

Polls tell candidates how to advertise; their media experts build campaigns in terms of what they learn from polls; blind advertising bit the dust a long time ago. In the 2004 campaign, for example, the polls gave advertisers information they needed to market their candidates to the small percentage of undecided voters who were considered so important in the campaign. To reach these voters, advertisers focused their efforts on 19 or 20 swing states that could decide the election. Out of the 210 TV media markets in the country, heavy political advertising occurred in only 93, which means that just 40 percent of Americans were exposed to television advertising. Those who lived in the big states (like California, Texas, and New York) where the vote was predictable, saw little if any advertising for the candidates.[7] But viewers in the swing states were blitzed with ads that pounded away at poll-driven issues like the Iraq War, the job market and the threat of terrorism.

Well, then, if virtually all political rhetoric is guided by expediency, why pay attention to it? If we can expect candidates to waffle, even to lie, why hear them out? The answer is that even waffling and lies can tell those of us who read between the lines a great deal about how candidates may perform if elected to office: Which sorts of lies they tell and what kinds of campaign promises they make tell us something about which groups and positions a candidate is likely to favor if elected. The promises made by Bush, Dick Cheney, and their advocates during the presidential campaign were somewhat different from those made by John Kerry, John Edwards, and their advocates, because somewhat different constituencies were being appealed to.

Nevertheless, it is true in the political arena at least as much as anywhere else that actions speak louder than words. It has to be true that a candidate's past performance is almost always a better guide to future performance than is his or her political rhetoric. Smart viewers of the political scene always evaluate current political advertising in the light of past performance. So a sensible evaluation of political rhetoric requires us to bring to bear good background information (nothing new here). (The other key ingredient, aside from background information is, of course, the desire and attempt to be intellectually honest—to set aside prejudices of all kinds and come to fair, cogent evaluations.)

Noncampaign "Campaign" Rhetoric

Politicians don't just campaign via advertisements or after they have thrown their hats into the ring. Image building is a day-in, day-out task—indeed, in terms of time spent, perhaps a successful politician's principal task. Of course, for those holding high office, particularly for the leader of a nation, image building often coincides with ceremonial

---

[7]From an interview with Ken Goldstein, director of the Advertising Project at the University of Wisconsin, on the *Lehrer News Hour,* July 18, 2004.

duties. At the start of the Gulf War, for example, President Bush was photographed going to church—symbolic of the seriousness of the step into war just taken—and evangelist Billy Graham was invited to spend the night with the Bush family in the White House. (Saddam Hussein prayed on camera nearly every day of that war in spite of being well known as a nonbeliever.) The second President Bush, who referred to the War on Terrorism as a crusade at one point, was photographed with all manner of religious figures from fundamentalist Christian delegates at the Southern Baptist convention to the Pope in the Vatican. Candidates challenging incumbents don't have the opportunity to improve their images via ceremonial activities, one reason incumbents are hard to unseat.

Another reason, of course, is that incumbents, at least of the United States Congress, can improve their images at taxpayer expense via their letter-franking privilege. Members of Congress aren't supposed to use this privilege for campaign purposes, but they do it anyway—by sending franked letters containing "questionnaires" and by answering letters from constituents.

Senator Milton R. Young of North Dakota was one of the first members of Congress to take full advantage of the opportunities offered by letters from constituents. He was expert at tailoring his responses so that they expressed sentiments recipients would be pleased to hear and would appear to have been individually written by the senator himself.[8] Nowadays, this practice has been honed to the point that computer software is available to make letter composition almost automatic. (It isn't possible for members of Congress to write an individual reply to every letter received; they have to use standard replies classified by issue and position taken on the issue.) Here is the main part of Young's standard reply to antiabortion letter writers:

> I thought you would be pleased to know that I have strongly supported the position you take. I have been a co-sponsor of a resolution in the Senate proposing a Human Life Amendment since the Supreme Court issued its decision liberalizing abortion. . . .

But here is the sort of thing you got in reply to a pro-abortion letter:

> I appreciate hearing from you and receiving your views on this matter. . . .
> I agree with you that a woman should have a right to decide whether or not she wants an abortion.

Officeholders who want to win reelection have to do this sort of thing.

Incumbents also have an advantage when it comes to garnering media coverage via press conferences. President Roosevelt was perhaps the first American president to exploit this kind of image-building opportunity, but the technique was perfected by President Kennedy, who, unlike Roosevelt, had television at his beck and call. Since Kennedy's time, presidential news conferences have generally been scheduled so as to gain the president free exposure on evening TV news programs. (President Carter arranged the Begin-Sadat Camp David agreement between Israel and Egypt so that the three leaders would sign on the dotted line and congratulate each other on television programs planned to have large national and international audiences.) Presidents are

---

[8] His nearly record-breaking length of service in the Senate—from 1945 until his retirement in 1980—was often credited to his considerable ability to talk out of both sides of his mouth when answering letters from constituents. See the *Washington Monthly* (October 1979) article by Mark Feldstein for more details.

Reprinted by permission of Paul Miller.

Typical politician at work.

coached beforehand so that they have ready-made "answers" to all likely questions, and they rarely are forced into on-the-spot improvisations. (The same was true, of course, of the 2004 presidential and vice-presidential candidates' debates.)

Of course, being a politician is not all sweetness and light, even for those who have managed to get elected. Being human, incumbents get into trouble now and then. Enter what columnist Richard Cohen referred to as the "totally insincere gesture."[9] For example, during the 1988 presidential campaign, when the Democratic party vice-presidential candidate, Senator Lloyd Bentsen of Texas, resigned from three private clubs, two of which had no black members, it wasn't because of a change of heart on the issue of restricted clubs. It was just a totally insincere gesture. After losing the election, he promptly rejoined all three clubs. (Yes, there still are clubs that do their best to keep out individuals belonging to whatever groups they want to exclude.)

Further Developments

The world does not stand still. New ways of doing things crop up now and then, mostly now these days.

Many years ago, virtually all political advertising was for candidates running for office. But with the advent of ballot initiatives and referendums—propositions put before voters for their direct decision—*issue advertising* entered the scene, and during the past few years it has become an extremely important kind of political advertising because voters in many states and localities now are regularly asked to decide all kinds of controversial issues. Interested parties now spend millions advertising their views on

---

[9] See the *Washington Post National Weekly,* December 4–10, 1989.

these measures. Philip Morris, for example, spent big bucks on a referendum measure that appeared to be antismoking but whose actual effect would have been to weaken existing antismoking legislation. (Unfortunately for Philip Morris, its originally concealed part in the campaign was revealed to the public, which then turned against the measure.) Another big change in political advertising stems from the increased ability of media experts to target specific audiences. This has enabled special interests to influence legislators indirectly by generating floods of letters and calls to their elected representatives. In 1993 and 1994, for instance, the health insurance industry spent millions on TV spots directed against the Clinton health plan (which was defeated). Seventeen million dollars were spent on the famous "Harry and Louise" TV spots, which generated more than 500,000 letters to members of Congress.

Nowadays even wars are marketed to the public. The first Gulf War, generally thought to be the first war tailored for the mass media, was "branded" "Operation Desert Shield" much the way brand names are given to toothpaste or cereal. The second war, "Operation Iraqi Freedom," was promoted by state-of-the-art marketing techniques that launched the "conflict" (not the war) with "shock and awe" (instead of bombing), wrapped it in patriotism and morality (stressing good versus evil), and downplayed the ugly realities with euphemisms like "decapitation strategy " (for kill Saddam Hussein). War propaganda has a long history, of course, but current marketing savvy has raised it to new heights (or sunk it to new depths, depending on your point of view). We can only roll our eyes at the recent Alice-in-Wonderland approach to marketing wars. Was Andrew Card (the second Bush's chief of staff) serious when he told the *New York Times* that the administration had waited until after Labor Day (2002) to make its case for military action in Iraq because "from a marketing point of view you don't introduce new products in August"?

Some of the more important developments in political advertising are simply vastly increased and improved versions of methods employed for some time now. Campaigning on television shows such as *Larry King Live* is a case in point. Politicians have come to understand that TV and radio talk shows can be used for free and very effective exposure. Ross Perot's 1992 campaign, for example, took off after his first appearance on the Larry King show and Clinton boosted his popularity when he played the saxophone on the Arsenio Hall show. But Arnold Schwarzenegger outdid them all when he sold himself to voters almost exclusively on talk and entertainment shows. He kicked off his campaign by announcing his candidacy for governor of California on the Jay Leno show, then did an end run around the establishment media (newspapers and serious news programs) and plugged himself mainly on talk radio, entertainment shows, and televised daily events. His highly successful mass media blitz enabled him to create the image of a decisive, optimistic visionary without addressing detailed policies and programs that the establishment media usually demand.

The *interactive viewer opinion poll* is another development, which hints perhaps at what the future may be like. For example, a CNN phone-in poll instructed viewers that "If you think the economy is getting better, press one, then the pound sign. If you think the economy is getting weaker, press two and then the pound sign," and so on. Not exactly what could be considered a scientifically designed poll.

Still another development trades on the fact that in most cases, when a legislative body considers a measure, some interests will be harmed and others served. Very few, if any, measures equally benefit everyone. So instead of employing mass advertising campaigns on TV, PR experts influence legislation by direct mailings to those affected by proposed laws, counting on those contacted to lobby elected officials. Although always used in one way or another, modern methods for selecting just the right group to contact (computer files and so forth) made this a favorite in the 1990s.

The great increase in negative telephone advertising that has occurred in the past few years is one of the more unfortunate recent developments in political advertising. The device itself is old, perhaps first being used on a large scale in 1946 when Richard Nixon first ran for Congress. A typical call in that telephone campaign went like this: "This is a friend of yours, but I can't tell you who I am. Did you know that Jerry Voorhis [Nixon's incumbent opponent] is a communist?" (Click.) Today's voters might be inclined to see that as a bit too dirty, so now the big item is "push polling," telephone calls disguised as opinion research, in which negative "information" about opposing candidates is revealed.[10]

Another development in political advertising, as in advertising in general, results from the dramatic increase in those who regularly surf the 'Net. During the 2004 presidential campaign, all candidates had Web sites dispensing "information" to Web browsers. Political action groups like MoveOn.org and Take Back America have Web sites that attract a wide range of people not usually reached by paid media. The tremendous increase in the number of people who have access to computers also has provided political advertisers with a cheap, quick way to marshal loyal troops for rallies and to raise money, generate talk show callers, and so on. Telephone solicitations and direct mailings are much more expensive and time consuming than e-mail.

The upshot of all the new ways to advertise is that the 30-second TV spots that played the major role in elections to high office during the previous 40 years or so have now become just one of several important devices used to influence the electorate (although still the most important). In 2004, tens of millions of Americans tuned in to at least one presidential debate, and at least that many heard candidates give their spiels on TV talk

---

Chevron's "People Do" ad campaign, in which Chevron is portrayed as a friend of the environment, is perhaps the most successful of a growing genre of identification advertisements. Each Chevron ad describes some kind of environmental project. One, for example, was about their construction of wooden platforms on high-voltage wires to shield eagles from electrocution, ending with the question, "Do people really reach that high to protect a natural wonder? People Do" (displayed under the Chevron logo).

One point of these ads is to get environmentally conscious motorists to identify with Chevron and to switch to that brand of gasoline. Another point is to influence legislation indirectly by picturing Chevron, and the oil industry in general, as environmentally sound, thus blunting criticism based on the industry's actual environmental record, which is extremely poor. (Think, for example, of the Exxon Valdez Alaskan disaster.)

Well, then, are these completely misleading ads effective? (Hint: Chevron has been running this series of ads for over ten years now.)

---

[10]For more on push polling, see "When Push Comes to Poll," by Larry J. Sabato and Glenn R. Simpson, *Washington Monthly* (June 1996). The article also discusses push polling employed by, among others, Governor Lawton Chiles, Democrat, Florida; and Oliver North, Republican, Virginia.

shows. What this electronic age has in store for us next is an interesting and exceedingly important question to which politicians and their media masters would very much like to know the answer. (So should we, so as to better defend ourselves against deceptive or emotively driven advertising.)

SUMMARY OF CHAPTER 10

1. Most ads can be divided into either of two groups. *Promise ads* promise to satisfy desires or allay fears. *Example:* Use Old Spice deodorant and get rid of body odor. *Identification ads* sell the product by getting us to identify with the product. *Example:* The Virginia Slims cigarette ads, "You've come a long way, baby," tailored to specific audiences.

2. Although ads provide us with useful information about products, often in an entertaining way, they also are designed to manipulate us via sophisticated ploys.
   a. They invite us to reason fallaciously. *Example:* Appeals to the authority of famous figures such as golf star Tiger Woods.
   b. They employ repetitive slogans and meaningless jargon. *Example:* "Nike: Just do it."
   c. They play on our weaknesses, prejudices, and fears. *Example:* The "ring around the collar" TV commercials.
   d. Ads draw on trendy issues. *Example:* The low-fat, low-sugar, low-salt, low-carb ads aimed at overweight Americans.
   e. They use sneaky rhetoric, including fine-print disclaimers and weasel words. *Examples:* Using the word *free* when the product isn't free; weasely expressions like "fights bad breath."
   f. They play on our patriotism, loyalty, and identification with members of our own group. *Example:* The ads wrapped in patriotism after September 11, 2001.

3. Although most ads hawk consumer goods, a few actually attempt to educate us and warn us against harmful activities. *Example:* The ads aimed at combating drug use in this country.

4. Old marketing techniques have been improved with new wrinkles, including new qualitative and quantitative procedures. *Example:* The Tennessee department store direct-mail ads based on in-store records of specific customer purchases.
      What the future holds is, of course, uncertain. *Example:* How will the latest Internet wrinkle, in which customers can see ads and immediately buy products with a few mouse clicks, ultimately play out?

5. Political candidates and issues are sold in pretty much the same way as any other products.
   a. In the age of television, elections are won or lost via exposure on the tube, whether in debates, paid 30-second TV spots, press conferences, or whatever. And it is *image,* not rationality, that often wins in this arena. *Examples:* The Daisy/Girl/Peace TV spot that portrayed Barry Goldwater as too trigger-happy to be trusted with the nuclear bomb button; Dukakis's "wimpy" response to Bernard Shaw's challenging question.

In addition to exposure on television, some of the fringe benefits of office provide opportunities for elected officials to gain added exposure with voters. *Example:* Campaigning via franked mailings.

When candidates are in trouble, there are ways in which they can sometimes beat the rap, one being by making a "totally insincere gesture." *Example:* Senator Bentsen resigning from private clubs that discriminated against blacks only to rejoin them after the election.

It also should be noted that the campaign rhetoric of candidates running for high office generally is guided by the results of polls. It's always safer to tell voters what they want to hear, not what candidates intend to do if elected. That is why we can expect candidates to lie, exaggerate, or otherwise distort when necessary to curry the favor of voters. (But savvy voters still can learn from political rhetoric by reading between the lines and paying attention to past performance so as to figure out what candidates are likely to do if elected.)

b. Politicians in a democracy "campaign" virtually all of the time, not just when actually running for office. They always have to be intent on projecting the right *image* to the voters, and once in office, they have several standard ways of doing this. One is by using their franking privilege to curry the favor of their constituents; another is by performing the ceremonial duties of their office well; still another is by holding press conferences.

c. Views on issues now are advertised just like candidates. The point is to influence voter preferences and thus legislation that is before Congress or state or local legislatures. *Examples:* Philip Morris's promotion of a referendum that would weaken existing antismoking laws; the health insurance industry's multimillion-dollar ad campaign against President Clinton's health plan; and the marketing of two Gulf Wars.

d. The made-to-order TV spots that dominated campaigning during the past 40 years or so have received serious competition recently from TV talk shows that provide candidates with free exposure to mass audiences; prefabricated TV spots that save candidates tons of money; and interactive telephone polling of television audiences (with additional electronic campaigning marvels in the wings).

EXERCISE 10-5

Write two letters to one of your senators or representatives in Washington, D.C., in one taking a short, strong stand on an issue of importance to you, in the other taking an equally strong but different stand (completely opposite, if possible) on the same issue. Compare the two replies that you get. (Remember that you can't expect instantaneous replies.) Send each letter from a different address and use different names (because some members of Congress keep track on computers).

EXERCISE 10-6

These days, the mass media (in particular, newspapers and magazines) spend a modest amount of time and effort covering and evaluating the political advertisements, especially TV spots, of candidates for high office. Look into some of this reporting; then (1) present and explain the content of at least two such analyses of advertisements for candidates in your state or locality; and (2) evaluate their accuracy and cogency.

EXERCISE 10-7

Recall Len Deighton's remark quoted on page 248 about straight teeth and blow-dried hair and consider what Andy Rooney had to say in his syndicated column (August 5, 1996) about what he called a candidate's "X-Factor"—what makes a person likeable. Rooney noted that Eisenhower, Kennedy, and Reagan had it, whereas Johnson, Nixon, and Bush (the elder) did not, and he speculated that if Dole lost the 1996 election, it wouldn't be "because of any one stand he took on an issue. The loser will be the one who, for some unfathomable reason, appears least attractive [he meant in the sense of being likeable] to the American public. Never mind the issues."

Rooney meant to imply that the X-Factor goes much deeper than what can be manipulated by makeup artists. Do you agree? Is Rooney right that being liked by voters is frequently more important than differences over issues or past records in determining who wins elections? Do you think personality was crucial in the victory of Bill Clinton over Bob Dole in 1996? What about George W. Bush's over Al Gore and John Kerry? Defend your opinions.

EXERCISE 10-8

1. In the 2000 presidential campaign, George W. Bush characterized himself as a *compassionate conservative.*
   a. What do you think this means?
   b. Once he was in office, did his policies satisfy your conception of that expression? Explain.

2. If past experience is any guide, it is very likely that if Al Gore had been elected president in 2000 or John Kerry in 2004, they would have broken quite a few of their campaign promises.

   But what about George W. Bush? In his case, we now have direct evidence on this point. He made lots of promises and either did or didn't keep them, or at least made token efforts to do so. According to one of his campaign promises in 2000, part of his plan called "A Comprehensive National Energy Plan," he was going to "work to make our air cleaner" while promoting electricity. "We will require all power plants to meet clean air standards in order to reduce emissions of sulfur dioxide, nitrogen oxide, mercury, and carbon dioxide within a reasonable period of time."

   Well, then, did President Bush keep this promise? Did he at least make token gestures? In particular, did he work for stringent and mandatory reductions in the emission of carbon dioxide, a known "greenhouse" gas, into the air by power plants?

EXERCISE 10-9

Here is an excerpt from a syndicated political column by William Pfaff that appeared in newspapers around the country in March 1990:

The Threat of Demagogic Oligarchy

Chicago—**Pressure is mounting** for campaign reform in American politics. Campaigning in cities like Chicago has always been rough, but now character assassination has become the privileged instrument of political ambition in national as well as local politics, excluding virtually all serious debate on issues. . . .

We are in fact witnessing the decline of American democracy towards a form of demagogic oligarchy. Individuals and groups with access to the vast sums now essential in American politics manipulate to their electoral advantage powerful images, some latently violent, some xenophobic.

. . . What prompts fear about what is happening in the United States is the general substitution of irrelevant emotional appeals for debate. More than half the population now fails to vote in national elections and there is a clear trend towards political alienation among those who do vote. Combine that with the mounting rates of illiteracy and general ignorance in the society and the substitution of manipulative oligarchy for representative democracy comes steadily closer.

For once there is a simple solution. It is possible, at a stroke, to solve the campaign money problem and deal a severe blow to demagogic image-manipulation. This solution is to prohibit political advertisements on television and radio. [Great Britain already does this.]

American political campaigns now are all but totally dominated by broadcast political advertising. The need to purchase time is responsible for the huge inflation of campaign costs in recent times. More than $250 million was spent on campaigns in the presidential year of 1988. Half a billion in current dollars will be spent during House and Senate campaigns in the 1990s. [The figures for 1992, 1994, and 1996 were much higher than for 1988 and 1990 and well over one billion for 2000 and 2004.]

The need for money to pay for advertising has made the single-issue political action committee the most powerful actor in American politics. It has made it all but impossible for an incumbent congressman or senator successfully to be challenged: the incumbent gets the PAC money because he can deliver what the PAC wants. Support for a challenger is speculation.

. . . No other serious democracy tolerates this. Virtually nowhere else is paid campaign advertising permitted. Ours is a mad system, perversely American, jeopardizing democracy itself. Banning advertising will hurt only the broadcasters. They are a powerful lobby, and one that politicians rightly fear, but even broadcasters not obsessed with their private interest must recognize the gravity of the situation.[11]

1. Summarize the part of Pfaff's column that explains his view as to what the problem is.

2. State his proposal to solve this problem in your own words.

3. State whether you agree or disagree with him about there being the problem that he describes. Explain.

4. Critically evaluate his solution.

---

[11] Copyright 1990, *Los Angeles Times* Syndicate. Reprinted with permission.

Drawing by David Levine. Copyright © 1975 NYREV, Inc.
Reprinted by permission.

In this drawing, David Levine pictures the television-viewing audience as contented sheep. Do you agree?

*When covering the Capitol, the first
thing to remember is that every
government is run by liars.*

—I. F. Stone

*Freedom of the press is guaranteed only
to those who own one.*

—A. J. Liebling

*Has any reader found perfect accuracy
in the newspaper account of any
event of which he himself had inside
knowledge?*

—Edward Verrall Lucas

*Journalists separate the wheat from the
chaff . . . and then print the chaff.*

—Adlai Stevenson

*I really look with commiseration over
the great body of my fellow citizens
who, reading newspapers, live and die
in the belief that they have known
something of what has been passing in
the world during their time.*

—Harry S Truman

*The Press, like the public, has room in
its brain for only one story at a time.*

—E. L. Doctorow

*People who read tabloids deserve to be
lied to.*

—Jerry Seinfeld

Chapter

11

MANAGING THE NEWS

Earlier, we stressed the fact that reasoning well requires a good stock of background information. This certainly is true with regard to information—news—about what is going on in the world. The good news about the news is that there is more and better news out there than ever before in history. The bad news about the news is that not all of the more is better. The trick is to know how to separate the wheat from the chaff and, thinking of the remark, above, by Adlai Stevenson, concentrating on the wheat. (Another bit of bad news is that masses of people pay more attention to news schlock than to news pearls.)

1. The Media and the Power of Money

In France, the expression is "Cherchez la femme" (find the woman). In America, at any rate, and perhaps in France and just about everywhere, a more apt expression would be "follow the money."

The Power of the People

The chief sources of news for most people these days are the mass media—ABC, *Newsweek* magazine, the *Boston Globe,* and their cohorts. And the one overriding fact about these news sources is that they are businesses. They exist to make money. They sell a product and we buy it. Or we don't, in which case they go out of business. This means that we, the viewers of television programs, listeners to the radio, and readers of newspapers and magazines, have the most important say as to what sorts of news stories are reported in the mass media and how they are presented. That is why, for instance, the mass media so often play up relatively unimportant events while slighting more important ones— most people tend to be more interested in certain kinds of relatively trivial goings-on than in extremely important events. A case in point is the low priority often given to foreign news (unless, of course, the United States is involved, as in the Iraq War). Since the news is now driven by ratings and foreign news ranks low in public interest, foreign coverage has been slashed in the past decade by up to two-thirds, some media watchdogs estimate.

Item: During the week in which the Soviet Union disintegrated and the Ukraine and other parts of the defunct Soviet Union declared a new union, TV news featured the William Kennedy Smith Florida rape trial.

Large audiences also tend to be quite provincial, so the mass media concentrate on national affairs and home-grown celebrities, slighting news events from other countries.

Item: Coverage of the 2004 Olympic Games in the United States featured American athletes like Mike Phelps while slighting those of other countries. For example, NBC ran a glitzy biopic about swimming star Amanda Beard just before she placed second in the Individual Medley finals. She won a silver medal and was immediately interviewed and congratulated by the press, but little mention was made of the Ukranian swimmer, Yana Klochkova, who came in first, winning her second gold medal in less than a week. This type of provincialism is common to all countries, alas.

Similarly, because mass audiences are more interested in light-hearted material, human interest stories, and fantasy than in hardheaded reality, human interest also tends to crowd out more important matters.

Item: The media time given over to the Laci Peterson case played almost as big as the war during long stretches of 2003. And during the month that *60 Minutes II* broke the news of prisoner abuse in Abu Ghraib, NBC's *Dateline* ran some five hours of specials on the series finales of *Friends* and *Frazier* and on the season finale of *The Apprentice* (all NBC shows). When the network was criticized for cheapening the newsmagazine format with celebrity and entertainment news (not to mention touting other NBC shows), network executives countered that they were serving their audience. And they were. The specials drew larger audiences than all other shows in their time slots.

As mentioned in Chapter 6, large numbers of people are superstitious or believe in pseudosciences of one kind or another, and we all are wishful thinkers to some degree. That is why many TV programs feature so many more pseudoscience programs than they do those concerning genuine science.

NBC and the Fox network are probably the worst TV networks when it comes to showing pseudoscientific and other fantasy junk programs. Fox, for example, pandered to audience interest in the supernatural with its April 2000 two-part series "Ghosts: Best Evidence Caught on Tape" and "UFOs: Best Evidence Caught on Tape." Even CNN gets into the act with *Larry King Live,* which often features psychics and other pseudoscientific offerings. King's uncritical presentation of spiritualists is particularly troubling because his impressive stature as a journalist gives credence to their claims. He regularly interviews political leaders and heads of state like Tony Blair, Bill Clinton, Vladimir Putin, and George Bush on CNN—the network that bills itself as the "most trusted name in news." So, when mediums like John Edward and Sylvia Browne get the same kind of coverage, with little or no critical perspective to counter their claims, gullible viewers are more likely taken in by their paranormal shenanigans than if they appeared on an entertainment network like Sci Fi.[1]

Revealing fact: There is a science fiction channel on many cable systems but no science channel.

It's also true that the mass media pander to the extremely short attention spans of so many people in their mass audiences.

Item: Shorter and shorter sound bites have become the mainstay of all network daily news programs. In 1968, sound bites lasted a mere 40 seconds on average. By 1988, they had shrunk to an average of 10 seconds. Nothing, absolutely nothing, of any consequence can be dealt with in 40 seconds, much less in 10. It is true, though, that the news on PBS is presented in modestly larger and somewhat more sophisticated chunks, but PBS audiences are minuscule compared to those of the major networks. (Some news programs on NPR—National Public Radio—tend to be a bit more detailed and sophisticated and are the best source of news on the radio or TV.)

The Power of Advertisers

The media are beholden not just to the people, as just mentioned, but also to advertisers. Advertising revenue is the most important source of income for virtually all newspapers and magazines and also the principal source for television stations and TV networks.

---

[1] For more on this see "King of the Paranormal," by Chris Mooney, *Skeptical Inquirer,* November/ December 2003.

This Modern World by Tom Tomorrow. © 1991 Tom Tomorrow.
Reprinted by permission of Dan Perkins.

Exaggeration used to make a serious point about local news coverage on TV.

Since money translates into power, the media must cater to the interests of advertisers as well as to those of the general public. Commenting on this fact years ago, H. G. Wells, in his classic *Outline of History,* remarked:

> [T]hose fathers of America thought also that they had but to leave the Press free, and everyone would live in the light. They did not realize that a free press could develop a sort of constitutional venality due to its relations with advertisers, and that large newspaper proprietors could become buccaneers of opinion and insensate wreckers of good beginnings.

Wells would not be a bit surprised at the way things have been going on the tube.

Item: After Proctor & Gamble announced that it would withdraw all of its advertising from any TV station that ran a 30-second spot (produced by Neighbor to Neighbor, a grassroots political group) that publicized a boycott of Salvadoran coffee in general and P&G's Folger's brand in particular, only 2 of 30 local TV stations approached to run the spot were willing to do so. When television stations lose P&G advertising revenue, they fritter away millions of dollars in income.

Item: When an editor for *The Pioneer Press* (publisher of many papers in suburban Chicago) ran a review critical of a restaurant that advertised in the *Press,* she was told by higher-ups that the paper was "not in the business of bashing business." A while later, a favorable review of the same restaurant was written by someone in the marketing division—not a journalist. (*Extra!,* May/June 2004)

The Power of Government

Government has the right and often the power to regulate business activity. It thus can harass a news agency by being strict about the rules it sets up (it usually isn't) and the licenses it requires. The mere threat of government action has a "chilling" effect on the media.

One way of exerting control is by slapping fines on the media for broadcasting indecent material. The Federal Communications Commission (FCC) has raised its fines considerably for obscenity and indecency under a new bill (HR 3717). CBS was fined $550,000 after Janet Jackson's breast was famously bared during her halftime Super Bowl performance in 2004 with Justin Timberlake (who euphemistically called it a "wardrobe malfunction"). Later that year Clear Channel paid a whopping $1.7 million for indecency charges, mostly against Howard Stern for a graphic on-air exchange with a caller, and against deejay Ted Clem (Bubba the Love Sponge) for sexual material aired over a three-month period. With fines this hefty, the media quickly come into line. Clear Channel fired Clem, dropped Stern from all six channels that ran his show, and instituted a zero tolerance policy for indecent and obscene content.

It is true, of course, that the United States Constitution guarantees freedom of the press as one of several freedoms necessary to make representative government function. But governments occasionally censor certain kinds of material anyway, one example being material alleged to be obscene, which is not covered by the First Amendment. The problem comes in trying to legally determine what is obscene. The FCC sidesteps this issue by levying fines (as in the above cases) and revoking licenses, not by censoring material.

One of the main reasons for government censorship involves national security. Courts have upheld the federal government's right to forbid the publication of classified material—items, it is said, that need to be kept secret for "security reasons." In practice, this means that the federal government also is able to keep all sorts of chicanery secret simply by claiming that news stories about them would harm national security. (Perhaps the classic case of U.S. government censorship is classification until 2036 of certain parts of the Warren Commission report on the assassination of President Kennedy.)

Government officials also can, and do, manipulate the news by playing favorites among reporters, leaking only to those news people who play ball in return. Since leaks are such a large source of media information (see the discussion of news-gathering practices a few pages forward), reporters have to think twice before crossing their government informants. Similarly, reporters have to be careful in press conferences not to ask embarrassing questions or follow-up questions; those who are too brash or persistent don't get called on in future.

Although many items leaked to the media are on target, the fact that their sources can be concealed gives government officials a good deal of power. They can rig stories to serve their own interest without being accountable.

Item: As reported in an *Extra!* "Update" (April 1995), "A Feb. 11 *New York Times* report from Mexico by Tim Golden was loaded with anonymous sources: 'government officials said,' 'one official said,' ' . . . according to one official, . . .'" *Extra!*'s comment: "The article was about the alleged 'unmasking' of Zapatista leader Commander Marcos; how about unmasking the *New York Times'* sources?"

A failed attempt to rig the news on a grand scale occurred during the Iraq War when the Pentagon developed the short-lived Office of Strategic Influence designed to modify views about the United States in other countries. As the *New York Times* reported (February 19, 2003), the idea was to develop plans ". . . to provide news items, possibly even false ones, to foreign media organizations as part of a new effort to influence public sentiment and policy makers in both friendly and unfriendly countries," according to military officials. This Orwellian attempt at disinformation came to an abrupt end before it got off the ground. Nonetheless, it is just one of many attempts to manage the news. The military and the State Department have long conducted various kinds of information warfare, ranging from factual press releases to outright lies.

Government censorship can take subtle forms. The *Washington Post* reported that the White House deleted statements from government Web sites that have subsequently proven to be untrue. For example, Andrew Natsios, the head of the U.S. Agency for International Development, reassured the public on *Nightline* (April 23, 2003) that the American taxpayers' contribution to reconstruction in Iraq would amount to no more than $1.7 billion. But when the president asked Congress for a whopping $166 billion (later reduced to $87 billion) the government ". . . purged the offending commentary by Natsios from the agency's Web site. The transcript and links to it have vanished."[2] Other sins of omission: The White House ordered the Department of Labor to stop publishing its regular mass layoff reports when the unemployment crisis loomed large, and ordered the government to stop publishing regular reports on budget cuts to states when the cuts became substantial.[3]

When government passes censorship laws in response to pressure from big business, the result can be a serious threat to the constitutional right to free speech. For example, more than a dozen states in the U.S. make it "a criminal offense" to "unscientifically disparage food." Talk show host Oprah Winfrey was one of the first to be prosecuted under these laws in 1998. Texas cattlemen took her to court, charging her with violating the law by discussing the dangers of mad cow disease on her TV program. According to a story in the July 1999 New Internationalist, "Other U.S. journalists, chastened by the fear of such legal quagmires, are increasingly reluctant to report on other food-safety and environmental issues." (So do these laws violate the First Amendment right to free speech?)

---

[2] "White House Web Scrubbing," by Dana Millbank, December 18, 2003.
[3] From *The Daily Mislead,* December 18, 2003, *latest@daily.misleader.org.*

This Modern World by Tom Tomorrow. © 1991 Tom Tomorrow.
Reprinted by permission of Dan Perkins.

Of course, no U.S. government agencies have censoring powers that are anywhere near those regularly exercised in quite a few foreign countries. In China, Burma, Liberia, and many other countries, newspapers rarely are allowed to criticize governmental policies or actions. (At the start of the October 2000 uprising in Yugoslavia that toppled the regime of dictator Slobodan Milosovic, TV viewers in foreign countries around the world were shown films of mass demonstrations and the burning of the Parliament Building in Belgrade, but at the same time state-controlled TV featured a classical music concert, as though nothing whatever was happening in the streets a few blocks away, until protestors took over the Belgrade TV station and broadcast the news to the citizens of their own country.)

Worse still, in some nations, reporters often are threatened, even with death, making the "news" from these places extremely unreliable. Reporters in Turkey, for example, have been subject to a reign of terror that is bound to intimidate all but the hardiest—one might say foolhardiest—of investigators. The very real threat of being murdered cannot just be sloughed off, and those who forge ahead anyway run the risk of ending up as did Ugur Mumcu, described in a *Columbia Journalism Review* (May/June 1993) item as "a gritty veteran investigative reporter . . . [for] one of Turkey's most respected newspapers," known "for his reports on Kurdish separatists, drug smuggling, and the rise of Islamic fundamentalism in Turkey, . . . killed this past January [1992] by a car bomb."

The relative safety enjoyed by journalists in this country doesn't extend to dangerous countries abroad. In 2003, Daniel Pearl, a *Wall Street Journal* reporter, was kidnapped in Karachi by a group called the National Movement for the Restoration of Pakistan while he was working on a story about the Islamic military underground. Repeated efforts to rescue him failed and eventually his captors beheaded him, claiming, among other things, that he was an agent for the CIA and (later) for the Massad, the Israeli intelligence agency. The murder of Daniel Pearl and others like him is enough to dis-

---

The shock of Dec. 7 [1941] can be well imagined. When the last Japanese plane roared off, five American battleships had been sunk and three damaged, three cruisers and three destroyers badly hit, 200 planes destroyed, and 2344 men killed. For the loss of only 29 planes, Japan had virtually crippled the U.S. Pacific Fleet at a single blow.

The American service chiefs immediately decided that news of a disaster of such magnitude would prove unacceptable to the American people, and steps were taken to ensure that they did not learn about it. So effective were these measures that the truth about Pearl Harbor was still being concealed even after the war ended. The cover-up began with an "iron curtain" of censorship that cut off the United Press office in Honolulu from San Francisco in the middle of its first excited telephone report.

So drastic was the suppression of news that nothing further, except for official communiqués, came out of Pearl Harbor for another four days. These claimed that only one "old" battleship and a destroyer had been sunk and other ships damaged, and that heavy casualties had been inflicted on the Japanese. It cannot be argued that these lies were necessary to conceal from the Japanese the extent of the disaster they had inflicted on the U.S. Pacific Fleet. The Japanese knew exactly how much damage they had done, and reports in Tokyo newspapers accurately stating the American losses meant that the Americans knew that the Japanese knew. The American censorship was to prevent the American public from learning the gravity of the blow.

After flying to Hawaii on a tour of inspection, the Secretary of the Navy, Colonel Frank Knox, held a press conference in New York at which, with President Roosevelt's approval, he gave the impression he was revealing the full extent of the American losses at Pearl Harbor. Colonel Knox told correspondents that one United States battleship, the *Arizona,* had been lost and the battleship *Oklahoma* had capsized but could be righted.

This must have made strange reading for anyone actually at Pearl Harbor, who had only to lift his eye from his newspaper to see five United States battleships— the *Arizona,* the *Oklahoma,* the *California,* the *Nevada,* and the *West Virginia*— resting on the bottom.

—From *The First Casualty*
by Phillip Knightley

In wartime, truth is the first casualty, censorship the first expedient.

courage any reporter from investigating provocative stories in dangerous parts of the world.

The Power of the Media

The media are not simply beholden to the three powerful groups just discussed. They themselves are a genuinely separate power faction. This is particularly true of the mass media: television, major newspapers and magazines, and so forth. Investigative reporters can, and sometimes do, unearth governmental chicanery as well as stories not in the best interests of advertisers, although we have gone to some pains to show why they often hesitate.

This doesn't mean that the media constitute a monolithic, organized group but, rather, that individual mass media organizations have a certain amount of power and that, taken as a whole, the mass media have great power and frequently common interests. Cases such as the *Washington Post* Watergate exposés, which set in motion events that drove Richard Nixon from office, are well known. But plenty of less striking examples could be cited. In any case, the mass media do on occasion provide their audiences with information about government and big business chicanery. The *Time* magazine series on corporate welfare is a good case in point. The articles catalogued government subsidies to corporations at the expense of individual or other corporate taxpayers. The headline and lead-in material in the February 7, 2000, exposé illustrates the hard-hitting nature of the *Time* magazine series:

> **How the Little Guy Gets Crunched**
> When powerful interests shower Washington with millions in campaign contributions, they often get what they want. But it's ordinary citizens and firms that pay the price—and most of them never see it coming.

The article in question then went on to list several ways in which ordinary taxpayers get it in the neck:

> You pick up a disproportionate share of America's tax bill. You pay higher prices for a broad range of products, from peanuts to prescription drugs. You pay taxes that others in similar situations have been excused from paying. You must pay debts that you incur while others do not. . . .

It then listed some of the benefits enjoyed by "the fortunate few who contribute to the right politicians:

> If they make a bad business decision, the government bails them out [recall the famous Chrysler Corporation bailout]. If they want to hire workers at below-market wages, the government provides the means to do so. . . . If they want immunity from certain laws, the government gives it. If they want to kill legislation that is intended for the public good, it gets killed. . . .

Unfortunately, exposés such as this one by *Time* magazine that hit at special privileges for the rich and powerful do not get heard with great frequency in the mass media; in particular, not on mainstream TV. (But they do in the *non–mass* media!)

Although the *Time* magazine series didn't result in any great reform of the corporate welfare system, it did inform the public about a great many government subsidies. So with all of their shortcomings, the media are our first line of defense against government gone wrong and against the very advertising power to which they themselves so often have to knuckle under.

Of course, one media giant's power has to compete with that of the others. CBS's power to determine what will be shown on its network programs is held in check by the identical power wielded by NBC, ABC, Fox, CNN, and the rest of its competitors, not to mention competitors in the print media, just as the power of one politician may be reduced by the power of others and by the power of the media. Vive le competition!

Every country has its own influential media, of course. A good case in point, given our current involvement in the Mideast, is the increasing importance of the media in the Arab world. Probably the most influential network in that area is Al-Jazeera, established in 1996 by the British-educated, progressive emir of Qatar. The network reaches over 35 million people and is reputed to have as much power as the *New York Times.* In a recent analysis of the network, two U.S. academics explained how the coverage of controversial issues in the Arab world revolutionized the way Arabs think about themselves and others.[4] Previously, the media were controlled either by Arab governments or by companies kowtowing to government interest. But Al-Jazeera changed all that. By featuring interviews and talk shows with open-air debates on provocative issues ranging from the role of secularism to human rights abuses under Arab regimes, the network has had a profound influence on the Middle East. Arab networks, in general, had a strong global impact during the Iraq War as well. Media around the world used footage from Al-Jazeera and other Arab stations that gave a much different perspective from the coverage by networks in the United States and other countries. As might be expected, the graphic footage of wounded soldiers and civilians, a staple of Al-Jazeera, has been highly controversial in this country and strongly criticized by the Bush administration.

The Power of Big Business

The days are long gone when most business in countries like the United States was conducted by individuals or small organizations. "Ma and pa" stores have given way to Wal-Marts and Safeways. Individual doctors hanging out their shingles have been replaced by group practices and HMOs. Most family farms have been replaced by huge agribusinesses. These days, virtually all industries are controlled by large corporations—in particular, by huge multinational conglomerates. Large corporations, individually and collectively, thus have great power, which they exercise almost exclusively in the interests of maximizing their own profits.

Corporate power affects the dissemination of news in two ways: first, by getting the viewpoints of big business reported favorably in the mass media; second, by preventing conflicting viewpoints from being reported or stressed. This censoring power of large corporations stems in part from their power as advertisers (a point already discussed). Large corporations, after all, are by far the largest advertisers in the mass media. But it also stems from the power money has in the political arena (a point to be discussed later). When the mass media cooperate with political power, they thus indirectly also cooper-

---

[4] *Al-Jazeera: How the Arab News Network Scooped the World,* by Mohammed El-Nawaway and Adel Iskandar, Westview Press, 2002.

ate with large corporate interests. Furthermore, the mass media themselves have become controlled in large part by very large media conglomerates, which often are parts of even larger corporate structures (a point also to be discussed shortly). In general, the interests of media conglomerates coincide with those of other large businesses—for example, in favoring lower wages for on-the-line employees—so that the mass media tend to have a built-in bias in favor of big business. (Interestingly, many conservative commentators regularly accuse the media of having a left-wing bias.)

The result is that news and opinion in the mass media tend to be skewed strongly to the interests of the rich rather than ordinary citizens or the poor. Ordinary people, of course, also have great power in determining how the mass media portray the world—they can switch channels or otherwise tune out. They also can go to non–mass media news and opinion sources (yes, these will be discussed shortly), but most people do not do so, one reason being that the average person does not understand how the news is slanted in the interests of those with great political power.[5] (Another reason is that large numbers of people—in particular, those in the lower half of the economic pecking order—tend to concentrate on their own personal lives and problems and to be inattentive when it comes to the important economic and political issues of the wider community, even though a good deal of what happens in their lives is seriously influenced by what happens in the broader social arena.) The increasing bias of the media is ironic at a time when an incredible amount of raw data is available on the Internet. But unless the media use that information to challenge the assumptions of those in power, the average person will never understand how the news is slanted.

Item: Most big city dailies have "business" sections that report the goings-on of large corporations and of the various financial markets—almost exclusively from the point of view of investors and other large money interests. But no daily newspapers have labor sections or report on business from the point of view of individual workers or, except on occasion, organized labor. Similarly, several business news programs are aired on TV during the day (when MSNBC is devoted almost exclusively to stock market goings-on), but no labor programs or programs regularly reporting from the point of view of ordinary workers. (But consider the fact that a majority of daytime TV audiences prefer to watch the soaps, sports news, and sitcom reruns. How then could a labor channel be a paying proposition?)

Have you ever noticed that the heads of labor unions frequently are referred to as "union bosses" but that expressions like "big business bosses" or "the boss of XYZ corporation" are almost never used in the mass media? Big business bosses go under nice labels like "CEO" and "President."

---

[5] The idea is widespread in America that there are no classes in the land of the free and the home of the brave. The truth in this idea is that in every generation some individuals move from lower into higher economic classes, even occasionally into the highest. The falsehood in this idea is that most of those born into rich families remain rich and most of those born into average- or lower-income households never become rich. Class membership in large industrial democracies is not carved in stone in the way it was in the monarchies of old, but this surely does not mean that there are any truly classless societies on this planet, other than in tiny hunting-and-gathering groups.

Item: When labor union stories are reported in the press they often have a negative slant. For example, a ten-year study of labor coverage (1991–2001) in the *Chicago Tribune,* conducted by Robert Bruno, of the University of Illinois, revealed that 77 percent of the descriptive language used to characterize labor was negative. In articles about labor disputes, 95.3 percent of the descriptors were negative and less than one story a year focused on unions improving working conditions. Interestingly, the most extensive coverage of labor relations was about player unions in the sports section, but more than three-quarters of these stories were negative in tone as well. The study concluded that the paper had an anti-union bias and that both the workers and their leaders were negatively characterized. The findings are a reflection of the fact that media sympathy for labor, once strong in big cities, has slowly evaporated. There may be a revival, though, now that Enron and other corporate scandals have hit the news.

Item: The media tell viewers about how Social Security payments and the nation's health expenses (in particular, for Medicare) need to be reduced if financial disasters lurking down the road are to be averted. But they don't often delve deeply into the extremely bloated military budgets that were barely reduced at the end of the Cold War (when there was supposed to be a drastic reduction in military spending) and have spiraled out of sight with the wars in Afghanistan and Iraq. The rich don't depend on Social Security payments and can afford first-rate medical insurance policies that provide them with the kinds of coverage HMO policies don't allow. (By the way, is the Social Security system in financial trouble and in need of drastic revision? Is there a good term paper topic here?)

It's also interesting that so much more attention is given to welfare for the poor than to welfare for the rich—the *Time* magazine exposés were not the norm—yet government handouts and tax breaks for the rich total several times more than do those granted to the poor. (Note that handouts to the rich rarely are referred to as "welfare" or as "handouts" in the mass media.)

Power Tends to Cooperate with Power

Although the interests of big business and government often coincide with those of the media, sometimes they do not. Scandals may sell newspapers and increase TV news audiences, but they also tend to sink political careers. What is bad for Microsoft may be good for CNN. (But see the section at the end of this chapter on recent trends!)

In a majority of cases, however, it's better for the various power factions to cooperate rather than to fight. That is why, for instance, reporters covering the White House quickly learn which sorts of questions can be asked at presidential press conferences, how far follow-up queries can go, what sorts of editorial comments they can make in news reports, and the like. Journalists who don't play the game, who persist in challenging the standard self-serving replies to their questions, don't get called upon in the future. Columnists who tear into an administration in Washington with a great deal of gusto are less likely to receive leaks or other tidbits.

Talk show hosts with guests who bash the government suffer as well. For example, when Phil Donahue interviewed a number of anti-war, anti-Bush guests, his show was abruptly cancelled in February 2003. An internal NBC memo leaked later that month (on All Your TV Web site) revealed that the network was concerned that Donahue presented "a difficult public face for NBC in time of war" and that the show could be "a home for the liberal anti-war agenda at the same time that our competitors are waving the flag at every opportunity."[6]

Of course, when the interests of politicians or big business moguls happen to coincide with those of the masses, coverage of interesting or important events will be automatic, perhaps even large-scale.

> *Example:* This is especially true in time of war, particularly when the media and the government cooperate, as they did in the Iraq War. Partly in response to severe press restrictions during the Gulf War, the second George Bush's administration decided to "embed" reporters with the troops. They were sent to media boot camp, trained in military behavior, and shipped off to Iraq, where they were assigned to military units around the country. These embedded journalists gave up-close coverage of the war with plenty of human interest stories about men and women in battle for the folks back home. The interests of the media, the government, and the public converged in this riveting event. (An ongoing event that is newsworthy is the dream of everyone in the news business.)

It's true that, in practice, the system does not work in precisely this way every time. There is slippage due to inefficiency and to the fact that middle-class interest is worth more (to advertisers, for instance) than is that of the poor, coupled with the fact that it takes lots of audience interest to overcome serious political opposition. The media will generally buck political power only when buttressed by support from very large numbers of people or by competing powerful forces. But when all or most power blocks line up and the public is perceived to be receptive, the media will go for broke and public opinion will be moved.

> *Example:* In August, 1996, the *San Jose Mercury* news, one of the better big-city newspapers, published an exposé called "Dark Alliance" by their then star reporter Gary Webb about the connection between the CIA and the drug-trafficking Nicaraguan contras (a group supported—some would say created—by the United States because it perceived the opposition [the Sandinistas] to be communistic). The three-day, 15,000-word series revealed how drug dealers worked with the contras to bring tons of cocaine into California in the 1980s, much of it being sold as "crack" cocaine to Los Angeles street gangs. The articles claimed that this drug distribution played an important role in the subsequent widespread crack addiction in urban America. Webb reported that some of the dope money went to the contras and that federal law-enforcement reports suggested the CIA knew about the drug smuggling and protected its existence. Although Webb had no smoking gun, he had a great deal of circumstantial evidence to support this claim, including information contained in a U.S. Senate subcommittee report.
>
> The CIA denied the story; the mass media on the whole discounted it, and eventually the *Mercury News* backed away from it. The role of the trendsetting newspapers, the *New York Times,* the *Los Angeles Times,* and the *Washington Post,* in debunking Webb's exposé was especially egregious, as were accounts on

---

[6] Quoted in "Dissent Unwelcome in Wartime," *Extra!,* May/June 2004.

major TV networks. Webb was moved from Sacramento, where he was assigned to big state news stories, and then to Cupertino, where he covered local events (the newspaper business's analog to the common police department practice of reassigning nosy or otherwise annoying cops to beats in the "boonies"). Some time after Webb's more-or-less forced resignation, short mass-media stories—on back pages of major newspapers and so forth—began to surface. (As usual, the non–mass media had long since beaten the mass media to the punch.) Finally, in October 1998, a declassified version of the report by the CIA's inspector general revealed that the CIA had known of the contra plan to sell drugs in the United States and had done little or nothing to respond to hundreds of drug-related allegations against contra officials. The major mass media news sources, as is generally the case, had accepted the CIA lies and again been burned. And will they own up the next time that they get used?

News as Entertainment

For all the reasons discussed so far, the news has increasingly become a source of entertainment more than an information source. Because money is the bottom line, because vested interests like big business and government shape the news to their advantage, and because the public wants entertainment more than information, news items tend to morph into Hollywood action stories. A good example is the saga of Jessica Lynch that dominated human-interest stories during the Iraq War. True, her story was hard to beat, crafted as it was into a hair-raising thriller. Small town girl joins the Army, winds up in Iraq where she is injured in battle, suffers multiple fractures, and becomes a prisoner of war. Freed in a rescue mission eerily filmed by the military, she becomes a national hero, receives the Purple Heart, the Bronze Star, and the POW medal, and lands a million-dollar book deal. The public lapped up her story, despite the inconsistencies that surfaced. No, she really didn't empty her gun firing on Iraqi soldiers as was originally reported. Her gun was jammed and she fell on her knees in prayer. Her captors tried to return her to the Americans before the rescue mission, but were fired on by U.S. troops who mistook them for invaders. Her story unfolded in the media like a riveting sitcom, transforming her into a symbol of the war, which to her credit, she apparently found embarrassing and wrong-headed. Stories like this, played up by the media and skewed by vested interests, glamorized the war and overshadowed the day-to-day activities.

The war itself was filmed like a TV movie, starting with the buildup of tension for months in advance. Anticipation grew as we learned that journalists embedded with the troops would cover the war as it really was. Once the action began, we watched bombs bursting in air and cruse missiles toppling tall buildings. We saw victorious American troops marching across Iraq into Baghdad, and along the way journalists reported from the battlefield, with gunfire in the background and troops on the attack. As Peter Arnett commented on NBC, "An amazing sight, just like an action movie, but this is real."[7]

The news as entertainment is just as prevalent in domestic politics as it is on the battlefield. When Arnold Schwarzenegger ran for governor of California, he avoided the

---

[7]Quoted in "That's Militainment," *Extra!,* June 2003, a well-researched analysis of press coverage of the Iraq War.

hard news media and, instead, appeared on entertainment shows throughout the campaign. Starting when he announced his candidacy on the Jay Leno show, he moved on to field softball questions on *Oprah* and *Larry King Live,* managed to avoid political reporters, appeared in only one quasi-debate, and came full circle when Jay Leno introduced his acceptance speech on election night. As Orville Schell, Dean of the U.C. Berkeley Graduate School of Journalism, said, "It's one more nail in the coffin that divides entertainment from news."[8] But the public loved it, electing Schwarzenegger out of a field of 135 candidates to succeed Gray Davis as governor of California in the 2003 recall election.

2. NEWS-GATHERING METHODS ARE DESIGNED TO SAVE MONEY

The all-important fact about the mass media, as we have been at pains to point out, is that they are in business to make money, not lose it. When they regularly spend more money gathering the news than they take in, they go out of business. The result is that true investigative reporting tends to get slighted, because it is so very expensive in time, effort, and thus money. More "efficient" news-gathering techniques are used whenever possible, even though spending greater amounts of money might produce more accurate accounts, not to mention dredge up dirt the powerful are trying to hide. Media people generally do try to be careful in what they report, so as not to leave themselves open to libel charges, and (in most cases) because of a desire to adhere to professional ethics. But they rarely get to dig below the surface.

The principal way in which news is gathered is through established "beats." The major wire services, television networks, and a few top newspapers and magazines routinely assign reporters to cover the major news-developing institutions—the White House, Congress, and so on. At the local level, they cover city hall, the police, and the like. Roving reporters are assigned to cover breaking stories in business, medicine, and so on, by interviewing interested parties—representatives of large corporations giving press conferences, "experts" in relevant fields, union leaders.[9] In effect, then, *most news is given to reporters by government officials or by others who have or represent power or wealth.* The news thus is bound to reflect established interests much more than those of the general public, given that it is the rich and powerful who have the means to call press conferences, provide video footage, or issue fancy press releases.[10]

That is an important reason why *very few important news stories in the mass media result from true investigative reporting!* It's much easier, quicker, and cheaper to interview heads of government agencies or representatives of big business than it is to find out what actually is going on by tedious digging. (It's also safer; recall the discussion a

---

[8]Quoted in the *San Francisco Chronicle,* October 2, 2003.

[9]Experts can be found on every side of virtually all issues. Which experts are consulted depends on the way in which a story is to be slanted, and that, of course, usually is determined by the various factors we have been considering in this chapter.

[10]An important exception to this rule is that ordinary people often are interviewed to impart "human interest" to stories that otherwise reflect the opinions and viewpoints of power or money. Another exception is the coverage of local news events such as fires—reporters actually go to the scene and interview those affected by the event.

"Hey, do you want to be on the news tonight or not? This is a sound bite, not the Gettysburg Address. Just say what you have to say, Senator, and get the hell off."

while back about the power of government and why power tends to cooperate with power.)

Anyway, there is a bit of good news on the topic of true investigative reporting. In recent years, newspapers, and occasionally TV and radio programs, have been recycling items from non–mass media magazines and from the major newspapers (which have set up syndicates for this purpose to compete with feature syndicates). Reprinting someone else's investigative efforts is a good deal cheaper than digging on one's own. So items from *The Washington Monthly, The Atlantic, The New Republic, The National Review,* and other non–mass media publications, as well as from the *New York Times,* the *Washington Post,* and the *Los Angeles Times,* appear now and then in local rags and on network news programs.

Another good bit of news is that the media are now using electronic marvels to lower the costs of true investigative reporting. For example, two *St. Louis Post-Dispatch* specialists in computer journalism, George Landau and Tim Novak, checked thousands of Missouri death certificates via computer and proved the locally well-known fact that citizens who have passed over into another constituency sometimes manage to register and vote. They also checked Missouri's computerized death certificate records to identify coroners who "repeatedly failed to investigate suspicious deaths," listing the cause as "unknown" when an autopsy might have revealed child abuse, elderly abuse, or other evidence of homicide.[11]

3. MISDIRECTION AND LACK OF PROPORTION

An important lesson to be learned from what has been said so far in this chapter is that the news, as presented to us by the mass media, tends to misdirect our attention away from important, underlying, day-to-day occurrences and trends in favor of "breaking news" (assassination of a foreign leader, Superbowl coverage), "human interest" stories, particularly celebrity coverage, and what the powerful want to tell us.

It hasn't always been this way. In the years before the media mergers and increasing demands that news divisions show a profit, the coverage of celebrities was a small part of mainstream news. *Extra!* (October 1997) reports that Elvis Presley's death in 1977 was covered in 29 minutes over the following five weekdays. When John Lennon was killed in 1980, his murder received 59 minutes over the next five weekdays. But coverage of Princess Diana's death in 1997 totaled 197 minutes on nightly newscasts over a five-weekday period—almost two-thirds of all nightly news coverage in the first week of September 1997. And allegations against Michael Jackson for child molestation got around-the-clock coverage for months in 2003.

The mass media also tend to play into the average person's lack of a good sense of proportion. That is why, for example, the media often pay just as much attention to an economic issue concerning, say, $100 million as to one about $10 billion. (It's well known that a great many people are able to distinguish rightly between relatively small amounts—for instance, between $500 and $5,000—but tend to get hazy when the numbers get larger than the kind that directly relate to their own lives.) For example, when

---

[11] See "Quantum Leaps: Computer Journalism Takes Off," in the *Columbia Journalism Review* (May/June 1992).

prescription drug benefits were added to the Medicare health program in 2004, most people easily grasped the amount involved for each person: Seniors would pay $35 a month, and after they met a $250 deductible, insurance would pay 75 percent of drug costs up to $2,280. But people's eyes tended to glaze over at the astronomical cost of the program—at least $400 billion by 2013 and possibly trillions by the time baby boomers retire. (Do you know how much a billion or a trillion is?)

Although satisfying the public's liking for human interest stories doesn't have to result in relatively trivial news getting a bigger play than more important items, in fact that is often the way it works. For instance, when an abandoned alligator turned up in a San Francisco lake in 1996, the local media had a field day (actually, several field weeks) with the story; relatively neglected were reports of increasing invasions of nonindigenous marine species into San Francisco Bay, causing million-dollar losses to local fishermen and threatening to wipe out several local marine species. The alligator and efforts to catch it were appealing to a large audience even though of trivial importance to anyone's life, while the more serious threat to local fishermen and the Bay Area economy lacked pizzazz.

4. NEWS REPORTING: THEORY AND PRACTICE

People don't often stand back and look carefully at what they're doing from a wider perspective; they don't often theorize about their activities. On the whole, media workers do so more than most, but their theories frequently are self-serving.

The Unusual Is News, the Everyday Is Not

Theory says that news is what is new—the unusual—not the commonplace. Yet what happens every day is generally more important than the unusual occurrences that make the headlines. For example, over the past 20 years or so, many kinds of bacteria slowly

---

Pete Hamil, on the trend of journalists to degenerate into gossip hounds:

[Reporters in the 1950's] were conscious of their limitations; they knew that they never once had turned out an absolutely perfect newspaper, because the newspaper was put out by human beings. But in their separate ways, they tried very hard never to write anything that would bring the newspaper shame. They would be appalled at the slovenly way the word "tabloid" is now used. [*Tabloid* describes the shape of the page, not the content.] They didn't pay whores for stories. They didn't sniff around the private lives of politicians like agents from the vice squad. Even in large groups, on major stories, the photographers didn't behave like a writhing, snarling, mindless centipede, all legs and Leicas, falling upon some poor witness like an instrument of punishment. Somehow, they found ways to get the story without behaving like thugs or louts.

—Excerpted from *News Is a Verb*
by Pete Hamil (1998)

but steadily have been developing resistance to present-day antibiotics. Millions of people who would have been saved just a few years ago are dying, or being seriously impaired, and everyone is at an increasing risk from diseases once thought to be virtually conquered by miracle drugs. (Tuberculosis is an example.) The media pretty much ignore this vitally important story or relegate it to newspaper back pages, except every once in a while, when a news magazine or TV news program runs a story that turns a few heads for a short time and then disappears—buried in the minds of media audiences under a mass of information about relatively trivial, or quickly unimportant, events. Yet without question, microscopic organisms—bacteria, viruses, and so on—constitute one of the two most serious threats to human life and health on this planet, the other being pollution and other swift environmental changes that threaten to unravel most, or at least an important part, of the ecological web on which human life depends and to result in immense suffering for millions of people. (A third serious threat—eliminating human life on Earth via a massive atomic war—has diminished considerably since the breakup of the Soviet Union in 1991, but worldwide terrorism and the threat of biological or chemical warfare and "dirty" bombs may be taking its place.)

Part of the reason for this slanting of the news to cover what is new compared to more important everyday ongoing realities surely has to do with audience interest. The media provided mountains of coverage about Monica Lewinsky, Laci Peterson, Michael Jackson, and others, but much less time on detailed reports of problems that more directly affect readers. For instance, there was very little coverage of a series of articles on HMOs in the prestigious *New England Journal of Medicine* (May 1998), stories that explained how some HMOs push cost-cutting procedures—often to the detriment of patients—and punish doctors who resist. The *Journal* showed how physicians who participate in HMO plans can earn significant fee increases by holding down hospital admissions, emergency room use, and referrals to specialists. These statistics certainly provide more valuable information to the average reader (who may be one of those patients denied adequate treatment) than facts about the DNA on Ms. Lewinsky's dress, but the media expended mountains more time on the dress and its evidence than it did on the serious problems with HMOs and what is euphemistically referred to as "managed care."

Another unfortunate consequence of the idea that only what is new constitutes news is that after a politician once is reported, say, as having lied on an important issue, in most cases the lie itself then no longer counts as a new event, although the politician's denial generally does count as news.

One of the consequences of uncritical objectivity is that too often the press reports political spin without analyzing it to separate fact from fiction. In just about every campaign, candidates either distort their opponents' positions or speak in half-truths, or just plain lie, but in the 2004 campaign this type of chicanery reached an all-time high. Candidates in both parties repeatedly distorted information that was technically accurate to suggest conclusions that were inaccurate.[12] for example, George W. Bush accused John Kerry of voting against six popular programs, including an increase in child credit and

---

[12]Examples are taken from "Tsunami," an excellent article by Bryan Keefer on the problems with campaign coverage, in the *Columbia Review of Journalism,* July/August 2004, page 18.

decreases in the marriage penalty and the tax rate on dividends. It comes as no surprise that the average person assumed that Kerry voted no on six separate issues, but in fact all of these programs were included in Bush's two major tax cuts, which Kerry opposed, yet this distortion was not reported in the mainstream media.

Kerry used similar tactics. Early in the campaign he launched a "middle-class misery index" that selectively picked a few damning statistics—like health care costs, college tuition, and bankruptcy rates—to show how bad the economy was under Bush. Most newspapers ran the bogus index without explaining what the more extensive, traditional "misery index" would show, which was a good deal better than the one cooked up by the Kerry campaign. When the press treats political spin as though it were legitimate argument, the public has little hope of separating fact from fiction.

News Reporting Is Supposed to Be Objective, Not Subjective

Those who work on the news in our country often say that facts are objective; conclusions or value judgments, subjective. Media workers are supposed to be objective—they are supposed to report only the facts. This is not the case in other countries, by the way. In England, for instance, the political bias of newspapers is openly expressed in news articles and not confined to the editorial pages as it is in the United States. The *Guardian* champions liberal causes, for example; *The Times,* conservative ones. But even in the United States this theory of objectivity is erroneous. Reports of facts generally depend on somebody's judgment that they are facts. A reporter must reason to the facts, or at least report someone else's reasoning to the facts, just as one reasons to anything else. Facts are not like fruit on trees, to be plucked at one's leisure.

We just mentioned, for example, the fact that mutant bacteria are becoming an extremely serious health problem, but there is no single observation, or series of observations, that demonstrate this truth. Medical experts have to reason to this fact from what they observe (for example, that syphilis, tuberculosis, and malaria cases now often do not respond to previously effective antibiotics).

Similarly, the idea that media hands should not make value judgments is foolish. They *must* make value judgments, if only about which items are important enough to be featured, which should be mentioned only briefly, and which should be tossed into the round file (where most items that go over Associated Press wires end up). The point is that *editing,* one of the chief tasks performed by media workers, requires value judgments about the relative importance of events.

In any case, theory is one thing; practice, another. Practice is driven primarily by the various forces we have been at pains to describe and only to a small extent by abstract theory. The theory of objectivity serves as a convenient cover under which this can be done. Its cash value is that reporters are motivated to stay within the narrow, middle-of-the-road social consensus when they make judgments or draw conclusions. So one effect of the theory of objectivity is to discourage the reporting of nonestablishment or nonconsensus points of view, satisfying instead the desires of media audiences, advertisers, and others who have great power. Objectivity turns into not rocking the boat. (Interestingly, some of the cable TV talk shows allow a bit wider range of opinion than can be found on network news programs.)

It's also true, and worth noting, that journalists often confuse objectivity with its close relative—being evenhanded. It has become common practice, for example, for the major networks to present rebuttal from the "other side" when they carry major presidential addresses, so that both major parties get their say. Comments about the truth of whatever is at issue tend to get lost—they would be considered value judgments anyway and so would not satisfy the criteria of the theory of objective reporting.

Note, by the way, how the expression "other side" masks the fact that there are *many* sides to most issues and that the viewpoints championed by the two major political parties often run the range only from A to B. During the 2004 presidential campaign, for example, the mass media were more or less "evenhanded" in their coverage of Democratic and Republican candidates, but they did very little reporting concerning candidates of the Green, Reform, Libertarian, and other "minor" parties.

News Is Supposed to Be Separated from Analysis and In-Depth Reporting

The theory of objectivity requires that facts be reported separately from conclusions or evaluations (which are thought of as "subjective"). But this separation of news from analysis further aggravates a defect already in evidence in most media reporting: *the failure to tie what happens to any explanation as to why it happened and why it is important.*

For instance, in 1998, when Hurricane Mitch wreaked havoc in Honduras, Guatemala, and Nicaragua, the mass media reported horrendous destruction and a large number of deaths. But they failed to explain *why* the destruction was so great. To do that, they needed to explain how the Central American policies of the United Fruit Company and of the United States in the 1950s and 1960s led to intense deforestation that undermined the landscape. They failed to stress the important point that this deforestation, undertaken to replace local farmers with large-scale agriculture, was a major part of the cause of the massive flooding and landslides that resulted when Hurricane Mitch hit. See, for example, *Counterpunch,* November 1–15, 1998—a left-wing non–mass media publication—or many good histories of Central America. Moral: To know what is really going on, you can't rely on the mass media.

Typically, when covering a story, a reporter consults those directly involved or affected by it. Writing, say, about civil service employee salaries, a reporter would very likely interview civil servants who, naturally, will say that their salaries are lower than for comparable jobs in industry, and critics who, having raised the issue, can be expected to say that the salaries in question are higher than in the nongovernment business world. In fact, this routine has been gone through several times in recent years. Most reporters, of course, have no idea which side is right—they don't know enough about the topic to

---

Thoughtfully written analysis is out, "live pops" are in. . . . Hire lookers, not writers. Do powder-puff, not probing, interviews. Stay away from controversial subjects. Kiss a ___, move with the mass, and for heaven and the ratings' sake don't make anybody mad. . . . Make nice, not news.

—Dan Rather (of CBS's *Evening News*)

make an intelligent judgment. They don't know, for example, whether civil service job specifications truly describe what happens on the job day to day. How could they, given that the topic they investigated the week before might have been water pollution in Pennsylvania, while next week's topic will be job flight to Mexico?

Although the theory of objective news reporting often tends to deter journalists from saying what they believe or even know to be true, as just described, it doesn't absolutely forbid the mixing of news with evaluation or analysis. In fact, reporters have a modest amount of freedom to spout off, at least when no toes of the powerful are being stepped on. Nevertheless, the impossibility of being experts on every topic they must investigate, coupled with the need to seem authoritative, whether they know what they are talking about or not, often produces rather mixed results. For example, the journalists embedded with the troops during the Iraq War reported a piece of the action as they experienced it, but they had no concept of the big picture. And since much reporting was instantaneous, aired on television or radio as it was happening, they had no time to sort through the information and give it context. As a result, the audience got a slice of the battle but little evaluation or analysis that would come from mature deliberation over time.

Another example is the way in which the mass media handled the story about the possible discovery that there once was life on Mars. For a short time, after which it disappeared into the great maw, news magazines ran feature stories, evening news programs played the story up to the hilt, and newspapers ran long articles about it. What generally was lacking in these mass media accounts was the balanced, questioning appraisal that could be found in non–mass publications—for example, in the October 1996 issue of *Scientific American* magazine. The story there was placed into its historical context (including the fact that a similar 1961 story played up in the mass media turned out to be incorrect) and stressed the tentative, iffy nature of the August 1996 claim about Martian life, citing a great deal of contrary opinion by scientists in the field. (Note that the media played the story incorrectly even if it should turn out that indeed there was once rudimentary life on the Red Planet.)

The Opinions of the "Right" Authorities Take Precedence

Since the reporters who gather the news are not usually experts in the fields they have to cover, they must, and do, seek out expert opinion. The trouble is that experts can be

Even though TV reporters arriving on the scene of a breaking story generally know very little about what is taking place or about the topic that is at issue, they still must appear to be authoritative and not merely people reading someone else's news to us. That is why, for example, evening news anchors may turn up anywhere, reporting as someone "on the spot" and thus presumably knowledgeable about what is going on. The recent wars provided ample opportunity. During the War in Afghanistan, Fox audiences were treated to a gun-toting Geraldo Rivera, reporting live from the battlefield claiming he'd kill Osama bin Laden if he had a chance. War wraps reporters in an aura of authority and makes them much more exciting than anchors who read the news.

found on all sides of virtually every issue that is even mildly controversial. Which experts they consult thus becomes crucially important, and usually is determined by just a very few factors.

Perhaps the most important consideration is whether an expert's opinions might be unpopular either with the intended audience or with advertisers or other power groups. Experts with views that might raise too many hackles tend to be overlooked (or, sometimes, used as foils). Mainstream experts dominate the field. These days, for example, positions on race, gender differences, pollution problems, and so on, generally have to stay within bounds set by PC. There is, of course, still a great deal of racism in America, as in most other countries, but there also is an "official line" on the matter. Racism is definitely not PC. An expert who holds a contrary view is not going to be heard, except on very rare occasions.

Anyway, books not in conformity to the PC line on race, as well as many other topics, tend either to get trashed or to be ignored. A case in point is the publisher's withdrawal of the book *The g Factor: General Intelligence and Its Implications,* by Chris Brand, a psychology lecturer at Edinburgh University. The publisher, John Wiley & Sons, said that Brand had made "repellent" assertions in his book—for example, that "It is a scientific fact that black Americans are less intelligent than white Americans and the IQ of Asians is higher than blacks." (Note that the publisher's reason for squelching the book was not a belief that its claims about race were false but rather that they were repellent. Do we need to be reminded of Voltaire's famous comment "I disapprove of what you say, but I will defend to the death your right to say it"?) This brings to mind, by the way, the many times in recent years that college audiences around the nation have hooted down scheduled speakers, denying them the right to have their say.

For the most part, the media rely on the same pool of punditry for expert advice, but occasionally an event that requires highly specialized experts to interpret makes such big news that journalists have to search for new faces. No one anticipated that the California recall election in 2003 would make headlines across the country, let alone the world, until Arnold Schwarzenegger entered the race. Suddenly the national media had to scour the state for experts in California state politics (aside from the usual political workhorses who were out in full force). They came up with a group of history and political science professors in state colleges and universities who managed to educate us about the state's political process as well as offer opinions.

In order to report the news accurately, journalists need to draw from a variety of reputable sources, particularly when covering controversial issues of national importance. Failure to do so can result in biased coverage that could have a significant impact on the country. A case in point is the *New York Times* coverage of Iraq's alleged weapons of mass destruction (WMD). Some reporters relied heavily on Ahmad Chalabi, then Iraq's opposition leader, as their principal source. Chalabi steered them to Iraqi defectors willing to talk about Hussein's government and the weapons program. Although the *Times* published some articles critical of Chalabi, he was the main source. The overall picture that emerged was an alarming image of the threat posed by Saddam Hussein, but it turned out that no one managed to unearth evidence of WMD and many of the defectors were later discredited as unreliable sources. (Chalabi disingenuously claimed that he just steered reporters to the defectors but never said they were credible.) The *Times* editors at least had the sense to apologize in a public letter indicating that their coverage wasn't as rigorous as it should have been. They weren't the only ones hyping the WMD story, though; the media as a whole were consumed by it. The end result was that the country bought into the notion that Iraq had WMD—our main reason for going to war. Had a wider range of reputable sources been used, we would have been much better informed about the real state of affairs.

Self-Censorship

The theory that news reporting should be objective does not require that all of the news, even all of the very important news, be reported. During wartime, for example, national security takes precedence. When United States troops were poised to invade Afghani-

One of the most prevalent sources of "experts" is the think tanks that the media have used increasingly in recent years. Here are the most widely quoted think tanks in the past few years (cited in *Extra!*, May/June 2004). Note the political orientation of each group and figure out the ideological shift in coverage over the years in study.

Citations of Think Tanks in Media

Think Tank	Political Orientation	2002	2003	% Change
1. Brookings Institution	centrist	4,323	4,784	11 %
2. Council on Foreign Relations	centrist	2,738	3,393	24
3. Heritage Foundation	conservative	2,356	3,141	33
4. American Enterprise Institute	conservative	1,859	2,645	42
5. Center for Strategic and International Studies	conservative	1,830	2,386	30
6. Cato Institute	cons/libertarian	1,836	1,873	2
7. Economic Policy Institute	progressive	850	1,091	28
8. RAND Corporation	center-right	1,413	1,066	−25
9. Carnegie Endowment	centrist	779	910	17
10. Urban Institute	center-left	658	892	36
11. Hoover Institution	conservative	520	756	45
12. Family Research Council	conservative	746	731	−2
13. Center on Budget and Policy Priorities	progressive	439	623	42
14. Public Policy Institute of California	centrist	440	565	28
15. National Bureau of Economic Research	centrist	624	531	−15
16. Washington Institute for Near East Policy	center-right	507	502	−1
17. Manhattan Institute	conservative	576	492	−15
18. Center for Defense Information	progressive	347	488	40
19. Carter Center	centrist	861	458	−47
20. Center for Public Integrity	progressive	593	444	−25
21. Institute for International Economics	centrist	390	433	11
22. Hudson Institute	conservative	606	397	−34
23. Institute for Policy Studies	progressive	330	358	8
24. Aspen Institute	centrist	161	301	87
25. Progressive Policy Institute	centrist	283	225	−20

Number of Media Citations by Ideology	2002	%	2003	%
Conservative or Center-Right	12,249	47	13,989	47
Centrist	10,599	41	11,605	39
Progressive or Center-Left	3,217	12	3,896	13
Total	26,055	100	29,490	100

Source: Nexis database on major newspaper and radio and TV transcripts
Note: Percentages may not add up to 100 percent due to rounding. The numbers for the Heritage Foundation were adjusted to correct for false positives. Approximately 15 percent of the time in 2003 and 20 percent of the time in 2002, the words "heritage foundation" appeared in Nexis without referring to the Washington-based think tank.

From *Extra!*, May/June 2004. Reprinted by permission of *Extra!*

stan in 2001, the media knew a full day in advance the exact time that the strikes would begin, but virtually no major media organization reported this information in the news. Even in peacetime, the media sometimes voluntarily suppress news out of a sense of duty. Perhaps the most famous instance of this kind occurred during John Kennedy's time as president, when the *New York Times* decided not to print reliable information about the impending attack on Cuba by U.S.-trained forces intent on overthrowing Fidel Castro.[13]

But not all self-censorship has to do with national defense. A more common reason, mentioned before, is to placate advertisers. Here is a little item from *The Nation* (December 16, 1996) illustrating this point:

> As a protest against consumerism, the Media Foundation has for the past four years sponsored Buy Nothing Day on the day after Thanksgiving. This year the group wanted to run a thirty-second spot promoting its buy-out but was turned down by all three major networks. ABC said the ad violated its policy on "advertising of controversial issues"; CBS said it was an "advocacy ad"; NBC was more honest, saying that the ad was "inimical to our legitimate business interests."

The other important reason for media censorship has to do with the power of media audiences to switch channels or to not buy a newspaper. Television, in particular, has to be sensitive to its audience, because its product comes into living rooms with such immediacy (and children may be watching). The way in which Elvis Presley was allowed to appear on an Ed Sullivan TV show in 1956 constitutes a classic example; Elvis was shown only from the waist up so that TV audiences wouldn't be exposed to his pelvic gyrations. (That sounds silly today, but what may or may not be objectionable differs considerably from one time to another.) Another famous case occurred in 1952 when Lucille Ball became pregnant and the story line of the *I Love Lucy* show was adjusted

---

[13] The invasion turned into a fiasco that was terribly embarrassing to the Kennedy administration. Kennedy himself is alleged later to have had the chutzpah to take the *Times* to task for this self-censorship on grounds that publication of the story by the *Times* might have resulted in the aborting of that ill-fated venture!

accordingly: the TV Lucy could be said on camera to be "expecting" and *enceinte* (French for "pregnant"), but the word *pregnant* could not be used. Even in the 1950s, this sort of censorship seemed ridiculous to lots of people, but media moguls considered it to be a very serious matter; too many viewers were likely to be offended by use of the term *pregnant.*

Times change, of course, so that in the 1990s, when TV's Murphy Brown was allowed to be an unwed mother, only a slight fuss was made about referring to her as pregnant. But media self-censorship still is with us, as it always will be. It's just that standards and the topics subject to censorship change. Back in the 1950s a program about homosexuals would have been unthinkable—absolutely out of the question—so much so that the lack of such programs hardly could be considered to constitute self-censorship. Gays simply did not exist as far as television was concerned. But today they do, yet programs featuring gays sometimes are censored by one segment of the media or other. When Ellen deGeneris's character "came out" on the sitcom *Ellen,* several stations refused to carry the episode.

But those who see self-censorhip as automatically evil might consider the right of individuals to privacy in their nonpublic life. Should detailed accounts of Clinton's sex life—even down to his "distinguishing mark"—have been broadcast in the media? At what point does one draw the line? A person in the public eye is still, after all, entitled to a private life. Anyway, things are not as bad here as in, say, England, where the press hounded Princess Diana up to her death and continues to cover every move of Prince Charles and Camilla Parker-Bowles.

In days long gone, the media felt more constrained in its reporting of the private lives of important public figures. It was well known to some in the press, for example, that both before and after his marriage—as a congressman, senator, and president—John Kennedy was quite a lady's man. But the media, on the whole, chose not to divulge this feature of his private life. In those days, matters of this kind were usually passed over, even though they would have found an eager audience. And yet, self-censorship of similar stories concerning Kennedy's brother, Ted, may well have been a mistake, given what happened at Chappaquiddick. Knowledge of a person's sex life may, in some cases, be relevant to character and thus to potential performance as a public figure.

5. DEVICES USED TO SLANT THE NEWS

So far, we have been considering why the media slant the news and how that affects story selection. Now let's take a brief look at a few of the many devices used to accomplish this task. (The examples are taken primarily from newspapers and magazines, but television and radio have their analogs.)

Stories Can Be Played Up or Down

Breaking news of immense interest, like the capture of Saddam Hussein, for instance, is always played up in the news. Photos of the haggard Hussein and his squalid hideout flashed across television screens and newspapers around the world within hours of his captivity. But not all news is that compelling. Often stories are played up because of audience interest or media bias. If the interest isn't there, the story may be buried by placing it on page 59 or by packing the undesirable material toward the end of an otherwise

Last year, 300,000 Americans were arrested for smoking an herb that Queen Victoria used regularly for menstrual cramps.

It's a fact

The herb. of course. is *cannabis sativa*. Otherwise known as marijuana. pot. grass. hemp. boo. mary-jane. ganja—the nicknames are legion.

So are the people who smoke it.

By all reckoning. it's fast becoming the new national pastime. Twenty-six million smokers. by some accounts—lots more by others. Whatever the estimate. a staggeringly high percentage of the population become potential criminals simply by being in possession of it. And the numbers are increasing.

For years. we've been told that marijuana leads to madness. sex-crimes. hard-drug usage and even occasional warts.

Pure Victorian poppycock.

In 1894. The Indian Hemp Commission reported marijuana to be relatively harmless. A fact that has been substantiated time and again in study after study.

Including. most recently. by the President's own Commission. This report stands as an indictment of the pot laws themselves.

And that's why more and more legislators are turning on to the fact that the present marijuana laws are as archaic as dear old Victoria's code of morality. And that they must be changed. Recently. the state of Oregon did. in fact. de-criminalize marijuana. Successfully.

Other states are beginning to move in that direction. They must be encouraged.

NORML. has been and is educating the legislators. working in the courts and with the lawmakers to change the laws. We're doing our best but still. we need help. Yours.

Used with permission of NORML.

Ad censorship. NORML marijuana ad rejected by Time *and* Newsweek, *accepted by* Playboy.

acceptable story. For example, hundreds of thousands of people sought refuge from the violence in the Darfur region of Sudan in 2003, yet few Americans knew about it. The Sudanese who fled into Chad when their villages were bombed and crops were burned to the ground got little international assistance and not much press coverage. The refugee crisis was voted one of the most underreported humanitarian stories in 2003 by Doctors Without Borders (Médecins Sans Frontières, winners of the 1999 Nobel Peace Prize). American audiences tend to be relatively uninterested in much of Africa and most Far Eastern countries. Back pages are relatively unread, and readers tend not to get past the first few paragraphs of anything (including, alas, material in school textbooks, but that is another matter; if you've read this far, place an *X* at the end of this sentence). On TV, stories get buried by being run toward the end of a news program when attention may be wandering (although, interestingly, not usually at the very end) and by being cut to run for less than 10 or 15 seconds.

The way in which the 1993 and 1994 debates concerning health care reform were covered in newspapers provides an interesting example. Opinion polls at the time showed that a small majority of Americans favored a "single-pay" plan much like the Canadian system, but this happened to be the plan that powerful factions in the United States (in particular, the health insurance industry) most strongly opposed. For whatever reasons (readers are invited to draw their own tentative conclusions), newspapers typically ran stories whose headlines and first few paragraphs were hostile to Canadian-style systems, although buried further down they often provided a great deal of favorable information, including the fact that a majority of Canadians like their system. This last fact still is not often reported on American television.

Of course, the chief way in which TV buries a story is simply to pass it over. TV news programs, by their very nature, are able to deal with many fewer items than daily newspapers, so that it is easier to get away with failure to report a news event. But even newspapers omit items for one reason or another. For instance, they often inform readers about which movies are drawing the largest audiences, which records are selling best, and so on. But the *New York Times,* for obscure reasons of its own, routinely excludes religious books (Bibles and so forth) and "romance" (Harlequin) paperbacks from its lists of best-selling books, even though together these two kinds of publications account for a very large slice of the book market.

Misleading, Sensational, or Opinionated Headlines Can Be Used

Many more people read the headlines on stories than read the accounts that follow. So even if an account itself is accurate, a misleading or sensational headline (generally not written by whoever wrote the news report itself) distorts the news for many readers. For example, on June 12, 2003, the *Philadelphia Inquirer* understated a Hamas terrorist bombing in Jerusalem with the headline[14]

Violence Tests Road Map

The *New York Daily News* sensationalized it in this headline with religious implications:

Hell on Earth in Holy Land Bus Blast Kills 16 in Jerusalem

But other major dailies announced the event in a matter-of-fact, informative way. Here, for example, is the *Boston Globe* headline—a little long, but accurate:

16 Killed as Palestinian Blows Up Jerusalem Bus. Israeli Raids Follow in Gaza, Nine Die

Some headlines are misleading because inaccurate, as in this *New York Times* error (August 17, 2003).

British Cameraman Shot Dead Near Baghdad

Actually the victim was a Palestinian, Mazan Dana, a well-known, award winning Reuters cameraman who deserved headline recognition, but apparently the headline writers didn't read the accompanying story.

Other headlines mislead through ambiguity in an attempt to dramatize the news. Here is a CNN.com attention grabber (October 28, 2003).

Pet Alligator Gets Loose Aboard Airliner

It turns out that an alligator in the cargo hold was discovered out of its crate after the plane had landed, but it was still in a burlap sack with its snout bound up—hardly the threat to passengers that the headline implied.

Images Can Slant the News

Image has been important in American politics ever since George Washington refused the crown and declined a third term in office because he didn't want to create the wrong image. Abraham Lincoln played up his image as a rail-splitting back woodsman reared in a log cabin in the Illinois wilderness. But in those days news traveled slowly and photography was either nonexistent (in Washington's time) or in its infant stages (in Lincoln's). With the advent of television, visual images began to dominate the scene. Starting with John F. Kennedy and his photogenic family, the emphasis on visual imagery

---

[14]www.camera.org., the Web site for the Committee for Accuracy in Middle East Reporting in America lists a couple dozen headlines for this tragedy.

began to increase. Kennedy's impressive showing against Nixon in the presidential debates was due more to his handsome, debonair image than to the content of the debates. (People who listened to the debates rather than watched them on TV considered two out of three a draw.) Today image triumphs over content for most people.[15]

Think of the images that have flashed on the screen in recent years. President Bush, as victorious commander-in-chief, posed triumphantly on an aircraft carrier in front of a banner proclaiming "Mission Accomplished." Saddam Hussein, as defeated tyrant, was humiliated in footage of military personnel examining his hair for lice. John Kerry, as war hero and presidential candidate, was photographed with his Vietnam swiftboat crewmates gliding into Boston Harbor in a water taxi, headed for the Democratic Convention. Today candidates have to look presidential to succeed. Even the great George Washington, with his pockmarked face, decaying teeth and big nose might have trouble getting elected without a skin abrasion, capped teeth, and a nose job.

Now that photos can be transmitted instantaneously around the world, the power of imagery has enormous impact internationally as well as nationally. Knowing full well the effect of disturbing pictures on the public, the second Bush administration refused to allow coverage of the flag-draped coffins that were returned from Iraq to Powers Air Force Base. But provocative photos tend to slip through the cracks no matter how carefully they are guarded. (The coffin footage eventually surfaced.) The most notorious example was the graphic photos of U.S. soldiers abusing and humiliating Iraqi prisoners at Abu Ghraib. The *60 Minutes II* airing of this footage sent shock waves around the world. Americans were horrified, Iraqis were alienated, and the popularity of the Bush administration plummeted in the polls. The Arab media were quick to respond. Although some of the coverage was even-handed, media outlets opposed to U.S. intervention used the photos to inflame anti-American feelings. In the case of Abu Ghraib, the image was the story.

Follow-Up Stories Can Be Omitted or Played Down

Follow-up stories rarely make headlines, primarily for three reasons. The first is that they are more difficult to obtain than breaking news stories. It takes much less time and effort to record the fact that a bank has failed than to follow up details of an ensuing court case against its directors. The second is that the public (and media) conception of "news" is what is new, and follow-up stories are just more of the same, or just plain humdrum.

Breaking news is often sensationalized, but follow-up stories usually aren't sexy enough to grab the audience's interest, so the media ignore them. For example, the media tend to play up outrageous verdicts against big corporations like Philip Morris, McDonald's, and Firestone, but when these verdicts are overturned on appeal, they go unreported or are buried in the back pages. Molly Ivins in her syndicated column (August 27, 2001) cited a famous case in point, of an 81-year old woman who sued McDonald's after she spilled a cup of its coffee on herself and suffered third-degree burns. The big news was that the jury awarded her $2.9 million after learning that McDonald's ignored

---

[15] For more on this see "The Triumph of the Image," by Richard C. Wahl, in the *Columbia Review of Journalism,* November/December 2003.

700 similar cases over time. The underreported news was that the verdict was reduced to $480,000 on appeal, was later settled out of court for an undisclosed amount, and McDonald's no longer serves scalding hot coffee. The point here is not so much that juries make idiotic awards for frivolous lawsuits as was implied in the original story (after all, hundreds of people had been burned in the past by McDonald's coffee), but that civil litigation often works well in correcting wrongs—a lesson that didn't make the news.

Another reason for the paucity of follow-up stories is that most of us have short attention spans. Except for "ongoing" stories—wars providing the best examples—people tend to tire of any topic quickly (the truth behind Andy Warhol's remark "In the future, everyone will be famous for 15 minutes"). When bored, it's all too easy to flip the switch to another channel or to put down the newspaper and instead watch Oprah do her thing on the tube.

Well, no one can be in favor of boredom. The problem is that in the vast majority of cases it is the time-consuming details that make all the difference. Ten-second news sound bites aren't all that different from "Chevrolet—the heartbeat of America" or "Magnavox—smart, very smart." Short and easily remembered usually drives out long and complicated. That may well be the chief reason relevant background information and follow-up tend to be in short supply on TV news programs.

The public's lack of interest in or general weariness with the Iraq War may account for the scant attention the news paid to the second President Bush's announcement—six months after the war—that there was no evidence linking Saddam Hussein to the September 11th attack on the World Trade Center. Buried in the back pages of most newspapers, this was a belated follow-up story to the headline news months earlier that the administration wanted to wage war partly because it believed Hussein's government had links to Al Qaeda and the terrorist network led by Osama bin Laden. Although Bush never claimed that Hussein was responsible for the attack, 70 percent of Americans inferred he probably was involved, based on their assumption that the administration was right about his links to Al Qaeda. (As it turned out, the 9-11 Commission found no evidence of this connection either.) Unless they read deep in the paper or paid attention to ten-second sound bites, they may still be unaware of this important clarification.

Points of View Can Be Conveyed via Cartoons and Comic Strips

According to the old saying, a picture is worth a thousand words, which may account for the ability of cartoons and comic strips to effectively—graphically—make a point. In any case, it most certainly accounts for the large number of these handy little devices that have been reprinted in this particular textbook. A clever practitioner of the cartoonist's art can puncture prejudices and force us to open our eyes to unpleasant truths in a way that few others can match. The Tom Meyer cartoon on the next page, for example, forcefully brings home the point that the so-called "three strikes and you're out" laws—mandatory life sentences for those convicted of a third felony—don't really get at the nub of the crime problem, and it ironically suggests what needs to be done if we are to make a serious dent in that problem.

The *Doonesbury* strip, crafted by Garry Trudeau, deserves special mention here because it has been in the forefront of a minor trend on newspaper comic pages to feature strips that at least occasionally touch on social or political issues rather than just

Cartoon by Tom Meyer. © *San Francisco Chronicle*. Reprinted by permission

tickling the funny bone. A particular favorite of the authors of this text (one of whom is a UCLA alum) is the 1994 *Doonesbury* series that poked fun at the hiring of junk bond ex-con Michael Milken to teach a business course at UCLA. In one panel, Milken is pictured saying, "Who is Professor Milken, the genius who created a new world of financial instruments? Well, I'm many things, of course. But most of all, I'm a survivor. After a 98-count indictment and a 6-count plea bargain, I'm still here—and with $1 billion to show for it!" after which students repeat his code: "Greed works! Crime pays! Everybody does it!" In another strip, Milken states what must certainly be his actual opinion on the matter: that government attempts at regulation are a joke and government employees no match for "a true visionary and his defense team." Students are shown booing the student who has the temerity to ask a pertinent question: "As the key player of the greatest criminal conspiracy in the history of finance, do you think justice was served by your brief stay in a country club prison?"

Unfortunately, this ability of comic strips to graphically make a point sometimes results in their being censored. *Doonesbury,* of course, bites the dust now and then. But even normally nonpolitical strips occasionally get the axe. For example, when a young boy in the *For Better or for Worse* comic strip summoned the courage to tell his parents that he was gay, the resulting furor came as a shock to the strip's creator, Lynn Johnston. The series of strips on this theme ran for just 10 days but was censored during that time in 40 papers, with 20 more canceling the strip outright. In Memphis, Tennessee, to cite just one city, about 2,000 readers canceled their subscriptions to the *Commercial Appeal*

Aaron McGruder's Boondocks *sometimes gets in trouble for its political satire.* Extra!
*(December 2001) noted that this strip along with several others were pulled from
some newspapers after September 11 because it was critical of U.S. foreign policy.*

because that paper ran the strips they objected to. Johnston was flooded with mail, both
pro and con, and stung by the anger and hate some letters exhibited. She wrote the series, she said, because several friends had died from AIDS, and one of her closest gay
friends recently had been robbed and killed. "He was nothing more than a wonderful
person and a good friend to me," she said. "My intent was to show that Lawrence [the
gay boy in the strip] was different but that he's still the kid next door, still a member
of the community, someone who should be judged on his moral character, not his genetic code." [16] (Interesting, by the way, was the failure of protests by gays across the
country against an impending [September 2000] television talk-show featuring Dr.
Laura Schlessinger, well known for her stand against homosexual sex. ABC, sponsors,
and producers did not knuckle under to this threat to free speech. But Dr. Laura didn't
do as well on TV as on radio.)

6. TELEVISION, FILM, AND ELECTRONIC INFORMATION SOURCES

Although still a relative baby, television is by far the most important of the mass media.
More households own television sets than bathtubs or showers. (Interesting fact: One
family in four in the United States has three or more television sets.) TV gives us the
closest thing we have to a way of bringing a whole diverse nation together. It is the town
crier, certifier, authenticator, and grapevine of modern life. That's why political campaigns are fought, and won or lost, on it; the news is broadcast on it; and a nation's mood
and tone are set by it.

It would be hard to overestimate the effects of television on everyday life. (One
thinks, for a parallel, of the ways in which the automobile has transformed the world.)
When film shot from a privately owned camcorder caught police in the act of beating up

---

[16] See, for instance, the *San Francisco Examiner,* April 25, 1993.

Rodney King, pictures of their brutality on TV news programs had a profound effect on the way in which police everywhere thenceforth carried out their duties. (Fear of being filmed in the act constitutes a powerful deterrent.) Similarly, the way in which the Los Angeles police department took it on the chin during the O. J. Simpson murder trial undoubtedly did much to improve police crime procedures everywhere. And more recently, footage of prisoner abuse at Abu Ghraib spiked an internal investigation that raised questions about the military flouting the Geneva Conventions.

All of the media, of course, have the power to force dramatic changes—to expose the bad and publicize the good. But television's power to expose and publicize is vastly greater and more immediate than all of the other mass media combined. Its power, therefore, is awesomely—indeed, frighteningly—greater. Consider, for example, what Americans know about Nazi Germany's extermination camps compared to what they know about Soviet labor camps. Only a few Americans know that many more civilians died in Soviet labor camps than were murdered in Nazi extermination camps. The names Auschwitz, Buchenwald, and Treblinka are familiar to us—well, to some of us—while extremely few Americans have heard, say, of Kolyma.

We also shouldn't forget the way in which news reporting has helped break down prejudices. It was a very important event indeed when the first woman, Barbara Walters, read the evening news to us on national TV and an equally important event when the first African American, Max Robinson, did so.

But perhaps the most graphic illustration of television's power to change the world is in its effect on the nature of war and associated diplomacy. It is a commonplace today that television shortened American involvement in the war in Vietnam through its living-room coverage, but insufficient notice has yet been taken of the way in which TV influenced the conduct of the Gulf War, the NATO bombing in Kosovo, and the Iraq War. The American government and its coalition allies were exceedingly careful to reduce the number of casualties, not just of their own forces but also of enemy civilians, in a way that (in the long history of warfare) has rarely, if ever before, been true. Compare that, for instance, with the American and British record of mass bombings of civilians in World War II, when television was not peeking over every general's shoulder.

Even sitcoms and the other prime-time entertainment programs sometimes have positive effects—in addition to providing entertainment—a case in point being their role in reducing ethnic and gender prejudice, one of the great improvements that has taken place in the United States (and most other democratic nations) since World War II. African Americans are portrayed as middle-class workers, not just as janitors or (the very expression is odious) cotton pickers, and women as business executives, not just housewives.

But we don't want to go overboard here. Television generally caters to the tastes of mass audiences in ways that have nothing to do with breaking down audience prejudices.

Television is the first truly democratic culture—the first culture available to everybody and entirely governed by what people want. The most terrifying thing is what people do want.

—Clive Barker

Think only of the titillating program *Who Wants to Be a Millionaire?* or the fabulously successful *Survivor* dramas, or the courtroom programs on which real people make fools of themselves in front of Judge Judy or on *People's Court.*

Television Is the Best News Source for Many People

When we think of the mass media, it's important to remember that at least one-third of American adults are or come close to being functionally illiterate. For them, and for many others, a picture is worth more than a thousand words. So for the mass of people, by default, television is the best news source. (Note, by the way, that it's much easier to become a couch potato and endlessly watch the tube than it is, say, to search the Internet for interesting material.)

But capturing and informing this kind of mass audience requires extremely tight editing (matched in print only by advertisements). The average attention span is short and comprehension, limited. TV does a better job than the other media in editing the news so that it can be understood, somewhat, by most Americans. However, a recent trend in cluttering the screen with multiple images tends to undermine otherwise concise editing. Even the most focused viewer gets distracted by split-screen pictures with headlines underneath and crawling commentary at the bottom.

Television and Videos

One effect of the recent computer revolution is that the various mass media have begun to meld together. Many people now view television programs on their PCs, and more and more have access to the Internet via their television screens. In addition, while going to the movies is still popular, especially among the young, millions watch films at home via their VCRs and TV sets. One screen now serves many purposes.

The trouble is that so much of what is watched on that screen which might inform people about the world is not accurate, to say the least. Blockbuster movies, for instance, generally distort reality or history in one way or another to increase dramatic impact or excitement.

The year 2000 hit *The Patriot* is a good example. The hero, played by Mel Gibson, pretty much wins the Revolutionary War single-handedly, with a little assist from

George Washington and a few others, by reforming military tactics and then defeating British General Cornwallis at Yorktown, while along the way audiences are treated to a completely fictional and absolutely horrible massacre by loyalists and the British in which a town's inhabitants are burned alive. (The film's director defended his historical bloopers by saying that "On certain kinds of points, we had to decide what is most important, historical accuracy or the dramatic impact." Exactly.)

There is nothing new in this, of course. Typical Western "shoot-'em-ups" have always presented a more or less fictional account of what the frontier West was like. No John Wayne westerns ever had much to do with the reality of life in the old West, nor do the several movies about Wyatt Earp and the "gunfight" at the O.K. Corral conform to historical fact. The damage done by movies of this kind is much worse nowadays than it used to be because their influence goes on for years via video rentals, cassette copies, and endless replays on television.

The Internet

The good news, of course, is that the Internet provides another way to obtain useful information and opinion. It can be, and often is, more up-to-date than the best reference books; it allows people everywhere to read some of the best newspapers and magazines in the land; and it often is more readily available than books or other print media. The world of online journalism continues to expand. Just about all of the major media outlets have Internet access, including broadcast networks, cable networks, newspapers, and news magazines. In addition, Google News, a new player in the field, provides unparalleled access to English-language news sites around the world. An outgrowth of the Google search engine, Google News draws on stories from 4,000 news sites, updating items on a second-by-second basis.

As the 2004 presidential campaign heated up, the Internet became an important source for campaign news. Although television was still the main source, the Pew Research Center noted that the number of people who got news of the campaign from the Internet had nearly doubled (13 percent up from 7 percent) since the last election. Young people in particular turned increasingly to the Internet for political news. (But, alas, about the same number, 21 percent, got their news from comedy shows like *Saturday Night Live* and *The Daily Show*.) Another interesting finding was that people who followed the campaign on the Internet were more knowledgeable about it than the average American, who knew little about the candidates and events. It comes as no surprise that those who got their information from comedy shows were least likely to know what was going on.[17]

The downside to the Internet is that so much more schlock is on the Web than even the TV networks provide. It takes a rather sophisticated Web browser to separate wheat from chaff. Of course, this is always a problem; the point is that it becomes more urgent to be able to do this well when surfing the Net. (Instructors regularly tear their hair out when students turn in papers based on second-rate Internet material.) Other problems

---

[17] For more information about the Pew survey on campaign news and political communication see http//people-pres.org/reports/display.

are looming on the Internet horizon. Project Censored has listed the reduction of access to information technology as one of the most significant underreported news stories in 2002–2003. So far we have had open access to 7,000 Internet Service Providers (ISPs), but our options are dwindling as the large cable and phone monopolies are buying them out. Up to now, telecom regulations prevented the big ISPs from blocking out other companies, but these rules no longer apply now that the FCC has relabeled high-speed cable Internet connections as "information services" rather than "telecommunication services." In doing so, the FCC has freed cable broadband from telecom regulations. The upshot is that cable and phone companies can refuse to give other ISPs access to their cable lines. Since more and more people are switching from dial-up to broadband Internet, they may well have their options limited to the cable company's own ISP, which would have the option to filter information as it saw fit. These are early days, though. We'll have to see what develops down the line.[18]

7. THE NON–MASS MEDIA TO THE RESCUE

The mass media are a reasonably good source of information about breaking stories — speeches made by important officials, fluctuations in the Dow, bills passed by Congress (but not about a bill's value or who benefits and who is harmed!), and so on. Television does these stories rather well, at least when it can get good visuals. But for detailed, sophisticated, in-depth accounts, and for analysis that doesn't just parrot what powerful people are saying, the non–mass media are indispensable.

The commercial networks do feature several rather good investigative, in-depth programs—namely, *60 Minutes, Nightline, 20/20, 48 Hours,* and *60 Minutes II.* But PBS, the Public Broadcasting Service, is the best everyday television news source—best, without doubt, for in-depth reporting and analysis. Indeed, in most ways, PBS is perhaps the brightest spot on the television spectrum. But those viewers who are on the cable, which means an ever-increasing majority, also can click to the Discovery channel, the Arts and Entertainment channel, C-Span, and, of course, CNN, which still gives its viewers a good deal more news and analysis than the major networks. Those people on cable can now choose among two NBC news channels and a Fox news channel, in addition to others just mentioned, and for coverage in the sciences, *Nova* (PBS) does an excellent job of reporting interesting developments. (Lots of young people prefer instead to watch channels like MTV, alas.)

Nevertheless, TV still easily is eclipsed by the few good daily newspapers and especially by small-circulation magazines and journals. The mass media, even the big-city newspapers, generally focus on what is current, in the air, neglecting the underlying forces that ultimately determine what will be big news at a later date. For example, in January 1999, the mass media finally got onto the story of corruption in the International Olympic Committee (they shake down cities competing for the games) and even occasionally got into the shady pasts of the IOC heads and how they may be on the take. But

---

[18]For more on this story see projectcensored.org/publications/2004, item #6, Closing Access to Information Technology.

readers of several non–mass media publications (e.g., *The Nation*) read about this long before it appeared in the mass media. Moral: If you really care what's going on in the world, you either won't find out from the mass media, or if you do, you'll get late and incomplete news. *Time, Newsweek,* and *U.S. News & World Report* do do a bit of digging under the surface, but they tend to sensationalize what is going on and to be flighty, blowing with the winds of public opinion. Yet it is precisely the underlying forces that are the bread and butter of small-circulation periodicals, some of which deal with these matters very well indeed. (See the annotated list of publications at the end of the book for examples and for some thoughts by the authors of this text concerning some of these important information sources.)

Finding out what is really going on, however, isn't so much a matter of mass versus non–mass media as it is of learning how to be selective—learning how to separate pearls from schlock. Those interested in science, for example, would do well to avoid newsstand magazines that pander to the appetite so many people have for stories about ESP and other matters on the edge of legitimate science and that try to sensationalize science to increase sales. (Will stories about "close encounters of the third kind" ever go away?)

The point is that the non–mass media contain lots more pearls per square inch and are, on the whole, a good deal more sophisticated in their discussions of what is going on in the world than are newspapers, TV, and even mass-sales books. Best-selling books—for instance those concerning politics, economics, and the like—often are shallow or sensationalist.

Of particular note are the self-serving memoirs of "distinguished statesmen," such as Henry Kissinger, that are often little more than bald-faced attempts to rewrite history in their favor. Presidential memoirs, supposedly written by former presidents, are perhaps the most self-serving of these tomes. Example: Ronald Reagan's *An American Life* (Simon & Schuster, 1990), apparently written by Robert Lindsey (whom Reagan credits by saying "Robert Lindsey, a talented writer, was with me every step of the way"). Also, Bill Clinton's, *My Life* (Knopf, 2004), written in longhand by Clinton himself, he claimed, played up his triumphs and played down his failures (as do most presidential memoirs), though he did take full blame for the Monica Lewinsky affair.

We should note, by the way, that National Public Radio (NPR) does a better job of presenting the news and analysis than does any television channel or most other radio outlets. Some examples of their regular programs are *All Things Considered, Talk of the Nation, BBC World News, Fresh Air, Science Friday,* and *As It Happens,* an excellent Canadian news program broadcast widely in the United States. There is even at least one major network entertainment program, *Law and Order,* that provides a good deal of information about how the legal system really works, as opposed to how it is supposed to work (more will be said in the next chapter about the great gulf between theory and practice) in addition to straight entertainment.

Finally, a word or two more about newspapers and magazines. The best newspapers in the United States, overall, probably are the *New York Times* (unfortunately sans comic strips, which means no *Doonesbury*), the *Los Angeles Times,* and the *Washington Post.* Even so, most large metropolitan areas have at least one reasonably good newspaper that is a better source of information than any of the major networks or cable news channels, for that matter.

8. RECENT DEVELOPMENTS

During the past 20 years or so, dramatic changes have been taking place in the news business. Perhaps the most important of these is the ever-increasing concentration of media ownership, and thus power, in fewer and fewer hands.

The first and much smaller concentration of media power occurred way back in the late nineteenth century with the development of newspaper chains—the most important, perhaps, being the one put together by William Randolph Hearst and fictionalized in the movie classic *Citizen Kane.* The power of these early media magnates is illustrated in that film by a scene in which a journalist sent to Cuba in 1898 reports back that there is no sign of war in Cuba, only to be told that Kane (Hearst) would supply the war. (The scene is a takeoff on what is held by some to be true: that the United States' involvement in the Spanish-American War was in large part due to the Hearst publications' sensationalistic journalism. More likely, though, it was just one of many factors leading to that one-sided, unprovoked, war.)

The power of the Hearst media empire was illustrated again in 1941 when Hearst forced RKO, the producer of *Citizen Kane,* not to show that film in its theaters nationwide. The threat was to refuse ads listing any RKO theater offerings in Hearst's many newspapers around the country, which would have caused RKO a tremendous financial loss.

This blacklisting of *Citizen Kane* nicely illustrates the great censorship potential of concentrated media power. But back in those days, all big cities had more than one newspaper so that no small group or individuals could effectively control the newspaper business. (It was not until the 1950s that television usurped the role of newspapers as the principal news source for a growing majority of people in the United States and Canada.)

Today's media conglomerates are a good deal more worrisome than were the newspaper chains of old, because they concentrate power into an extremely few hands in all of the major news media—television, radio, mass-circulation magazines and newspapers. Independent newspapers still exist in some cities and towns, but their number shrinks every year, and most big cities now are down to just one daily paper, usually owned by a large and powerful chain. So today, a single individual may control quite a few TV outlets as well as newspapers and magazines, as does, for example, Rupert Murdoch (the Fox TV network, the New York *Post,* and many other newspapers, including the prestigious *London Times,* and magazines worldwide).

The founders of this country believed a free and rambunctious press was essential to the protection of our freedoms. They couldn't envision the rise of giant megamedia conglomerates whose interests converge with state power to produce a conspiracy against the people. I think they would be aghast at how this union of media and government has produced the very kind of Imperial power against which they rebelled.

—Bill Moyers, on media and democracy,
www.media.reform.net, November 25, 2003

This problem was compounded when the FCC voted to ease restrictions on media ownership in June 2003. This decision allows companies to own even more TV and radio stations, as well as cross-own newspapers and radio and TV stations in the same market (previously banned by the FCC). The measure has prompted widespread opposition from groups as diverse as the Christian Coalition, the National Rifle Association, and the National Organization of Women. In response to these massive protests, the Senate voted to overturn the FCC's new rules allowing TV networks to own stations that reach as much as 45 percent of the country's market. It reduced the percentage to the previous cap of 35, but the cap was later revised upward to 39 percent under pressure from the White House.

Equally frightening is the fact that the giant media empires have multiple business interests outside the news media world that provide enormous opportunity for product sales and promotion. The ruling principle of these megacorporations is the bottom line, not the best possible dissemination of news. Here is a list of some of the holdings of four of these huge media giants:

Time Warner owns or controls the Turner Broadcasting System (CNN, TNT, TBS, and other networks), HBO, Warner Brothers Studios and Television, Warner Books, Little Brown and Company, and dozens of music groups and recording labels. It has over 50 magazines, including *Time, Fortune, Sports Illustrated, Money,* and *People,* and though it dropped AOL from its corporate name, it still has holdings like AOL Instant Messenger and AOL Movie Fone. If that isn't enough, add to the list Netscape Communications, the Atlanta Braves, and a bunch of theme parks.

Viacom merged with CBS in 2000 to become one of the largest media conglomerates in the world. It owns CBS, UPN, Infinity Broadcasting (with 185 radio stations, second only to Clear Channel), over a dozen cable networks (including MTV and Comedy Central), Paramount Pictures, Blockbuster Video, and CBS Internet Group. Other holdings include Simon and Schuster, Scribner, Pocket Books, and MTV Books, not to mention various theme parks, the Star Trek Franchise, and Viacom Outdoor, the largest outdoor advertising group in North America.

Walt Disney owns ABC (*ABC Network News, Prime Time Live, 20/20,* TV stations serving a quarter of U.S. households, and over 65 radio stations), Fox Family Worldwide, Walt Disney Pictures, Miramax Films, Hyperion Books, Disney Publishing Worldwide, and the Walt Disney Internet Group. Then, of course, there are Disneyland, Disneyworld, and a host of other theme parks, plus more than 400 Disney stores selling Disney products. It owns a nice slice of ESPN, A&E, and the History Channel, and a chunk of Sid R. Bass (crude petroleum and natural gas, ranked high on the Forbes 500 list).

General Electric has primary interests elsewhere but is heavily invested in the media. It owns 80 percent of NBC (Vivendi controls 20 percent), including *NBC Network News, Dateline NBC,* the *Today* show, and cable networks (CNBC, MSNBC, Bravo, and USA). It owns Universal Studios and the Telemundo Communications Group, an investment group that includes Sony and Liberty Media. Big as they are, the media investments are just part of GE's vast empire. GE manufactures aircraft engines, power generators, and a wide array of consumer products. It owns an important insurance division and is involved in industrial, transportation, and power systems.

If all this is not frightening enough, consider that most of the media conglomerates are furiously moving into the new electronic arenas, in particular into the Internet. Oh, yes, we've forgotten to mention the international conglomerates, like the German-owned Bertelsmann AG or Rupert Murdoch's News Corp (Fox) that spread their tentacles worldwide. Then there are the gigantic newspaper and media service corporations such as The New York Times Co., The Washington Post Co., The Dow/Jones Wall Street Journal, The Tribune Co., Knight Ridder, and Gannett—groups that control an ever-larger portion of the newspaper business in America.

Well, then, why should the rest of us care about this concentration of media power into fewer and fewer hands? Doesn't size, after all, yield efficiency? Aren't large news companies better able to afford large staffs of reporters gathering news items around the world? The answer to both of these questions may well be yes. But three other nagging questions immediately arise. Will being *able to afford* larger staffs automatically translate in practice into larger staffs? Will greater efficiency generally translate into better news reporting or simply into greater profits? Will media moguls resist the temptation to further their own interests, including the interests of their own nonnews subsidiaries, at the expense of news quality and fair evaluation? The answer to all of these questions, unfortunately, seems to be *no.*

Item: Serious radio news reporting is rapidly being reduced as local stations increasingly come under the control of media giants. Here is an excerpt from an excellent article in the *Columbia Journalism Review*[19] describing what is happening:

> The new radio entrepreneurs have slashed station budgets and eliminated what they view as costly nonessential operating expenses such as news staffs and even wire services. The current trend is to "outsource" radio headline news without letting the audience know—not just cutting back on station news coverage but eliminating all reporters. . . . Out of approximately 10,000 commercial radio stations throughout the nation, only about fifteen are all-news outlets that employ substantial news staffs to report on what is going on in their communities.

The result is that almost all radio stations that bother with the news (music now is their principal focus) primarily broadcast canned news reports composed of "sound bites"— tiny snippets lacking sufficient content to enable listeners to adequately evaluate what they hear.

Item: Since media consolidation leads to news staff reductions, local news, including emergencies, may well go unreported. A notorious example (cited in *The Public I,* November 2003) occurred in Minot, North Dakota, where Clear Channel, by far the biggest player in the midwest radio industry, owned six of the eight commercial stations in the area. The public was never warned of a chemical spill in January 2002 because emergency workers were unable to find a living person at any station to broadcast the news.

Since mega corporations are profit driven and risk averse, one consequence of their dominating the industry is that the quality of programming has gone down in recent years, so instead of getting high-caliber, innovative sitcoms like the Mary Tyler Moore productions in the 1970s, for example, we get reality TV—cheap thrills that cost a fraction of a good sitcom to produce. Even more important, though, is that big media have the ability to limit the free exchange of ideas and thus undermine democracy. Because they are able to control the news, they can (and do) limit the range of information and debate from diverse sources, slant the news to their advantage, and kill stories that threaten their own interests.[20]

Item: When the lead singer of the Dixie Chicks, Natalee Maines, criticized President Bush during a London concert, Cumulus Media ordered its 50 country music stations not to play the group's songs for a month. Her comment, "We're ashamed the president of the United States is from Texas," was made the summer of 2003, soon after the U.S. invasion of Iraq.

Item: In 2004, the Walt Disney Company prevented Miramax, one of its subsidiaries, from distributing Michael Moore's Bush-bashing documentary *Fahrenheit 9/11.* A *New York Times* article (May 5, 2004) reported that Moore's agent said Disney's chief executive had asked him to pull out of financial arrangements with Miramax the year before

---

[19] "The Death of Radio Reporting: Will TV Be Next?" by Lawrence K. Grossman (September/October 1998). A fascinating article containing a good deal more information on this dumbing down of radio news reporting.

[20] For more on this see Ted Turner's article "My Beef With Big Media," in *The Washington Monthly,* July–August 2004. Turner focuses in particular on the way big media increasingly shut out independent entrepreneurs with diverse points of view but not enough cash or clout to compete with the big guys.

because the deal would endanger the tax breaks Disney got from various business interests in Florida. Disney execs denied that this was their motive, claiming instead that "It's not in the interest of any major corporation to be dragged into a highly charged partisan battle."

Having just trashed Disney brings to mind one of the few definite advantages of mass media control by powerful megacorporations. As you might imagine, Disney would like very much to get a nice slice of the growing Chinese market for films and other entertainment products. So Disney was confronted with a very tough choice when Chinese authorities warned Disney executives in late 1996 that China would be forced to "reconsider" Disney investment plans in that country if Disney failed to put the kibosh on a movie that portrayed the current situation in Tibet from the point of view of the exiled Tibetan Dalai Lama. Smaller companies might well have felt unable to withstand the threat of being shut out of the Chinese market and have caved in to the threat, but Disney, to its great credit, stood fast and continued production of the film—which, of course, will not be allowed to be shown in China. (For more on this, see, for example, the November 26, 1996, *New York Times*.)

Talk of Disney and Turner Broadcasting brings to mind the fact that all of the news outlets owned by the huge media conglomerates are not quite like peas in a pod. Some are a bit more true to professed journalistic ideals than others. Turner's CNN and CNN News channels, for instance, occasionally appear to be more willing to report the news accurately when it goes against the interests of big business or other powerful organizations than are, say, the Rupert Murdoch–owned Fox news channels.

Getting back to the topic at hand, another positive development in the mass media is Oprah Winfrey's use of her TV pulpit to convince audiences that reading books can be both fun and informative.[21] When Oprah selects a book for discussion on her program, it usually rises quickly onto best-seller lists. People write to her about how they have started reading and love it. Hooray for Oprah Winfrey! (On the negative side, Winfrey engages in some of the shoddy news practices that are routine on TV and radio talk shows—for example, concerning health news.)

Which brings us to the Internet, interactive television, and the other electronic wonders. Of course, no one can be sure how these new media will work out with respect to the news and other kinds of information. Bill Gates, for example, says that within a few years people will regularly be watching TV programs on their computer screens. TV sets now are available that can do some of the simple things done by computers. HDTV (high-definition TV) has arrived. Most computers these days are programmed to handle CD-ROMs containing whole dictionaries, almanacs, encyclopedias, and the like. Billions are being wagered one way or another in the attempt to get in on the ground floor of the new ways in which the electronic marvel industry is going to change our lives.

Perhaps the biggest threat to current news dissemination on these new electronic media has to do with advertising and the Internet. Newspapers get most of their revenue from ads, including classified ads. If a good deal of this advertising revenue is diverted to the Internet, newspapers will suffer greatly, and many, perhaps most, could go out of business. (The flip side of this is that advertising on the Internet, so far, has not been as successful as it still is on the relatively old-fashioned TV outlets, but it is rapidly catching up.)

---

[21] See, for instance, Caryn James's "Critics Notebook" (*New York Times,* November 21, 1996).

It also has been argued that the Internet is going to increase the division in large, industrial countries between the resources available to the rich as compared to the poor. Public libraries, for example, traditionally (well, for the past 100 years or so) have been free sources of all kinds of information, but the Internet seems to be headed more and more toward information provided at a price that may seriously limit access by the poor.

Nevertheless, many viewers on the scene see the Internet as a wonderful democratizing force, counteracting the concentration of media power now taking place. Increasingly the Internet provides news coverage from major publications, like the *New York Times,* and from on-line magazines. In addition, it provides information that may be slighted by mainstream news outlets. A case in point is the Internet coverage of the political conventions in the 2004 presidential campaign. When broadcast networks cut back on airtime for the conventions, the Internet filled the gap with around-the-clock coverage that included polls, live chats, and interactive events. When used this way, the Internet provides a megaphone for ordinary people, allowing all of us to tell the world what is on our minds. (Whether the world will be tuned in is another matter.) Correspondence via e-mail also has great promise as an information source. But so far, the now-traditional media (television, radio, newspapers, periodicals, libraries) still remain the principal news and information sources for the vast majority of people, though that may change in the near future.

SUMMARY OF CHAPTER 11

1. The mass media are businesses intent on making money. So they have to satisfy their audiences, advertisers, and governments.

   They cater to their audiences by simplifying the news to make it more easily understood—by breaking news items into small sound bites that stay within the average attention span in length and by arranging coverage of news so as to conform to audience interests and prejudices. *Example:* The 2004 Olympic Games coverage on NBC larded over with human interest stories. (Note that organized groups of people—for instance, the NRA—have more clout than do isolated individuals.)

   The media cater to advertisers by suppressing news that reflects badly on them or their products and by touting advertisers' products free as "news" items. *Example:* Proctor and Gamble pressuring TV stations into not running an item critical of Folger's coffee.

   The media also have to take account of the power of government to harass by rescinding licenses or censoring anti-CIA exposés, by playing favorites in the dissemination of news, and by fining networks for broadcasting indecent material. *Example:* The half-million-dollar fine slapped on CBS for airing Janet Jackson's indecent exposure during her halftime Super Bowl performance. The media often give in to this power of government by treading more carefully in criticizing government actions. *Example:* Reporters at press conferences who are careful not to ask overly pointed follow-up questions. (Note that the power of government to censor is much greater in many other countries than in the United States and in some other industrial democracies.)

But the mass media have a good deal of power of their own, stemming from their ability to expose and publicize whatever they care to. *Famous example:* The *Washington Post*'s dogged exposé of the Watergate scandal that forced President Nixon to resign in disgrace.

The business world—in particular, very large corporations—have a large say in the dissemination of news. They often use this power, first, to suppress stories unfavorable to their own narrow interests and, second, to get favorable stories included in media presentations. This power of big business stems from its power as advertisers (to withdraw advertising), from its ability to influence politicians and governments (principally through "campaign contributions") and from its ownership of a good deal of the mass media. *Example:* Disney media outlets touting Disney products.

Of course, in practice the media tend to try to satisfy all of the various power factions and not to needlessly throw their weight around. It almost always is more profitable to cooperate with power than to fight it. *Example:* Politicians and the media cooperating to produce sound bites: The pols get exposure and the media get cheap footage to show on the evening news. Unfortunately, the news has increasingly become a source of entertainment more than information, playing up human interest stories like the saga of Jessica Lynch at the expense of hard news.

Since the bottom line is, as they say, the bottom line, news-gathering methods tend to be designed to save money, which means that regular beats are set up to gather the news from those able to regularly supply it (the rich and/or powerful and the government). True investigative reporting is very costly and thus relatively less common than a mere gathering of the news from other sources. *Example:* The regular attendance at presidential press conferences as compared to the amount of journalistic digging below the surface.

2. For reasons already mentioned, the media tend to misdirect audience attention away from important, underlying issues and events to human interest stories. In doing this, they tend to take advantage of the average person's lack of a good sense of proportion.

3. What happens every day is not new and is therefore not usually considered to be newsworthy by the mass media. *Example:* The ongoing and extremely serious threat posed by bacteria and viruses that tends to get only sporadic coverage.

The media's theory of objectivity, to which lip service is widely paid, requires that news stories be separated from speculations, judgments, evaluations, and the like, which are considered to be subjective. But this theory is off the mark. Facts don't just lie around waiting to be picked up; reporters must reason to the facts. Similarly, decisions as to what will be covered and what will not depend in part on value judgments, so that news and evaluations cannot be completely separated.

In practice, however, the theory of objectivity simply keeps the media from straying too far in their judgments and evaluations from the mainstream social consensus. *Example:* Their attempts to be objective by being "evenhanded" merely result in our hearing what the Democrats have to say as compared to the Republicans.

Because the theory of objectivity says that news reporting must be separated from judgments, speculation, and background information, the mass media tend to be short on explanations as to why things happen as they do. Of course, reporters cannot be expected to be experts on every topic they cover. But they still want to appear to be authoritative—to appear to know what they are talking about whether they do or don't. *Example:* Geraldo Rivera reporting from Afghanistan.

The media generally want to play it safe when featuring expert opinion. They want to satisfy all relevant power factions, if possible. So they tend to consult establishment figures, including media bigwigs, and not to annoy their audiences. The result often is silly pontificating. *Example:* The political correctness of almost all political discussion on TV.

Note that the media sometimes act as self-censors, either out of patriotic intent (as in wartime), or in order to placate their audiences or advertisers, or to avoid the possibility of libel. *Example:* Showing Elvis Presley doing his stuff only from the waist up on the old Ed Sullivan TV show.

4. The media need to slant the news can be accomplished in quite a few different ways: playing a story up or down, using a misleading or sensational headline, omitting or playing down follow-up stories, using (or not using) emotive language, using suggestive photos and other imagery, and using cartoons to convey a point of view. *Example:* Burying reports on the virtues of the Canadian single-payer health care system at the end of articles after presenting critical material at the beginning.

5. The most important mass medium these days is television, which serves as town crier, certifier, and grapevine. It is the chief medium on which political contests are fought and news about major events such as wars is disseminated. No other medium comes close to television in the size of its audience or the immediacy of its offerings.

The result is that the television industry has greater power than the other media and indeed can and does influence the course of events in the world on which it reports. *Example:* The way in which TV coverage of war affected the NATO bombing of Kosovo.

Even prime-time television entertainment sometimes has positive features. *Example:* It has helped to break down prejudices against ethnic and religious groups and women—portraying blacks and women in important jobs in the business community. Note also the positive effects of employing African Americans and women on TV news programs. (TV also is superior in explaining the news to ordinary people on the street.)

6. Although the mass media are a modestly good source of breaking news, smaller-scale outlets are much better at analysis, at supplying background information, and at investigative reporting.

PBS is a relatively good source of news, generally better than most mass media outlets, in particular in providing background information and analysis. But lots of small-circulation magazines are significantly better than PBS and CNN, being crafted so as to appeal to more sophisticated audiences. *Example:* The *Washington Monthly* coverage of politics.

But the point is selectivity, not mass versus non–mass media. This is true not only with respect to television, newspapers, radio, and magazines, but also to books. Popular books tend to be lighter weight than some that are less popular, because mass audiences tend to be rather unsophisticated. *Example: Discover* and *Omni* magazines, which hoke up science in the attempt to make it interesting to a mass audience. (Note that presidential memoirs and those of other high government officials tend to be particularly shoddy products. *Example:* President Reagan's rearrangement of facts called *An American Life.*)

7. The intense concentration of media power in the hands of giant conglomerates is one of the more ominous recent developments in the media business. *Example:* Walt Disney owning ABC, dozens of radio stations, hundreds of Disney stores, and so forth. Although size theoretically can yield efficiency and better news coverage, in general it hasn't worked that way so far. But large scale does occasionally enable a news source to resist pressure to censor by foreign governments. *Example:* Disney standing up to Chinese pressure to censor. Finally, what the Internet and computers hold for the future is an interesting and as yet unanswered question, but each year more news coverage is provided by on-line publications.

EXERCISE 11-1

1. Evaluate the coverage in your local newspaper of a particular event or issue of national importance, with respect to (1) objectivity, (2) original versus second-hand reporting, (3) use of headlines, (4) establishment or mainstream point of view compared to minority opinions, and (5) any other matters discussed in this chapter.

2. Do the same for a recent issue of *Time, Newsweek, U.S. News & World Report,* or one of the on-line magazines such as *Salon.*

3. Do the same for an ABC, NBC, or CBS national evening news program.

4. Get a recent copy of *The Economist,* a British news magazine that widely circulates in the United States and Canada. Select a story in it about a particular event, and compare how it is handled with the way it is dealt with in one of the major American news magazines.

5. Compare news reporting on the BBC world news program carried on National Public Radio (NPR) with news reporting on any network TV or radio station. Which is better, and why?

6. Watch several TV episodes of *ER* and explain how doctors and the medical industry are portrayed. Be sure to explain how their portrayal is similar to and different (if it is) from the real medical world. Do you think this program influences how viewers tend to see doctors and medical care?

7. How are the elderly and teenagers portrayed on network TV programs, both in news stories and, especially, in popular entertainment programs? Back up your conclusions with details. How about women as compared to men?

8. Check the front page of a single issue of your local newspaper and determine as best you can the sources of their stories. (In the case of wire stories—Associated Press, Reuters, and the like—try to determine their sources.) How many of these stories are based primarily on a single handout or speech, how many were compiled from several such sources, and how many from reporters going out and finding for themselves what is going on?

9. Read through a single issue of three non–mass media magazines, one liberal (for instance, *The Washington Monthly*), one conservative (say, *The National Review*), and one libertarian (for example, *Reason*). Are their points of view evident? How do you think they compare to mass media magazines such as *Time* or *Newsweek* or to network national TV news programs?

10. How do you think the news would be presented to us if the federal government controlled and managed the mass media? Be specific and defend your answer with some thoughtful analysis.

11. Suppose that you owned a local television station or newspaper, or a whole television network. Would you report the news any differently from the way that the outlets in your area do now? If so, how, and why? If not, why not? (Assume that, while rich, you can't withstand losses forever. And be realistic, not goody-goody.)

12. Many more women are working in the mass media today than in the old days, but fewer women than men rise to the top. Do you think the fact that men hold so many of the top positions in the mass media and thus make most of the important policy decisions seriously influences work conditions and news content in ways that would be different if women were equally represented in news media high management? If so, how? If not, why not?

13. For the energetic: Go to the library or the Internet and dig through back issues of some mass media publication and evaluate its coverage over time of some important, underlying, or long-term national issue or problem (for example, under- and unemployment, crime, pollution). Defend your evaluation.

14. Also for the energetic: Write your own news story about a personal event that truthfully makes you look bad. Write it as though it were to appear in your local or school newspaper, including headlines and the rest. Now rewrite the story to show your part in it in the best light possible without actually lying. Compare the two. Was this little exercise educational? (Answer: Very definitely, if you did it well.)

15. Examine the photographs accompanying a news story and explain how they slant the news.

16. The thrust of the discussion about the recent intense concentration of media power into fewer and fewer hands was that on the whole this is bad for the ef-

fective dissemination of the news. We noted, for example, that the chief concern of these large corporations is the bottom line, not the best presentation of the news. But isn't it possible, perhaps even likely, that these megacorporations will find that the highest profits are obtained by best satisfying their audiences, thus putting all of us (collectively) into the driver's seat—being given the sort of news coverage we most prefer? And if so, isn't that all to the good? So why worry about the concentration of media power that has been taking place lately?

By Handelsman, from *The New Yorker*. Reprinted by permission of Tribune Media Services.

"Do your owners treat you well? Mine are very kind."

This New Yorker drawing depicts what many critics claim is the principal problem with the political process in industrial democracies like the United States today—politicians are beholden to fat-cat contributors who provide most of the cash required to campaign successfully for high office. (By the way, what do you think are the chances that a social studies text containing this cartoon would be adopted by your school?)

Not to know what has happened before one was born is always to be a child.

— Cicero

A high school teacher, after all, is a person deputized by the rest of us to explain to the young what sort of world they are living in and to defend, if possible, the part their elders are playing in it.

—Emile Capouya

A child educated only at school is an uneducated child.

— George Santayana

The less people know about how sausages and laws are made, the better they'll sleep at night.

— Otto von Bismarck

Germany has taught me that an uncritical view of the national past generated an equally subservient acceptance of the present.

—Hans Schmitt (who grew up in Nazi Germany)

If a nation expects to be ignorant and free, . . . it expects what never was and never will be.

—Thomas Jefferson

Chapter

12

TEXTBOOKS: MANAGING WORLDVIEWS

Public schools are one of the earliest sources of information about the world that most of us are exposed to. So it is important to have a good idea about how accurate what we have been told while growing up might be.

One way to get an idea about this is to examine typical textbooks used in public school classrooms. Most teachers, after all, tend to coordinate classroom instruction with textbook content. This is particularly true in history courses, where the textbook is often the backbone of the curriculum. Since most history teachers in middle and high school haven't majored or minored in the subject, they tend to rely heavily on the content of the textbook. So let's discuss, first, the ways in which history texts tell high school students about the history of the United States.

1. HIGH SCHOOL HISTORY TEXTBOOKS

Textbooks don't stay the same for very long. Ups and downs in quality and content are bound to occur every so often.

The Good News

The good news is that since about 1960, the quality of high school history textbooks has improved in many significant ways. The first of these improvements was in the portrayal of African Americans. Blacks had been close to invisible in texts published before that time. They were mentioned, of course, with respect to slavery and its elimination via the Emancipation Proclamation, and reference generally was made to two "token" Negroes, Booker T. Washington and George Washington Carver. But by some time in the 1970s, virtually all history and civics texts had been revised to include more, and fairer, material about African Americans and their place in American history and everyday affairs.

Improved treatment of other minority groups and of women quickly (as these things go) followed, reflecting changing attitudes and roles in the body politic. In older textbooks no mention was made of the atrocities committed by European explorers against Native Americans or of their later subjugation by the government. Today, virtually every high school history textbook mentions the "Trail of Tears" (the forced move of the Cherokee Indians from their homeland in the South to the Oklahoma territory), the illegal incarceration of loyal Japanese citizens in concentration camps during World War II, and so on.[1]

Coupled with the improved treatment of minority groups has come a moderately large step toward objectivity in the portrayal of the darker side of American history. Imperialistic interference in the affairs of other countries—for example, of the so-called "banana republics"[2] of Central and South America—sometimes is hinted at (although the nasty details are never gone into in any depth).

> He that reads and grows no wiser seldom suspects his own deficiency, but complains of hard words and obscure sentences, and asks why books are written which cannot be understood.
>
> —Samuel Johnson

[1] Interestingly, hardly any texts mention homosexuals (about 5 percent of the population?), and, while Jews are referred to, anti-Semitism in this country rarely is discussed except in connection with the Ku Klux Klan. Some books do mention the discrimination against the Irish that was common in times past, but never with more than a line or two. (The paucity of textbooks that talk about homosexuals has made the selection of texts quite difficult in the very few places—the most prominent being San Francisco—where gays have a certain amount of political clout.)

[2] The expression derives from the way in which the United Fruit Company dominated the political affairs of many of these countries for many years.

The Bad News

Oh, yes—the bad news.

History Texts Are Dull and Overly Long   Public high school history books, as virtually all junior and senior high school textbooks, are exceedingly dull and full of misleading verbiage, so that only the brightest and most diligent students who do a good amount of reading between the lines are apt to learn much from them about the true history of their country. Very little in these texts is likely to raise student interest in these matters. Most of the better-selling senior high school history textbooks now run to at least 800 large pages of double-column type (most contain more than a thousand pages), with endless "learning aids," questions, special features, and the like.[3]

Students are snowed by the mountains of facts ladled out one after the other in an "and then this happened and then that happened" style that is completely devoid of what English teachers refer to as *voice* or *tone*. Names that even professional historians would not always be able to identify—for example, of some of the failed early nineteenth-century vice-presidential candidates—pile up one after the other as details concerning the election of 1816, the election of 1820, the election of 1824 . . . are described. Interesting topics have the guts wrung out of them. Even accounts of the good features of the American social system tend to fall flat.

That detailed facts spewed out one after another don't easily become part of the working knowledge of students is supported by all sorts of surveys (in which, for instance, students identified J. Edgar Hoover as a nineteenth-century president, Jefferson Davis as a guitar player, and Socrates as an Indian chief). But students also don't seem to grasp the general, or approximate, kinds of knowledge that are more important than most precise facts. It's more important, for example, that students know the approximate size and

---

Overly long books, overstuffed with facts, facts, facts, are not just dull, dull, dull. They're also heavy, heavy, heavy, often weighing more than six pounds. Students now carry these books home with them in backpacks, homework assignments being a regular feature of today's educational system (as opposed to the one in effect when the authors of this text attended high school—we're talking ancient history here).

The result is that backaches and strained back muscles have become all too common these days among public school students. One-third of the students in a study by researchers at Simmons College in Boston said that their backs hurt so much that they had missed whole school days, or had missed physical education classes, or had needed to visit their doctor.

So the overstuffed texts in use today not only fail to increase student comprehension but also harm student health.*

*See, for instance, "Weighty Backpacks Straining Schoolkids," *San Francisco Chronicle,* February 14, 2001, p. 1.

---

[3] Interestingly, units labeled "critical reasoning" now tend to occur here and there in most of the newer social studies and history textbooks.

population of their country rather than precise statistics on this matter, and the evidence indicates that the ideas of most students concerning these important matters are either way off the mark or nonexistent.

Evidence of this is apparent in the results of periodic general knowledge polls. For instance, in a 2000 survey of seniors at prestigious colleges around the country (Amherst, Duke, Harvard, Grinnell, and some others), more students named Civil War general Ulysses S. Grant as the commander of the Continental Army in the final battle of the Revolutionary War than selected George Washington. Only one in five correctly identified the source of the famous and wonderful phrase "Government of the people, by the people, and for the people." (And who did utter that immortal line, and when?)[4]

History Texts Have Been Dumbed Down   Another part of the bad news is that in the past several years a great many textbooks have been "dumbed down" with respect to vocabulary and sentence construction, although a few more linguistically sophisticated texts still are available. Dumbed-down texts shortchange students in several ways. One is the failure to stretch the already low student reading abilities that have led some educators to prefer the dumbed-down texts. Another results from the difficulty in presenting any complicated material using just simplified linguistic structures, forcing authors to oversimplify inherently complicated material.

History Texts Have Gone Overboard on Multiculturalism   Still another part of the bad news is that history textbooks in recent years have reflected a general tendency to carry good, worthwhile improvements too far. If minorities and women were once seriously neglected in public school history texts, they now receive attention that distorts the history of the United States. History texts, in current lingo, have become *politically correct* and *multicultural*. (Recall the discussion in Chapter 1 concerning these trends.)

One of the myths adopted by a great many who have gone overboard on multiculturalism is that of the "noble native Americans," formerly called "Indians." Atrocities committed against them by European interlopers are featured; atrocities committed by native Americans to each other (one tribe to another) and to European opponents get short shrift when mentioned at all. (The alleged conservationist practices of native Americans also are usually distorted all out of proportion, but let that pass.)

American History Is Distorted   But arguably the most serious defect in today's history and social studies textbooks is that they still tend to distort American history and how the social/political system actually works in the United States, even if less so than in the past. Although those who ultimately decide what sorts of textbooks will be adopted surely do not intend to adopt books that stray too far from the truth, they also always have in mind the need to make students into loyal, proud citizens when they take their places in adult life, and they are influenced by the opinions and prejudices of those who have political power (a point to be discussed later).

---

[4] Is television, or rather the great amount of time young people typically spend in front of the tube, also a causal factor here?

United States History Is Sanitized   History texts "clean up" our past so as to maintain student pride in America. As much as possible, our leaders are pictured as better than human, all dressed up and minus their flaws (except, of course, for a very few Benedict Arnolds whose transgressions can't be papered over). Take the way in which Theodore Roosevelt, affectionately referred to as Teddy (the teddy bear was named after him), is spruced up in virtually all public school texts. Typically, he is portrayed as an energetic, hard-driving, exuberant, brave, trust-busting conservationist, reformer, and progressive, who was against monopolistic big business—a great man deserving of his place on Mount Rushmore.[5]

And perhaps he was. But no textbooks the authors of this text have ever seen, or even heard of, tell students about another side of good old Teddy. They don't describe him as a bloodthirsty bigot who, though unusually brave, reveled in the slaughter he personally engaged in and witnessed during the Spanish-American War; a man who expressed pleasure after 30 men had been shot to death in the Civil War draft riots ("an admirable object lesson to the remainder"); a man who justified slaughtering Indians on the grounds that their lives were only "a few degrees less meaningful, squalid, and ferocious than that of the wild beasts," and who said that "All the great masterful races have been fighting races. . . . No triumph of peace is quite so great as the supreme triumph of war." Not exactly a teddy bear, this Teddy Roosevelt. (History texts also falsely pump up the part played by Roosevelt's "Rough Riders" in the famous charge up San Juan Hill in Cuba during the Spanish-American War at the expense of the black American soldiers, who did the most effective fighting.)

Embarrassing Facts and Topics Are Omitted or Played Down   Although outright lying is frowned upon, the writers of public school textbooks have other devices at their disposal enabling them to satisfy the various kinds of social and political demands

---

The soul of historical research is debate, but that sense of uncertainty and contingency seldom finds its way into textbooks. By its nature, the textbook must pretend that its condensation of events and its presentation of their meaning are correct. In reality, every textbook has a point of view, despite a façade of neutrality; the authors and editors select some interpretations and reject others, choose certain events as important and ignore others as unimportant. Even when they insert sidebars with point and counterpoint on a few issues, they give the false impression that all other issues are settled when they are not. The pretense of objectivity and authority is, at bottom, just that: a pretense.

—Diane Ravitch
The Language Police

---

[5] But Roosevelt's role in the machinations that went on before construction of the Panama Canal, now seen as definitely not politically correct, sometimes are mentioned as a minus, whereas his role in the building of the canal previously was cited as one of his more glorious achievements. ("The more things stay the same, the more they change."—Harold Gordon)

It's interesting to compare how native Americans are portrayed in public school textbooks with how historians picture them. Here, for instance, are excerpts from an account of Indian atrocities committed during the French and Indian War, discussed in a review in the New York Review of Books *(May 11, 2000) of a book about that war by historian Fred Anderson: ***

Indians at war followed cultural conventions that eighteenth-century Europeans could not, at least openly, condone. Indians gave no quarter and did not expect any. . . . [W]hen they were enticed into large-scale actions of British and French military operations, they still carried the expectation that victory meant the right to do what they wished with prisoners of whatever age or sex. What they wished was to torture and kill some of them, maybe eat a few, and to adopt some of the rest into their own depleted ranks, procedures that continued to horrify and mystify Europeans.

The review quotes Anderson:

The only rewards that the Indians—whether Christian or heathen—had expected were plunder trophies to prove their prowess in battle, and captives to adopt or sacrifice as replacements for dead warriors or perhaps to hold for ransom. When it became clear that the man whom they called "Father" [French General Montcalm] intended to do what no real father would and deprive them of the reward they had earned, most of the warriors decided merely to take what they have come for and then to leave.

The review continues:

The immediate result was "the massacre of Fort William Henry," familiar to all readers of *The Last of the Mohicans.* Despite all efforts to restrain them, Montcalm's Indians killed close to two hundred of the garrison, troops and civilians alike, and carried off more than three hundred captives, at least one of whom was ritually boiled and eaten just outside Montreal.

Nothing like this ever appears in today's politically correct public school textbooks.

* The Crucible of War: The Seven Years War and the Fate of the Empire in British North America, 1754–1766 (Knopf, 2000).

made on them. The most commonly employed of these devices is the complete omission of embarrassing historical events or facts. For example, most of the CIA "dirty tricks" and other sorts of interferences in the internal affairs of several foreign countries over the years—for instance, in Chile—get passed over. (Interestingly, the "Irangate" scandal that occurred during President Reagan's administration usually is mentioned.) Similarly, although all textbooks expend dozens of pages on World War II, most omit reference to the terrible firestorm bombing of Tokyo that killed more people than either of the atomic bombs we dropped on Japan, and they frequently fail to mention the deliberate policy of the American and British air forces to bomb German civilians, mostly women and children, as a way of breaking down German will to continue fighting.[6]

Embarrassing events also sometimes are papered over by carefully controlled emphasis, especially by simply expending relatively little space on a topic. For example, most history textbooks these days, unlike those of times past, do tell readers about the war that occurred between American troops and Philippine guerrillas intent on gaining independence after the United States annexed the Philippine Islands at the end of the Spanish-American War, but they do so quickly, thus masking the extreme nastiness of the way in which the Filipinos were subjugated. The war with Spain gets relatively lots of space in most texts; the war against Filipino patriots extremely little, even though many more deaths and much greater destruction resulted from the war to force the Philippine people to knuckle under than from the war against Spain (itself quite a blot on the American escutcheon).

These devices are very hard for uninformed or unsophisticated readers to see through, particularly because we all want very much to believe in the greatness of our own society and tend to see national warts only after a good deal of experience has forced us to do so.

As might be expected, the role of the United States in foreign wars such as World War II is puffed up and cleansed. But it might also be supposed that the suffering and dying of American fighting troops would be explained in a way that would let students understand the extent of their sacrifices and the terror they endured, as they did, for instance, on June 6, 1944 ("D-Day"), when several thousand American troops lost their lives on the beaches of Normandy, in France.[7] After all, this would show how brave and self-sacrificing American troops have been. But telling students about this would require explaining what modern warfare really is like: about what it means to advance into concentrated machine gun fire that is certain to mow down most of those who find themselves in this terrible and terrifying circumstance; about flying on bombing missions with the knowledge that sooner or later most bombers in your unit are likely to be shot down and their occupants killed[8]; about suddenly being covered with the splattered

---

[6] Absolutely no texts provide anything like an accurate depiction of the nature of these cataclysmic bombings of German cities and of Tokyo (although there are hints—tiny hints—about the horror of the atomic bombings of Hiroshima and Nagasaki). Only a very few even mention the infamous firestorming of Dresden in which about 50,000 to 100,000 civilians were killed, an extremely ugly blot on the American and British escutcheons because Dresden had next to no military importance, and in any case the war was all but won when the thousands of bombers turned that once architectural gem into an inferno. An accurate count of the dead was impossible because all that was left of many people were heaps of ashes or a layer of gelatin covering the floors of cellar air raid shelters. See, for instance, *Target: Hitler's Oil,* by R. C. Nesbit (Kimber, 1985), or *Brute Force: Allied Strategy and Tactics in the Second World War,* by John Ellis (Viking, 1990).

[7] A great many died or were permanently maimed, by the way, because of a lack of cooperation between air and ground forces. But even most reasonably good histories of that great invasion gloss over this disgraceful fact, so we can't realistically expect public school textbooks to mention it. Similarly, no textbook can be expected to mention the large number of men who deserted during World War II, as in every major war fought by this country.

[8] That is one of the important points made in the well-known and excellent novel *Catch 22.*

brains of a buddy who has just been hit by an unseen sniper; about the last moments of men drowning on submarines; about incinerated tank crews or the soldiers blasted into thousands of tiny pieces by enemy shelling. (Back in high school did you notice the total omission of pictures of dead American soldiers in history textbooks or of anything that graphically conveys the true horror of modern warfare?)

2. A TYPICAL HIGH SCHOOL HISTORY TEXTBOOK

So far, we've described high school history texts as dull, lacking tone or voice; too long; too fact filled; dumbed down compared to texts of the old days; overboard on multiculturalism and the roles of minorities and women; and sanitized so as to picture the history of "our great nation" in the best possible light. Let's now see how some of this works out in a better than average but otherwise typical and widely adopted high school history textbook.[9]

This textbook, *America: Pathways to the Present,* contains 1,187 huge, double-columned 8½ by 12-inch pages, chock full of teaching devices (graphs, critical thinking questions, and so on). As might be imagined, this text is also chock full of facts about American history ladled out one after another in a deadly flat tone of voice. Here, for example, is a short excerpt from this book's account of the presidential election of 1880:

> As the 1880 presidential election approached, the Republican party was split into three factions. The Stalwarts, followers of Senator Conklin, defended the spoils system. The Half-breeds, who followed Maine senator James G. Blaine, hoped to reform the spoils system while remaining loyal to the party. Independents opposed the spoils system altogether. James A. Garfield, a congressman from Ohio, won the party's presidential nomination. Garfield was linked to the Half-breeds. To balance the ticket, the Republicans chose as their vice-presidential candidate Chester A. Arthur, the New York Stalwart whom Hayes had fired two years earlier.
>
> In the 1880 election Garfield won a narrow victory over the Democratic candidate, General Winfield S. Hancock. . . [*ad infinitum*].

Fascinating. But how many students ever remember even the tiniest bit of this dreary account?

The fact that students do not learn even a tiny portion of the mountain of facts textbooks like this one try to stuff into their (the students') minds is illustrated by the outcry during the 2000 presidential election fight over Florida's electoral votes. This text, like many others, expends more than 50 pages on the adoption of the Constitution of the United States and even prints the entire document, including amendments. Yet it surely did not surprise most high school teachers when, during the fight for Florida's 25 electors, surveys showed that many Americans did not know that the candidate with the most popular votes does not automatically win election.

---

[9]This textbook, *America: Pathways to the Present,* by Andrew R. L. Cayton, Elisabeth Israels Perry, and Allan M. Winkler (Prentice Hall, 2000), is reviewed in *The Textbook Letter* (March/April 1999), the premier journal dealing with junior and senior high school textbooks.

Oh, yes. Multiculturalism and all of that. *America: Pathways to the Present* expends 30 of its 48 pages on World War II to the topics of race prejudice and black soldiers, Japanese Americans, Mexican Americans, and so forth. The battles engaged in during that great war get 18 pages or so, by themselves telling students much more than they are likely to remember.[10]

Here is a passage from a book that absolutely never will find its way into public school classrooms. It describes how a great many of the American GIs who fought in the front lines against the Germans in World War II felt about it at the time:

"The Real War Will Never Get in the Books"

What was it about the war that moved the troops to constant verbal subversion and contempt? [This was described earlier.] It was not just the danger and fear, the boredom and uncertainty and loneliness and deprivation. It was rather the conviction that optimistic publicity and euphemism had rendered their experience so falsely that it would never be readily communicable. They knew that in its representation to the laity what was happening to them was systematically sanitized and Norman Rockwellized, not to mention Disneyfied. They knew that despite the advertising and publicity, where it counted their arms and equipment were worse than the Germans'. [The author doesn't mention here that GIs had a vastly greater supply, at any rate, of weapons than did their opponents, and that American and British airplanes were as good as or better than those of the Germans.] They knew that despite official assertions to the contrary, the Germans had real smokeless powder for their small arms and that they did not. They knew that their automatic rifles . . . were slower and clumsier, and they knew that the Germans had a much better light machine gun. . . . They knew that their own tanks, both American and British, were ridiculously under-armed and under-armored, so that they were inevitably destroyed in an open encounter with an equal number of German panzers [tanks]. . . . And they knew that the greatest single weapon of the war, the atomic bomb excepted, was the German 88-mm flat-trajectory gun, which brought down thousands of bombers and tens of thousands of soldiers. The Allies had nothing as good, despite one of them designating itself The World's Greatest Industrial Power. The troops' disillusion and their ironic response, in song and satire and sullen contempt, came from knowing that the home front then (*and very likely historiography later*) could be aware of none of these things. (Italics added.)*

* Wartime: Understanding and Behavior in the Second World War, by Paul Fussell (Oxford University Press, 1989).

---

[10] No public school textbooks come remotely close to conveying the important fact that soldiers of the Soviet Union did most of the fighting and dying that defeated the German war machine, nor do any texts convey what is perhaps the most vital fact about modern warfare—namely, its absolute horror. Pictures of dead American soldiers are *extremely* rare; none appear in the photo-filled text we have been examining.

What is the point of stuffing the minds of students with so many details about World War II when surveys regularly show that, for example, about a third of young adults are unable to name a single country the United States fought against in that indescribably terrible conflict and don't know that we dropped an atomic bomb on Hiroshima, much less Nagasaki? Most students, of course, do not have a clue about the equally awful firestorm bombings of Tokyo, Hamburg, and Dresden—none of which are mentioned, by the way, in the textbook we've been discussing.

One of the really annoying features of today's texts is the questions they ask students ("What evidence does this photo give of the depth of their poverty?"—under a photo that clearly shows the extreme poverty of the people pictured) or the allegedly "critical thinking" sidebars. ("What kind of president do you think Americans were looking for after Watergate and the Nixon resignation?")[11] Not much critical thinking is needed to answer these make-work questions.

Another troublesome feature of today's textbooks is that they are completely uneven, haphazard, or even irrational in the way in which they present their topics. The text we have been examining, for instance, discusses Jack Dempsey at length (also Jackie Robinson) but passes over Joe Louis and Muhammad Ali; expends two pages on author Sandra Cisneros but makes only a tiny reference to Saul Bellow and completely neglects Philip Roth, Emily Dickinson, and Alice Walker; refers to George M. Cohen and Duke Ellington but not to Irving Berlin, Cole Porter, or Ella Fitzgerald; and mentions Helen Willis (with photo) but not Jesse Owens, Florence Griffith-Joyner, or "Babe" Didrikson.[12]

Before passing on to other matters, perhaps we should point out that the worst distortions of American history occur in grade school texts and that as students move up in grade level, textbooks become less goody-goody and quite a bit more accurate. The idea, which certainly is not without merit, seems to be that tiny tots are not ready for unvarnished truth and need to be gently introduced into the "facts of life" over time. What we have stressed here is that even in high school, students are provided a dolled-up version of reality, an account that fails to square with the true history of the United States. (Similar remarks apply to the social studies—civics, government, politics—texts about to be discussed.)

> Who controls the past controls the future; who controls the present controls the past.
>
> —George Orwell (*1984*)

---

[11] This text also contains a gazillion boxes titled "Internet Activity" and "Writing Activity" (no student could possibly write anything sensible in one or two semesters on even 1/50th of the topics suggested), as well as more than 100 maps; 139 graphs, charts, and tables; a section with short biographies of every American president (with photos); a special list at the end of the book containing short descriptions of exactly 50 Supreme Court cases (with discussions of 23 of these cases in the body of the text); a glossary (yes, Rosie the Riveter is in it); a Spanish glossary; and so forth.
[12] Stephen Foster, of course, is a no-no in today's textbooks, as he is in current music classes. Textbook content does indeed mirror classroom curricula, and vice versa.

Drawing by David Levine. Copyright © 1969 NYREV, Inc. Reprinted
by permission of Kathy Hayes Associates, agent for David Levine.

Hamburger Hill

*David Levine's drawing of Hamburger Hill (a hill in Vietnam on which many
soldiers lost their lives) pictures two American presidents as jolly mass murderers.
Would the Texas State Textbook Committee give its approval to a book containing
this caricature?*

3. SOCIAL STUDIES (CIVICS) TEXTBOOKS MINIMIZE THE GREAT GULF BETWEEN THEORY AND PRACTICE

In the constant struggle for power and wealth that goes on in every country, national
ideals, customs, and laws get violated. Thus, a great gulf always exists between the official story about how a system is supposed to work and actual, everyday practice. It is

extremely important that we know the extent of this gulf if we are to have even a mod-estly good idea about what is likely to be in store for us as we go through life. We need to know, for example, what our chances are of getting justice if we have to go into court,[13] how far we can trust the leaders of our nation to consider our economic and other interests, and to what extent elected officials are influenced by lobbyists to do what is in their, but not necessarily our or the nation's, best interests.

For example, one of our official myths is that no one is above the law—that a Rock-efeller can't break into someone else's property with impunity any more than you can. Civics texts try as much as possible to stress the positive and play down the negative, so they don't tell students that this particular official myth really is a myth—that the rich and/or powerful frequently are above the law in ways we common folk never are, and that a Rockefeller can (because one actually did) sometimes break into someone's else's property and get away with it. Here, for instance, is a *Washington Post* (December 1, 1981) tidbit you're not likely to run across in any public school texts, although it reveals a great deal about privilege differences between the "aristocracy" and the rest of us:

Rules Are Made to Be Broken, for Some People

Late one night in Kansas City, [Nelson] Rockefeller [later, by the way, one of the two unelected vice presidents in American history] couldn't find his Water Pik. "He had dental work that debris would catch in sometimes," recalls Hugh Mor-row, the former Rockefeller spokesman. "So with the aid of the local police, [aide] Joe [Canzeri] broke into a drugstore, got the Water Pik and left the money on the counter. . . ."

During the 1968 New York City garbage strike, [then New York Governor] Rockefeller was once in all-night negotiations with the union. By 5 a.m. the group was tired and hungry. Canzeri broke a kitchen lock at the nearby Gotham Hotel, then made bacon, scrambled eggs, coffee and toast for the group of 30.

Other cases in which the rich, or the politically powerful, apparently violated the law and got away with it quickly come to mind. Think, for example, of the way in which Sen-ator Ted Kennedy was treated after his escapade at Chappaquiddick. Although the evi-dence strongly suggested negligent homicide and quite likely more serious crimes, he was never tried and received no legal punishment whatsoever. (One wonders how the 2000 Florida election scandal will be dealt with in the next crop of civics and history textbooks.)

Nevertheless, today's social studies textbooks are miles better than the ones in use un-til about 20 years or so ago. In the old days, civics texts restricted themselves almost entirely to descriptions, detailed and quite accurate, as to the theory of American gov-ernment and social practices, more or less ignoring everyday reality. A typical text went on for pages about the "checks and balances" of government, provided minute details concerning the Constitution, the various departments and bureaus of the federal gov-

---

[13] It may very well be true, as some have suggested, that many young people learned more about the difficulty of getting justice when going to court from television and newspaper coverage of the two O. J. Simpson trials—in one of which he was declared innocent of murder while in the other guilty—than from anything they learned in public schools.

ernment, and so on, but hardly ever discussed the ways in which the system fails in actual practice to operate as it is supposed to.

Today's textbooks, unlike those in the past, often at least hint at everyday reality—for example, mentioning ways in which bribery, graft, and incompetence reduce and skew the performance of government. Here, for instance, is an example from a social science textbook typical of those on the market today:

> Why would voters want to remove the "Ins" and replace them with the "Outs"? Sometimes . . . a political scandal of some kind may cause voters to wonder whether officials at city hall or at the state or national capital are honestly serving the public. In a democracy, elections provide the people with a powerful means of "cleaning house" and ridding government of those who, in their opinion, are not properly fulfilling their duties.[14]

Note that the bad news about occasional scandals is followed by the good news about how the guilty can be voted out of office.

And what about corruption due to the power of big business? Here is what the same text has to say on that score:

> Another issue that challenged and changed the two [political] parties was the rising power of big business. For a while [!!], it seemed that railroad companies and other businesses could buy votes in a state legislature. Big businesses could use their money and influence to pass laws that gave them special privileges. When a politician accepts bribes from rich supporters, it is known as corruption.
>
> In the early 1900s, a Republican president, Theodore Roosevelt, made himself popular with voters by trying to regulate big business. Later, a Democratic president, Woodrow Wilson, did much the same thing. Because of their leadership, the two major parties became less corrupt. Also, businesses came to be regulated by laws enforced by the national government.

In most other social studies textbooks, even the better ones, the issue of bribery via "lobbying" and corruption in general are even more sanitized than in the one just discussed. Here, for instance, is how one venerable text that has been much improved in recent years discusses lobbying:

> The typical lobbyist of today is a far cry from those of an earlier day—and from many of the fictitious ones still found on television and in novels and the movies. The once fairly common practice of bribery and the heavy-handed use of unethical practices are almost unknown. Most present-day lobbyists work in the open, and their major techniques come under the heading of friendliness, persuasion, and helpfulness.
>
> Lobbyists are ready to do such things as buy lunches and dinners, provide information, write speeches, and prepare bills in proper form. The lunches and dinners are good, the information usually quite accurate, the speeches forceful, and the bills well drawn [!]. Most lobbyists know that if they behaved otherwise—gave false information, for example—they would damage, if not destroy, their credibility and so their overall effectiveness. . . .

---

[14] *Government for Everybody,* by Steven L. Jantzen (Amsco School Publications, 1992).

Lobbying abuses do occur now and then, of course. False or misleading testimony, bribery, and other unethical pressures are not common, but they do exist.[15]

Obviously, textbook accounts of this nature don't come close to revealing the way in which legislators are bought by the rich and powerful. (Notice then-Senator Bob Dole's unusually candid comment, quoted by Edward Sorel in his drawing reproduced on p. 327: "When these political action committees give money, they expect something in return other than good government.") But most of today's public school textbooks do at least hint at something close to the truth, and this is a great improvement over the way in which the topic of graft was discussed in times past. Students carefully reading between the lines now may be able to get at least a vague idea as to how the system works in practice.

4. TEXTBOOKS AND INDOCTRINATION

The obvious question to ask is why public school textbooks are written in the way just described. There is no easy answer to this question, but one thing is clear: The ultimate purpose of public schools is to educate the young to fit into adult society. This means, first, giving them the knowledge they will need to be productive citizens and, second, inculcating in them the values, attitudes, and practices that will make them good citizens. Education thus inevitably involves a certain amount of indoctrination.[16]

Applying these thoughts to public school textbooks yields some tentative conclusions as to their likely content, conclusions that are borne out by examining these works. The first is that history and social studies texts are bound to distort their material. The history of every nation has its dark spots as well as bright, and no system works the way it is supposed to. Public school history and civics texts therefore inevitably distort their subject matter so as to make "Our Great Nation" appear better than it really is. No society wants disaffected citizens. Embarrassing matters have to be papered over somehow or other; exactly how depends on social and political factors that change from time to time. Today, these factors are more favorable for providing students with greater accuracy and less indoctrination than ever before. (But not all is sweetness and light by any means, as we shall see shortly.)

The second tentative conclusion is that noncontroversial topics, such as mathematics, will be presented in a much more straightforward way than are history and social

---

[15] *Magruder's American Government,* by William A. McClenaghan (Prentice Hall, 1995.) This book has been a popular one since 1917. The quotes here are from a four-page account of lobbying that almost in its entirety is a whitewash of the topic. Still, anyone who wants to see how much better today's texts are than those of even 20 or 30 years ago would do well to look at earlier editions of this work.

[16] Although the primary intent of the adults who write and adopt public school textbooks is indeed to educate the young of their society, human nature being what it is, they also have other motives: to defend their own collective contribution to the history of their nation and to deny or play down their collective mistakes and misadventures. It's always difficult to notice how this creeps into the content and tone of the works of one's own group, but it becomes more evident when we examine those of other societies.

Dependence Day, 1993

EDWARD SOREL

This July 4, Senator Dole has a special reason for celebrating. The American political system has been good to him. According to reports filed with the Federal Election Commission, his campaign receipts for 1991-92 totaled $2,362,936—almost all from special interests. His agribusiness contributors include Philip Morris, Dow Chemical, John Deere, Kellogg, General Mills, Archer Daniels Midland and Farmland Industries. (Dole is a senior Republican on the Agriculture, Nutrition and Forestry Committee.)

Finance and real estate interests also contribute. These include Equitable Life, Goldman Sachs, American Express, Glendale Federal Savings and Loan, PaineWeber, First Boston, Chemical Bank, Mutual of Omaha and Prudential Insurance, among others. (Dole is *the* senior Republican on the Finance Committee.)

Senator Dole insists that his interventions on behalf of his contributors are perfectly legal, and while being interviewed by *The Wall Street Journal* was surprisingly frank about how Congress operates: "When these political action committees give money, they expect something in return other than good government."

Drawing by Edward Sorel from *The Nation,* July 1993. Reprinted by permission of Edward Sorel.

This drawing (with comment) by Edward Sorel, whose excellent work frequently graces the pages of The New Yorker, The Nation, *and* Atlantic Monthly *magazines, nicely illustrates the point that lobbying in the United States today is quite different from, and a good deal more insidious than, the lobbying described in public school textbooks.*

studies texts, with indoctrination at a minimum. Society wants just about everybody to be able to do arithmetic. (But see the comments later concerning recent trends in math textbooks.)

Finally, a third tentative conclusion is that controversial or "touchy" topics will be approached gingerly, papered over, or simply not discussed at all. Examples include the effects of campaign contributions on the performance of elected officials; so-called *regressive* taxes—indeed, most controversial economic issues; and social justice or its lack. As remarked on before, all of these tentative conclusions turn out to be accurate.

An unexpected new trend in education may modify the indoctrination built into American textbooks and, for that matter, the schoolbooks of other countries as well. Education, like big business, is going global. For example, a Swiss-based secondary school program developed by the International Baccalaureate Organization is being used in hundreds of schools throughout the world, and curricula for elementary and middle schools are in the works. Since publishers will be selling to an international community with potentially far more consumers than any single country could provide, textbooks will be much less likely to favor the bias of any one nation. It's worth keeping an eye on this trend.

5. Textbooks and Politics

When discussing the mass media in the previous chapter, we pointed out how the various interested parties—media owners, governments, big business, readers, and viewers—exert their power both in the political and the business arenas. The textbook arena also is the scene of power encounters, although, as should become evident, the various strengths and roles of the players are modestly different from what they are in the mass media. The players in the textbook political arena are voters, in particular, parents of schoolchildren and organized groups of interested individuals; teachers, educators, and other scholars; and textbook manufacturers. Governments, of course, particularly on the state and local levels, have a large say in the matter, but they more or less act in response to guidance and pressure from the interested parties and in particular to voter demands.

There is nothing new in the fact that politics plays an important role in determining textbook content. It has always played a big role in the field of education. Even the idea of universal literacy was once fought over in the political arena. Until well into the nineteenth century, education in Europe and America was confined to the upper classes, with very few exceptions. Indeed, the dominant upper-class worldview held that the masses of people were easier to control if they remained ignorant. (It also self-servingly held that the lower classes were too loutish to be able to learn to read and write with any facility.) The push for universal literacy began only with the nineteenth-century growth in the size and political power of the middle classes. Textbooks, in fact, themselves are an invention, more or less, of nineteenth-century educators. In Shakespeare's day, for instance, studying the great classical writings and other treatises constituted a relatively large part of grammar school education.

Nineteenth-century textbooks had just as strong a political orientation as those used in schools today. For half a century after the Civil War, southern states insisted on a sympathetic account of their part in the war, whereas northern states demanded inclusion of the South's treason, so publishers came up with the two different versions of the war for their respective clients. After the First World War, patriotic groups like the American

Legion and Veterans of Foreign Wars criticized textbooks that failed to arouse patriotic fervor, and ethnic groups insisted that their heroes be included in history books, much as ethnic and women's organizations do today. Then as now, textbook publishers complied.[17]

How Textbooks Are Selected

In the United States today, textbooks are selected and purchased on the local level. School boards either select the texts to be used or provide teachers and school principals with lists of approved books from which to select. In practice, of course, local boards follow the advice of teachers, except when under political pressure or higher-level direction of the kinds about to be described. Teachers, quite naturally, are influenced in their selection of texts by what they were taught in schools of education and thus by dominant members of their disciplines. (Similar remarks apply to the way things work in most democratic countries, including Canada and most of the European democracies.)

School boards, elected by the public or appointed by elected officials, tend to be rather vulnerable not only to the advice of teacher and educational theorists but also to lobbying by politically active groups. These groups thus indirectly influence textbook publishers intent on satisfying the requirements of local and state boards. This is perhaps the most important reason for the textbook revisions in the treatment of class, gender, and race briefly described a while back. Publishers today wouldn't dream of using a title like *Man and His Changing World,* to cite a 1930s example, any more then they would illustrate a textbook exclusively with pictures of white, middle-class males. Minority groups with increasing political power are insisting that textbooks reflect more accurately the historical and cultural experiences and contributions of nonwhites, of women, and of other minority groups. Women's rights organizations have successfully reduced the use of sexist language in textbooks, and the hotly debated traditional canon of Western literature has been broadened to include a wider selection of multicultural writers. All of these changes have been politically driven.[18]

Another skirmish currently being fought on the textbook battlefield concerns the liberal versus conservative interpretation of traditional values. In 1995, for instance, the decision to use textbooks depicting nontraditional families (including homosexual parents) in certain San Francisco public schools sparked a controversy that threatened government funding. There also still is a good deal of infighting going on over the issue of evolution versus creationism (more about that later). And the controversial issue of birth control has motivated some textbook writers either to skirt the subject or to take a moral position on it. For example, in a review of the high school text *Global Science,* Max G. Rodel noted that the excellent discussion of birth control in the previous edition had all but disappeared in the 2000 edition. It was replaced by a chapter called

---

[17] For more history on textbook bias see Chapters 3 and 4 in *The Language Police,* by Diane Ravitch.

[18] Of course, as in most cases of this kind, success usually depends on a readiness to change on the part of many ordinary citizens, the point being that perhaps organized groups can succeed only to the extent that the times are ripe, even though, without organized political pressure, little change might take place. In any case, organized political agitation surely was (and is) an important cause of widespread changes in attitude concerning minorities and women.

"The Case for Abstinence for Young People."[19] Revisions like this reflect the tenor of the times.

Nor should we overlook political fights over ideological issues concerning the quality and standards maintained in textbooks. Over the past two decades, the American school system has been intensively scrutinized and extensively criticized. Textbooks have come under fire, in particular, for being "dumbed down" in both content and linguistic sophistication. Educators are under pressure to raise textbook standards, to standardize content, and to link material to an increasing number of state and national achievement tests.

In times now long gone, funds spent by local boards in America came exclusively from local taxes—chiefly property taxes—and each district controlled its own choice of textbooks. Nowadays, a great deal of school money comes from state coffers, and even from the federal government, with the inevitable consequence that school boards are restricted from above as to their textbook choices. Political power concerning education thus has been dispersed from being almost exclusively local, to spreading to entire states and even, to a lesser extent, to the nation as a whole. Nearly half of the states in America now have state textbook adoption committees that screen publisher offerings—in particular, those concerning basic or "sensitive" topics and books intended for the first six school grades. Local boards in states with textbook committees must choose books from lists approved for adoption within their state. Inevitably, politicking on the state (and to a much lesser extent) national levels increasingly shapes the content of the textbooks from which local boards must choose.

The Power of Big Business

All of this means, by the way, that big business has less power in determining textbook content than it does in shaping the news offered by the mass media. But textbook publishing companies still exert a good deal of power in the textbook arena. State and local boards, after all, are forced to choose from the books offered to them by textbook publishers (whose number grows smaller every year because of the same market-driven forces that have been shrinking the number of mass media outlets). But publishers, in their turn, are guided by the demands of state and local agencies, especially of textbook committees in two key states: California and Texas. (Pressure groups are particularly strong in Texas. And when you consider that one adoption alone—the 2003 social studies texts for all grades—amounted to $345 million, you can understand the clout that state has.)[20] That is why the power that publishers derive from their role as commodity supplier is not as large as one might suppose.[21] A textbook that makes neither the California nor the Texas list is going to have a hard time hanging around long enough to find a sufficiently large constituency in other states, and so the major publishers pretty much have been forced to tailor

---

[19] See the July/August 2000 *Textbook Letter* for what is a generally favorable review of *Global Science: Energy, Resources, Environment,* Kendall/Hunt Publishing, 2000.

[20] A state committee in California approves all books used in kindergarten through the eighth grade; in Texas, through grade 12. But California does lay down requirements that all texts used in every grade must meet.

[21] If the idea that the supplier of a commodity has great power in determining the nature of those goods is foreign to you, think only of the way in which Microsoft, by gaining a controlling portion of the computer software market, has been able to influence the computer revolution.

their offerings accordingly. (The very few low-budget books intended for use in a single state or locality are obvious exceptions.) Furthermore, because local boards also generally specify a pool of potential texts from which individual schools in their districts must select, publishers also have had to take these boards' preferences into account. The requirements of big city school boards (remember the extent to which the United States has become an urban society) thus are an important influence on textbook publishers.

But the large textbook conglomerates, just like other large corporations, can and do influence the marketplace for their products in another way—namely, by lobbying. (Ironically, one of the important defects of social studies textbooks is that they must pussyfoot around controversial issues such as the effect of lobbying on the political process.) In 1996, for example, after intense lobbying by publishers, the California State Board of Education voted six to one to approve three new series of math textbooks for use in California schools even though they had been given very low scores by a special review committee of math instructors. Eliminated from the approved list, and thus ineligible for adoption in any California public school, was the rigorous math series developed by the University of Chicago and adopted by many prestigious private schools

---

Here is part of what Texas textbook laws stipulate concerning the selection of texts to be used in Texas public schools:

Illustrations and written materials shall avoid bias toward any particular group or individual and should present a wide range of goal choices. Particular care should be taken in the treatment of ethnic groups, roles of men and women, and the dignity of workers, and respect for the work ethic. [Textbooks] shall present examples of men and women participating in a variety of roles and activities and shall further present the economic, political, social, and cultural contributions of both men and women, past and present. . . . Traditional and contemporary roles of men, women, boys, and girls shall be included. . . .

Textbook content shall promote citizenship and understanding of the essentials and benefits of the free enterprise system, emphasize patriotism and respect for recognized authority, and promote respect for individual rights. [They shall not] include selections or works which encourage or condone civil disorder, social strife, or disregard of the law, [nor shall they] contain material which serves to undermine authority . . . or which would cause embarrassing situations or interference in the learning atmosphere of the classroom. . . . [They] shall not encourage life styles deviating from generally accepted standards of society.

But Texas State Board of Education members find ways of stretching definitions. In an article about the board's annual battle over textbook bias, the Christian Science Monitor (July 22, 2003) cited two examples: "The state board rejected an environmental science book last year in part because it put the U.S. and the free enterprise system in a bad light as significant players in global warming. And, earlier this year, a history text was withdrawn by the publisher after board members objected to references of rampant prostitution in the 1800s."

(including, interestingly, Sidwell Friends Academy, the school attended by Chelsea Clinton).

How Authors Influence Textbook Content

Authors and experts in the various fields also inevitably have a say as to textbook content. Although under the thumb of political and market forces of the kind just discussed, authors do generally have scruples concerning truth telling and do tend to be constrained by professional standards. They aren't inclined to stray from the straight and narrow (as they see it!) any more than they are forced to do so. (There no doubt are rotten apples in this barrel, just as in every other, and let's pass over the charge occasionally heard that some authors of public school history and social studies texts do not have a realistic grasp of their subject matter.) But they rarely, if ever, have a genuinely free hand to "write it as they see it." (We also should mention the disgraceful fact that the authors listed on some public school textbooks sometimes have had little or nothing to do with the actual writing of their books.)

Although content is the most important element of textbooks, the clarity, the style, and the author's ability to engage the reader's interest go a long way in making the material palatable. It's little wonder that students' eyes glaze over when the style is turgid, the presentation dull, and the writing unclear. Too often books written by committees fall into this category. Once in a while, though, a textbook comes along that is not only packed with information but is interesting as well. One such book is *Environmental Science: The Way the World Works* (Prentice Hall, 2000), a science book for high school honors courses. In a very positive review of this book, *The Textbook Letter* made particular note of its narrative flair and engaging style.[22] Instead of plunging into scientific explanations, each chapter begins with a descriptive scene that sparks the reader's interest in what will follow. For instance, one chapter starts with the description of a dense fog that settled over the town of Donora, Pennsylvania, for five days in 1944. The reader's natural tendency is to wonder why there was such a dense fog and to read on for the answer. Similar techniques are used in fiction to draw the reader into the action of the story. How much more interesting textbooks would be if they used some of these narrative devices.

But Students Have Little Influence on Textbook Content

Oh, yes, students also have an indirect say in textbook content, particularly as to style and level of difficulty. Unliked books, or those that are too difficult, tend to be unread books. Teachers want the textbooks they select to be read—indeed, to be studied.[23] Anyway, that's why, in the case of public school textbooks, the term *indoctrination* isn't far off the mark. In the case of the mass media, the ultimate users of the commodity wield

---

[22] See "This Is a Fine Textbook, All in All, and I Recommend It," by Max Rodel, *The Textbook Letter,* September–October 2004.

[23] Occasionally, students make their dislike of texts known via direct political activity—for example, as some Latino and Asian ESL (English as a second language) students did in 1994 in San Francisco. But flurries of activity of this kind are unusual.

The Weekly Reader *and Channel One are not alone in this field. Here are excerpts from an article in the August 2000 issue of* The Hightower Lowdown *describing a more recent entry:*

The ZapMe! Corporation, an Internet provider that's backed by such giants as Microsoft and Dell Computer, has contracts with 6,000 schools and, on the surface, the contracts look great. The company provides computers, Internet access, maintenance, and support services free of charge. What the company gets in return, however, is an agreement that their computers will constantly flash ads at the bottom of the screen, for the four hours a day the students are supposed to be online[!]. Plus the schools must agree to hand out sponsors' promotional materials for the kids to take home. Plus ZapMe! tracks where the students go on the Web and delivers that as demographic information to its sponsors—with no control over how the information is used or to whom it can be sold.

The point, of course, is to sell students products in ways that resemble those discussed in the advertising chapter in this book. As noted earlier, in Chapter 10, math texts engage in a special kind of product advertising, asking students questions like, "How many square inches of label are on a box of Kellogg's Cocoa Frosted Flakes?" and "If a package of M&Ms includes 56 pieces and 16 are brown, what fraction of the total are brown?" But now that California, the largest textbook-adopting state, has passed a statute outlawing this sort of practice in taxpayer-financed textbooks adopted for use in California public schools, this type of plugola may soon be a thing of the past. No publisher wants to lose that vast market for their products. (For more on this, see, for instance, the June 16, 1999, San Francisco Chronicle.)*

great power (as should be evident from the discussion in the last chapter). In the case of public school textbooks, the ultimate users, students, have relatively little say. (But then, most mass media audiences consist of "responsible" adults, while public school textbook audiences are considered to be "just children" or, extrapolating from other currently popular lingo, just "preadults.")

6. CENSORSHIP

It's very difficult to determine in particular cases whether books have been censored, but the earlier discussion about the ways in which local and state boards influence textbook content should make it clear that censorship does occur. Government agencies, from the federal government down to local school boards, do in fact force changes in the content of public school texts (and also nonprint materials). Authors definitely are not free to write the books that they might prefer to; at least they cannot do so with any serious hope of having their efforts published and adopted. Textbook writers these days try very hard to tailor their works so as to be politically correct (more will be said about this shortly), just as, you will recall, do writers in the mass media.

Cartoon by Tom Meyer. © *San Francisco Chronicle*. Reprinted by permission.

The Controversy Concerning the Teaching of Evolution: An Instructive Example

All even remotely controversial topics are subject to censorship, or at least to serious attempts at censorship. The theory of evolution is an especially interesting case because, perhaps more than any other scientific theory, it goes against the grain of many deeply held religious beliefs.

Starting in 1859 with the publication of Charles Darwin's great work *On the Origin of Species,* the theory of evolution has been challenged and denied countless times and for several different reasons. But the most important of these reasons has always been that evolution theory runs counter to literal interpretations of the Old Testament. In a famous 1924 court case, commonly referred to as the "Scopes Monkey Trial," John Scopes was convicted of violating a Tennessee law against the teaching of the theory of evolution in public school classrooms. In more recent times, however, courts have systematically struck down laws like the old Tennessee statute, notably in 1962 when the United States Supreme Court declared unconstitutional an Arkansas law that banned the teaching of evolution.

After the 1962 Supreme Court decision, religious fundamentalists invented the theory they call "creation science" in an attempt to make their biblical view at least be taught alongside that of evolution theory in science classes. But in 1987, after several lower court decisions, the U.S. Supreme Court declared creation science to be religious advocacy, not science, and thus not to be taught as science in public school science classes. Although this has dealt a blow to those advocating creationism as science, it has not stopped attempts at state and local levels to flout the law; in fact, creationism is still espoused in some schools where community sentiment is highly in favor of this being done, and evolution theory is slighted in many others because of that pressure. (Interestingly, because of the Supreme Court's ruling, fundamentalists now often eschew the terms *creation* and *creation science,* instead employing the euphemism *intelligent design.*) Fundamentalists still attempt to picture evolution as just one theory (as the name "theory of evolution" implies to those who don't understand scientific lingo) and to get the biblical account in Genesis taught alongside it. In Alabama, for instance, textbooks must warn students that evolution is "controversial" and an "unproven belief." [24] (In fairness, it needs to be said that at least some advocates of creation science believe it to be scientific.)

Nevertheless, the relative failure of religious fundamentalists in their attempt to counter the teaching of evolution and to get creation science taught in science classes has not reduced their efforts. Indeed, in recent years pressure on state and local school

---

Evolution is often discounted as "just a theory," and, in fact, the concept was extremely controversial in the past. But with the continued gathering of substantiated evidence for 150 years, it has finally been validated. Here is an explanation of why scientists today would accept evolution not merely as a theory, but as an overarching set of principles or laws. *

In the physical sciences there are many observations or facts that have given rise to generalizations. . . . The statements of facts and their convenient generalization to laws are expressed in terms of macroscopically observable and weighable quantities. The overarching explanation for these laws is achieved in atomic theory, which is expressed in terms of invisible atoms and molecules. No one thinks that atomic theory is "just a theory," for it possesses extraordinary explanatory power and provides the context in which many of the conveniences of our civilization depend. Thus we proceed from many observations or facts to their generalization in terms of laws, both levels macroscopic, to a theory expressed in terms of invisible entities.

   If we now apply this scheme to biology, we see that the concept of evolution is at the law level, as it summarizes the results of a large number of observations or facts about organisms. The analogous theory is natural selection or other means by which evolution is achieved. Unknown nearly 150 years ago to Darwin, explanations of macroscopic evolution in terms of microscopic genes and molecular sequences of nucleic bases in DNA are known to us. Placing the concept of evolution at the law level clarifies its status; it is not a theory.

*Taken from "Neither Intelligent nor Designed," by Bruce and Frances Martin, *Skeptical Inquirer,* November/December 2003.

---

[24] For more on these recent trends, see "Monkey Business," by Eugenie C. Scott, in *The Sciences* (January/February 1996), or the November–December 1996 issue of *The Textbook Letter.*

boards and on individual schools has increased, no doubt due to the increase in enthusiasm for fundamentalist religion in the United States (as in many other countries).[25]

The fight that went on in Kansas in 1999 and 2000 illustrates this point. In spite of previous failures, in August 1999, the Kansas Board of Education voted to remove almost all references to evolution from its required curriculum, making it optional for teachers to cover the origins and history of life on Earth or any evolutionary principles that make the Earth older than creationists believe. (They included astronomical, geological, and cosmological theories such as the "Big Bang," plate tectonics, and so on.) But in August 2000, citizens in Kansas voted out several members of the board who had favored the creationists' position, and the new board has rescinded the antievolution directive. A similar reversal occurred in Texas, in November 2003, where the State Board of Education rejected previous attempts by religious conservatives to water down the theory of evolution, and adopted instead a new approach to biology textbooks, acknowledging that the theory is widely enough accepted to be considered a cornerstone of scientific research.

Before going on to other matters, it is worth noting, first, that many high school science teachers believe in the creationist position and would like to teach creationism alongside evolution theory in biology classes and, second, that a significant number of high school science teachers do not have a satisfactory grasp on their subject matter, as many studies have shown.

Interestingly, Darwin himself did not believe that his theory of evolution was antithetical to belief in the existence of a creator. In fact, the last sentence in his classic book *On the Origin of Species* affirms such a belief:

> There is a grandeur in this view of life, with its several powers, having been originally breathed by the Creator into a few forms or into one; and that, whilst this planet has gone cycling on according to the fixed law of gravity, from so simple a beginning endless forms most beautiful and wonderful have been, and are being evolved.

It is difficult to be sure why the very well-organized fundamentalists are not winning more battles than they do, but one reason has to be the pressure exerted by an aroused scientific community, worried that a generation of scientific illiterates will be raised in the United States. Eminent scientists, for example, testified in the court cases mentioned before that creation science is not a science and convinced courts to hold that this is the case. Nevertheless, fundamentalists have not given up the fight by any means and, indeed, have had success at the local level in many places where large numbers of parents do not want students to be taught that evolution theory is a fact.

Interestingly, religious fundamentalists are largely responsible for one of the improvements in recent public school textbooks—namely, the very modestly improved treatment of the topic of religion in American life. After World War II, and up to just a

---

[25] Note, however, that other sorts of books espousing the creationist viewpoint sometimes are used in public schools, especially in states such as Louisiana and Texas, where fundamentalist interpretations of the Bible are widely accepted. Also of interest is the fact that the influence of fundamentalist Jewish and Muslim groups on public school education has been comparatively slight because these groups constitute only a tiny minority in America today.

Although the majority of biology textbooks in use today in public schools in America hold the line, more or less, against fundamentalist censorship demands, they do so in different ways. In some cases they teach evolution theory as a very well-confirmed scientific theory and simply ignore creationism entirely. That is the way the problem is handled, for instance, in one of the best biology textbooks.* In other texts, creationism is briefly mentioned and then dismissed, as illustrated by this excerpt from a rather good, although "linguistically simplified" text:†

When [H.M.S.] *Beagle* sailed from England [in 1831, Charles] Darwin, like most people of his time, believed in creationism. . . . According to creationists, God designed each kind of animal and plant to match its particular habitat. Thus, places with similar environments have similar kinds of plants and animals. Moreover, creationists believe that species are unchanging.

During his journey Darwin often left the ship to collect specimens of animals, plants, and fossils. His observations led him to doubt creationism and its assumption of unchanging species.

This text then describes some of Darwin's findings, including those concerning the famous finches on the Galápagos Islands, findings that provided Darwin with very good evidence for what became his theory of evolution and natural selection.

Another way in which biology texts respond to religious challenges to evolution theory is illustrated by this excerpt from a somewhat better-than-average high school biology textbook, in which "Creation science" is dealt with in a section titled Pseudoscience:‡

"Creation science" is not science because its working assumptions cannot be examined by scientific methods. The word *creation* is associated with religion and a supreme being. It is, therefore, a matter of faith—not of scientific investigation. Furthermore, creationists resist modifying their model even when observations fail to support it. These characteristics do not exclude creationism from a place in the school curriculum. Rather, they strongly suggest that creationism should be taught as a religious belief and not as a scientific theory.

* Modern Biology, by Albert Towle (Holt, Rinehart & Winston, 1999).
† Biology: Visualizing Life, by George B. Johnson (Holt, Rinehart & Winston, 1994).
‡ Biological Science: A Molecular Approach, 6th edition (Heath, 1996). The revision is by a team of seven writers from Colorado College, Colorado Springs.

few years ago, religion tended to get mentioned only in the colonial period, except for accounts of the Mormons' great trek west in the nineteenth century and the inauguration of the first (and so far only) Catholic president, John F. Kennedy, in 1960. Most of the newer texts today provide much more information than that about the role religion has played in American life, even if their accounts still have a bit of the flavor of a token gesture. (Now that a Jew—Joseph Leiberman—has been nominated by a major political party for the vice presidency of the United States, we can expect Jews and the Jewish religion to become a more noticeable feature of public school textbooks. Will the extent

From about the time just after World War II until very recently, science textbooks steadily improved both in accuracy and in content. But the "dumbing down" of public school textbooks mentioned before has affected some science texts, just like those concerning history and social studies. The idea seems to be to make science texts easier to read (by shortening sentences and limiting vocabulary), more interesting (by making science "relevant" and by pandering to pseudoscience), and, of course, politically correct (by fudging facts of geography, anthropology, and so forth). A great many excellent textbooks are still available, but there also are some that seriously cross over the line. An example is Prentice Hall's *Exploring Earth Science* (1995). This science text goes out of its way to discuss astrology (without ever using that term) in a chapter dealing with astronomy, leaving the impression that astrology has some scientific merit, or at least some truth to it. (Interestingly, the account of astrology is historically false.) At the end of the short discussion, students are asked, "Under what sign were you born? Do you know how your emotions are supposed to be affected by your sign?" No mention is made of the fact that emotions are not affected by signs of the zodiac. (This text also contains a gratuitous discussion of the completely unscientific Oriental theory of yin and yang—included to make the text "multicultural"?).*

*For more about this and two other poor-quality science textbooks, see the September–October 1996 issue of *The Textbook Letter.* Every issue of this excellent publication discusses and evaluates recent public school textbooks in the various disciplines.

of anti-Semitism during the course of U.S. history now be mentioned? If what happened after the election of Catholic John F. Kennedy provides a clue, we can expect only a token gesture in this direction.)

Publisher Self-Censorship

Given what has been said so far, it shouldn't come as a surprise that publishers have become exceedingly cautious in the editing of public school textbooks or that they try very hard not to offend powerful special-interest groups. This is especially true with respect to grade school textbooks, as might be expected, because most parents want their children apprised of the harsher realities of life rather slowly. (Few see anything wrong in telling tiny tots that there is a Santa Claus or a tooth fairy.)

This caution on the part of publishers sometimes has rather ludicrous consequences. For example, a West Coast publisher asked one of its illustrators to remove the stem from a picture of a plum because it cast a shadow that might be construed as phallic. Harcourt Brace, a very large textbook publisher, once had an artist remove a mother's apron from a drawing picturing a typical eighteenth-century family scene because the apron was seen to be "demeaning to women." (Never mind that the portrayal was accurate.) Some publishers no longer allow udders on drawings of cows or flies on the trousers of little boys.

In the old days, when Dick and Jane reigned supreme, the world was portrayed as having a gardenlike quality. Slums did not exist, nasty people were restricted to fairy tales, almost everyone was white, and women were primarily pictured as housewives and mothers. The pressures on publishers were different, so the product was different.

Textbook publishers inevitably try to make their products be as politically correct as possible; what changes over time is what counts as politically correct.

Currently the most significant source of self-censorship is the bias guidelines issued by every educational publisher. They all conduct bias and sensitivity reviews that regulate the way textbook authors discuss ethnic and minority groups, including women, the disabled, and the elderly, and they respond to both liberal and conservative pressure groups. In one sense, this is understandable, given the strong impetus to eliminate discrimination since the 1960s, but guidelines have gone way beyond their original intent, as Diane Ravitch points out in *The Language Police,* an excellent analysis of test and textbook bias. Here are a few examples she cites to give you the flavor of constraints placed on authors. (These are drawn from the Scott Foresman-Addison Wesley and McGraw Hill guidelines.)[26]

Writers must include women in equal numbers with men in both the text and illustrations (despite the fact that men have dominated Western culture up to and including much of the twentieth century—like it or not). But they must avoid such stereotypes as passive, weak, gentle, illogical, short, or emotional women and active, strong, brave, logical, tall, or unemotional men. Sexist terms like *sissy, tomboy, lady, hen-pecked husband,* and *forefathers* are out. Disabled people must never be referred to as "the disabled" but as "people with disabilities." The blind and the deaf should be called "people

---

"Make Sure It's Not Iceberg"

Irene Trivas, an artist, stopped accepting assignments to illustrate children's readers partly out of frustration over publishers' efforts to be "everything to everybody," as she put it. Here is her account of the instructions she received for one book:

It's etched in acid in my mind. They sent 10 pages of single-spaced specifications.

The hero was a Hispanic boy.

There were black twins, one boy, one girl; an overweight Oriental boy, and an American Indian girl.

That leaves the Caucasian.

Since we mustn't forget the physically handicapped, she was born with a congenital malformation and only had three fingers on one hand.

One child had to have an Irish setter, and the setter was to be female.

The Hispanic kid had two parents. The father has a white-collar job. The mother is an illustrator and she works at home.

At one point, they are seen through the kitchen screen door making dinner, having spaghetti and meatballs and a salad. The editor appended a note that said: "Make sure it's not iceberg; it should be something nice like endive."

They also had a senior citizen, and I had to show her jogging.

I can't do it anymore.*

*Copyright © 1990 by the New York Times Company. Reprinted by permission.

---

[26] See Chapter 12 of *The Language Police* for a full account of these bias and sensitivity reviews.

who are blind" and "people who are deaf," and midgets and dwarfs are "people of small stature." But it's just as bad to call someone "normal" or "able-bodied"; the correct term, instead, is "a person without disabilities" or "a person who is nondisabled"!

The discussion of ethnic and racial groups is closely monitored as well. Writers must present "a fair and balanced representation" of racial, ethnic, and gender groups in text and illustrations. Here is a random sampling. Authors cannot refer to "primitive cultures" because there are no primitive cultures. African tribes have been replaced by ethnic groups, and they don't live in huts but in little houses. Illustrators must not draw African Americans in loud colors or prints, straw hats, and white suits—or in middle-class clothes. They can't show these people in tenements and bright cars or in "dull, white picket-fence neighborhoods." Given these constraints, one wonders how African Americans *can* be depicted, or for that matter, why anyone would want to write a textbook to begin with (except, of course, the intrepid authors of this text).

Nontextbooks Also Often Are Censored

Books that are not explicitly textbooks often are subjected to censorship. The censor in most of these cases is the local school board, but state boards have been getting into the act in recent years.

The number of books and magazines censored out of public school classrooms and libraries runs into the thousands every year. Here are a few striking examples: *

Of Mice and Men (John Steinbeck)
The Sun Also Rises (Ernest Hemingway)
The Catcher in the Rye (J. D. Salinger)
The Grapes of Wrath (John Steinbeck)
Look Homeward Angel (Thomas Wolfe)
The Invisible Man (Ralph Ellison)
Native Son (Richard Wright)
Brave New World (Aldous Huxley)
Slaughterhouse Five (Kurt Vonnegut, Jr.)
To Kill a Mockingbird (Harper Lee)
The Naked Ape (Desmond Morris)
I Know Why the Caged Bird Sings (Maya Angelou)
Ms. magazine
(The *American Heritage Dictionary* was banned because it includes "gutter words" like *ball, nut,* and *tail* and cites certain uses of the term *bed* as a transitive verb.)

Oh, yes. Perhaps in an attempt to prove that George Orwell is the Nostradamus of the twentieth century, lots of school districts have banned use of . . . 1984.

*See the American Library Association's *Newsletter on Intellectual Freedom*.

Almost any kind of book may be censored, but most that are contain passages alleged to be obscene, racially or ethnically biased, slighting or demeaning of women, or providing a favorable portrayal of a lifestyle claimed to be immoral. A Tennessee county school board, for example, removed the old standby *Drums Along the Mohawk* from an assigned list because it contained words judged to be obscene, such as *hell* and *damn.* Shakespeare's *The Merchant of Venice* is sometimes censored because Jewish groups object to its portrayal of Shylock, and a New Hampshire school banned *Twelfth Night* because it violated a school board ruling that prohibited alternative lifestyle instruction. (Viola, the heroine, is disguised as a boy who inadvertently becomes romantically entangled with another woman, Olivia.)

A bit sillier was the removal from California's annual English exam list for tenth graders of the short story "Am I Blue," by Pulitzer Prize–winning author Alice Walker—removed primarily because it was "anti-meat-eating." But perhaps silliest of all, surely the most ironic, is the fact that one of the most frequently censored books is *The Adventures of Huckleberry Finn.* Sam Clemens would have been amused, but not surprised. The Clemens classic has two groups on its back: fundamentalists and others offended by its portrayal of religion and by the way Huck flouts conventional morality, and African Americans offended by its portrayal of Negroes and by the racist language it puts into the mouths of bigoted slave owners. Irony of ironies: One of the schools that has censored *Huck Finn* turns out to be Mark Twain Intermediate School in Fairfax County, Virginia. Censoring *Huck Finn* is ironic, of course, because Clemens intended his great work to expose the evils of slavery—precisely what civil rights groups today want every American to remember.

It would be provincial, however, to conclude that public school book censoring is a uniquely American phenomenon. On the contrary, this sort of censorship, like most other kinds, is less frequent and less severe in the United States than in most, perhaps all, other countries. Every nation dolls up its past, for the same reasons that we do so in the United States, and many censor on religious grounds or out of a sense of propriety. In Germany, starting after World War II and continuing to a lesser extent until the mid-1990s, history texts have understandably played down the atrocities committed by Germans during that most horrible of all wars—so far!—and teachers still often engage in their own kind of censorship by simply never quite finding sufficient time to cover that period in German history adequately. Similar remarks, incidentally, apply more or less to the teaching of Japanese history in Japan. And Soviet texts didn't bother to mention the millions killed by the Soviets during Stalin's reigns of terror or the smaller but still extremely large number of people worked to death in Siberia even after his death.

Needless to say, authoritarian regimes have absolute control over the education of their young. Before Saddam Hussein was ousted, schoolbooks in Iraq were vehicles for Baathist party propaganda. History books traced the dictator's ancestry back to a cousin

---

[W]hen American scholars talk about . . . Soviet texts which blatantly indoctrinate, they are called brainwashing. When our own texts are biased, prejudiced, one-sided and unfair, it is called "transmitting a favorable view of our democracy.

—S. Samuel Shermis

of the prophet Muhammed and compared him to great leaders of the past. His quotes were sprinkled throughout math texts, and his name was incorporated into English primers in birthday greetings and songs to Father Saddam. Iraqi teachers are now at work deleting this garbage from their schoolbooks.

Although the censoring of books outside public schools' walls (and also most schools that are religiously sponsored) always has been, and still is, much less common than it is within these walls, it does occur, and this obviously limits what students as well as adults can read. Favorite targets are books with sexual content and those affecting national security.

In the long history of censorship, however, all sorts of books have been banned. Way back in 1526, the first English translation of the New Testament was banned and printed copies burned; in Spain, a similar fate awaited the first translation into Spanish. Indeed, the Bible may be the most censored book in history. For decades, *Lysistrata, Canterbury Tales, Decameron, Moll Flanders,* and versions of the *Arabian Nights* were banned from U.S. mails under the Federal Anti-Obscenity Act (the Comstock Law of 1873), and *Fanny Hill,* the story of a prostitute told with explicit sexual descriptions, has been suppressed on and off since its publication in 1749. D. H. Lawrence's *Lady Chatterly's Lover* was in and out of obscenity trials until the 1960s and James Joyce's *Ulysses,* voted the best novel of the 20th century by the Modern Library, was banned in this country for 11 years (1922–1933) because of its obscenities.

In the 1980s censorship focused more on sex and swear words, but as we moved into the new millennium, the emphasis switched to witchcraft and wizardry. For several years the Harry Potter series headed the American Library Association's list of most challenged (that is, banned) books. Although most readers enjoy as fantasy the tales of sorcerers and magic spells, some take them literally as corrupting forces of evil; others are concerned about the clash between Christianity and witchcraft, still others by the depiction of family dysfunction and violence. In 2003, the Alice series (*Alice in Agony, Simply Alice, Alice the Brave,* and so on) topped the Harry Potter series, criticized for the usual reasons—too sexually explicit and too many swear words. If fairy tales were as popular now as the Alice and Harry Potter series, they'd probably be banned too. (In fact, they have been cleaned up over the years—for example, in Grimm's version of "Cinderella," her mean stepsisters were brutally punished at the end when pigeons plucked out their eyes in the wedding procession. How many kids hear that version today?)[27]

7. TEXTBOOKS FAIL TO GIVE STUDENTS GENUINE UNDERSTANDING

From what has been said so far, it should be clear that public school textbooks fail to give students a true understanding of the history and workings of their society. They, and schools in general, fail to orient students in space and time—fail to help them understand how life is different from place to place and, in particular, from one time to another. These failures are due primarily to defects in style and content of the kinds we have been at pains to describe—defects, we have suggested, that result from the various forces at work shaping the finished products, in particular, conflicting pressures from interested social groups.

[27] See Banned Books Online for further examples. Digital.library.upenn.edu/banned-books.htm

If you're still wondering whether all that much progress has occurred in textbook quality in recent years, this snippet from a really bad textbook still in circulation as late as 1970 should provide a bit of evidence:

As you ride up beside the Negroes in the field they stop working long enough to look up, tip their hats and say, "Good morning, Master John." You like the friendly way they speak and smile; they show bright rows of white teeth. "How's it coming, Sam?" your father asks one of the old Negroes. "Fine, Marse Tom, jes fine. We got more cotton than we can pick." Then Sam chuckles to himself and goes back to picking as fast as he can.

—Mentioned in *The New Republic* (July 25,1970);
the book's title is best omitted here.

If that sort of writing doesn't make every current textbook look wonderfully good, nothing will.

But it is important to understand that these defects do not result from something peculiar to the American system. The textbooks of any democratic society are bound to reflect the different opinions and interests of its citizens. To have it otherwise would be to surrender control of this important part of our lives to others, as is the case in most authoritarian societies around the world. While fighting to make textbooks better than they are today, we should not forget how much they have improved since, say, the authors of this college text went to school (eons ago, when dinosaurs still roamed the Earth).

One final comment. The praise that has been somewhat begrudgingly given to today's public school textbooks [28] in this chapter should not cloud the fact that the writers of this college text do not care for the large doses of indoctrination they contain. This text was written in a completely different spirit. A student who accepts its contents uncritically, without thinking carefully about the subjects discussed, has missed its main point, which is that in important or controversial matters, free men and women must become their own experts, or at least must be able to judge for themselves the opinions and advice of those who call themselves experts. The success of a free society depends on an informed and thinking electorate, not on an indoctrinated one.

8. POSTSCRIPT ON COLLEGE TEXTS

The question naturally arises about college textbooks: Do they distort American history and practice as do public school texts? Do science texts fudge in their portrayal of evolution theory? If the forces at work are the same with respect to college as public school

---

[28] The history and social studies books used in private schools are, with rare exceptions, quite similar to those discussed here, except for some of the textbooks used in schools run by organized churches. Of course, in some of the very best private schools, original sources—books intended for adult readers—are more in evidence than are texts designed explicitly for schoolroom use. (Yes, the schools attended by the offspring of the rich are indeed better than the ones the rest of us are subjected to.)

texts, we should expect the results to be roughly the same (taking into account the greater maturity of college students). If they aren't, we should expect the finished products to be different. What do our worldviews tell us about this question?

Note first that the publishers of college texts have exactly the same motives as those who produce public school textbooks. In fact, most publishers in one field also publish in the other. Second, most college texts are adopted by the teachers who will use them in their own classes (or, in the case of courses having several sections, by group faculty decisions), not by school boards or state agencies. (Students buy them but can't choose which ones to buy.)

The reason for this important difference is the history and the current funding of higher education in the United States as compared to primary and secondary education. Primary and secondary school traditions are largely "homegrown" and intended for a mass audience. Public school teachers have always had their rights to academic freedom infringed upon by local school boards or, more accurately, never had such rights. But American colleges and universities evolved on the model of their European counterparts (chiefly in Germany and England), which were intended for an elite clientele. Professors, at least, were granted a great deal of academic freedom. (They were, of course, more constrained under monarchical systems, and professorial freedoms were nonexistent during the Nazi period in Germany and, to a lesser extent, during the Fascist period in Italy.) The result of transplanting this tradition to the United States, the freest Western society, has been academic freedom for almost all faculty members; thus, college teachers have always had the privilege of selecting the books they and their students will use.[29] It follows, then, as night follows day, that college textbook publishers will try to produce books that please college teachers—their potential adopters.

College teachers, however, do not operate in a vacuum. They, too, have an audience to consider—their students—and many students, unfortunately, are not as well prepared to do college work as typical students were, say, 40 years ago. (This obviously tends to be less true of students in "elite" colleges and universities.) One reason for this fact is that a larger proportion of young people go to college today than in times past, when only brighter students (and a few who were merely rich) went to college. But another reason is that over the years, more and more students have become victims of the "dumbing down" of grade and high school texts mentioned a while back and find it difficult to comprehend some of the more high-powered college texts. They are more easily intimidated by thick books or those written in past centuries in a dense or a different style. College teachers, being human, often react (consciously or unconsciously) to the problem this raises by selecting textbooks and works of literature that are relatively brief and more easily understood. Reading lists have been shortened; books perceived as "weighty tomes" tend to get neglected in introductory courses.[30]

---

[29] More precisely, almost all *tenured* faculty members. Nontenured faculty still have to worry about offending those who determine who will be rehired and who "terminated." This benefit of the tenure system often is overlooked but is of great importance. (Nontenured faculty also usually are paid a good deal less than the tenured variety. But that is a topic for another time, another class.)

[30] There also is the fact that what is "in" at one time may well become "out" at another; textbook selection tends to reflect these changes, especially the dramatic changes in course offerings. Forty years ago, for example, there were no courses in critical reasoning. Most schools required courses

Anyway, college texts, wherever they may rest on an absolute scale, are genuinely unlike their public school counterparts. College teachers want widely differing textbook content and levels of difficulty, creating a market in which all sorts of views and qualities find a constituency. College texts even tend to be less dull than their lower-level counterparts, a happy note on which to end this particular—immensely interesting, entertaining, and completely unbiased—college textbook.

SUMMARY OF CHAPTER 12

Public school textbooks in America have improved a great deal in the past 25 years or so.

1. History and social studies texts are more accurate in their portrayal of minorities and women and in the way in which they deal with the dark side of the social system and history of the United States. But textbooks still are written in a dull, one-fact-after-another style that makes true understanding, and also retention of specific facts, quite difficult. They also have reflected the general "dumbing down" that has occurred in public schools and colleges during the past several years.

2. History texts tend to bombard students with almost endless lists of forgettable facts that tend to bury important information. They also distort reality so as to satisfy the various interested pressure groups and to mold students into good, loyal citizens. They portray American presidents and heroes in a one-sided manner (for instance, not mentioning the vicious, bloodthirsty side of President Theodore Roosevelt). They also exaggerate the American role in world affairs (as in World War II) and play down the nasty side of U.S. history. *Example:* Putting down the Filipino attempt to gain independence.

3. Although today's social studies texts are light-years better than those of even 30 years ago, they still say relatively little about the large gulf between theory—how the American social system is supposed to work—and practice—how it actually works in everyday life. For example, they don't tell students about the preferential treatment often given to the rich and powerful (how they are sent to cushy jails when they are convicted of crimes, for instance) and play down the corruption that is common in government. *Example:* At best only hinting at the extent to which governments are corrupted by lobbying and by campaign contributions.

4. The ultimate purpose of public schools is to educate the young to fit into the adult world. Textbooks are intended to provide students with the knowledge they will need to be productive citizens and to inculcate the values, customs, and attitudes of the society as a whole. (That is why it is accurate to speak of indoctrination.)

---

in formal logic, usually taught in philosophy or math departments, and these obviously did deal with the principles of good conclusion drawing. Critical reasoning was taught by English department instructors primarily in the context of the writing of argumentative essays. That is why there was only one true critical reasoning textbook (Monroe Beardsley's *Thinking Straight,* mentioned in Chapter 7) in common use prior to *Logic and Contemporary Rhetoric*'s appearance on the scene in 1971.

We can expect, then, that noncontroversial topics will be presented in a more or less straightforward manner, while topics that are controversial, or sensitive—in particular, those connected to the history and social practices of society—will tend to pull punches and portray matters in the best light possible.

5. Just as in the case of the mass media, politics enters into the textbook business. Because they are a commodity, textbooks are written so as to satisfy potential buyers, which means primarily local school boards, state agencies, and the professional educators who are empowered to make selections. Political considerations enter in at every level—local, state, and national.

   Although the details change from time to time, there is nothing new in this intrusion of politics into the educational arena. Even the very idea of public school education is political, there being no public schools whatsoever in the United States until some time in the nineteenth century.

   Big business, of course, has some power over textbook content, but less than it does, say, concerning how the news is presented in the mass media. But it does have some power, including power derived from its ability to lobby state legislatures and local school boards.

   The most important of the state agencies concerned with textbook selection are those of California and Texas.

6. Pressure groups have been rather successful—indeed, sometimes oversuccessful—with respect to their demands that textbooks be politically correct by increasing coverage of minorities, women, and religion in American history and life, leading publishers to tailor their products to fit expected pressure group preferences. Many of these demands have been incorporated into bias guidelines that are the most significant source of self-censorship for educational publishers. But attempts to have discussions of creation science included in biology texts, either alone or alongside evolution theory, on the whole have not been successful.

   It should be noted that nontextbooks also sometimes are censored by public schools, including classic works of literature (by such writers as Ernest Hemingway, Mark Twain, and more recently J. K. Rowlings for the Harry Potter series) as well as dictionaries listing four-letter words.

7. The result is that textbooks fail to provide students with genuine understanding or even, because of their dull styles and piling on of facts, knowledge of particular facts that is retained for any length of time. They do, however, reflect what organized groups and professional educators want students to read, which is as it should be in a democratic society.

8. But college texts, having a different sort of clientele, are different. (Vive la difference.)

EXERCISE 12-1

1. Here is a famous quote by Northrop Frye: "Censorship is to dissent (and democracy) what lynching is to justice." Evaluate this quote, in particular, discussing the charge that it contains a fallacy.

2. Now here is a (fortunately) much less famous quote by Mel Gabler, of Educational Research Analysis (a pressure group that has had success, particularly in Texas): "When a student reads in a math book that there are no absolutes, suddenly every value he's been taught is destroyed. And the next thing you know, the student turns to crime and drugs."

    a. What is Gabler's (unstated) point? What is he advocating, and why?

    b. Evaluate his argument, again considering the charge that his reasoning is fallacious.

3. The Alabama State Education Department requires that the following disclaimer be included in all biology texts used in Alabama public schools that include an account of evolution and evolutionary theory:

    > This textbook discusses evolution, a controversial theory some scientists present as a scientific explanation for the origin of living things, such as plants, animals, and humans. No one was present when life first appeared on the earth; therefore any statement about life's origins should be considered as theory, not fact.

    Critically evaluate this disclaimer.

EXERCISE 12-2

1. At what point in their educational careers do you think students are ready to be taught the biological facts concerning human sex and reproduction? Or do you think these topics should not be broached in public schools? Defend your answers.

2. Recall the excerpt on page 321 from Paul Fussell's book about GIs in World War II and the textual remarks about the horrors of war (soldiers being blown apart and so forth).

    a. In your opinion, should high school textbooks tell students things like this about war? Defend your view on this.

    b. In fact, they never describe these things. Why do you think this is so? Again, defend your answer.

3. It has been forcefully argued that very young children are tender shoots who need to find out the bad features of their society (as of life in general) rather gradually, so that it would be wrong to tell them too quickly that quite a few presidents (including such "heroes" as Franklin Roosevelt and John Kennedy) had mistresses, that the bribes taken by the "Keating Five" were just the tip of the iceberg, or that America's history is filled with nasty deeds and steeped in blood and conquest. The point of these arguments is that we don't want to destroy the pride and loyalty of the young, and we don't want to make future citizens into cynics.

    a. Do you agree or disagree with this line of reasoning? Defend your answer.

    b. Does it tend to undercut one of the themes of this chapter—that less indoctrination means better education?

    c. At what age, if ever, should students be given a completely accurate and balanced account of these matters?

d. It has been argued that, in a society such as exists today in the United States, where several religions flourish and there is no single moral code accepted by all, public schools should not attempt to teach students about alleged values, customs, or traditions of the culture. What is your opinion on this question and, of course, why do you think so?

*4. Does the term *creation science* ring a bell with respect to a topic discussed in an earlier chapter in this book? Explain.

5. Recall how the Boston Massacre was described in your history textbooks back in high school. Then look up that event in a first-rate history book and describe the differences. (Hint: If there are no differences, either your high school history text was the best ever published, or your memory is poor or your new source is not a first-rate book.)

6. Evaluate the following argument:

Because evolution cannot be reproduced in the laboratory, it should not be taught as though it is the only theory believed by sane individuals concerning the origins of life on Earth.

EXERCISE 12-3

Here is Lewis Lapham in *Harper's* magazine essay (August 2000) explaining why he believes that today's public schools are as poor as he thinks they are:

Why . . . do the public schools continue to decay . . . [?] Possibly because the condition of the public schools is neither an accident nor a mistake. The schools as presently constituted serve the interests of a society content to define education as a means of indoctrination and a way of teaching people to know their place. We have one set of schools for the children of the elite, another for children less fortunately born, and why disrupt the seating arrangement with a noisy shuffling of chairs? Serious reform of the public schools would beg too many questions about racial prejudice, the class system, the division of the nation's spoils. A too-well-educated public might prove more trouble than it's worth, and so we mask our tacit approval of an intellectually inferior result with the declarations of a morally superior purpose. . . .

What do you think of some of Lapham's claims, for instance, that we have a two-tiered school system, that issues concerning racial prejudice and our class system (is there one?) intrude, and that there is tacit approval of the intellectually inferior result?

EXERCISE 12-4

Here is a short excerpt from a video, *Fueling America's Future,* produced by the Shell Oil Company and distributed to many high schools:

[Two young people of about high school age are driving through the countryside.]

FEMALE: Oh, what a beautiful day, . . . Hear the sounds, smell the smells.
MALE: Ah, birds, flowers, newly mowed grass.

FEMALE: I'm talking about the sound of an internal combustion engine! The smell of the open road!

MALE: But what about the wonders of nature?

FEMALE: What about the wonders of cars and trucks? Planes and gasoline?

MALE: What are you talking about?

FEMALE: That's how we travel. See the sights. Live where we want. Work where we want.

MALE: What about nature?

FEMALE: It takes gasoline to power the vehicles that get us to nature. And gasoline comes from nature.

MALE: Gasoline comes from nature?

FEMALE: Sure! . . . [F]rom the sea! Millions of years ago, . . . billions of tiny sea creatures and plants lived there, and when they died, their remains sank to the bottom of the sea floor. . . .

MALE: Right. Scientists think that the earth's crust buckled and shifted and got all mangled and turned all that sea life into petroleum products. . . .

FEMALE: [I]n 1908, horseless carriages started to be mass produced. That's what they called cars.

MALE: . . . Because they didn't need horses to pull them?

FEMALE: Right. But they did need . . .

MALE: Gasoline. . . .

FEMALE: Right. . . . This person looks at a horse and a carriage, thinks about it, and invents the impossible—a car with an engine to run it, instead of a horse!

MALE: *Now that is amazing.*

FEMALE: Hey, it's the spirit of America! . . . doing something that can't be done! Thinking and trying and figuring until you can do the impossible. . . .

MALE: But with all those cars, we also got smog.

FEMALE: Well, that's why the spirit of America went to work again. New gas nozzles introduced in 1976 take 120 tons of smog out of the air every day! . . .

1. In your opinion, how accurate is this snippet from the Shell Oil video? Why do you think so?

2. Do you think this video is appropriate for use in high school classrooms? Why, or why not? (Isn't it appropriate to teach sutdents about where gas and oil come from and how they are a natural product whose use enables us to take drives through the countryside?)

*EXERCISE FOR THE ENTIRE TEXT

This text, like all others, is based on certain presuppositions (only some made explicit) and no doubt contains fallacious reasoning, in spite of the authors' best efforts to reason cogently. So, as the final exercise, write a brief critique of this textbook with respect to (1) its major presuppositions (that is, the worldviews of the authors as stated or implied in the text); (2) possible fallacious arguments; (3) biased selections of material; and (4) rhetorical devices used to persuade readers to accept the authors' opinions on this or that. (Be sure to defend your findings, including examples to back up your claims.)

Dennis the Menace® used by permission of Hank Ketcham
and © by North America Syndicate.

"It'll stop, Joey. It always has before."

A youthful inductionist at work.

APPENDIX: MORE ON COGENT REASONING

1. MORE ON CAUSE AND EFFECT

In Chapter 1, we said a few words about how inductive reasoning is used to discover causal relationships—to discover how one thing causes another. But just as in the case of most interesting concepts, that of causation is really a cluster of related concepts, mostly with blurred edges. When we call one thing the cause of another, we can mean simply the **sufficient condition** for bringing it about. In this sense, the cause of Marie Antoinette's death was being guillotined—having one's head cut off certainly suffices to bring about death.

On the other hand, we often mean by the cause of a thing or event whatever is a **necessary condition** for bringing it about. Striking a match on a rough surface (thus heating it) can be thought of, for example, as a necessary condition of the lighting of a match, even though it is only part of what must be true for the effect—the lighting of the match—to occur. It is a necessary condition, but not a sufficient condition: Matches also need to be dry and struck in the presence of oxygen if they are to light. Being in the presence of oxygen and being dry and being heated together constitute both the necessary and the sufficient conditions for a match to light.

The point here is that, even though striking a match (heating it) cannot alone cause a match to light, we still in everyday life talk as though striking a match is what makes it light. It usually makes perfectly good sense to say, for instance, that the match lit because it was struck on a rough surface (which heats the match to the required temperature), even though a match struck on a rough surface in a vacuum will not light (because of a lack of oxygen). But we would not say, for example, that it lit because it was in the presence of oxygen. The difference, roughly speaking, is *human agency*—in everyday life, it's easy to make a match light by striking it (heating it), but we can't usually make it light by providing oxygen. (For one thing, the oxygen already is there; for another, the match still won't light because ordinary air temperatures are too low.)

Also of interest is the fact that we sometimes need to distinguish between **proximate causes** and those that are more **remote.** Suppose that a truck jackknifes on an icy highway, blocking three of four lanes, and that an auto, call it auto A, has to swerve into the unblocked lane and that another auto, B, then crashes into auto A. The ice on the road would be said to be the proximate cause of the truck's jackknifing but a much more remote cause of the accident between autos A and B.

The difference between proximate and remote causes can be important in everyday life, in particular in legal cases. Clearly, auto A's swerving into the last unblocked lane is a proximate cause of the crash between A and B, yet the driver of A may well not be held responsible, since his need to go into that lane was caused by more remote events. The guilty party more likely will be held to be the driver of the truck for driving without sufficient care on an icy highway.

This example brings to mind the fact that, in everyday life, a given effect can be explained in terms of more than one cause. Which one we select usually depends on our particular interest in that effect. In assessing blame, say, in the case of a knife murder, we don't care about the neural and muscular causes of the murderer's arm movement, but we do care very much about his having consciously willed to do the act. A biologist, on the other hand, might be very interested indeed in neural firings in the guilty party's body, and in a court of law might well testify to neural and muscular causes of the knife blow. So it makes sense to say either that the willing caused the event or that the neural firings and muscle contractions did so.[1]

2. SCIENTIFIC METHOD

Scientific method is just common sense writ large, sharpened, fine-tuned, and applied (in the best cases) with creative persistence and patience. There is nothing mysterious or impenetrable about how scientists go about justifying their hypotheses.

Common sense requires that beliefs about the nature of the world be justified, more or less, by cogent arguments, as discussed in earlier chapters. Scientists have no other way, no magic formulas or wands, for coming to justified beliefs about the nature of the world. Science's "secret" lies in the persistent accumulation of knowledge by thousands (now literally millions) of practitioners who have required of each other the elimination so far as is possible of the shoddy, wishful thinking that peppers everyday reasoning. The rules of the scientific game force scientists to reject unjustified theories[2] and to give up their most cherished ideas when experience shows that they are false (or unsupported by good evidence).

Typical scientific theories result from a complicated mixture of deductive and inductive arguments, but the key arguments are inductive. Good scientists try to find **patterns** in what they have observed so far, in particular in their scientific experiments,[3] and pro-

---

[1] For more on causation and related matters, see Howard Kahane and Paul Tidman, *Logic and Philosophy,* 9th edition (Wadsworth, 2003).

[2] Scientists use the terms *theory* and *hypothesis* in at least two ways. In one sense, both of these terms refer to untested speculations or to insufficiently confirmed patterns. In another, they refer to well-established, well-confirmed, and accepted patterns. The second sense is synonymous with the expressions "scientific law" and "law of nature."

[3] A scientific experiment is just a kind of deliberately arranged experience. Instead of waiting for an event to happen, scientists arrange for it to happen, perhaps in their laboratories. For instance, they may mix two chemicals in the laboratory that rarely, if ever, are found mixed in nature, to see the result. But whether an event is "found" in the laboratory or found in "nature" is irrelevant to scientific procedure.

ject these patterns via inductive reasonings to larger slices of reality. In everyday life, common sense reasons by inductions from past experiences that sugar sweetens, vinegar sours, bread nourishes, and drought kills crops. Scientists, using the same common-sense methods, but much more persistently and stringently, conclude that copper conducts electricity, cigarette smoking causes cancer, the Earth's path around the sun is an ellipse, and radioactive substances have half-lives. (They also, of course, use viewing instruments they have learned to construct by means of inductive reasoning—telescopes, microscopes, X-ray machines, and so on—that we ordinarily don't have at our disposal in daily life.)

So science is just the accumulated knowledge gained by huge numbers of individuals observing nature, proposing theories (patterns) that explain what has been observed, and testing by additional observations to confirm their theories (hypotheses). When scientists claim to have discovered a new pattern, others will try to duplicate their findings; when they succeed, a theory tends to be accepted into the scientific canon; when they cannot successfully duplicate the findings, a theory will be discarded, or at least modified so as to take account of what has been learned by the failure to confirm. It is this that distinguishes science from pseudoscience: A scientific theory predicts what will be experienced under certain conditions; if it is not experienced, the theory must be rejected or revised to conform to what has been discovered. Those who believe in pseudosciences—for example, extrasensory perception—cling to theories that are disconfirmed by experience and that do not make successful predictions about what will be experienced in the future.

Speaking of pseudoscience brings to mind the fact that a truly scientific theory must conform not just to evidence directly supporting it but also indirectly to all scientific theories whatsoever. Pseudosciences, on the other hand, never conform to the whole body of scientific knowledge or even, sometimes, to ordinary everyday thoughts. Creation science, for example, asserts that all human beings except for Noah and his family perished about 5,000 or so years ago in the biblical flood. This means that all of the human genetic variety we see today—all racial differences—must have evolved in just a few thousand years from the common Noah family stock, and this contradicts everything we know about how human beings, or any mammals, evolve and propagate. So anyone who accepts creation science on this point must reject virtually everything known about genetics, along with a great deal of the rest of modern biology.

Note, by the way, that failure to confirm a proposed scientific theory does not mean that the attempt to do so was of no value. On the contrary, failure can be very revealing; indeed, it often is more enlightening than success. For example, the failure of experiments conducted in the 1880s to prove the existence of an "ether," believed in those days by scientists to be the medium through which light (and other electromagnetic waves) traveled through space, led to a crisis in Newtonian physics that was finally resolved by Einstein's special theory of relativity. So, in a sense, one of the most important scientific advances of the twentieth century grew out of the failure to confirm a previously widely accepted scientific theory.

Students often misunderstand this aspect of scientific investigation. They often object, for example, to biological research done on animals because what works with respect to other animals frequently does not do so in the case of human beings; students often see this as proof that animals were made to suffer with no offsetting increase in knowledge about how human diseases can be conquered. They don't understand that failures of this kind may lead investigators away from a wrong path and on to a right one. (They also often overlook the many cases in which, say, drugs that work well on close mammalian relatives also do so when tried on human beings.) Note, by the way, that those who champion pseudosciences generally do not learn from failures to confirm their theories; they tend simply to sweep this sort of counterevidence under the nearest metaphorical rug.

Pseudoscientists also tend to ignore ways in which their theories run counter to simple facts and ideas about how things work that we all hold in everyday life. Creation science, for example, fails to take account of what we all know about the abundance of species in today's world. There are thousands of mammal species, thousands of bird species, thousands of amphibian and reptilian species, and millions of insect species, all of which could not have fitted into one ark that even today's technology might with great effort construct. So even forgetting that lions can't be expected to lie down with lambs; forgetting that the ark would have had to be stocked with an incredible amount and variety of food and water so animals would not starve or dehydrate; forgetting that literally millions of plant species would have had to be collected; forgetting the physical impossibility of Noah and his family going around the world to collect all of these animals and plants and food; forgetting about bacteria and viruses; and forgetting fussy details about getting rid of huge amounts of fecal material, it should be clear that the creation science story violates not just dozens of extremely well-confirmed, high-powered scientific theories but also all kinds of everyday ideas about how the world works, *while predicting nothing about what sorts of (earthly!) experiences the future may hold for us!* The scientific theory of evolution, on the other hand, is consistent with every other well-confirmed scientific theory and has predicted all sorts of things that have been and continue to be discovered to be true, including how and where fossils might be found, and so on.

Finally, let's take a look at a rather simple and truly scientific theory—the "sea-of-air" hypothesis—and at how scientists test and confirm their hypotheses. The theory was proposed by the seventeenth-century mathematician and physicist Evangelista Torricelli, a disciple of Galileo. It was well known then that water can be pumped from a well only from a maximum of about a depth of 34 feet (without the aid of auxiliary power); Torricelli proposed to explain this and other facts by his theory that a sea of air surrounds the surface of the Earth and presses down on it because of the force of gravity, just as water presses down on something at the bottom of the ocean. Pumps thus can raise water from a well (at most) to a height of about 34 feet, Torricelli theorized, because of this *air pressure*.

Torricelli's theory can be, and was, confirmed by performing several different sorts of experiments. For instance, if the limit that water can be pumped from a well is about 34 feet, and if mercury is about 14 times heavier than water (it is), then if the sea-of-air theory is correct, it follows that air pressure will hold up a column of mercury only $\frac{1}{14}$ as high as a column of water. So we can confirm the sea-of-air hypothesis by constructing a mercury device (we call these things *barometers*) and finding that this is the case. Torricelli's followers also confirmed his theory by testing at higher-than-sea-level elevations where, according to the sea-of-air theory, a column of mercury should be held up a lesser amount than at sea level, because there is less air pressing down on the mercury. (We now use this fact in other ways—for instance, in measuring fluctuations in air pressure at a given elevation, part of the knowledge needed to predict changes in the weather.) Notice, by the way, that had the results of experiments not conformed to Torricelli's theory, his hypothesis would not have been accepted by the scientific community.

The point of all this is twofold. First, scientific method is not some mysterious entity; and second, although in practice it leads to extremely complicated experiments and arguments, the basic underlying patterns of scientific inquiry are rather simple. We also should mention that it is the incredibly diverse evidence that supports scientific theories that is the reason why they are so reliable and why we should not reject what science has to say on any subject without having *extremely good reasons* for doing so.

3. CALCULATING PROBABILITIES AND FAIR ODDS

Billions of dollars are legally wagered on games of chance each year in the United States, and billions more are wagered illegally. The popularity of Atlantic City, Reno, and Las Vegas testifies to the fact that many millions of people in America gamble every year. Yet most who gamble have no idea how to calculate fair odds, one reason almost all gamblers lose in the long run. (Another reason, of course, is that the odds on all legal gambling games, including in particular slot machines and state lotteries, are rigged against the player—the odds *always* favor the house.)

Legitimate, fair odds depend on the *likelihood* (*probability* or *chances*) that a given outcome will occur. For example, when you flip a symmetrical coin, the chances are *one out of two,* or $\frac{1}{2}$, that the coin will land heads up because there are two possibilities, and both are equally likely. **Fair odds** on heads thus should be even money—one to one—and someone who bets a dollar and wins should win a dollar. (Note, though, that very few coins are absolutely symmetrical. They tend to be very slightly heavier on one side or the other. Also notice that the dice at places like Las Vegas are specially made to be as close to asymmetrical as possible. Just any old pair of dice will not do, because of possible numbers "bias" favoring some numbers over others.)

Most games of chance are designed to present players with a specific number of equally likely alternatives, or combinations of alternatives, on which they must wager. To find the **probability** of combinations of outcomes, simply divide the number of favorable outcomes by the total number of possible outcomes, favorable or unfavorable. (Remember, though, that this works only in cases in which all individual outcomes are equally likely and outcomes are *independent* of each other—a matter to be discussed soon.)

Suppose we want to calculate the chances of getting a 7 on the next toss of an honest (symmetrical) pair of dice. There are exactly 36 possible outcomes on each toss, of which exactly 6 add up to 7 (namely, the combinations 1 and 6, 2 and 5, 3 and 4, 4 and 3, 5 and 2, and 6 and 1). So the probability of getting a 7 on a given toss equals $\frac{6}{36}$, or $\frac{1}{6}$. Out of 6 tosses, the average wagerer will win once and lose five times. That is why fair odds on 7 in a dice game are 5 to 1 and why someone who wins a dollar bet should win \$5.

At a casino, someone who bets a dollar is required to place it on the table, so that, if winners were paid fair odds, they would get back \$6—their own dollar plus five in winnings. But no casino in history has ever paid fair odds. Gambling establishments are in business to make money, not to run fair games of chance!

At Las Vegas and other places where gambling is legal, perhaps the best odds for average players are at the dice tables. Slot machines provide the worst odds (except for wagers on sporting events or horse races). Yet the slots are without doubt the most popular way to lose money at every legal gambling casino. But state lotteries very likely offer players (one is tempted to say "suckers"!) the worst odds of any legal popular games of chance, since they pay back in winnings only from one-half to at best two-thirds of what they take in.[4]

Anyway, probabilities being what they are, when the odds are less than fair, virtually everyone who gambles must lose in the long run. But people being as so many of us are, all sorts of foolish theories have gained wide currency among those who like to gamble. The most foolish theory, of course, is that there is something called luck and that in certain situations luck is on our side—an idea that was discussed earlier.

But there are also two other, more sophisticated theories that should be mentioned. One is the belief that doubling a bet after a losing play, say, at the dice table, assures victory in the long run even when the odds are stacked against you. After all, you must win sooner or later, thereby recouping all losses plus a nice profit.

Alas, there is no gambling Santa Claus. First, the odds are against you on every play; doubling the bet cannot change that fact. Second, unless you are a Bill Gates or a Warren Buffett, the house always has a very much larger pile of reserve cash than you do and therefore can withstand a greater run of losses. In the battle between house and gambler, the gambler thus almost always gets wiped out first by a streak of bad luck. (There are old stories and even a song about "the man who broke the bank at Monte Carlo," but if it ever happened, it wasn't in living memory.)

According to a variation of the double-the-bet gambit, a bet made after previous losses should cover just what has been lost so far plus just a small amount extra—say, the amount of the first bet—so that if you bet $2 on the first play and lose, the second play is for $4, the third for $8, and so on until you win, at which point you start over with a $2 bet. This method certainly increases the average number of plays until a gambler will get wiped out, but it still can't change the inevitable failure lurking in the distance. This method also has the disadvantage that, even if you beat the odds and end up a winner, you've just won the tiny amount of your initial wager. (A friend of the authors of this text tried this system at Las Vegas several years ago—at $10 a pop—and actually lasted over two hours before losing her bankroll.)

The other cute fallacy that gamblers fall for is to believe that the less often, say, a 7 has shown up lately at the dice table, the more likely it is that it will show up on the next toss of the dice. The odds, gamblers are fond of saying, have to "even out." Wait until 7 has not shown up for a specified number of tosses, say, 10 in a row, and then bet heavily on 7.

The trouble with this system is that each toss of the dice is *independent* of every other toss, which means that what happens on one toss is independent of what happens on any other. The point is that the dice don't know (or care!) what has shown up on previous

---

[4]That is why playing a state lottery amounts to paying a voluntary state tax. Thomas Jefferson, among other illustrious figures, favored lotteries for that very reason. Ordinary taxes are compulsory; lottery "taxes" are completely voluntary. Good point. Of course, human nature being what it is, plenty of people who regularly toss money away on state lotteries complain bitterly about having to pay state sales and income taxes.

tosses. The conditions that determine the odds on any given toss determine them to be the same for all tosses, no matter how previous tosses turned out. The dice, after all, are still the same symmetrical devices obeying the same laws of physics on every toss.

True critical reasoners, of course, don't need to know anything about correct odds to be sure that systems like this don't work. The house is in business to win; if they let you play, you can bet your system is no good.[5]

Although the theory about how to calculate fair odds in general is quite complicated, there are a few simple rules that cover most common cases. Using the lowercase letter *a* to stand for a first event or outcome and *b* for a second, and *P* as shorthand for probability, here are four such rules:

Restricted conjunction rule:

If two events are **independent** of each other (the occurrence of one has no effect on the occurrence of the other), then the probability of both occurring is equal to the probability of the first times the probability of the second. In symbols, this reads:

$P(a \ \& \ b) = P(a) \times P(b).$

For example, the probability of getting two 7s in a row with a fair pair of dice is equal to the probability of first getting a 7 ($\frac{1}{6}$) times the probability of 7 on the second toss ($\frac{1}{6}$), and thus is $\frac{1}{6} \times \frac{1}{6} = \frac{1}{36}$.

General conjunction rule:

$P(a \ \& \ b) = P(a) \times P(b, \text{given that } a \text{ occurs}).$

For instance, the probability of drawing two spades in a row out of an at-first-complete deck of cards is equal to the probability of drawing the first spade ($\frac{13}{52}$, because 13 of the 52 cards in a deck are spades) times the probability of drawing a second one, given that the first spade is not replaced in the deck ($\frac{12}{51}$), and thus is $\frac{13}{52} \times \frac{12}{51} = \frac{1}{17}$.

Restricted disjunction rule:

If *a* and *b* are mutually exclusive events (an outcome cannot be both *a* and *b*), then

$P(a \text{ or } b) = P(a) + P(b).$

For example, the probability of drawing a spade or a heart on a given draw is equal to the probability of drawing a spade ($\frac{1}{4}$) plus the probability of drawing a heart ($\frac{1}{4}$), and

---

[5]There have been very few exceptions to this rule. One occurred many years ago when "card-counting" systems were devised for blackjack that changed the odds so that they were in favor of adept card counters. At first, casinos refused to let card counters play—they actually kept lists—but then they simply increased the size of blackjack decks or used mechanical devices spewing out an endless series of cards, thereby ruining the card-counting game. (The card counters proved to be not much of a problem, because extremely few players were sufficiently adept at keeping track of cards played, and anyway, the idea that there is a way to beat the odds is good for business.) Another exception also occurred many years ago when college students discovered the tiny bias of a particular Las Vegas casino roulette wheel by patient observation over several days. They were allowed to win several thousand dollars, because of the great publicity, before the house ruined the game simply by changing the wheel.

thus is ¼ + ¼ = ½. (Drawing a spade and drawing a heart are mutually exclusive because no card can be both a spade and a heart.)

General disjunction rule:

$P(a \text{ or } b) = P(a) + P(b) - P(a \& b).$

For instance, the probability of getting at least one head in two tosses equals the probability of getting a head on the first toss (½) plus the probability of doing so on the second toss (½) minus the probability of getting heads on both tosses (¼), and thus is ½ + ½ − ¼ = ¾. (Note that we can't just say it is equal to ½ + ½.)

It should be obvious, by the way, that the probability of a contradiction equals zero and of a tautology (logical truth), one.

Exercise A-1

*1. What is the probability of getting either 2 or 12 on a given toss of an honest pair of dice?

2. How about one or the other in two tosses?

3. What is the probability of getting a red jack, queen, or king with an ordinary deck of cards on one random draw?

*4. If a state lottery paid fair odds, how much should a $2 wager pay a winner who picked the correct five-digit number?

5. Can we use the general disjunction rule in cases in which the events are mutually exclusive, as in the spade/heart example just mentioned? Explain your answer, and give an example.

Exercise A-2

Here is a "system" promoted in a book on gambling.[6] (A tiny part of the system has been omitted here.) Explain why it doesn't work (hard question, but well worth figuring out).

There is only one way to show a profit. Bet light on your losses and heavy on your wins.
Bet minimums when you're losing.
You recoup losses by betting house money against the house, not your own. When you win with a minimum bet, let the winnings ride and manage to come up with a few more wins. . . .
Bet heavy when you're winning.
Following a win with your minimum bet, bet the original minimum plus the amount you won. On a third win, drag [keep?] the minimum and bet the rest.

---

[6]Clement McQuaid, editor, *Gambler's Digest: The World's Greatest Gambling Book,* 2nd edition (DBI Books, 1981).

You now have a one-minimum-bet profit on the round, regardless of what happens. . . . As soon as you lose, go back to the minimum bet. . . .

Always make your heavy bets with the other fellow's money, not your own.

The worst thing you can do betting house money against the house on a bet is break even on that particular wager. Actually, you've lost money on the round—but it was money that you got from the other fellow, not part of your original venture money. . . .

Don't limit your winnings.

Always ride out a winning streak, pushing your skill to the hilt. . . .

Quit on a losing streak, not a winning streak.

While the law of mathematical probability averages out, it doesn't operate in a set pattern. Wins and losses go in streaks more often than they alternate. If you've had a good winning streak and a loss follows it, bet minimums long enough to see whether or not another winning streak is coming up. If it isn't, quit while you're still ahead.

ANSWERS TO
STARRED EXERCISE ITEMS

These answers certainly are not presented as revealed truth. They represent the authors' thoughts on the matter, which it is hoped will prove useful to the reader.

Exercise 1-1 (pp. 3–4)

4. *Premise:* We are sinners all.
   Implied premise: All sinners should forbear to judge (others).
   Conclusion: We all should forbear to judge (others).

6. *Premise:* Since 18-year-olds are legally allowed to vote,
   Premise: Since they can be drafted into war,
   Conclusion: Eighteen-year-olds should be allowed to drink alcoholic beverages.

Exercise 1-2 (pp. 4–6)

1. *Premise:* If we keep burning so much coal and oil, the "greenhouse" effect will continue to get worse.
   Premise: But it will be a disaster if it happens.
   Conclusion: So we've got to reduce our dependency on those fossil fuels.

4. No argument. Just a narrative of summer activities.

9. *Premise:* We all think ourselves so abundantly provided with good sense that we don't desire any more.
   Implied premise: If everyone is satisfied with the amount of good sense he has, then good sense must be equally distributed.
   Conclusion: Good sense is equally distributed.

   (The bit about it being the most equally distributed item is, we can assume, a rhetorical flourish. By the way, do you suppose Descartes was being a bit ironic?)

Exercise 1-5 (pp. 20–21)

3. $10.9 billion is a drop in the bucket these days for military expenditures. The United States spends a great many times more than that every year on the military.

Exercise 2-3 (pp. 36–37)

4. Disjunctive syllogisms have the form

    A or *B*

    Not *A*

    B

    If we replace the *A*s by the *sentence* "Snow is white" and the *B*s by the *sentence* "Snow is pink," we get the following argument:

    Snow is white or snow is pink.

    Snow isn't white. (Not snow is white.)

    Snow is pink.

    The term *or* in this disjunctive syllogism serves as a *sentence connective* (grammarians would say it serves as a coordinating conjunction); it connects whole sentences. In this case it connects the sentences "Snow is white" and "Snow is pink." "Snow is white or snow is pink" is said to be a *compound sentence* composed of the two *atomic sentences* "Snow is white" and "Snow is pink," joined together by the sentence connective *or.*

    Contrast this with the following syllogistic form and argument:

All *S* are *M.*	All sinners are betrayers.
All *M* are *P.*	All betrayers are untrustworthy.
All *S* are *P.*	All sinners are untrustworthy.

    In this case, we replace the *S*s, *M*s, and *P*s not by the whole sentences but by parts of sentences—namely, sentence *subjects* or sentence *predicates*. The term *are* serves not as a sentence connective but rather as a *verb* (the verb *to be*); it connects the subject of a sentence with its predicate. In the case, say, of the atomic sentence "All sinners are betrayers," the verb *are* connects the subject *sinners* with the predicate *betrayer* to form the atomic sentence "All sinners are betrayers." (The term *all* serves as a *quantifier,* indicating how many sinners, but that is another story, discussed in formal logic texts.)

Exercise 2-4 (p. 38)

3. *Contingent.* It certainly is not a contradiction, and it also is not a tautology because there is no law of logic that forbids one from running for both president and vice president in the same election. (Is there a legal law of the land?)

Exercise 3-1 (pp. 66–70)

1. *Appeal to authority.* Doctors are specialists in medicine. They don't necessarily know anything more about moral issues than anyone else. Anyway, don't we all need to make up our own minds about moral matters?

2. Johnson came very close to being inconsistent. If he meant that under no circumstances should the right to dissent be exercised, then he was indeed inconsistent. But if he meant that under the actual circumstances at the time, dissent was not warranted, then he was not inconsistent. (Whether he was then guilty of a questionable belief—that things then were as they should be—is another story.)

15. *Suppressed evidence.* Most of us are in our own home a lot more than we are in these other places. The rape rate per unit of time is much greater in the other places mentioned by Dr. Brothers than in one's own home.

23. *Inconsistency.* Doesn't the phrase "heritable disposition" mean a disposition caused by a genetic inheritance?

Exercise 4-1 (pp. 86–89)

4. *Irrelevant reasons.*

6. *Slippery slope.*

13. *Equivocation.* You don't have to make the past or future present in thought. What you make present, the "it," is thoughts about the past or present. The term *it* is used equivocally, the first use denoting the past or present and the second the thought of the past or present.

23. *Equivocation.* To imagine our own death is to visualize what it would be like to experience it. In this sense we can and do imagine our own death. Freud changes the meaning of *imagine* so that to imagine it we would have to not visualize it, which, of course, is impossible.

Exercise 5-1 (pp. 109–110)

6. Students taught this way could be, and very likely are, different from "average" students in having more concerned parents (than average), more affluent parents, homes in which books and the like form a larger part of life, and so on. We already have good reason to believe that "booked" households produce children who, on average, score higher than average.The point is bringing background beliefs to bear. You may have specific, relevant background beliefs, as above, or just general ones that should lead you to have some doubts about the implication of the stat—that home teaching is better than public schools.

Exercise 5-2 (pp. 110–112)

13. *Questionable cause.* Lewinsky's peccadilloes had nothing to do with the decrease in crime or the robot economy in 1998.

19. If LaPierre intended his analogy to prove anything, then he was guilty of the fallacy *questionable analogy.* But since he then provided reasons for believing gun bans do not reduce crime rates, we have to assume he meant his analogy to be illustrative, not demonstrative.

21. *Questionable statistics.* We can roughly estimate what is spent on illegal drugs, say, give or take $10 billion, but precise figures have to be unknown since they are illegal, therefore unrecorded actions people want to keep secret.

Exercise 5-3 (pp. 113–116)

1. *Questionable analogy.* Here's an example for which some background information is essential. (Precise figures aren't necessary.) On a trip to Saturn, the *Titan 4, Cassini,* carried 72.3 pounds of plutonium—the most carcinogenic substance known to man—with far greater radioactivity than was in the Chernobyl reactor at the time of its meltdown. The failure rate of *Titan 4* is 1 in 12.5. If *Cassini* disintegrated at its closest point (500 miles) in encircling the Earth, scientists estimate that millions of people would die—vastly more than the fatalities in a car crash. It's also worth noting that the chances of having an accident when driving a car are very much less than 1 in 12.5.

2. *Suppressed evidence.* In a nation where most people live in cities, where pigs cannot be kept, forbidding the sale of pork, bacon, and such is tantamount to forbidding the eating of these items. *Inconsistency.* So Rabbi Shapira came close to being inconsistent when he

claimed that the ultrareligious Jews in Israel want the sale but not the eating of these kinds of meat to be forbidden, since the one is tantamount to the other.

7. *Questionable statistics.* Having extolled scientists for their generally correct handling of statistics, here is a case where they goofed. The problem isn't that a rough statistic did not follow from their evidence but rather that precise ones such as 968.1 billion tons of carbon stored 18,000 years ago did not. Note, for instance, that they estimated how much carbon dioxide was locked within plants, and so on.

9. *Suppressed evidence.* (1) Superstition is more accurately defined, in part, as belief without good evidence or in the face of contrary evidence. (So the article changed the meaning of the term *superstition,* and some readers may have been guilty of falling for the fallacy *equivocation.*) (2) Some of the greatest scientists may have been superstitious, Isaac Newton being perhaps the best candidate. But the parts of their beliefs that became incorporated in science were not superstitions, Newton again furnishing perhaps the best example. (3) In addition, a great deal of what scientists once accepted, *on good evidence,* they now reject, or have modified or sharpened, because of better evidence (for example, the rejected ether theory). Rejecting or modifying well-supported theories because of better evidence in favor of more accurate theories is the heart of science and is definitely not superstition.

13. No fallacy. His analogies are apt.

19. *Hasty conclusion.* The evidence cited certainly is relevant to the question and favorable to Peirce's claim that the ads caused a rise in teen smoking, but it is not conclusive. Many other factors were at work (was there a similar increase in the use of other harmful drugs such as alcohol or marijuana?) and need to be evaluated along with the ads. *Questionable statement.* Why isn't banning cigarette ads a First Amendment issue? It's true that we don't think a ban on ads for illegal substances would violate the First Amendment prohibition on censorship of speech, but, on the other hand, we wouldn't be inclined to agree that nothing can be advertised which causes serious illnesses (for instance, high-fat foods).

20. *Hasty conclusion.* There certainly are plenty of good background reasons for concluding that raising the speed limit will increase traffic fatalities. But we can't automatically credit the 55-mph speed limit with reducing fatalities. (For one thing, that limit was generally flouted anyway; for another, cars have been made safer, and perhaps drivers on average are more sober.) Still, it would have been a good guess, based on background beliefs, that increases in speed would result in increases in fatalities. (Experience so far is mixed as to whether in fact the new higher maximum speed limits have resulted in increased highway deaths.)

22. *Questionable analogy.* The issue is not the similar sizes of California and Iraq, but the populations. There are 35 million Californians but only 140,000 U.S. soldiers in Iraq. California homicides would amount to 125,000 if people in that state were actually killed at the same rate as our soldiers were dying in Iraq.

Exercise 5-4 (p. 116)

Questionable cause/Hasty conclusion. To begin with, if we subtract the United States' figures, the stats look much different (suggesting the criminal population in the United States is high for other reasons). Also, Ireland, with 88 percent church attendance, has a lower jail rate than four of the six low-church nations and lower than the average. This raises all kinds of questions. Are the Irish secret sinners? Are their police incompetent? How many criminals are behind bars in the

United States because they committed victimless crimes (such as smoking dope) or because of race prejudice?

In any case, the statistics cited completely fail to support the implication that churchgoing leads to criminal behavior, nor do any other statistics known to the authors of this text.

Exercise 5-6 (p. 117)

Questionable cause. According to ACLU claims, they've opposed bans on commercial ads on First Amendment grounds for more than 50 years.

1. If true, are opponents guilty of *questionable cause?*
2. Is it true? Do research (for example, *Public Citizens' Health Letter* [April 1999]; *The Progressive* [February 1999]).

Exercise 7-1 (pp. 168–169)

3. *Translation:* Printed on paper that is at least 10 percent recycled, with a minimum of 40 percent new material.

   Is there something sneaky about this? Yes, indeed. Starting out with the statement "Printed on recycled paper" leads one to suspect that the item is printed on 100 percent recycled paper, thus playing to those who like to use recycled materials. The bit about post- and preconsumer materials is bound to be confusing to most of these people, who will then rely on the (misleading) first statement—the one they can understand. At the same time, the manufacturer is protected from fraud by the statements about pre- and postconsumer materials.

6. What the good admiral said in militaryese was that navy teams had gone around the country trying to find ways to get naval installations to spend more money. (It was close to the end of the fiscal year, and the navy had not used up its appropriation for that year. Yes, bureaucracies, with very few exceptions, do work this way.)

Exercise 7-3 (p. 170)

2. Actually, two of the sayings might be challenged. Charles Beardsley's quote may be thought to be doublespeak, and the Chinese proverb clearly does use the pronoun *he* when people in general are meant. But Beardsley deliberately employed "pompous prolixity" in order to rail against that very kind of language. And it makes not a great deal of sense to change ancient sayings (or should we commit to flames the King James version of the Bible with its sexist sayings, such as "Let him who is without sin cast the first stone"?).

   Confucius's precept does exaggerate the slipperiness of the slope he describes. But it is slippery!

Exercise 8-1 (pp. 178–180)

3. *Thesis:* None of the historical or anecdotal parts of the Bible are the word of God.
   Reason (premise): What I've seen (or know?) needs no revelation.
   Conclusion: Revelation is that which reveals what we don't know (haven't seen) before.
   Reason: Revelation is that which reveals what we don't know (haven't seen) before.
   Conclusion: Revelation can't tell us about earthly things men could witness.

Reason: Revelation can't tell us about earthly things men could witness.

Conclusion (thesis): None of the historical or anecdotal parts of the Bible count as revelation. (Paine assumed an equation between revelation and the word of God.)

Exercise 9-4 (pp. 217–218)

It is very difficult to construct margin notes or a summary for material such as these excerpts from *Mein Kampf,* because confusion and ambiguities abound. Nevertheless, here is a reasonably accurate summary (omitting Hitler's anthropomorphization of laws of nature):

1. It is a law of nature that animals mate only with members of their own species.
2. Breeding higher with lower within a species produces a medium that will lose out eventually to the higher.
3. If a law of nature did not exist forbidding breeding higher to lower, still higher could not develop.
4. The struggle for food and mates results in a higher development of a species.
5. Just as mating stronger with weaker *individuals* goes against nature, so does mating higher with lower races.
6. Proof: Aryans in North America remained pure and became masters of the continent; Latins in Central and South America mixed with the natives and produced an inferior culture, of which they are not complete masters. (This isn't exactly what Hitler says, but it is what he means. Remember that a good deal of Latin America was still in a colonial status in the 1920s when Hitler wrote his tome.)

Exercise 10-1 (pp. 239–240)

2. Clearly there's a contradiction here. Certificates that cost $1 aren't free.
9. This Nike commercial wins the *Logic and Contemporary Rhetoric* "Most Offensive Commercial of the Decade" Award for telling those who have just proved to be the second best at an activity (perhaps by the tiniest margin) among the several billion people on the planet that they are losers, instead of crediting them with their great accomplishment. (The underlying offensive message is captured by Vince Lombardi's famous remark, "Winning isn't everything; it's the only thing." Compare that to "It isn't whether you win or lose but how you play the game.")
10. *Questionable statements.* Everything those who have their eyes wide open have observed indicates that Dean Witter plans first and foremost for its own benefit, not for any client's future, and measures success in terms of its own profits (as do virtually all corporations?).
13. *Appeal to authority.* Agronsky is no authority on the subject. *Straw man.* No one claims coconut oils are "poisoning" America. *Suppressed evidence.* (1) While some fats are healthier than others, coconut oil is low on the healthy list. (2) It is total amount of fat intake that is most important. (3) No single fat source supplies more than a small portion of total intake of fat, so that "only" 1.5 percent coming from coconut oil proves nothing. The point is that it's prudent to reduce one's total amount of fat intake well below the national average and to reduce intake of some kinds of fat—coconut oil being a prime example—more than others. (4) If true that the fatty acids in coconut oil are beneficial, that would be a good reason to prefer this oil to others—say, when cooking. But this claim is generally not accepted by the medical profession. On the contrary, it is fats such as olive oil that seem to be the most beneficial.

Exercise 10-2 (pp. 240–241)

3. This commercial points to a profitable use of air travel—to foster face-to-face business relationships. That is why this has been an extremely successful ad—it reminds business executives of the value of catering to customers in person. But the commercial gives no reason to fly United instead of other airlines. (The implied reason that United flies to more than 200 locations is not a good reason for choosing United. For one thing, some other airlines fly to that many cities; and for another, what difference does it make if you intend, say, to fly to Chicago, whether the airline you choose also flies to 199 other cities or just to half that many?) *Jargon-type slogan.* "United. Come fly the friendly skies." *Identification.* Casting the right actors for TV commercials is crucial, and this ad does it beautifully. Ben is someone most people in business will identify with.

Exercise 12-2 (pp. 347–348)

4. The topic is the one discussed in Chapter 7 entitled "Those Who Control the Definitions"—defining oneself into victory. Those who favor teaching the biblical account of creation in science classes were trying to define themselves into victory by calling the biblical account "creation science," very much like businesses do who call employees "subcontractors."

Exercise for the Entire Text (p. 349)

You didn't really expect an answer to this one, did you? (If you did, go back to page 1 of Chapter 1 and start reading—carefully this time.)

Exercise A-1 (p. 358)

1. Since it isn't possible to get both 2 and 12 on a given toss, we can use the restricted disjunction rule. And given that the probability of getting a 2 = $\frac{1}{36}$ and of a 12 = $\frac{1}{36}$, the probability of getting 2 or 12 = $\frac{1}{36} + \frac{1}{36} = \frac{2}{36} = \frac{1}{18}$.

4. There are 100,000 five-digit numbers, each one equally likely to be picked. Thus, the odds on any given number are 100,000 to 1. So a winning $2 bet should pay $200,000 plus the $2 wagered. (None do. But note that in lottery cases of this kind, how much is paid to winners usually depends on how many people pick the correct number and whether there was a winner of previous plays. When there is no winner for several plays and the pot becomes very large, the number of people who play increases dramatically [people are not always rational!], so that, even though the amount of prize money increases, the probability that there will be several winners increases, thus dividing each winner's share. Of course, when the odds against winning anything are 100,000 to 1, the chances of winning are so miniscule that it is a waste of time to play. It almost never makes sense to wager at such poor odds, even if they are statistically in your favor; doing so loses you the opportunity to profit in some more likely ways. Human irrationality makes most of us see things differently, but that's just one of the tendencies that a good rational thinker fights against.)

BIBLIOGRAPHY

Asterisks indicate works mentioned in the text.

Cogent Reasoning

Carroll, Lewis. *Symbolic Logic and the Game of Logic*. New York: Dover, 1958.

Dewey, John. *How We Think*. Lexington, Mass.: Heath, 1910.

Kahane, Howard. "The Proper Subject Matter for Critical Thinking Courses." *Argumentation* 3 (1989).

*Kahane, Howard, and Tidman, Paul. *Logic and Philosophy,* 9th ed. Belmont, Calif.: Wadsworth, 2003.

Lemmon, E. J. *Beginning Logic,* rev. G. N. D. Barry. Indianapolis, Ind.: Hackett, 1978. (A strictly formal logic text.)

Fallacious Reasoning

*Bentham, Jeremy. *The Handbook of Political Fallacies*. New York: Harper Torchbooks, 1962. (A reprint of a classic nineteenth-century tract.)

Broad, C. D. "Some Fallacies in Political Thinking." *Philosophy* 29 (April 1950). (Interesting article by an important twentieth-century philosopher.)

*Cerf, Christopher, and Navasky, Victor. *The Experts Speak: The Definitive Compendium of Authoritative Misinformation*. New York: Pantheon, 1984.

*Dixon, Paul. *The Official Rules*. New York: Delacorte, 1978.

Ekman, Paul. *Telling Lies: Clues to Deceit in the Marketplace, Politics, and Marriage*. New York: Norton, 1992. (Fascinating book that will help readers to perceive when they are being lied to.)

Hamblin, C. L. *Fallacies*. Newport News, Va.: Vale, 1986. (A reprint with new preface of the definitive history of fallacy theory.)

Huff, Darrell. *How to Lie with Statistics*. New York: Norton, 1954.

*Kahane, Howard. "The Nature and Classification of Fallacies." In *Informal Logic: The First International Symposium,* ed. J. Anthony Blair and Ralph H. Johnson. Inverness, Calif.: Edgepress, 1980.

Miller, James Nathan. "Ronald Reagan and the Techniques of Deception." *Atlantic Monthly* (February 1984). (Nice illustration of how statistics can be misused for political advantage.)

Morgan, Chris, and Langford, David. *Facts and Fallacies: A Book of Definitive Mistakes and Misguided Predictions*. Exeter, England: Webb & Bower, 1981. (One of several excellent books illustrating expert feet of clay.)

Morgenstern, Oscar. "Qui Numerare Incipit Errare Incipit." *Fortune* (October 1963). (Still one of the best explanations of how government statistics on business and such can be and are manipulated for political purposes.)

*"Real World Macro: A Macroeconomics Reader from Dollars and Sense." 1996. (How statistics can be manipulated, in particular by the federal government.)

Smith, H. B. *How the Mind Falls into Error.* N.p.: Darby, 1980. (Reprint of the 1923 edition.)

Thouless, Robert H. *Straight and Crooked Thinking.* New York: Simon & Schuster, 1932.

Wheeler, Michael. *Lies, Damn Lies, and Statistics: The Manipulation of Public Opinion in America.* New York: Dell Laurel, 1977.

Impediments to Cogent Reasoning

Batholomew, Robert E., and Goode, Erich. "Mass Delusions and Hysterias: Highlights from the Past Millennium." *Skeptical Inquirer* (May/June 2000). (Fascinating article on human irrationality during the just-completed thousand years. Great companion to the Charles MacKay book listed later.)

*Bentham, Jeremy. *The Handbook of Political Fallacies.* New York: Harper Torchbooks, 1962. (A reprint of a classic nineteenth-century tract.)

*French, Christopher C., Fowler, Mandy, McCarthy, Katy, and Peers, Debbie. "Belief in Astrology: A Test of the Barnum Effect." *Skeptical Inquirer* (Winter 1991).

Gardner, Martin. *Science: Good, Bad, and Bogus.* Buffalo, N.Y.: Prometheus, 1981. (Debunking of pseudoscience.)

———. *Fads and Fallacies in the Name of Science.* New York: Dover, 1957. (The classic debunking of pseudoscience.)

*Gilovich, Thomas. *How We Know What Isn't So.* New York: Free Press, 1991.

*Goffman, Erving. *The Presentation of Self in Everyday Life.* New York: Anchor, 1959. (A classic.)

*Goleman, Daniel. *Vital Lies, Simple Truths.* New York: Simon & Schuster, 1985. (The best understandable explanation of recent scientific ideas about self-deception, its biological functions, and the unconscious.)

MacKay, Charles. *Memoirs of Extraordinary Popular Delusions and the Madness of Crowds.* New York: Harmony, 1980. (Reprint of 1841 edition, with foreword by Andrew Tobias. An excellent account of several disasters — the Crusades, the seventeenth-century Dutch tulip madness, the South Sea Bubble — driven by mass hysteria.)

Nickell, Joe. *Inquest on the Shroud of Turin.* Buffalo, N.Y.: Prometheus, 1982. (An example of sanity on a foolishness-provoking topic.)

Nisbet, Robert. *Prejudices.* Cambridge, Mass.: Harvard University Press, 1986.

Peirce, Charles Sanders. "The Fixation of Belief." *Popular Science Monthly* (1877). (A classic article by America's premier philosopher.)

Sagan, Carl. *The Demon-Haunted World.* New York: Random House, 1996. (A protest by an eminent astronomer against superstition and the uncritical acceptance of pseudoscientific claims.)

Shermer, Michael. *Why People Believe Weird Things: Pseudoscience, Superstition, and Other Confusions of Our Time.* New York: Freeman, 1997.

Twain, Mark. *Mark Twain on the Damned Human Race,* ed. Janet Smith. New York: Hill & Wang, 1962. (The great American humorist on all sorts of human foibles. If you think of Sam Clemens as just a writer of stories, you should read this book. For one thing, it will make evident to you how ridiculous it is to censor *Huckleberry Finn* on grounds of racism.)

Vyse, Stuart A. *Believing in Magic: The Psychology of Superstition.* New York: Oxford University Press, 1997.

Language

*American Philosophical Association (APA). *Guidelines for Non-Sexist Use of Language*. (Publication of the APA, available from their national office in Washington, D.C.)

*Carroll, Lewis. *Alice's Adventures in Wonderland*. New York: New American Library, 1960. (Reprint. The Reverend Dodgson, by the way, was a first-rate logician.)

"Guidelines for Equal Treatment of the Sexes in McGraw-Hill Book Company Publications." (Eleven-page, in-house statement of policy that has been generally adopted in the publishing business.)

Hall, Edward T. *The Silent Language*. New York: Doubleday, 1973.

*Lakoff, George. *Moral Politics: How Liberals and Conservatives Think*. Chicago: University of Chicago Press, 2002.

Lutz, William. "Notes toward a Description of Doublespeak." *Quarterly Review of Doublespeak* (January 1987).

*Orwell, George. *Nineteen Eighty-Four*. New York: New American Library, 1949. (Shows how language control helps control thoughts and thus behavior.)

*————. "Politics and the English Language." Reprinted in *A Collection of Works by George Orwell*. New York: Harcourt Brace, 1946.

Postman, Neil. *Amusing Ourselves to Death: Public Discourse in the Age of Show Business*. New York: Penguin, 1986.

Solomon, Norman. *The Power of Babble: The Politician's Dictionary of Buzzwords and Doubletalk for Every Occasion*. New York: Bantam Doubleday Dell, 1992.

Evaluating and Constructing Extended Arguments

Cavender, Nancy, and Weiss, Len. *Thinking/Writing*. Belmont, Calif.: Wadsworth, 1987.

Flew, Antony. *Thinking Straight*. Buffalo, N.Y.: Prometheus, 1977.

Lanham, Richard. *Revising Prose*. New York: Scribner's, 1979. (A good guide to clear writing.)

St. Aubyn, Giles. *The Art of Argument*. Buchanan, N.Y.: Emerson, 1962. (A beautifully written little book on argument.)

Writing Cogent (and Persuasive) Essays

*Hayes, John R., and Flower, Linda S. "Writing as Problem Solving." *Visible Language* 14:396–398.

*Kahane, Howard. *Contract Ethics: Evolutionary Biology and the Moral Sentiments*. Lanham, Md.: Rowman & Littlefield, 1995. (Helpful in bringing value judgments to bear when evaluating arguments.)

Advertising

Baker, Samm Sinclair. *The Permissible Lie*. Cleveland, Ohio: World, 1968.

*Beiler, David. *The Classics of Political Television Advertising: A Viewer's Guide*. Washington, D.C.: Campaigns and Elections, 1986. (Companion guide to a 60-minute videocassette containing some of the great TV campaign spots. Great fun and educational, too.)

Benn, Alec. *The 27 Most Common Mistakes in Advertising*. New York: AMACOM, 1978.

*Clark, Eric. *The Want Makers*. New York: Viking, 1988.

*Collins, Thomas L. *Beyond Maximarketing*. New York: McGraw-Hill, 1994.

Faucheux, Ron. "How to Win in '94." *Campaigns and Elections* (September 1993). (Interesting to compare with how campaigns were run in 1994.)

*Feldstein, Mark. "Mail Fraud on Capitol Hill." *Washington Monthly* (October 1979).

Glatzer, Robert. *The New Advertising: The Great Campaigns from Avis to Volkswagen.* New York: Citadel, 1970.

Hopkins, Claude. *Scientific Advertising.* New York: Crown, 1966. (Reprint of one of the classics on advertising.)

Iyengar, Shanto, and Ansolabehere, Stephen. *Going Negative: How Political Advertisements Shrink and Polarize the Electorate.* New York: Free Press, 1996.

Jamieson, Kathleen Hall. *Dirty Politics: Deception, Distraction, and Democracy.* Oxford University Press, 1992. (How campaigns dominated by 30- and 10-second TV spots fail to provide voters with adequate information.)

———. *Packaging the Presidency: A History and Criticism of Presidential Campaign Advertising,* 2d ed. New York: Oxford University Press, 1992.

*Kilbourne, Jean. *Deadly Persuasion: Why Women and Girls Must Fight the Addictive Power of Advertising.* New York: Simon & Schuster, 1999.

*Lemann, Nicholas. "Barney Frank's Mother and 500 Postmen." *Harper's* (April 1983).

McGinnis, Joe. *The Selling of the President 1968.* New York: Trident, 1969. (Still the best inside account of a presidential campaign—Nixon's successful run for the presidency.)

*Ogilvy, David. *Confessions of an Advertising Man.* New York: Atheneum, 1963.

Preston, Ivan. *The Great American Blowup: Puffery in Advertising and Selling.* Madison: University of Wisconsin Press, 1975. (Interesting account of what legally counts as mere puffery rather than false advertising.)

Rowsome, Frank, Jr. *They Laughed When I Sat Down.* New York: Bonanza, 1959. (Perhaps still the most interesting book on the history of advertising.)

*Sabatim, Karry J., and Simpson, Glenn R. "When Push Comes to Poll." *Washington Monthly* (June 1996).

Savan, Leslie. *The Sponsored Life: Ads, TV and American Culture.* Philadelphia: Temple University Press, 1995.

Stauber, John, and Rampton, Sheldon. *Toxic Sludge Is Good for You: Lies, Damn Lies, and the Public Relations Industry.* Monroe, Me.: Common Courage Press, 1995.

In addition to the books already listed, several excellent videocassettes are available from Campaigns and Elections, Washington, D.C., including the June 1986 *The Classics of Political Advertising* (with an accompanying booklet by David Beiler); *Prime Time Politics,* a 1989 cassette primarily concerned with the 1988 elections; and *The 25 Funniest Political TV Commercials* (actually, not all that funny, but instructive). There also are several other modestly interesting videocassettes available, including *30-Second Seduction,* a 1985 cassette by Consumer Reports.

Managing the News

Bagdikian, Ben. *The Media Monopoly,* 4th ed. Boston: Beacon, 1992.

Bennett, James. "The Flack Pack: How Press Conferences Turn Serious Journalists into Shills." *Washington Monthly* (November 1991).

Cohen, Jeff, and Solomon, Norman. *Adventures in Medialand: Behind the News, Beyond the Pundits.* Monroe, Me.: Common Courage Press, 1993.

Cohen, Richard. "Making Trends Meet." *Washington Post Magazine,* September 28, 1986. (How *Time* and *Newsweek* exaggerate and invent trends and fashions.)

Crossen, Cynthia. *Tainted Truth: The Manipulation of Fact in America.* New York: Simon & Schuster, 1994.

Croteau, David, and Hoynes, William. *By Invitation Only: How the Media Limits Political Debate.* Monroe, Me.: Common Courage Press, 1997.

Day, James. *The Vanishing Vision: The Inside Story of Public Television.* Berkeley: University of California Press, 1995. (A good account of how and why public television [PBS] succeeds in some ways and comes short in others.)

*El-Naway, Mohammed and Iskandar Faraq, Adel. *Al-Jazeera: How the Arab Network Scooped the World.* Boulder, CO: Westeview Press, 2002.

Fallows, James. *Breaking the News: How the Media Undermine American Democracy.* New York: Pantheon, 1996. (Important book by the now [1997] editor of *U.S. News & World Report.*)

Faludi, Susan. *Backlash: The Undeclared War against American Women.* New York: Bantam, 1991.

Fineman, Howard. "The Power of Talk." *Newsweek,* February 8, 1993. (How "call-in democracy"—TV and radio talk shows—are influencing elections and the legislative process.)

Hansell, Saul, and Harmon, Amy. "Caveat Emptor on the Web." *New York Times,* February 26, 1999.

Hausman, Carl. *Lies We Live By: Defeating Double-Talk and Deception in Advertising, Politics and the Media.* New York: Routledge, 2000. (One of the best books on these related topics.)

Hess, Stephen. "Television's Self-Fulfilling News." *Washington Post,* National Weekly Edition, October 30–November 5, 1989. (How TV shops around for expert opinion that conforms to the view they want to air.)

Hitt, Jack. "Warning: CIA Censors at Work." *Columbia Journalism Review* (July/August 1984).

*Jensen, Carl, and Project Censored. *Censored: The News That Didn't Make the News—and Why.* New York: Seven Stories Press, 1996. (A [hopefully] yearly publication about censored news stories.)

*Knightly, Phillip. *The First Casualty.* New York: Harcourt Brace Jovanovich, 1975. (The first casualty in war is, of course, truth.)

Levine, Richard M. "Polish Government versus the Workers: Why TV Is the Prized Weapon." *TV Guide* (November 7, 1981). (An illustration of how important TV has become for politics everywhere.)

Lieberman, David. "Fake News." *TV Guide* (February 22, 1992). (How video press releases, created by public relations firms, are surreptitiously slipped into TV news programs.)

McChesney, Robert. *Corporate Media and the Threat to Democracy.* New York: Seven Stories Press, 1997. (Interesting critique of corporate media power, plus some suggestions for improving the fairness and accuracy of the mass media.)

Miller, John J. "MLK, Inc." (How the Martin Luther King family is making big bucks by charging high permission fees to reprint from King's "I Have a Dream" speech and other writings, thereby inadvertently acting as censors.)

Perkins, Ray, Jr. *Logic and Mr. Limbaugh.* Chicago: Open Court, 1995. (A nifty account of how Rush Limbaugh mangles truth and logic.)

*Perry, David L. "No Way to Celebrate." *Columbia Journalism Review* (July/August 1990). (On how increasingly large jury awards in libel cases are putting a chill on investigative reporting.)

Smiley, Xan. "Misunderstanding Africa." *Atlantic Monthly* (September 1982). (How government intimidation and interference mangles news from Africa. An old article, but not that much has changed.)

Waters, Frank. *The Earp Brothers of Tombstone.* Lincoln: University of Nebraska Press, 1976. (The most accurate account of the exploits of the famous "Wild West" Earp brothers, Wyatt and Virgil, including a reasonably accurate account of the so-called "gunfight" at the O.K. Corral. A good antidote to the baloney the media dish out on this and other aspects of western U.S. history.)

*Zepezauer, Mark, and Naiman, Arthur. *Take the Rich off Welfare.* Tucson, Ariz.: Odonian, 1996.

In addition to the books just listed, there are several excellent videocassettes on managing the news, perhaps the most revealing being *Fear and Favor in the Newsroom,* distributed by California Newsreels, dramatically illustrating how corporate power influences news coverage.

Textbooks: Managing Worldviews

American Indian Historical Society. *Textbooks and the American Indian.* San Francisco: Indian Historical Press, 1970. (Shows how textbooks in those days—pre-1970—covered up the horrible treatment of Native Americans by European invaders.)

Barzun, Jacques. "The Wasteland of American Education." *New York Review of Books,* November 5, 1981. (Still very relevant.)

Black, Hillel. *The American Schoolbook.* New York: Morrow, 1967.

Chubb, John E. *Politics, Markets, and America's Schools.* Brookings Institution, 1990.

Cockborn, Alexander, and St. Clair, Jeffrey. *Al Gore: A User's Manual.* New York: Verso, 2000.

DelFattore, Joan. *What Johnny Shouldn't Read.* New Haven, Conn: Yale University Press, 1992.

*Elson, Ruth M. *Guardians of Tradition: American Schoolbooks of the 19th Century.* Lincoln: University of Nebraska Press, 1964.

*Fussell, Paul. *Wartime: Understanding and Behavior in the Second World War.* New York: Oxford University Press, 1989.

Henry, Jules. *On Sham, Vulnerability, and Other Forms of Self-Destruction.* (Unfortunately out of print.)

"History/Social Science Framework for California Public Schools, Kindergarten Through Grade Twelve." (The basic document governing California schools.)

Kasarda, John D. "The Jobs-Skills Mismatch." *New Perspectives Quarterly* (Fall 1990). (The economy needs highly educated workers; schools produce "low achievers.")

Loewen, James W. *Lies Across America: What Our Historic Sites Get Wrong.* New York: New Press, 1999.

———. *Lies My Teacher Told Me: Everything Your History Textbook Got Wrong.* New York: New Press, 1995. (Terrific book explaining how and why public school textbooks distort history the way they do. Probably the best book on the topic ever written.)

Lynch, Michael W. "Rampaging Toward Choice." *Reason.* (Libertarian slant on the issue of school vouchers and charter schools.)

*Nelson, Jack, and Roberts, Gene. *The Censors and the Schools.* Boston: Little, Brown, 1963. (The best book on the topic up to 1963.)

Paulos, John Allen. *Innumeracy: Mathematical Illiteracy and Its Consequences.* New York: Hill & Wang, 1988.

Raloff, Janet. "Errant Texts." *Science News,* March 17, 2001. (Very good article on the poor quality of public school science textbooks.)

*Ravitch, Diane. *The Language Police: How Pressure Groups Restrict What Students Learn.* New York: Knopf, 2003.

Schrank, Jeffrey. *Understanding Mass Media,* 2d ed. Skokie, Ill.: National Textbook, 1986. (One of the best public school social science texts.)

*Shenkman, Richard. *Legends, Lies and Cherished Myths of American History.* New York: Morrow, 1988.

Stotsky, Sandra. *Losing Our Language: How Multicultural Classroom Instruction Is Undermining Our Children's Ability to Read, Write, and Reason.* New York: Free Press, 1999.

Washburn, Katharine, and Thornton, John. *Dumbing Down: Essays on the Strip-mining of American Culture.* New York: Norton, 1996. (Several fascinating essays on how the dumbing down of American public schools is harming society.)

Zinn, Howard. *A People's History of the United States.* New York: Harper & Row, 1980. (Perhaps the easiest-to-understand antidote to the history learned via public school history texts.)

Selected List of Periodicals

One of the themes of this text is that good reasoning requires reasonably accurate background be-liefs, and one of the best ways to acquire a good stock of general information and theory is by read-ing some of the literally thousands of periodicals—magazines and journals—that are readily available these days. Here is a selected list of (primarily) non–mass media periodicals, the ma-jority concerned mostly with social/political issues, the media, or science, which the authors of this text happen to dip into at least now and then. (The comments represent our opinions and are not to be taken as some sort of revealed truth.) Most of these publications have Web sites. For a complete list of magazine reviews see *Magazines for Libraries,* ed. Cheryl LaGuardia, available in the reference section of most college libraries.

American Heritage. Perhaps the most interesting history magazine, featuring fascinating articles about American history. A good antidote to dull public school history texts. *Examples*: The Feb-ruary–March 2004 article on the history of plastic surgery (dating back 2,500 years) and the July 2004 article "Democratic Debacle" on how the 1964 Democratic convention did lasting damage to the party.

American Spectator. Wild-swinging right-wing publication. *Examples:* The July–August 2004 is-sue features a laudatory article and photos of Ronald Reagan and a not so complimentary one on Seymour Hersh, who is described as "a balding conspiratorial anti-American retread."

Amnesty Now. Publication of Amnesty International reporting on government torture around the world. (Reading this publication makes one appreciate living in a democratic society.) Recent ar-ticles include "Political Profiling: Police Spy on Peaceful Activists" and "False Confessions: Scar-ing Subjects to Death."

Atlantic Monthly. One of the best general magazines, with some excellent fiction and articles. *Ex-amples:* A July–August 2004 article, "Dumb and Dumber" on why campaign commercials are so lousy; another, "Kerry Faces the World," comparing John Kerry's foreign policy to that of the first President Bush.

Black Enterprise. A business magazine oriented toward African Americans in the business world. *Examples:* Special issues featuring topics like "Careers and Opportunities" and "Money Manage-ment"; monthly editorials covering health care, start-up opportunities, and the best cities for Af-rican Americans to work in.

Business Week. Good business magazine, written for those in business and much better than, say, *Money,* written for the masses. *Examples:* The August 2, 2004, article on how Charles Schwab plans to revive his ailing brokerage and the August 9, 2004, article on why investors should pro-ceed with caution in buying Google's IPO.

Columbia Journalism Review. One of the better journalism publications. *Examples*: Monthly "Darts & Laurels" awards; an article in the July–August 2004 issue on how Ahmed Chalabi, Iraqi opposition figure, played the press; another on why the press must rethink its coverage of the cal-culated descriptions and outright lies that were characteristic of the 2004 presidential campaign.

Common Cause Magazine. Liberal magazine sent to Common Cause contributors. *Example:* The Autumn 2001 article on trafficking women in Pakistan.

Consumer Reports. Publication of Consumers Union, an unbiased, nonprofit organization; a very good source of information about consumer products. *Examples:* Any one of the several articles every year on new cars; the June 2004 article on the truth about low-carb foods; and the August 2004 article about how to make over your kitchen, covering everything from cabinets to dish-washers.

Discover. Perhaps the best of a bad lot of mass media popular science magazines. *Example:* The entire September 2004 issue devoted to Albert Einstein with articles on his life, his theories, and his impact on the modern world.

The Economist. Quite a good British newsweekly concentrating on business news, but containing more general news than *Time, Newsweek,* or *U.S. News and World Report,* plus in-depth essays. *Examples:* A June 26, 2004, article on the problems Federal Reserve Board chair Alan Greenspan may face in raising interest rates too slowly to head off inflation; another on the difficult birth of the New European Union constitution.

Editor & Publisher. Important trade magazine. A good source of information as to how those in the business see things. *Example:* A recent article, "Can't We Just Get Along," about newspaper union issues.

Environmental Nutrition. A very good publication on diet, nutrition, and health that covers a wide range of topics, including food safety, nutrition comparison charts, herbal remedies, and best buys in brand-name foods.

Extra! The best magazine on the media. *Examples:* A December 2003 article about how journalists allow themselves to be manipulated by government leaks and a May–June 2004 report on a recent study showing that NPR uses the same influential sources as mainstream news and doesn't draw enough from diverse nonelite sources.

Free Inquiry. Secular humanist publication. *Examples:* The August–September 2004 article "What Use Is Religion?" by Richard Dawkins and an article by Peter Singer on the regressive stand of the Pope to keep alive indefinitely patients who are in a persistent vegetative state.

Harper's. Very good general monthly; the "Harper's Index" has become very popular, and editor Lewis Lapham's monthly columns often are very enlightening. *Examples:* A February 2004 editorial "Bad Medicine" on the corporate rip-offs built into the new Medicare drug prescription program, an article on what high school journalists are taught today (much of which involves politically correct coverage), and another on following the food chain back to Iraq.

Harvard Health Letter. A publication of Harvard University containing reasonably reliable medical information. *Examples:* The August 2004 article on low-carb versus low-fat diets, another on the possibility that statins may prevent cancer as well as lower cholesterol, and another on eating fish for cancer prevention.

Index on Censorship. Chronicles censorship around the world. *Example:* A recent article, "Inside the Axis of Evil," examining issues in Iran, Iraq, and North Korea.

Intercollegiate Review. Conservative journal of scholarship and opinion. *Examples:* Fall 2000–Spring 2001 articles on "The Foundations of Compassionate Conservatives" and a Spring 2002 article "Terrorism and the Intellectuals."

In These Times. Left-wing socialist publication. *Examples:* A November 26, 2003, article "Dishonorable Discharge" on how the Bush administration slashed veterans' benefits and an August 12, 2004, article on how labor unions reconfigured to battle huge multinationals.

Mother Jones. Successor to *Ramparts:* radical left viewpoint, with occasionally very good exposés. *Examples:* A December 2003 article by Molly Ivins on George Bush, "The Uncompassionate Conservative," and a July–August 2004 article, "Sidestepping Sanctions," about the "Axis of Evil's" corporate partners, U.S. companies that routinely manage to bypass economic sanctions.

Movieguide. A movie magazine that discusses and rates films from the point of view of fundamentalist Christian doctrine.

The Nation. Long-established left-wing magazine, very much improved under the current editor, and now very good indeed. *Examples:* The July 5, 2004, issue "State of the Union" given over to articles on the state of marriage in the United States, both straight and gay, and the July 29, 2004, article on how private prisons thrive on cheap labor in poor towns.

National Geographic. The long-established special-topic magazine. Tends to make the world look somewhat better than it is, but nevertheless has interesting articles, with very good, sometimes stunning, visuals about interesting places around the world. *Examples:* An August 2003 article on the hidden tribes of the Amazon and an August 2004 article "Crossing Patagonia's Ice Field," about traversing the largest expanse of ice on earth.

National Review. Perhaps the most interesting conservative magazine. *Examples:* A May 31, 2004, article about the Vietnam War veterans who came out against John Kerry and a June 29, 2004, issue devoted to Ronald Reagan and his legacy.

Natural History. A publication of the American Museum of Natural History. *Example:* The July–August 2004 article on the surprising characteristics of Gila monsters and beaded lizards.

Nature Conservancy. Magazine sent to contributors to the Nature Conservancy, an organization that purchases land in the attempt to preserve natural habitats. Recent articles discuss topics like overfishing and deforestation.

New Internationalist. Excellent, very-left-wing publication intent on reporting issues of world poverty and inequality, and the unjust relationship between the powerful and the powerless. *Examples:* The June 2004 issue on cooperatives, with articles on how people around the world come together in groups to work for their rights, including an article on sex workers in Calcutta and another on cocoa farmers in Ghana.

New Republic. Long-established liberal (sort of) political magazine. *Examples:* A June 26, 2004, article by Joe Biden criticizing the war in Iraq and one by John McCain defending it; an August 2, 2004, article on Ralph Nader's idealistic friends (including Republican campaign contributors).

Newsletter on Intellectual Freedom. American Library Association newsletter containing lists of censored books.

Newsweek. Mass media, general news weekly. Trendy, generally fails to scratch the surface. *Examples:* An August 16, 2004, article "Al Qaeda's Pre-Election Plot" about escalating terrorist threats before the November election, an entire section on the upcoming Olympics, and an article on the remake of hip hop music label Def Jam.

New Yorker. A very good general magazine, with funny cartoons (several reprinted in this textbook), great photos, plus information on goings-on in New York City. *Examples:* Regular, lengthy reports on the Iraq War by outstanding journalists like Seymour Hersh; an August 9, 2004, review of Bill Clinton's *My Life* that has an interesting perspective on the accomplishments and failures of the ex-president; also, nifty covers by some of the best cartoonists in the business.

New York Review of Books. Very good left-wing publication with excellent, indeed sometimes superb, lengthy reviews and articles. *Examples:* A January 2004 review of two Diane Arbus exhibitions and catalogs by Janet Malcolm; a review of two books on the economic highs of the 1990s by William D. Nordhaus; and an article by Oliver Sacks, "In the River of Consciousness." Also David Levine's great caricatures.

Nutrition Action Health Letter. Publication of the Center for Science in the Public Interest. An excellent source of information about food and health. Each issue tends to focus on topics in the news.

Reason. Perhaps the most interesting of the libertarian (pro free enterprise, con big government) publications. *Examples:* The November 2003 article "Show Us Your Money" about how the USA Patriot Act lets the government spy on your finances but doesn't necessarily help catch terrorists and a February 2004 article, "Dominate, Intimidate and Control," the sorry record of the Transportation Security Administration.

Science News. Very good weekly on what's new in science. *Examples:* The May 29, 2004, article on the effects of global warming on vineyards and wine quality; the July 17, 2004, article on the debate over low-carb diets.

Scientific American. Excellent science monthly, often difficult going for lay readers, but worth the effort. *Examples:* The October 2003 article on the environmental impact of Gulf War II; the May 2004 article on the way string theory modifies scientists' notion of the big bang theory, and a neuroscience article that links modern biological descriptions of the brain to Freud's controversial psychological theories.

Secular Humanist Bulletin. Addendum to *Free Inquiry* that will amuse nonbelievers and infuriate fundamentalists, in particular, with their accounts of Biblical passages that appear to be contradictory when taken literally. *Example:* The Summer 2003 article "Ending Discrimination Against the Nonreligious in the Military."

Skeptical Inquirer. Publication of the Committee for the Scientific Investigation of Claims of the Paranormal. The best periodical on pseudoscience. *Examples:* The October 2003 article on an investigation of the chicanery behind TV mediums' seemingly impressive results, and a May–June 2004 article on what college students really learn about science.

Textbook Letter. The best source of information about the quality of new public school textbooks. *Examples:* The March–June 2000 issue examining the treatment of religion in various schoolbooks—in particular, the way some of them promote religious tales as history; the January–February 2001 issue reviewing a very good molecular biology book for high school honors courses.

Time. Mass media general news weekly. Trendy, generally fails to scratch the surface. *Examples:* An article in the June 28, 2004, issue on new details revealed by the 9/11 Commission on Osama bin Laden's original plot and a section devoted to Bill Clinton's *My Life;* a July 12, 2004, article on the psychological damage suffered by veterans of the Iraq War and an article on the discoveries of the Cassini space probe.

TV Guide. Lists each week's TV offerings, plus sometimes interesting articles on TV programs and personalities.

Utne Reader. Reprints "the best of the alternative press," and is perhaps itself the best of the magazines that reprint material from other magazines. *Examples:* The July–August 2003 reprint "Myth of the Liberal Media" from *The Nation,* an article on why the pharmaceutical industry now targets healthy people from *World Watch,* and a reprint of "The Book of Matt," the Bible summarized in street English by the Dorchester Dog Hip Press.

U.S. News and World Report. A mass media general news weekly that is tilted a bit to the right but is considered somewhat more reliable than *Time* or *Newsweek. Examples:* The May 31, 2004, cover story on why America's obsession with plastic surgery is going out of control and the August 9, 2004, article on what the first Olympics were really like.

Washington Monthly. Neo-liberal. Our favorite magazine on how our political system works and might be improved. *Example:* The July–August 2004 article "My Big Beef with Big Media" about how government protects big media and shuts out independent operators, by Ted Turner, a man who knows all about it from the inside out.

The Washington Post National Weekly. A compendium of articles, columns, and cartoons from the *Washington Post. Examples:* The July 26, 2004, article on Bush's shrinking base of military support and the August 2, 2004, article on the fertile mind behind the 9/11 attacks.

Wired. Nerd's magazine on computing, the Internet, and so on. *Examples:* The September 2003 article tracking the surge of spam and the March 2004 article on the ways Americans are cheating more than ever, from P2P piracy to corporate research.

Women's Health Watch. A very good Harvard University health letter for women. *Examples:* May 2004 articles on heart risks that threaten women and ways to reduce air-travel-related problems like jet lag and blood clots; July 2004 articles on unanswered questions about hormone therapy and ways to boost our immune system.

World. A weekly news magazine reporting from a right-wing "Christian perspective."

GLOSSARY

Ad hominem argument   An attack on one's opponent rather than one's opponent's argument.

Analogical reasoning   Reasoning from the similarity of two things in several relevant respects to their similarity in another.

Appeal to authority   Accepting the word of an authority, alleged or genuine, when we should not.

Appeal to ignorance   Believing that something is true because there is no good evidence that it is false.

Argument   One or more statements (premises) offered in support of another statement (a conclusion).

Asserting the consequent   Arguing in a way that has the following invalid form:
   1. If A then B.
   2. B.
   $\therefore$3. A.

Background belief   A belief that is brought to bear in evaluating an argument's cogency.

Begging the question   Assuming as a premise some form of the very point that is at issue—the conclusion we intend to prove.

Biased statistics   Fallaciously reasoning from a sample that is insufficiently representative of the population from which it is drawn.

Categorical proposition   A proposition (statement) that asserts or denies a relationship between a *subject class* and a *predicate class.*

Cause   (of an event) Something necessary to bring about a particular result, or part of what is sufficient to bring it about.

Cogent reasoning   Valid reasoning from justified (warranted) premises that include all likely relevant information.

Cognitive meaning   The part of the meaning of a word or expression that refers to things, events, or properties of one kind or another.

Common practice   The fallacy in which a wrong is justified on the grounds that lots or most others do that sort of thing.

Composition   The fallacy in which it is argued that a particular item must have a certain property because all or most of its parts have it.

Concatenated reasoning   Reasoning that employs several inductions and deductions, concluding to a pattern that fits what has been observed so far.

Conclusion   What the premises of an argument are claimed to prove.

Contingent statement   A statement that is neither necessarily true (a tautology, logical truth) nor necessarily false (inconsistent, a contradiction).

Contradiction   A statement that is necessarily false (inconsistent, a contradiction), or a group of statements that taken together are inconsistent.

Deductively valid   An argument the truth of whose premises guarantees the truth of its conclusion, so that if its premises are true, then its conclusion must be true also.

Denying the antecedent   Arguing in a way that has the following invalid form:
1. If *A* then *B*.
2. Not *A*.
∴3. Not *B*.

Dilemma   An argument that presents two alternative courses of action, both claimed to be bad.

Disjunctive syllogism   A deductively valid argument having the following form:
1. *A* or *B*.
2. Not *A*.
∴3. *B*.

Division   The fallacy in which it is assumed that all (or some) of the parts of an item have a particular property because the item as a whole has that property.

Either-or fallacy   Mistakenly reasoning from two alternatives, one claimed to be bad (to be avoided), so that we ought to choose the other alternative in particular when there is at least another viable alternative.

Emotive meaning   The positive or negative overtones of a word or expression.

Equivocation   Use of a term in a passage to mean one thing in one place and something else in another.

Essay   A passage (usually consisting of at least several paragraphs) that argues for a conclusion.

Evading the issue   A fallacy in which a question at issue is avoided (usually) while appearing not to.

Fallacious   Reasoning that is not cogent, because it suppresses relevant evidence, contains a questionable premise, or is invalid.

False charge of fallacy   Wrongly accusing others of a fallacy.

False dilemma   A dilemma that can be shown to be false because either one of its premises is false or there is a third alternative.

Faulty comparison   A questionable analogy.

Form   (of an argument) Its logical or grammatical structure.

Hasty conclusion   The fallacious drawing of a conclusion from relevant but insufficient evidence.

Higher-level inductions   Very general inductions that can be used to evaluate those that are less general.

Hypothetical syllogism   A deductively valid argument having the following form:
1. If *A* then *B*.
2. If *B* then *C*.
∴3. If *A* then *C*.

Identification advertisement   An ad aimed to motivate its intended audience to identify either with a particular product or with the product's manufacturer or distributor.

Inconsistent   Contradictory.

Indirect proof   An argument in which the contradictory of a desired conclusion is assumed as a premise, leading to a conclusion that is false, contradictory, or patently absurd, justifying acceptance of the desired conclusion.

Induction   Reasoning that a pattern of some sort experienced so far will continue into the future.

Induction by enumeration   An inductively valid argument moving from a premise stating that all so far examined *A*s are *B*s to the conclusion that all *A*s whatsoever are *B*s.

Inductively valid   Correctly reasoning that a pattern experienced so far will continue into the future.

Ironic   Locutions that literally say one thing although their intended meaning is something else, usually opposite to its literal meaning.

Irrelevant reason   A broad fallacy category containing several narrower fallacies in which a premise of an argument is irrelevant to its conclusion.

Logical truth   A statement that is necessarily (logically) true; a statement that can be proved to be true by logic alone.

Major term   The predicate of the conclusion of a syllogism.

Margin note and summary method   A method for evaluating an extended passage by constructing a summary of that passage and evaluating the summary.

Middle term   The term that occurs once in each premise of a syllogism but not in its conclusion.

Minor term   The subject of the conclusion of a syllogism.

Modus ponens   A deductively valid argument having the following form:
1. If A then B.
2. A.
∴3. B.

Modus tollens   A deductively valid argument having the following form:
1. If A then B.
2. Not B.
∴3. Not A.

Mood   (of a syllogism) The classification of a syllogism depending on the kinds of propositions (A, E, I, or O) it contains.

Obfuscate   To be so confused or opaque as to be difficult to understand.

Particular affirmative proposition   A proposition having the form "Some As are Bs"; an I proposition.

Particular negative proposition   A proposition having the form "Some As are not Bs"; an O proposition.

Philosophy   The most important of one's background beliefs (including those about morality, God, the "meaning of life," etc.), usually but not always very general; one's worldview.

Plagiarism   Verbatim, or close to it, use of someone else's writings without acknowledging the source, making it appear to be one's own material.

Predicate class   The items referred to by the predicate of a categorical proposition.

Premise   A reason offered in support of an argument's conclusion.

Pro and con argument   An argument that considers reasons in favor of and against a thesis or conclusion.

Promise advertisement   An ad that promises to satisfy desires or allay fears.

Questionable analogy   Reasoning by an analogy that is not apt, not justified.

Quibble   To attempt to take advantage of the failure of one's opponent to cross every *t* and dot every *i*, to spell out what should be taken for granted.

Reasoning   Inferring from what we already know or believe to something else; the conclusion reached by reasoning.

Reasons   Statements (premises) offered in support or acceptance of another statement (conclusion).

Reductio ad absurdum argument   An argument in which the contradictory of a desired conclusion is assumed as a premise, leading to a conclusion that is false, contradictory, or patently absurd, justifying acceptance of the desired conclusion.

Refutation to counterargument   An attempt to refute one's opponent's arguments against one's own position.

Slanting   A form of misrepresentation in which a true statement is made to suggest something else (usually either known to be false or not known to be true). Also, the careful selection of facts so as to imply something else (usually something false).

Slippery slope argument   Objecting to a course of action on the grounds that once it is taken, another, and then perhaps still others, is bound to be taken; or arguing that whatever would justify taking the first step would justify the others, where, given that the last step is not justified, then neither is the first.

Slippery slope fallacy   Arguing that a slope is slippery without providing good reasons for thinking that it is.

Statistical induction   An induction that moves from the premise that a certain percentage of a sample has a particular property to the conclusion that the whole population from which it is drawn has the same percentage of that property.

Straw man   A fallacious form of reasoning in which an opponent's position, or a competitor's product, is misrepresented or a weaker opponent is attacked rather than stronger ones.

Subject class   The items referred to by the subject of a categorical proposition.

Suppressed evidence   The fallacy in which evidence contrary to one's position is neglected (overlooked).

Syllogism   An argument containing exactly three categorical propositions, two of them premises, one a conclusion.

Tautology   A statement that is logically, or necessarily, true or so devoid of content as to be practically empty.

Thesis   The conclusion of an extended argumentative passage; its conclusion.

Tokenism   Mistaking a token gesture for the real thing, or accepting a token gesture in lieu of something more substantive.

Tone   The attitudes or feelings expressed by a passage.

Traditional wisdom   Accepting an unsuitable practice because doing so follows a traditional or accepted way of doing things.

Two wrongs make a right   Justifying a wrong by pointing to a similar wrong done by others, usually by one's accuser.

Universal affirmative proposition   A proposition having the form "All S are P"; an A proposition.

Universal negative proposition   A proposition having the form "No S are P"; an E proposition.

Unrepresentative sample   Fallaciously reasoning from a sample that is insufficiently representative of the population from which it is drawn.

Valid   A criterion of cogent reasoning requiring that the premises of an argument genuinely support its conclusion, either deductively or inductively.

Warranted premise   A premise that is believable given one's background beliefs and other evidence.

Weasel word   A word that appears to make little or no change in a passage while in fact "sucking out" most of its content.

Worldview   The most important of one's background beliefs (including those about morality, God, the "meaning of life," etc.), usually but not always very general; one's philosophy.

INDEXES

Subject Index

Abortion
    moral values and, 192
    political advertising and, 254
Abu Ghraib scandal, 158
    images of, 292
    news media and, 264
    questionable analogy fallacy and,
        97
    television and, 296
A. C. Nielsen Company, 242
Academese, 147
Ad hominem arguments, 73–75
    guilt by association, 74–75
Advertising, 229–262. *See also*
        Drugs; Political advertising
    affluence and, 244
    apathy and, 244
    censorship of, 289
    comparative terms in, 236
    databased marketing, 245
    deceptive advertising, 239
    dynamic pricing, 243
    electronic ploys, 243
    e-mail marketing, 246
    equivocation fallacy in, 81
    fallacies in, 47–48, 233–234
    fine-print disclaimers, 156
    food labeling requirements, 53
    future of, 245–246
    identification advertising,
        230–232, 257
    implied conclusions in, 4
    on Internet, 245–246
    irrelevant reason fallacy in, 79
    jargon in, 234–235
    loyalty, appeal to, 237–239
    marginal needs and, 238
    news issues and, 235–236
    news media and, 265–267
    patriotism and, 237–239
    positive advertising, 242
    promise advertising, 230–232
    puffery in, 239
    slanting in, 155

slogans in, 230, 234–235
straw man fallacy in, 58
in textbooks, 333
trends in, 242–246
troubling trends in, 231–232
weaknesses, play on, 235
weasel words in, 236–237
Advertising: The Uneasy Persuasion
    (Schnudson), 244
Affirmative action programs, 76
Affirming the consequent fallacy,
    34–35
Afghanistan, war in, 160
    reporters in, 284
The Age of Reason (Paine), 179
AIDS, 15
Alabama, teaching evolution in,
    335
Alice series, 342
*Al-Jazeera: How the Arab News Net-
    work Scooped the World* (El-
    Nawaway & Iskandar), 272
Al Qaeda, 293
Alternatives, essays comparing, 174
Amazon.com, 243
Ambiguity
    equivocation and, 81–82
    interpretation of, 82
American Association of Health Plans
    (AAHP) statistics, 101
American Enterprise Institute, 286
American Heritage Dictionary, 340
American Legion, 328–329
American Library Association, 222,
    342
Analogies
    argumentative analogies, 98
    explanatory analogies, 98
    questionable analogy fallacy,
        96–98
    reasoning by, 39–40
Analogy of the cave, 98
Analysis of news, 283–284
An American Life (Reagan), 300
Anecdotes, 210
    evidence, anecdotal, 63

Answers to starred exercises,
    360–366
Anti-Semitism, 123
    textbooks mentioning, 314
Anxiety, self-deception and,
    132–133
Appeal to authority fallacy, 48–52
    expectations as to expert knowl-
        edge, 51
    field of expertise and, 50
    judging the experts, 50–51
    opposite of, 52
    past records of experts, checking,
        50–51
    personal expertise, acquiring,
        51–52
    trustworthiness of authorities,
        49–50
Appeal to force fallacy, 106
Appeal to ignorance fallacy,
    82–83
Arabian Nights, 342
Argentum ad baculum, 106
Argumentative analogies, 98
Arguments, 2–3. *See also* Cogent
        reasoning; Fallacies; Form of
        arguments
    affirming the consequent fallacy,
        34–35
    deductive invalidity, 34–35
    denying the antecedent fallacy, 34
    exposition and, 4–6
    extended evaluations, 186–191
    indirect proofs, 37
    modus ponens, 10
    modus tollens, 32
    pro and con arguments, 174
    stringing together of, 33
    theses, support for, 173
Argumentum ad ignorantiam, 83
Aspen Institute, 286
Assertions, 7
Association, guilt by, 74–75
Assumptions in essays, 177
Astrology, 134–135
Audience for essays, 211–212

Experts. *See also* Credentials
appeal to authority fallacy, 48–52
essays, consultation for, 205
legitimate appeal to, 174
news-gathering, 277, 284–286
questionable statement fallacy and,
61
textbooks, influence on, 332
think tanks, list of, 286–287
Explanatory analogies, 98
Exploring Earth Science, 338
Exposition, 4–6
Extended arguments, 107
Extended evaluations, 186–191
Extrasensory perception, 136–137
Exxon Valdez disaster, 257

Facts
background beliefs and, 15–16
cogent reasoning versus, 43
as objective, 191
slanting and, 155
value judgments blended with, 157
Fahrenheit 9/11, 251, 304–305
*Failing the Future: A Dean Looks at
Higher Education in the Twenty-
First Century* (Koloday), 169
Fair odds, calculating, 355–359
Fallacies, 1, 6, 47–70. *See also* specific types
ad hominem arguments, 73–75
advertising and, 233–234
affirming the consequent fallacy,
34–35
appeal to authority fallacy, 48–52
appeal to ignorance fallacy, 82–83
begging the question fallacy,
59–61
composition fallacy, 84
denying the antecedent fallacy, 34
division fallacy, 84
either-or fallacy, 59
equivocation fallacy, 80–82
evading the issue fallacy, 60–61
false charge of fallacy, 105–107
false dilemma fallacy, 58–59
fighting fire with fire fallacy, 76
in "The Futility of the Death Penalty" (Darrow), 189–190
gambling fallacies, 356–357
hasty conclusion fallacy, 91–92
inconsistency fallacy, 52–57
irrelevant reason fallacy, 78–79
master categories of, 48
overlooked evidence fallacy, 62
questionable analogy fallacy,
96–98
questionable cause fallacy, 93–96
questionable statement fallacy, 61
questionable statistics fallacy,
98–100
questionable uses of good statistics
fallacy, 100–102
quibbling, 107
slippery slope arguments, 84–85
small sample fallacy, 92
straw man fallacy, 58
tokenism, 64–65
two wrongs make a right fallacy,
75–78

unrepresentative sample fallacy,
92–93
Fallacies (Hamblin), 48
False beliefs, 15–16
False charge of fallacy, 105–107
False dilemma fallacy, 58–59
Family Research Council, 286
Fanny Hill, 342
Faulty comparisons, 214
in advertising, 233–234
fallacy, 97
FCC (Federal Communications Com-
mission)
on Internet connections, 299
media ownership restrictions, 302
obscenity and indecency fines, 267
Stern, Howard and, 251
Fears, advertising playing on, 235
Feminine logic, 12
Feminism. *See* Women
Fighting fire with fire fallacy, 76
Fine-print disclaimers, 156
in sweepstakes notifications,
236–237
First Amendment and censorship, 267
The First Casualty (Knightley), 270
First drafts, writing, 212–213
Follow-up stories, slanting news with,
292–293
Food
censorship and, 268
misleading labels, 159
requirements for labels, 53
For Better or for Worse, 294–295
Form of arguments, 9–10. *See also*
specific forms
deductive validity and, 31–34
Franking privilege, 254
Fraud
advertising, fraudulent claims in,
239
in e-mail marketing, 246
in science, 25
FTC (Federal Trade Commission)
e-mail marketing fraud estimate,
246
weight-loss ads and, 235–236
Fueling America's Future (Shell Oil
Company), 348–349
"The Futility of the Death Penalty"
(Darrow), 187–189

*Gambler's Digest: The World's Great-
est Gambling Book* (McQuaid),
358
Gambling, probabilities and, 355–359
Gannet, 303
Gender. *See* Women
General conjunction rule, 357
General disjunction rule, 358
General Electric holdings, 303
Generalized anxiety, 133
Genius, 6
Genocide, 123
Germany
Allied bombing of, 319
Nazi Germany's extermination
camps, 296
*The g Factor: General Intelligence
and Its Implications* (Brand), 285

*Global Science: Energy, Resources,
Environment,* 329–330
Glossary, 377–380
Gobbledygook, 147
Good statistics, questionable uses of,
100–102
Google News, 298
Gossip, news and, 280
Government. *See also* Statistics
censorship, 268
national security issues, 267, 287
news media and, 267–271
Government for Everybody (Jantzen),
325
The Grapes of Wrath (Steinbeck), 340
Grasping the horns of a dilemma, 59
The Great Gatsby (Fitzgerald), 127
Greenhouse effect, 61
Group identification advertising, 231
Guilt by association, 74–75
Gulf War, 254
marketing of, 256
television news and, 296
Gulliver's Travels (Swift), 196
Gun control
questionable analogy fallacy and,
97–98
questionable statistics fallacy and,
99

Half-truths in politics, 281–282
The Handbook of Political Fallacies
(Bentham), 75, 126
"A Hanging" (Orwell), 173
Harcourt Brace, 338
Harry Potter series, 342
Hasty conclusion fallacy, 102
HDTV, 305
Headlines, misleading, 291
Health care. *See* Medicine
Health insurance policy information,
243
Heart of Darkness (Conrad), 82,
129–130
Herd instinct, 120–122
Heritage Foundation, 286
Higher-level inductions, 40–41
Hiroshima bombing, 319
History textbooks, 314–323
distortion in, 316
dull and misleading information in,
315–316
as dumbed down, 316
embarrassing facts, omission of,
317–320
multiculturalism in, 316
sanitization of U.S. history in, 317
typical textbook, description of,
320–323
HMOs (health maintenance organizations), 281
questionable uses of good statistics
and, 101
Homosexuality
cartoon strips depicting, 295
self-censorship and, 288
textbooks mentioning, 314, 329
Hoover Institution, 286
Horoscopes, 135
Huck Finn (Twain), 341

Name Index

Media Index